SHARED PROSE
Process
to Product

SHARED PROSE

Process to Product

Robert Bator
The City Colleges of Chicago

Holt, Rinehart and Winston
New York   Chicago   San Francisco   Philadelphia
Montreal   Toronto   London   Sydney
Tokyo   Mexico City   Rio de Janeiro   Madrid

To my children,
Miranda and Aaron

"On Keeping a Journal" by Roy Hoffman, on pp. 9–10, is copyright 1983 by Newsweek, Inc. All rights reserved. Reprinted by permission.

Library of Congress Cataloging in Publication Data

Bator, Robert.
  Shared prose.

  Includes index.
   1. English language—Rhetoric   2. English language—Grammar—1950–   I. Title.
PE1408.B454   1985   808'.042   84-22456
ISBN 0-03-071427-3

Copyright © 1985 by CBS College Publishing
Address correspondence to:
383 Madison Avenue
New York, N.Y. 10017
All rights reserved
Printed in the United States of America
Published simultaneously in Canada
5 6 8   090   9 8 7 6 5 4 3 2 1

CBS COLLEGE PUBLISHING
Holt, Rinehart and Winston
The Dryden Press
Saunders College Publishing

To the Instructor

Shared Prose: Process to Product is intended for composition students who have not had much experience (or much recent experience) with the demands and rewards of carefully planned reader-based writing. As its title suggests, this text is designed to guide the reader from private to public written communication.

The book contains many aids to help students meet the complexities of what I call "shared prose."

1. Students often need a method to create content and discover form as they compose. They are shown a six-stage method which covers the entire prewriting–writing–rewriting process. FLOWER (for *find, list, organize, write, edit,* and *rewrite*) is an easy-to-use and easy-to-remember guide suitable for any kind of writing assignment. FLOWER demystifies the writing process while allowing for the recursiveness and complexity of that process.

2. The book contains many, many examples of student writing composed by college freshmen of varying ages and ability levels—not just that of exceptional students. Several of these are shown evolving from prewriting through multidraft writing and rewriting.

v

3. The book is both a rhetoric and a workbook, offering a balanced mix of instruction, examples, and exercises. Many of the exercises are progressive, leading to application in students' own writing. Even the more basic exercises are not overcoached. For example, students are not asked to find five comma errors in five sentences, each of which has a single comma error. Often, the exercises allow for optional ways of correcting error as opposed to the rigid rote enforcement of a single method.

4. Dozens of writing assignments to fit a wide range of student interest and experience are interspersed throughout the book. Almost all the assignments offer a wide range of options, and many instruct the student to direct them at specific audiences, not to the general reader. For these topics the emphasis is on the student's own experiences, not on research writing, which, it is presumed, will be the focus of a follow-up composition course.

5. In addition to the key mnemonic (FLOWER), several memory aids are offered throughout the text, especially for process items, for example, STAR for the four ways of revision: Substituting, Taking out, Adding and Rearranging. Not all of these student-tested aids need to be memorized. They are meant to encourage the student to touch all the bases of a particular aspect of writing.

Arrangement

The first chapter of *Shared Prose* keys the student to the distinction between self prose, such as journal writing and freewriting, and writing for an audience. Chapter 2 presents a process model for shared prose. The next section of the book (chapters 3–7) reviews the structures of writing: chapter 3 builds from sentence recognition and sentence skills drills to achieving variety in sentences; chapter 4 reviews the structure and arrangement of paragraphs; chapter 5 explains the traditional modes of discourse as they apply to paragraphs (comparison and contrast, definition, and the like); chapters 6 and 7 do for the essay what the two previous chapters do for the paragraph.

The last part of the book (chapters 8–11) covers writing systems: language, parts of speech, punctuation, mechanics, and manuscript format. The book concludes with an afterword that offers encouragement and advice to students to further improve their writing.

Except for chapters 1 and 2 which, as I explain to the student in a separate preface that follows, I feel should be covered first, you are encouraged to use the book in any order that suits your teaching style and your students' needs. If nothing else, I would like to have students who use this text come out with a sense of what the writing process is and how to make it work for them.

To keep the grammatical tail from wagging the writing dog, I have placed parts of speech and mechanics at the end of the book. This arrangement also mirrors where attention to such matters often comes to the writer—near the end of the writing process, not the beginning. On their own or as a class, some students may have to be dragged through participles earlier in the semester than the chapter order would suggest. Feel free to adapt the book to fit your circumstances.

Shared Prose aims to be (to borrow from today's computerspeak) "user-friendly," an intention that applies not just to the student user. For a teacher's guide which includes an answer key to the many exercises plus some advice on how to use conferencing to teach composition write to:

English Editor
Holt, Rinehart and Winston
383 Madison Ave.
New York, NY, 10017

One reviewer of this book in its manuscript stage claims that the tone used to describe writing is one of "I've been there. It is worth the trip." That is what I hope you, through this text, can succeed in demonstrating to your students. Convert that message to "We've been there. It is worth the trip."—something immensely important which many of our students have yet to discover.

Acknowledgments

To write a text is to incur a lot of literary debts. Here are some of mine.

For sharing sample student writing, I am indebted to many colleagues: Rita Thomson and Dick Lerner of Truman College and Julie Sharpe, Bill McGannon, Joyce Ewell, Florence Becker, Ed Dixon, Tom McKay, Gwen Ferguson, Lorraine Helmer, and Ron Naas of Olive-Harvey College, where I teach. Lorraine and Ron also read the manuscript in process. Others who read the text at various stages of its development were Lucien Agosta, Kansas State University; Michele Barale, University of Colorado, Boulder; Caroline Dobbs, William Rainey Harper College; Deborah Rosen, Broward Community College; and Carlene Walker, the University of Texas at El Paso. Where I have heeded them, my text is much the better for it.

I would also like to thank the following:

The National Endowment for the Humanities for two summer seminars on rhetoric and writing which enabled me to work with and learn from fellow writing teachers from around the country.

The seminar directors, Robert Gorrell and W. Ross Winterowd, for their efforts in making the teaching of writing the profession it is, not the sideline some departments pretend it to be.

Margaret C. Annan, a former Chicago public school teacher, for her inventive and useful organizing device—the chickenfoot.

Charlyce Jones Owen, English editor at Holt, Rinehart and Winston, for seeing the star in my sapphire before it was polished. And to Kate Morgan, developmental editor, and Herman Makler, senior project editor, for kindly and efficiently overseeing the polishing.

And I owe a special thanks to the many students who gave permission to reprint their writing, thus enabling this text to more fully become what it claims—*Shared Prose*.

                                                                    R.B.

To the Student

I seldom read prefaces. It would serve me right if you skip this one. Read it, however, not for my sake—I will never know if you do—but for your sake. I would like you to have an idea of what to expect from *Shared Prose*. Since teachers usually cannot cover an entire text, you will be using some parts of this book on your own. You also might want to read ahead on your own.

Here's a suggested plan: whatever else you do, read chapters 1 and 2 before you read any other part of the book. Why? Because these chapters start you out with writing for yourself before stepping you through the stages that writing for others will put you through. Once you review the writing process and see why it is needed, you are free to tackle any part of the book in any order you wish. Don't get involved in the smaller details until you know what you are about in the larger process of sharing your writing.

The book is designed to show you a method of writing that will enable you to create content and discover form. In the first two chapters that method is demonstrated. Chapters 3–7 deal with the forms that writing takes: sentence, paragraph, essay, and specialized paragraphs and essays. The concluding chapters cover writing systems: language, parts of speech, punctuation, capitalization, and spelling. The last chapter shows what your writing assignments should look like, and the book ends with suggestions to help you become a better writer.

To help you write better is the intention of this text. The instruction, examples, advice, and exercises are means to that end. Whether you know a participle from a popsicle, you can write. There will be plenty of help along the way to make sure you do. When I mention having to write, I expect to hear your groans and excuses (I was never good in English. I hate to write, etc.) and I won't deny your experience of them. Here, however, is what one writing teacher says about the difference between writers and nonwriters:

All kinds of people write. What distinguishes the writers is not that they have heads of stone and minds of steel. They probably run the range of anxieties and writing blocks as much as nonwriters. The main difference is that they write. They live with their uncertainties and difficulties, and they write.*

So check your excuses at the door. Hang on to your uncertainties and difficulties. Let's write.

---

*Frank Smith, *Writing and the Writer* (New York: Holt, Rinehart and Winston, 1982), p. 134.

Contents

PART II   Writing Structures

PART III   Writing Systems

9   Parts of Speech   252

10   Punctuation, Capitalization, and Spelling   291

11   Manuscript Format   311

Afterword: Becoming a Better Writer   327

PART I

The Writing Process

1

"Self Prose" versus Shared Prose

Just as you can talk to yourself, you can write for yourself. Such private communication can be very useful. Class notes, diary entries, even a shopping list, are examples of such "self prose." In this kind of writing you, the communicator, are the only intended audience.

Adding even one person to that audience puts many new demands on the writer. Take those notes that you keep for yourself. Assume a friend asks you to take notes for her in a history class. However well she knows you, will she automatically know that *H8* is your private shorthand for Henry VIII and that *PC7* stands for Pope Clement VII? Once you consider who else might have to read what you write, whether it is a recipe, an essay, or a report, "self prose" becomes a shared prose.

In shared prose the writer must anticipate who the audience is and what that audience already knows. Terms such as *poly sci* and *western civ* are convenient shorthand on many U.S. college campuses. You might have to drop these otherwise useful abbreviations when writing to someone who didn't go to college, something you wouldn't have to do when writing for your college newspaper. Whether you compose directions for assembling a bicycle, an ad for cornflakes, or a box score for a baseball game, you have to make many such writing decisions according to what the audience already knows about your topic.

In "self prose," where you, the producer of the writing, are also the sole consumer, there are few hurdles beyond remembering what you meant or deciphering your own handwriting. To the maker of a shopping list, the single word *shampoo* means a particular brand and size of liquid green goop. In shared prose such private, clipped communication will not do. Without you around to translate or expand on what you wrote, the reader must extract your intended meaning. For example, if you mention a "rat psych" course, be sure your audience knows you mean rational psychology, not the psychology of rodents. To extract meaning from writing is the reader's job; when you write for a reader, your job is to make that meaning extractable.

EXERCISE   "Self Prose" versus Shared Prose

Here is some student writing. Read it and decide whether it was written as "self prose" or shared prose.

> I went and got the Sunday morning papers, early in the morning. My Aunt did not cook breakfast so it was up to me. I cooked some pancakes and ham, the pancakes was easy because you just add water kind of pancakes. I washed the dishes after breakfast. I watched college football on TV because of the NFL strike, then watched Canadian football. When football went off I went outside. I saw some friends playing football so I joined. Soon as I got in I catch a touchdown, the game did not last long because it was getting dark. I went in and did a litle studying about half of an hour. My aunt had cook dinner some rice and pork steak with hot buttermilk biscuits.

1. The selection above is an example of

   a. "self prose"   **b.** shared prose

   Circle one answer by letter only.
2. Explain what helped you decide what kind of prose it is:

   _____

   _____

The writing selection in the preceding exercise seems rambling and in need of editing. It was, however, clear enough for the college student who made this entry in a journal he kept just for himself. He knew, for example, where he played football and with whom, so he did not have to add such details for his audience (himself). There are many such details that we as readers need that the writer did not need for himself.

Although often crude and unpolished, daily "self prose" is a great exercise for writers. It is like singing in the shower. So long as no one else is listening, you can sing off key, botch lyrics, and skip whole passages. The goal is to produce notes, not perform for the public. Likewise, when you keep a journal or diary you produce words, phrases, and sentences for yourself. The emphasis is not on a polished finished product for performance but on producing, at one sitting, some notes or observations that interest you, the writer.

Although some bits of what you jot down in these informal sessions might prove useful when you write for an audience, that is not the main purpose of keeping a journal. You do it to make writing an everyday occurrence, to make facing a blank page less of a threat. Singing in the shower does not mean you are ready to sing on stage, but if you will not sing even for yourself, how can you perform for others?

As you can judge from the sample from the student journal, that writing does not have to be profound or perfect. Why? It does not depend on feedback from an outside audience. Writing every day just for yourself will make all your writing more natural and comfortable. Just as a daily jog makes jogging easier, so will a daily log make writing easier.

A journal is similar to a diary with this important difference: A diary tends to center on events of *one day.* A journal offers no such restrictions. Students who grow tired of journal writing are often those who feel they have to list what they had for breakfast every day. On the contrary, in a journal you can write about anyone or anything you want—past, present, or future.

EXERCISE "Self Prose" versus Shared Prose

Here is another example of student writing. Read it and decide whether it is "self prose" or meant for an audience other than the person who wrote it.

One-Sixth of a Day

As I reach over to the bedside table to shut off the alarm clock, I say to myself, 6:15—time to start a new day. I slip my feet into my slippers and grab my robe off the foot of the bed. I make a sleepy-eyed attempt to reach the living room, where I turn on the radio to hear Bob Wall perk up my day. It's time to make coffee, so off to the kitchen I go. With that done, I'll lay out my husband's work clothes.

6:25—time to get up dear hubby, a new day is dawning as Michael Jackson sings "I wanna rock with you," as I prance into the living room with two hot cups of coffee, spilling the excess all over my burning hands.

With hubby off for the day, it is now time to wake the kids. "Carrie, time to get up," I yell as I do every weekday morning. "When you get finished, wake your sister." In turn, her sister will wake her brother. "OK, kids, time for breakfast. Now hurry and eat or you'll be late for school." *Family Affair*'s theme plays loudly on the television set as each one kisses me and says, "See you later, Mom."

Going from room to room, I clean up the house, being careful to omit the kids' rooms and finish my housework rather quickly. Time to get ready for school myself, I say as I start dressing. As I head out for the day, I notice the air is a little nippy; I'd better put on a hat. I miss both buses going toward my sister's house, so I decide to walk. Only six blocks: it'll be good exercise for me.

With my sister in tow, we freeze while we wait for the Stony Island 28 bus to come. Thirty minutes later it arrives, and we're all snuggly as we ride to school. I ease into a seat in my ten o'clock class. My English teacher wants us to write an essay describing our day. Not much happened today. I hope I can think of enough to write about.

Juanita Glees

The selection above was written

    a. for the writer   **b.** for a wider audience

Choose one answer by letter only.

EXERCISE Making Prose Sharable

The reading selections in the two preceding exercises described part of what happened to each student during a single day. Similar in subject, they differ in treatment—in how they approach their subject.

One obvious difference is that the writer of the second prose piece ("One-Sixth of a Day") arranged her writing in paragraphs. List two more specific things this writer did to make her prose sharable with an audience.

1. _____

2. _____

_____

Perhaps you are thinking that "One-Sixth of a Day" is better simply because its writer had a better vocabulary or is a better writer, period. Don't be so sure. The student who wrote the first reading selection in this chapter, the unedited journal entry, also wrote this paragraph:

Out Cold

I was ten years old at the time the accident happened. Some friends and I were playing in a parking lot by my house. It was about one-thirty in the afternoon on a bright sunny day in July. We were all playing on the thick, long silver chain that connects two small poles. Everyone would take turns swinging on the chain. One person would be on each end of the chain to swing it. The first time I got on the chain I clutched the cold thick chain tightly. At this moment, a chilling feeling went through my body. The next thing I noticed, I was swinging in the air. The only thing I remember is going up. An hour later, I woke up in a daze. Then I asked what happened to the people standing around me. They told me I had been out cold.

Darryl Brooks

This is far from perfect prose, but there is quite a difference when this writer (or any writer) decides to write with an audience in mind. When you jump from private to public communication, many new demands are placed on you, involving word choice, arrangement, and style. To create writing for an audience, you need a writing process. Chapter 2 reviews that process to guide you from process to product.

Summary of Differences between "Self Prose" and Shared Prose

"Self Prose"	Shared Prose
easier to write	easier to read
created for writer	created for outside reader
the writer as audience	the reader as audience
little or no revision and editing called for	much revision and editing called for

EXERCISE "Self Prose" versus Shared Prose

In questions 1–5, decide whether each form of writing listed is an example of "self prose" or shared prose. Circle your answer. Then answer questions 6–10.

1. A grocery list you write for yourself

   a. "self prose"   **b.** shared prose

2. A grocery list you write for someone else to use

   a. "self prose"   **b.** shared prose

3. A recipe someone asks for

   a. "self prose"   **b.** shared prose

4. A diary

    a. "self prose"   **b.** shared prose

5. Notes you take when you are studying a textbook

    a. "self prose"   **b.** shared prose

6. What is the last "self prose" you recall writing?

    _____

7. What are some of the ways you would have to change that "self prose" to make it a shared prose?

    _____

    _____

8. What is the last shared prose you recall writing?

    _____

9. Who was the audience?

    _____

10. Explain one important way shared prose differs from a conversation.

    _____

    _____

The Advantages of Keeping a Journal

It makes writing something you do every day.
It builds up your confidence because you are writing for yourself, not for an outside audience.
It makes facing a blank page less of a threat.
It provides a retrievable record of happenings of your life that you might want to keep for future reference.
It lets you, as one student put it, see what your thinking looks like.
It might provide some ideas or details to be used in your shared writing even though that is not the primary purpose of keeping a journal.

EXERCISE Journal Writing

Read the following article by a professional writer, and answer the questions that follow it.

On Keeping a Journal

Wherever I go I carry a small notebook in my coat or back pocket for thoughts, observations and impressions. As a writer I use this notebook as an artist would a sketch pad, for stories and essays, and as a sporadic journal of my comings and goings. When I first started keeping notebooks, though, I was not yet a professional writer. I was still in college.

I made my first notebook entries in the summer of 1972, just after my freshman year, in what was actually a travel log. A buddy and I were setting out to trek from our Alabama hometown to the distant tundra of Alaska. With unbounded enthusiasm I began: "Wild, crazy ecstasy wants to wrench my head from my body." The log, written in a university composition book, goes on to chronicle our adventures in the land where the sun never sets, the bars never close and the prepipeline employment prospects were so bleak we ended up taking jobs as night janitors.

When I returned to college that fall I had a small revelation: the world around me of libraries, quadrangles, Frisbees and professors was as rich with material for my journals and notebooks as galumphing moose and garrulous fishermen.

These college notebooks, which built to a pitch my senior year, are gold mines to me now. Classrooms, girlfriends, cups of coffee and lines of poetry—from mine to John Keats's—float by like clouds. As I lie beneath these clouds again, they take on familiar and distinctive shapes.

Though I can remember the campus's main quadrangle, I see it more vividly when I read my description of school on a visit during summer break: "the muggy, lassitudinal air . . . the bird noises that can not be pointed to, the summer emptiness that grows emptier with a few students squeaking by the library on poorly oiled bicycles." An economics professor I fondly remember returns with less fondness in my notebooks, "staring down at the class with his equine face." And a girl I had a crush on senior year, whom I now recall mistily, reappears with far more vitality as "the ample, slightly-gawky, whole-wheat, fractured object of my want gangling down the hall in spring heat today."

When, in reading over my notebooks, I am not peering at quadrangles, midterm exams, professors or girlfriends, I see a portrait of my parents and hometown during holidays and occasional weekend breaks. Like a wheel, home revolves, each turn regarded differently depending on the novel or political essay I'd been most influenced by the previous semester.

Mostly, though, in wandering back through my notebooks, I meet someone who could be my younger brother: the younger version of myself. The younger me seems moodier, more inquisitive, more fun-loving and surprisingly eager to stay up all night partying or figuring out electron orbitals for a 9 A.M. exam. The younger me wanders through a hall of mirrors of the self, writes of "seeing two or three of myself on every corner," and pens long meditations on God and society before scribbling in the margin, "what a child I am." The younger me also finds humor in trying to keep track of this hall of mirrors, commenting in ragged verse: "I hope that one day / Some grandson or cousin / Will read these books, / And know that I was / Once a youth / Sitting in drugstores with / Anguished looks, / And poring over coffee, / And should have poured / The coffee / Over these lines."

I believe that every college student should attempt to keep some form of notebook, journal or diary. A notebook is a secret garden in which to dance, sing, muse, wander, perform handstands, even cry. In the privacy of this little book, you can make faces, curse, turn somersaults and ask yourself if you're *really* in love. A notebook or journal is one of the few places you can call just your own.

Spring of my senior year I wrote: "This notebook shall be / A continuing inner sanctum, / Where my closest confidante / Will seem like a stranger." It's hard, but necessary, to sustain that conviction. Journal writing suffers when you let someone, in your mind, look over your shoulder. Honesty wilts when a parent, teacher or friend looms up in your imagination to discourage you from putting your *true* thoughts on the page. Journal writing also runs a related hazard: the dizzying suspicion that one day your private thoughts, like those of Samuel Pepys or Virginia Woolf, will be published in several volumes and land up required reading for English 401. How can you write comfortably when the eyes of all future readers are upon you? Keep your notebooks with the abandon of one who knows his words will go up in smoke. Then you might really strike fire a hundred years or so from now if anyone cares to pry.

By keeping notebooks, you improve your writing ability, increasing your capacity to communicate both with yourself and others. By keeping notebooks, you discover patterns in yourself, whether lazy ones that need to be broken or healthy ones that can use some nurturing. By keeping notebooks, you heighten some moments and give substance to others: even a journey to the washateria offers potential for some offbeat journal observations. And by keeping notebooks while still in college, you chart a terrain that, for many, is more dynamically charged with ideas and discussions than the practical, workaday world just beyond. Notebooks, I believe, not only help us remember this dynamic charge, but also help us sustain it.

Not long ago, while traveling with a friend in Yorktown, Va., I passed by a time capsule buried in the ground in 1976, intended to be dug up in 2076. Keeping notebooks and journals is rather like burying time capsules into one's own life. There's no telling what old rock song, love note, philosophical complaint or rosy Saturday morning you'll unearth when you dig up these personal time capsules. You'll be able to piece together a remarkable picture of where you've come from, and may well get some important glimmers about where you're going.

Roy Hoffman

1. How many excerpts from the diary Mr. Hoffman kept in college are cited in his article? _____
2. Hoffman says every college student should try to keep some form of notebook, journal, or diary. In your own words, list three of the major reasons he gives to support this statement.

     _____

     _____

     _____

     _____

3. Explain what the author means when he says, "Journal writing suffers when you let someone, in your mind, look over your shoulder."

     _____

     _____

     _____

     _____

Suggestions for Journal Writing

1. Find a regular time each day to make your journal. If you fall behind in your entries, it will be hard to catch up and recapture vividly what interested you on a particular day.
2. Make your journal entries in a notebook you use just for that purpose or set aside some looseleaf paper just for your entries.
3. You can write about anything! This is a breakthrough one student made after just one week of journal writing. She found she did not have to write about what she had for breakfast or the events of that day. She could take time just to describe a tree in front of her house or how mad she was at a certain teacher, and so forth. Take time for description or reflection.
4. There are no rules of length to follow: Some entries may be quite short; some subjects will draw more words from you. You can stay with a subject for more than one day if you wish.
5. Allow about fifteen or twenty minutes for your journal entries. Ten minutes may be enough on many occasions. If you have trouble squeezing in the time for the journal entries, use classroom time when you are waiting for class to begin or when a teacher is returning papers, calling roll, etc.

WRITING ASSIGNMENT   Keeping a Journal

Keep a writing journal every day for a week. You can write about anything you wish. The journal will not be corrected or graded. Your instructor might want to see it to credit it as a writing assignment, but try not to be conscious of the teacher as audience. Remember that in journal writing you are the audience that counts. Follow the suggestions given above. No matter how much you dread writing, try this assignment. Many very reluctant students attest that they gained a great deal from keeping a writing journal.

Freewriting

Another "self prose" exercise you should try is freewriting. This is nothing more than five or ten minutes of nonstop writing. Because the object is to keep writing quickly and not to hesitate over what to write next, it is even less structured than a journal. In journal writing you are free to change subjects any time you want, but you still have to plan consciously what will follow what. In freewriting you do not need an internal map of where you are headed when you start to write. Simply write what is going through your head. If you get stuck for something to say, you can write, "I am stuck for something to say," or write the days of the week or keep writing your name as many times as you want. Bizarre as that sounds, it works. You soon grow tired of writing the same thing and thus get over your block about what to write next.

Here is an example of some freewriting a student came up with in one five-minute session:

I love to write when it's serious. I love my boyfriend. I hate Rebecca. Man woman you me we us. A student walked in English late. Life is hard this writing assignment is easy. It's fun. Red blue black yellow. Red blue black yellow. Billy, Tony. McDonald's. I work at McDonald's. I have fun at work. I love pay day. School is boring I wish I had gone to school in Texas instead of Alabama. I can't think steadily can you? My mother's name is Juanita. James and Gerard and Maynard are her brothers. Christmas was wonderful. I wish I had today off. I can't wait till the weekend. Don't tell me what to do. I hope I have Friday and Saturday off. It's fun that I must buy note book paper. My hands are tired, very tired. Everyone is writing. I want to cough loud, but I'll hold it in. and yeah, Randy came over last night. I really miss him. I hope he feels the same way. Ohhhh he is so sweet. The clock has stopped. How stupid. I am 18 years old. I am an almighty Scorpio. I love Taurus, Virgo.

Such nonstop writing is cruder and more random than journal writing, but it provides many of the same advantages, especially making writing something you do regularly. Remember, it is nonstop writing. That means no long pauses to reflect on what to write next. Write what is on your mind without worrying if or how it connects with the previous sentence. In the freewriting selection shown above, notice how many times the writer changed topics. Because it is nonstop writing, freewriting is easier to write than a journal and therefore often even more effective in helping students get over their writing anxieties. Although it is only an exercise, freewriting will sometimes help you find a writing topic or discover how you really feel about a subject.

Suggestions for Freewriting

1. Freewriting should be done several times a week or even daily. Many instructors build five or ten minutes of freewriting into the class schedule. If you schedule freewriting on your own, do not, at first, go beyond five minutes. Later, you can expand the nonstop writing to ten or fifteen minutes.
2. Do not plan what you will write about beforehand. Let the freewriting be a record of the free associations going on in your mind as you write.
3. If you get stuck for something to write, do what the student did in the freewriting sample above: repeat a list of some sort. She chose colors. You could list those or the days of the week or anything else, *so long as you keep writing.* When you grow tired of the repeated items, some new topic to write about will pop into your head.
4. Freewriting is your own verbal doodling. Do not feel you have to save your freewriting or show it to anyone (unless a teacher wants to see it to credit you for an assignment). Freewriting, like journal writing, suffers if, in your mind, you let someone look over your shoulder.

WRITING ASSIGNMENT   Freewriting

Following the suggestions outlined above, do five or ten minutes of freewriting every day for a week. Your instructor may collect it to credit you with the completed writing assignment, but try not to think of any audience beyond yourself. Freewriting is a process, an exercise for yourself, not a finished product for someone else.

WRITING ASSIGNMENT   Linked Freewriting

Do five minutes of freewriting. The next day, use one of the ideas or images from the first day's freewriting to get started on another five minutes of freewriting. Use an image or idea from that freewriting to get you started on the next day's freewriting, and so forth. After the fifth freewriting session, write a paragraph on one topic that came up in the free-writing sessions.

WRITING ASSIGNMENT   Analysis of Journal Writing or Freewriting

After you have kept a journal for at least one week or done freewriting every day for at least a week, write a letter to someone explaining the benefits and the difficulties of journal writing or freewriting. Assume your audience has never heard of journal writing or freewriting.

Specify below the person you are writing to. My audience for this assignment is:

_____

Give the age and position of the person you are writing to—for example, "My niece, Zena, who is twelve and a sixth-grader," or "Mr. Steely Wool, my former boss, who is forty-six and a vice-president of a bank." Describe your relationship to this person (close friend, relative, etc.).

_____

2

The FLOWER Method

FLOW (Prewriting and Writing)

To produce any product, whether bricks or bologna, you need to know the process involved. The same is true of writing. To begin with writing as a product is to start at the wrong end of the process. A well-written product is the final goal, but the writer must first work through the writing process. Without some writing process, there would be no written product.

Many techniques are available to guide you through the writing process. Some of them you already know and use. To supplement and structure these, here is an easy-to-follow and easy-to-remember system to help with any writing assignment you are faced with, whether a single paragraph, a short response to an exam question, a full composition, or an extensive report.

FLOW
Finding a subject
Listing details the subject calls to mind
Organizing the details
Writing a first draft

Finding a Subject

In some writing assignments, the choice of a subject is already taken care of. If you are asked to evaluate a president's foreign policy or explain the dinosaur's disappearance, your work is, in part, cut out for you. But even when you are given something to write about, you often have at best a topic, not a subject.

A subject is a *restricted* or *limited* topic. For a short paper, a topic that is too general, such as crime, will lead to a general essay that lacks specific detail. That topic is too broad for a book, let alone a short paper. Try posing some questions. For example: What crime? Where? When? Why? Such basic questions not only help you limit your paper to a manageable topic, but also suggest interesting detail. Crime in one town or one neighborhood, or a single crime you may have witnessed, is a better subject than the unfocused topic "crime." In searching for a subject, you may start with a general topic, like pollution, inflation, or nuclear war, but you owe your reader (and yourself) a limitation of that generality which will make it a subject you can handle thoroughly in a short paper.

What is meant by making a topic limited or restricted? These relative terms mean that your subject is narrowed down to suggest more specific details to an audience. For example, if someone said, "Hand me a cooking utensil," you wouldn't know whether to look for a pot or a pan or any of a number of cooking tools, such as a spatula. If you were asked instead for a frying pan, you could form a picture of what was requested much more quickly. "Hand me the black frying pan from the shelf above the refrigerator," even though it is a mouthful, would prompt an even speedier response because it is so detailed.

Let's look these descriptions over:

A cooking utensil—could mean anything you can use to cook with, from a pot or pan to any of a number of cooking tools
A frying pan—one specific kind of cooking utensil (*a more restricted term is substituted*)
A black frying pan—a specific frying pan described by color (*modifying detail added*)
A black frying pan from the shelf above the refrigerator—a specific frying pan described by color and place (*more modifying details added*)

We learn, of course, to fit description to our audiences. Someone who has never been in your kitchen before would need to know where the frying pan is and what it looks like. Someone who has helped you before in your kitchen might know you have only one frying pan and where it should be. In speaking to that person, you could ask for a frying pan, period.

Here is another example.

I'd like some ice cream.
What kind?
Strawberry.
How much?
Two scoops.
Anything else?

"Some ice cream" is such an elastic general term that you might get as little as a spoonful or as much as a gallon. Notice that moving right into specifics communicates more effectively. "I'd like dessert" won't get you two scoops of strawberry ice cream with a cherry until you restrict or limit the general term (dessert) to specifics (how many scoops, what kind, etc.).

Writing topics also need to be restricted. To make sure they will find enough to write about, some students pick huge general topics. The problem is that such topics can't be treated with much real detail in a short paper. A short paper (about 500 words) calls for a shortened— that is, limited—topic. Stopping to ask some basic questions is a quick way to get to a more specific subject:

For example:

Inflation—Too general

Inflation *where?*
Inflation in the United States—Better; at least you have narrowed the subjects to a single country, but there are over 200 million people in fifty states.

Inflation as it affects *whom?*
The effects of inflation on U.S. college students—Ask another question; this country has been around for over 200 years.

Inflation *when?*
The effects of inflation on U.S. college students in the 1980s—Getting there, but can you speak for all college students?

Which college students?
Inflation in the 1980s and its effects on me—Now you are down to one time period, one place, and one person: you as a college student. Specifics should come to mind on this restricted topic, such as your latest tuition and book costs. The revised limited topic should generate more reader interest and be easier to write about than the general topic we began with—inflation.

general topic plus who, what, where, why, when, & how

= restricted or limited subject

EXERCISE   Getting Specific

Some pairs of topics are listed below. Decide which of each pair provides more detail—that is, which is more specific (easier to see, touch, etc). Circle the letter of your choice. For example:

a. children's books   **(b.)** *Peter Rabbit*

1. **a.** Cinderella   **b.** fairy tales

2. **a.** urban problems   **b.** rush hour traffic

3. **a.** dandruff   **b.** diseases

4. **a.** university   **b.** school of business

5. **a.** essay examinations   **b.** examinations

6. **a.** hang gliding   **b.** outdoor activities

7. **a.** drug problems in the United States   **b.** drug addiction among U.S. doctors

8. **a.** social studies   **b.** Afro-American history

9. **a.** employment opportunities in high-tech industries   **b.** employment opportunities in the computer field

10. **a.** educational problems   **b.** teacher burnout

Limitation is not simply a matter of picking one term of reference over another. Sometimes you have to keep working on a topic, restricting and limiting it again and again to come up with a topic that prompts details, not generalities. For example, "high school" is a more specific topic than the catchall word "education." Here is one attempt to move from the general topic of education to a more restricted and more manageable subject for a 500-word writing assignment:

Education—Too broad. Substitute a more *restricted* term.

High schools—One important sector of education, but still too much to cover. *Restrict* it even more.

High school students—One division of high school personnel. But there are millions of high school students. *Restrict* further.

Problems of high school students—All the possible problems of high school students, from acne to suicide? *Restrict* to some problems.

Three major reasons students drop out of our local high school—A much more limited topic: a specific number of problems of one category of high school students (dropouts) at a specific high school.

You can do such narrowing of a topic at any stage in the writing process. Doing it right off will, however, save many false starts. Restricting a subject is not "busy work" to please a teacher. Limiting what you write about will help lead you and your audience from thin generalities to meaty specifics.

EXERCISE   Restricting the Topic

Take any three of the general topics below, and restrict or limit them so they would be appropriate for a *short* writing assignment (approximately 500 words).

Hint: You might start by substituting a more specific word or phrase for the one given before adding specifics.

EXAMPLE: entertainment (broad topic)

Substitute a more specific word or phrase: *television*

Using several more narrowing or modifying phrases which answer questions such as *what?, who?, where?, when?, why?,* and *how?,* you will come up with a more limited subject, such as:

beer commercials on television
Saturday-morning children's cartoon shows
current televised game shows

General Topics (Choose any three.)

1. computers
2. poverty
3. hobbies
4. education
5. discipline
6. studying
7. alcoholism
8. inflation
9. jobs
10. exercise

General Topic Number _____
Restricted or limited subject:

General Topic Number _____
Restricted or limited subject:

General Topic Number _____
Restricted or limited subject:

For some writing assignments you get to pick your own subject. Picking a subject you know a lot about or can easily find out about will make the job of moving from topic to subject much easier. What you know firsthand should generate interesting details. Your first summer job, for example, would be of more interest to you and the reader than an essay about employment opportunities in the computer field if you have little firsthand knowledge about that topic. Even with a subject you know well, don't try to cover too much ground. For example, you might be tempted to describe an entire city, but a single neighborhood or block would suggest more specific details and therefore be more interesting to read.

If you cannot think of what to write about, survey your own interests: if you can fix a ten-speed bike or know your way around a darkroom or how to make strudel, share your expertise. Pick a topic that grows out of these skills. Work out of what currently interests you: music, psychology, dance, or whatever. You need a topic that can be covered in, at most, a few paragraphs. You don't want a book-length topic; you want the kind of topic covered in a short magazine article. The history of photography would take volumes. Your tips on photographing dogs should not.

Your own freewriting or journal writing is a good place to look for topics you have already paid some attention to: what's wrong with your boss, your fear of flying. Chances are there are dozens of topics that you have already started to deal with in writing.

Sometimes you are spared the job of picking your own topic. But even when you are assigned a topic, you still may have to restrict it to what can be treated adequately in a few pages. If you are asked to write about pollution or the peace movement or your hobbies, cut those general topics down by narrowing and limiting. For example, you might be asked to describe your neighborhood. While that is more restricted than a description of an entire city, it is still a large task. One student cut that topic to one block party. This single event offered the reader an instant close-up snapshot of her neighborhood.

Even with assigned topics, you will often have to refocus. That will take, as I have shown, a lot of adjustment. The following exercise gives you some practice with finding suitable topics for short writing assignments of around 500 words.

EXERCISE   Restricting General Topics

Decide which of the examples in each pair would be more suitable as a subject for a two- to three-page essay. Answer by circling one letter.

1. **a.** My relatives
   b. Strange Uncle Louie

2. **a.** How to survive your first rock concert
   b. The history of rock music

3. **a.** A movie I saw six times and why
   b. Western movies

4. **a.** Computers
   b. My roommate, the computer freak

5. **a.** A smooth-talking salesman
   b. Effective sales techniques

6. **a.** A decision I regret
   b. Important decisions

7. **a.** Photography
   b. How to develop black-and-white film

8. **a.** Comic books
   b. How the Superman comic books have changed

9. **a.** New England colleges
   b. Why I chose _____College

10. **a.** Video games are a waste of time.
    b. Video games

Obviously there are degrees of limitation of topics. It is possible you could get too restricted in a topic you select. To illustrate: most writers could not describe at any length a minor ailment like a hangnail or tell why they chew a particular brand of gum. (However, a magazine once published an article that focused entirely on Michael Jackson's sequined glove.) Many student essays, however, are too general rather than too narrow. The next step in the writing process will help you decide whether your topic is too general and, if it is, what to do about it. It will even rescue you from the unlikely choice of an overly narrow topic.

Listing Details

List details that your subject brings to mind, using the Listing or Brainstorming Sheets provided on pp. 319–326. Simply flood the paper with as many associations as you can. Do not, at this stage, stop to puzzle over correct spelling or punctuation or to compose full sentences. Your list is, at first, so much window shopping. Another caution: Do not rule out any images or ideas you come up with during this brainstorming session. Criticizing your work too soon can block the writing process. Of course, you will not use every memory marker you come up with, but until you compile a substantial list, you will not know what to keep and what to reject.

List-making serves as a check on the subject you have chosen or been given. If you were planning to write about children's literature but the only details you could list were Peter Rabbit and Foxy Loxy, either you are moving to a more restricted subject than you planned or you need to find a lot more about the one you have.

Making a list also helps you decide between competing topics. If, for instance, you were not sure you wanted to write about hang gliding or about surfing, window shopping both subjects would show which prompts a better batch of details.

Here is one student's brainstormed list. The general topic was a description of how hard someone works. The student chose to write about her mother, a letter carrier, so she sat down to list whatever came to mind about her mother's job. This is what she came up with:

1. Walking miles a day
2. Working in all weather
3. Lifting heavy mailbags
4. Driving old jeeps
5. Listening to irate customers
6. Long hours—six days a week
7. Children throw snowballs
8. Car and/or jeep stuck in snow & ice
9. Overloaded mail carts
10. Overloaded mailbags
11. Dogs that bite
12. Starts early in mornings
13. Cakes & cookies
14. Putting up with her boss
15. Housework when she comes home
16. Coming down sick
17. Money & cards at Christmas & birthday
18. Getting to know people
19. Some customers even know her birthday
20. People count on her

21. Invite in for coffee & lunch
22. Children help push cart/deliver mail
23. Discount rates

Yes, the list is random. At this stage the order is not important. Flooding out twenty-three details, some of which overlap, some of which contradict, and some of which will not prove useful, the student proved to herself that she had a topic she knew something about. Even though it lacks some specifics—for example, how much a mailbag weighs—the list served its purpose.

If, however, the student could not come up with enough details to prove her central point that her mother works hard, this would signal the need for more brainstorming or another subject. When your first list shows that you do not have very many specifics to support your topic, brainstorm your list once more. If you still do not like what you come up with at this stage, find another topic. When the list reveals enough support for the limited subject, you are ready for the next stage of shared prose: organizing that list.

Organizing Details

In the list-making session, ideas do not come in any reliable order. One idea may suggest another, but they are not necessarily related. Nor are all the ideas or images equally important. If, for example, you are writing about a favorite teacher, details about how he lectures would be more important than whether his socks match his suit. If you were arranging details on this topic, you might decide to play down or eliminate your notes about your prof's socks.

If you do enough brainstorming on a topic familiar to you, you will have much more detail than you need. You can then afford to cut out what is less important, repetitious, or irrelevant. If you find your list too general or not detailed enough, do not be afraid to go back and redo it. To revise and edit your list at this stage is a lot easier than dealing with large chunks of text later.

Unless you arrange the list you prune, the reader will have to struggle through the random order you generated. In "self prose" you know where your journal or diary entry is headed. In shared prose, however, readers need to see clearly where they are headed. Grouping or arranging the details before you write will save you much rewriting later.

Here is an example of that. In the preceding section you saw a list prepared by a student describing her mother's job. That list was enough to convince the student she had enough details to go on with her subject. But, since the list was put together just as the ideas and details came to her—in random order—she had to rearrange it. Compare the original random list with her revised list, which groups and rearranges the items from the first brainstormed list.

Original List	Revised List
1. Walking miles a day	−1. Starts early: 6:30 A.M.
2. Working in all weather	−2. Long hours—six days a week
3. Lifting heavy mailbags	−3. Lifting heavy mailbags
4. Driving old jeeps	−4. Working in all weather
5. Listening to irate customers	−5. Walking 10 miles a day
6. Long hours—six days a week	−6. Overloaded mailbags
7. Children throw snowballs	−7. Overloaded mail carts
8. Car and/or jeep stuck in snow & ice	−8. Car and/or jeep stuck in snow & ice
9. Overloaded mail carts	−9. Jeep breakdowns
10. Overloaded mailbags	−10. Children throw snowballs
11. Dogs that bite	−11. Dogs that bite
12. Starts early in mornings	−12. Irate customers
13. Cakes & cookies	+13. Cakes & cookies
14. Putting up with her boss	+14. Money & cards at Christmas & at birthday
15. Housework when she comes home	+15. Invite in for coffee
16. Coming down sick	+16. Children help push cart / deliver mail
17. Money & cards at Christmas & birthday	
18. Getting to know people	
19. Some customers even know her birthday	
20. People count on her	
21. Invite in for coffee & lunch	
22. Children help push cart / deliver mail	
23. Discount rates	

The original list has been trimmed. The student writer dropped the note on special discounts that postal employees receive and some other details, such as how her mother gets along with her boss. Note that the revised list is not only shorter, it offers more detail. We now know how many miles the student's mother walks every day and when she leaves for work. "Starts early" turned out to be too general. 6:30 A.M. tells exactly how early.

Not only has the list been trimmed and given more detail, it has also been rearranged. An idea that came to the writer halfway through the brainstorming list (item 12 in the first list) is, in the revised list, put first. In addition, the ideas are clustered in a more natural order. For example, the two complaints about the jeeps are put next to each other. Also, all the positive features of the job are put at the end after the main point: how difficult the job of a letter carrier is. Plus signs are put next to the affirmative or positive features, and minus signs are put next to details that show the negative or difficult aspects of a letter carrier's job.

Using plus and minus signs is one simple way of grouping or clustering ideas to see if they fit a pattern. Do not try to begin with a pattern. Let the content suggest the arrangement. And do not be afraid to add or delete any items you came up with in your first brainstormed list. It is not unusual for some details and additional ways of grouping the details to come to you later in the writing process.

Here are several organizing or grouping patterns to choose from:

Spatial

Spatial arrangement moves like a guided tour: left to right, right to left, inside out, top to bottom, and so on. Mostly used to describe physical objects (buildings, paintings, etc.), it means walking through a subject with your reader in mind, much as you might describe your bedroom to someone who has never seen it.

Chronological

This is the automatic mode of the storyteller—time order. Whether it is about a visit to the zoo or a heart transplant operation, readers expect a story to be linked by a time sequence. Even when the strict time order is turned backward, as in a movie flashback, stories and other forms of writing are still tied together by some chronological order.

Affirmative and Negative

Affirmative and negative order is one of the simplest forms of arrangement. As you go over your brainstorming list, you could label + or − as shorthand for the positive and negative features of your subject or those items you agree with or disagree with. These labels will help you decide whether your essay will be pro, con, or pro and con. Then you can decide the order of your arguments. You can, for example, present arguments in favor of a position and then arguments against or vice versa. Such a pattern could also be used to help find similarities and differences. This way of organizing is especially useful if you want to compare and contrast two subjects or different aspects of a single subject.

Logical

In logical order you can proceed from a generalization to specifics (deductively) or from specifics to a generalization (inductively). For example, if you were writing about "junk food," you could begin with a general statement about what is wrong with all junk foods before complaints about specific foods, such as soft drinks. That is deductive order. In inductive order you would move from specific junk foods, like candy bars or soft drinks, to a generalization about all junk foods. Logical order may seem very formal and complex, but you have, consciously or unconsciously, used it many times to structure paragraphs or entire essays.

In addition to formal logical order (induction and deduction), logical order can also mean any order that is a natural or logical fit for a given topic. For example, a logical division of a college population would be faculty, staff, and students. Or the logical parts of a microcomputer would be input devices, output devices, and central processing unit. In this looser sense, logical order refers to major elements that comprise any subject or typical ways of categorizing a subject. Restaurants, for example, could logically be categorized by the kind of food served (Chinese, French, etc.), by cost (inexpensive, moderately expensive, expensive), or by location (downtown, near a college campus, in the suburbs, etc.).

Emphatic

Emphatic arrangement—that is, organizing in order of emphasis—proceeds from the least important to the most important point or example. An essay on crime that moves from murder to mugging to purse snatching violates this order. Emphatic order would build from purse snatching to mugging to murder. Emphatic order *ends* with the most dramatic or most climactic point.

Summary of Organizing Patterns

Spatial

Left Outside Top
↓   ↓   ↓
Right In   Bottom

Chronological

Affirmative and Negative + –

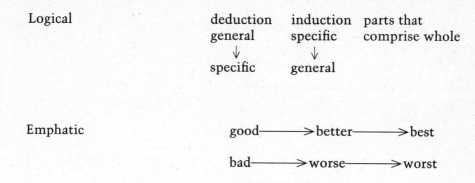

Logical

deduction   induction   parts that
general   specific   comprise whole
↓   ↓
specific   general

Emphatic

good——→better——→best

bad——→worse——→worst

The first letter of each way to organize spells:

S   C   A   L   E

Remember SCALE. It suggests many ways to organize your ideas from your head or from your notes into a structure that the reader needs to follow those ideas. As the writer, you know where your writing is headed; your readers do not. Clear organization will help keep them (and you) from getting confused or lost.

It is time to see how easy making and organizing a list can be. Before you start the following exercise, remember that list-making is not a commitment to write about everything that comes to mind. Rather, it is a check to see whether enough specifics come to mind to get started writing.

EXERCISE   Listing Details

In the space provided below, make up a list using the general topic "a teacher or teachers who stand out in my mind." You can make that topic more limited if you want. Do not write sentences. Instead, jot down single words or short phrases, one to a line. You will not be using all your jottings. Later, you can get rid of what overlaps and what does not fit. Think of your list as a shopping list of items, not all of which you will invest time in later.

General topic: A teacher or teachers who stand out in my mind.

Your limited or narrowed topic: _____

_____

Your brainstormed list:

1. _____

2. _____

3. _____

4. _____

5. _____

6. _____

7. _____

8. _____

9. _____

10. _____

11. _____

12. _____

13. _____

14. _____

15. _____

16. _____

17. _____

18. _____

19. _____

20. _____

You don't have to fill every line in the exercise above. On the other hand, if you need more room, make a second column above and number it from 21 on.

If some teacher or teachers stood out in your mind, you were able to generate several lines of details. If not, do more brainstorming. Chances are that you found enough for more than one topic, especially if more than one teacher stands out in your memory: for example, the third-grade teacher who scared you, and your favorite high school teacher.

Put your list away for a while. Then go back to it and scratch out what no longer interests you. Also add further details that now come to mind. When you have finished, decide on some way of organizing what you came up with.

If you need help in creating groupings, use one of the organizing patterns suggested below.

SCALE

S = SPATIAL—This order would work only if you are describing one teacher, say, from head to toe. Use this if your list turns up lots of description.

C = CHRONOLOGICAL—This order might work if you are discussing first a teacher you had earlier, then a teacher you had later in life, for example a grammar school teacher and a high school teacher.

A = AFFIRMATIVE and NEGATIVE—Since you are evaluating some teachers, this would fit. It would even work if you are dealing with a single teacher. You could use the plus and minus categories that were used in the list on the letter carrier.

L = LOGICAL—There are some natural groupings of teachers that would help you organize a discussion of them. One logical grouping is by subject matter: English teachers, gym teachers, and so on. You can probably come up with several more logical groupings that fit this catchall category: teaching methods, age, and the like.

E = EMPHATIC—Here you would save the strongest details for the end of your list: the teacher you feared most, the teacher you liked most, or what you liked or disliked about a particular teacher.

EXERCISE   Organizing Details

General topic: A teacher or teachers who stand out in my mind.

Your limited or narrowed topic: _____

_____

Your rearranged and organized list:

(List only those details from your first brainstorming list that you still are interested in. Put them in some grouping that makes sense to you. Use any of the groupings suggested by SCALE. You might have to try out several before you get one that seems right for your subject.)

1. _____
2. _____
3. _____
4. _____
5. _____
6. _____

7. _____

8. _____

9. _____

10. _____

11. _____

12. _____

13. _____

14. _____

15. _____

16. _____

17. _____

18. _____

19. _____

20. _____

Which organizing principle helped most?

spatial   chronological   affirmative and negative
logical   emphatic

Circle one of the above, or, if none of these helped, state below what did
help most. _____

_____

Outlines

There are more formal ways of organizing material for writing. The
most widely taught of these is the formal outline. To many students
this is a bewildering and overrigid system of Roman numerals and letters that reminds them of sixth-grade homework.

Although outlines can be tyrants, they can also lead you to order
and clarity. Outlines are especially helpful in working with topics that
otherwise might run away with you. For example, when asked to
describe the classroom they were in, most students plunged into
descriptive details without any formalized plan of attack. One student,
however, began with this formal outline:

Topic: Describe this room.
Limited topic: How this room affects my senses.

   I. Sound
      A. High-pitched drone of fluorescent lights
      B. Small talk
      C. Rhetoric coach having a student conference
      D. Creaking doors in hallway
      E. Footsteps in hallway
      F. Shuffling papers
      G. Scratching of pencils
  II. Sight
      A. Straining faces
      B. Sickly-green chalkboard
      C. Broken coat hooks
      D. Picture behind teacher
         1. Ridiculous
         2. Indescribable
 III. Touch
      A. Feel of wooden pasteboard under me
      B. Arctic air brushing the exposed flesh of students
 IV. Smell and taste
      A. Absolute lack of smell
      B. Dry mouth

EXERCISE   Outlines

The outline above uses what arrangement? Circle one answer by letter only.

a. spatial
b. chronological
c. affirmative and negative
d. logical
e. emphatic

    The above outline was not required. The student chose it because it provided a writing plan. Put into outline form, the five senses bring a logical order to an otherwise random grouping of details. The student also knew how to adapt his outline to fit his needs. Since he couldn't think of many details for taste and smell, he fused them into a single category. Some students mistakenly believe that all parts of an outline must have the same number of divisions. That is not so. In the student outline above, two details are used to explain the smell and taste conveyed to the student in the classroom, but eight details are listed to suggest the sounds heard while writing. Note that in outlines smaller divisions add up to the larger categories and all divisions must be lined up.

In addition to outlines, there are other ways of helping find connections and patterns in the details you come up with.

Trees

One way to organize is to keep drawing out more particular examples or categories until you get to what you want to write about. This is especially useful in moving from a general topic to a specific subject. Here is an example. A student was dealing with the topic "hard work." Here is how she got down to what she wanted to write about.

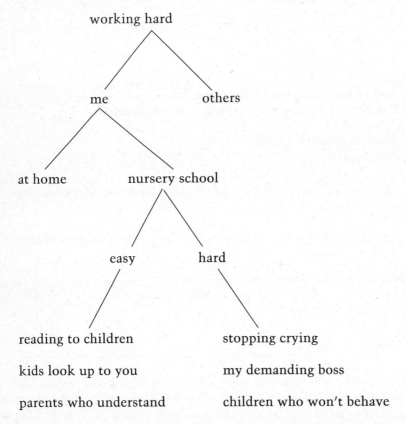

working hard

me   others

at home   nursery school

easy   hard

reading to children   stopping crying

kids look up to you   my demanding boss

parents who understand   children who won't behave

With this tree method, in contrast to the outline, you can fill in one area and leave others undeveloped. For example, in the student example above, hard work at home is mentioned but never developed. Simply by adding more branches you can often get down to the kind of details that are useful in short writing projects.

Clusters

Another informal way of getting at specifics is to have one detail suggest another in clusters or balloons. Here's an example a student used
in planning how to describe the experience of being pregnant.

She started out with this idea:

which suggested these ideas:

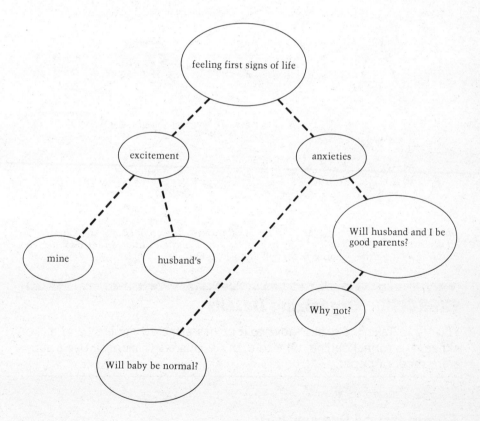

Clustering can be quite extensive. Look at this web which identifies
some topics found in *Morning Star, Black Sun,* a children's book on the
Northern Cheyenne Indians.

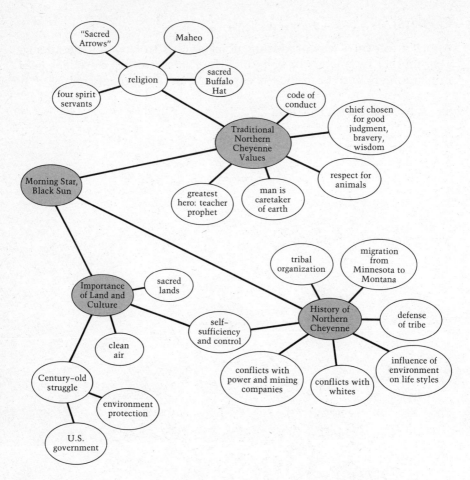

Donna E. Norton, *Update: 1983: Children's Literature: Research, Issues,* and *Children's Books: An Annual Update for Users of Through the Eyes of a Child: An Introduction to Children's Literature.* Charles E. Merrill Publishing Co.

EXERCISE Organizing Details

You try it. Take the topic "how college has affected my life" and make either (1) a formal outline, (2) a tree, or (3) clusters (balloons). Use a separate sheet of paper.

Summary of Prewriting

When you have found a subject, tested and expanded it with a list of details, you have finished prewriting. Prewriting is whatever you do to get ready to write from the first head-scratching over a topic to finally putting pen to paper to write. Since anything you have ever experienced or read is potentially useful in prewriting, do not be surprised if it takes at least half your writing time. In many cases it should! A formal application for a job will demand more prewriting than a letter to a friend, but no matter how well you know your audience and that audience knows you, all shared prose, even a love letter, needs some prewriting. The cartoon strip below shows what happens when a writer tries to do without prewriting.

Do not let prewriting consume the writing process. Some students find the search for a subject alone takes up the bulk of their time on a writing task. If you often wait until the night before a paper is due to come up with the right subject, you are letting the planning hold you back from the writing. Try this rough rule of thumb. When half of the time you have for writing a paper is up, start writing, even if you have not finished all the planned prewriting. For example, if you have two weeks to compose an essay, at the beginning of the second week stop prewriting and shift to writing. Some prewriting will be called for later. You can always go back to add details to your outline or to rearrange sections of your paper.

Prewriting is preparation. It should and will make writing easier. If prewriting gets too elaborate or time-consuming, cut it short. Many students and professional writers swear they never use formal outlines; they must know how to store up mental plans of what they will write about. Whether you use a formal outline or an informal grouping of details, you need an informed sense of where you are headed during the writing process. Prewriting sharpens that informed sense; writing tests out the promises and plans of prewriting.

You have reviewed and practiced finding a subject, listing details about that subject, and organizing those details you decide to keep. If you should find yourself changing your mind and moving back to the organized list to add more details or from the list to a new subject, that is fine. Since, at this stage, you have not yet written anything that your audience will see, it does not matter how many false starts or restarts you make. Better to shape and reshape your writing at this stage than to scrap much written work later. It is more convenient to move bricks

©1983 United Feature Syndicate

(words, phrases) than walls (sentences, paragraphs). Not every subject will pan out; not every listed detail will be used; not every organized grouping of details will work out. Expect a constant back-and-forthness with all three of the areas that make up prewriting:

Finding a subject
Listing details
Organizing details

Writing a First Draft

All writers follow some rituals when it is time to start writing. Some writers will compose only on yellow pads with a purple felt-tip pen. Any ritual that enables you to begin writing is fine, but some rituals can become avoidance mechanisms. I often write from notes scrawled on whatever is handy—backs of envelopes, cocktail napkins, and the like—so I easily manage to misplace some of these and then have to hunt for them. The last notes that turn up in the trunk of my car or under my bed are often duplicates or unreadable, but I still must launch a search for them before I can sit down to write. So a ritual that helps you write can become a delaying tactic. Some students report that their kitchens sparkle the day before a paper is due. They would rather face the drudgery of housework than the chore of writing.

WRITING ASSIGNMENT   Your Writing Rituals

There are many rituals writers use to get in the mood to write. Before sitting down to write every morning, Ernest Hemingway used to sharpen a dozen pencils. Other writers use long walks to get their prewriting sequence going. What do you do to get ready to write? Write a paragraph or essay in which you discuss the rituals you go through when you sit down to write. Do you have to have a certain kind of pen or pencil? Do you need music on or off? Do you write better at a particular time of day? If you prefer, write instead about those things you sometimes indulge in to *avoid* sitting down to write.

But whether you have sharpened every pencil in the house, scrubbed the stove, or misplaced your notes, a deadline will prompt you to get on with the writing. If you have followed any prewriting system (the one suggested in this chapter or your own), you are well ahead of the student who must stare at a blank page without the benefit of such organized prewriting. To guide you, you already have a list and an organizational plan.

Armed with whatever prewriting help you gave yourself, you are ready to face the dreaded blank page and start writing. Where to begin?

"Begin at the beginning" is the overworked, oversimplified advice given to storytellers, but may not be useful to you; where you begin to write is not always where your audience will begin to read. When you make the leap from prewriting to writing the first draft, it is OK—in fact, it is encouraged—to begin anywhere you want.

Many students find that starting with the middle is most comfortable. Often they know what they want to say, but they are not always sure at first how to introduce what they have not yet generated. Another reason for putting off the introduction is proportion. A two-page introduction to a four-page paper would be topheavy. Similarly, a short paragraph will very likely not be enough to launch a twenty-page report.

Once you have a rough draft of the body (middle section) of your paper, you can see how much room is left for the introduction and conclusion. In one of his novels, John Updike suggests that, when buttering toast, you start with the edges because the middle will take care of itself. Writing an essay is a lot more complex than buttering toast, but Updike's advice might work in reverse in your writing as it does for mine. The middle is what you really want to get to. Having written it, you can then draw out a conclusion, an introduction, and a title from what you have written. First do the middle (body of the paper), then the edges (conclusion, introduction, and title).

Of course, where you start often depends upon the topic and what you are comfortable with. One editorial writer claims that he could never start writing an editorial before first coming up with a title. You might be at ease with such a top-to-bottom movement, but do not feel locked into any one method. I still butter my toast contrary to Updike's suggestion and usually write the introduction and title last, for that is a writing mode I am used to. If a title comes to me first (as it did for this textbook), I use it and keep on writing, grateful that any part of the writing task is over. That title changed many times, but it got me going.

SALLY FORTH by Greg Howard, ©1983 Field Enterprises, Inc. Courtesy of News America Syndicate.

Likewise, if you are temporarily stumped for a title, don't let that keep you from getting on with the rest of a writing assignment.

No two writing assignments will be the same. The student who wrote about her mother, the letter carrier, tried to write her first draft following the numbered items she set up on her revised list (see page 24). She began with item 1: how early her mother starts work. When she brainstormed, that was not her first detail listed. Originally, that was detail number 12.

Here is her first rough draft:

Every morning at 5:30 A.M. Mom prepares to leave home. Her day begins at 6:30 A.M. and is scheduled to at 3:00. My mom is a Postal worker and delivers mail to many households each day.

Once she gets to work, she organizes heavy sacks full of mail to be deliered that same day. When Mom leaves the station it's already obvious the day. Its really true that Postal workers must deliver mail thru rain, sleet, snow or scorching high temp. My mom walks 10 miles a day pushing a cart full of mail for a countless # of households. Instead of walking, she could drive a jeep, but in most cases its better to walk. The old jeeps often break down. They easily get stuck in the snow & ice of winter or overheat in the high temperatures of summer.

Meantime after finally getting to the house to deliver the mail, some of the people are screaming "Why is my mail so late! Where you been! I should report you." Most of the time their bark is worse than their bite, but this is not the case with the canine resident of the neighborhood. Several times she has been chased, attaced and bitten by dogs whose owners ignore their pets behavior. Even the teenagers in the area have to get in on the act. A few of them throw snowballs at her and bury the postal jeep in mountains of snow.

Since there is a silver linning in every cloud, there is indeed a bright side to Mom's job. Most of the tots that live in the neighborhood help her push the mail cart along the route. On the cold days she's invited into the of many for coffee and the soothing warmth of a fire. Mom's birthday is never forgotten and Christmas always brings a shower of cakes & pies. Its these nice experiences that always manage to carry her thru the rough times.

Yes, there are mistakes in what this writer came up with. Many of them, especially the spelling and typing errors, will be corrected later. The student knew she would have to make corrections later. For openers, she wanted to see how long the writing assignment was getting and if the paragraphs were in the right order. This was an important concern because she used more than one organizing principle. Remember all those plus and minus signs? They were used to show the pro and con of a letter carrier's job. The writer thus used affirmative and negative order. Because she built up to the positive features of the job, she was also using emphatic order. The first three paragraphs follow her mother on the job in a single day. That is time order. Therefore, the writer used affirmative and negative, emphatic, and chronological order to organize her writing for an audience.

Lastly, on this first attempt at moving from organized list to first writing draft, she tried out a title: "Through Rain, Sleet, or Snow." Even though she was not entirely happy with the title, she kept it in hope of coming up with something better on the next draft.

Remember, your first draft can be composed in any order you want. The parts can be rearranged later. Think of a first draft as a base draft, a place to start. It does not have to be polished or error-free. Whether crude or well crafted, a first draft is where writing begins, not ends.

On a live TV program a famous cook once dropped a fish dish on the floor. Scooping up her damaged creation, she patched it up until it was presentable. Unruffled, she faced her viewing audience and explained, "Remember, nobody has to know what goes on in your kitchen." Her guests, she assured her listeners, would not be aware of her mishap when they saw the reconstructed fish dish presented to them. What has this got to do with writing a first draft? Plenty! Your audience does not care how bad or good your first draft was. They want a readable final draft, which is all they will see. No one but you has to know what your first draft looked like. No one has to know what went on in your writing "kitchen," just the final product you serve them.

Summary of the Writing Process: The First Four Stages

Prewriting		**Writing**
Finding a subject	+	Writing a first draft = FLOW
Listing details		
Organizing details		

FLOW will remind you of the four stages shared writing will often go through. Since you might have to find and test out more than one subject and refine the list of details you come up with, FLOW is simplified. It does, however, highlight the stages to which your prewriting and writing will lead. So go with that FLOW—find, list, organize, and write.

The Final Stages of the Writing Process: Editing and Rewriting

As the W stage (writing a first draft) suggests, there is more work ahead after FLOW. Prewriting and writing are two-thirds of the writing process. What is next?

Editing

Editing is your chance to go over your drafts to weed out error and to improve the style and content of what you wrote.

In the prewriting process you had to get used to two halves of your creative self: the creator of your writing and the critic of it. Your creative self brainstormed; your critical self trimmed and arranged that brainstormed list. The creator in you came up with a first draft; the critic wants to improve it. To the creator, the closer to the deadline, the better the writing looks. The critic, your writing editor, is not so easily deceived.

How do you switch from creator to editor? One sure way is to distance yourself from your work. Put the writing away for a while—minutes, hours, even a day or two if you have the time. Coming back to it, you can approach your writing with some of the freshness the reader will bring to it. You become, in effect, your own first reader.

Your job is not just to detect error. A sentence may be capitalized and punctuated perfectly but still not be effective. Before tending to misspellings or punctuation errors, get rid of wordiness, unnecessary repetition, and fuzzy diction. For example, why double-check the spelling of a word if that word may be edited out later? The end result of editing should be not just accurate writing but clearer writing. Clarity in writing calls for revisions in editing.

There are four major ways to revise written work:

1. *Substitute* better words, phrases, sentences, or paragraphs.
2. *Take out* unnecessary words, phrases, sentences, or paragraphs.
3. *Add* missing words, phrases, sentences, or paragraphs.
4. *Rearrange* words within sentences, sentences within paragraphs, and paragraphs within essays.

These four ways of revising can be easily recalled by the word:

S T A R

As STAR will remind you, there is much more to editing than proofreading for error.

Let's look at the student essay about the letter carrier, the first draft of which you read earlier. After putting the writing away for a while, the student came back to it. Here is some of the editing that was done to the first draft.

Every morning at 5:30 a.m. Mom prepares to leave home. Her day begins at 6:30 A.M. and is scheduled to/at 3:00. My mom is a Postal Worker and delivers mail to many households each day.

Here is some of the editing that was done to the first paragraph, as classified under the STAR method:

Substitute: many households ———⟶ dozens of households
and delivers mail ———⟶ who delivers mail

Take out: 5:30 A.M. every morning ———⟶ 5:30 every morning

Add: scheduled to at 3:00 ———⟶ scheduled to end at 3:00
prepares to leave home ———⟶ prepares to leave home for work

Rearrange: Every morning at 5:30 ———⟶ At 5:30 every morning

Here is the rest of the student writing assignment, marked to show much of the editing that took place. As you can see, many changes have been made.

Once she gets to work, she organizes *large* heavy sacks ~~full~~ of mail to be

delivered that ~~same~~ day. When Mom leaves the station it's already obvious the

day. *will be a long one* It's really true that Postal workers must deliver mail ~~thru~~ *through* rain, sleet,

snow or scorching high ~~temp.~~ *temperatures* (My mom walks 10 miles a day) pushing a cart

full of mail for a countless *number* ~~#~~ of households, ~~Instead of walking,~~ she could

drive a jeep, but in most cases it's better to walk. The old jeeps often break

down, ~~,and~~ They easily get stuck in the snow ~~&~~ *and* ice of winter or overheat in the

high temperatures of summer.

~~Meantime~~ (after *F* finally) getting to the house to deliver the mail, some of

the people are screaming "Why is my mail so late? Where have you been? I

should report you!" Most of the time their bark is worse than their bite, but

this is not the case with the canine resident, *s on her route⊙* ~~of the neighborhood. Several~~

~~times~~ she has been chased, attacked and bitten *several times* by dogs whose owners ignore

their pets' behavior. Even the teenagers in the area have to get in on the act. A

few of them throw snowballs at her and bury ~~the~~ *her* postal jeep in mountains of

snow.

~~Since there is a saying about a silver linning in every cloud,~~ there is *T*

~~indeed~~ *, however,* a bright side to Mom's job. Most of the tots ~~that live~~ in the area help

~~her~~ *her* push ~~the~~ mail cart along the route. On ~~the~~ cold days she's invited into ~~the~~

homes
of many/for hot coffee and the warmth of a fire. Mom's birthday is ~~never~~ *always*
remembered,
~~forgotten~~ and Christmas ~~season~~ always brings a shower of cakes *and* & pies. It's

these nice experiences that always manage to carry her ~~thru~~ *through* the rough times.

EXERCISE   STAR

Using the last three paragraphs of the essay above, list any two examples of specific editing changes for each of the categories of STAR:

Substituting

1. original word or phrase _____

   substituted word or phrase _____

2. original word or phrase _____

   substituted word or phrase _____

Taking out

1. original word or phrase _____

   word or phrase taken out _____

2. original word or phrase _____

   word or phrase taken out _____

Adding

1. original word or phrase _____

   word or phrase added _____

2. original word or phrase _____

   word or phrase added _____

Rearranging

1. original phrase or sentence _____

   _____

phrase or sentence as rearranged _____

_____

2. original phrase or sentence _____

_____

phrase or sentence as rearranged _____

_____

Notice that the editing changes are mostly to make the writing clearer. In her first sentence, the student did not mean to suggest her mother was leaving home, period, but that is what her first draft suggested. Making it "leaves home for work" certainly clarifies that vague statement.

Proofreading for spelling and typing errors, the student finally got around to correcting some of these mistakes. For example, she noticed that in paragraph two *delivered* was misspelled and that at the end of the same paragraph the symbol & should be spelled out as *and*. There are more such errors, but at this stage they do not preoccupy the student because, when she gets closer to the final draft, some of the words and phrases may be changed or eliminated altogether. The final hunt for surface error (in spelling, capitalization, and punctuation) she wisely leaves for later. Of course, if you catch a mistake at any stage, change it. But a concern for correctness *too soon* can sidetrack the major editing and rewriting.

Looking over the STAR corrections, the student sees she needs to think about another draft. She moves from editing to rewriting. Likewise, when you have gone over your first draft several times to improve it in each area (substituting better words or phrases, taking out what does not belong, adding what is missing, and rearranging elements), you are ready for the last area in the writing process—rewriting.

Rewriting

You have already done some rewriting when you substituted and arranged your brainstorming lists. Rewriting is much more than making another copy of your work; it means incorporating your many editorial changes in another draft. When you get close to final copy, you should take care with your typing or penmanship not only for neatness but also for accuracy. Surface error is a common problem in student writing. Spelling, capitalization, and punctuation errors plague all writers. Our brains running ahead of our hands, we make many unconscious slips when we type or write. You might even misspell (mistranscribe, actually) your own name. Why? The creator of the writing is not the best transcriber of that writing because he or she knows it too well. Knowing what a sentence should contain, the writer might leave out a word or mentally plan a comma that never gets inscribed onto the paper. Read each draft against a previous draft to see if, while concentrating as you had to on penmanship or typing, you made some new errors.

Ridding your paper of surface error is important, but professional writers, when they revise, do much more than that. Before they start another draft, they make many changes to improve what they have written. To illustrate, before delivering his speech to Congress just after the Pearl Harbor attack, Franklin Delano Roosevelt looked over his "final" draft. Rereading that draft's first line—"December 7, 1941, a day which will live in history"—he scratched out *history* and penciled in *infamy* to make the phrase read: "December 7, 1941, a day which will live in infamy." *Infamy*, which suggests great public disgrace, is certainly a better word than *history*. Until just before delivering his speech, FDR failed to see the need for that changed word. Such careful wordcraft as that single-word substitution helped create a memorable and often reprinted speech.

When a draft gets buried under the weight of multiple corrections, it is time to rewrite it. There is no way to know whether a writing project will be over in a couple of drafts or will take half a dozen. Once a draft compares well with your intentions, it becomes a final draft.

Sometimes you may do a lot of revision in your head, so you will not need many separate drafts. At other times, you will have to unearth your meaning within the editing and revising process. Often you will first have to see what you have written to know what you have said and then see if that compares with what you meant. As one famous American writer put it, "I don't know so well what I think until I see what I say; then I have to say it again." Writing is as much a self-discovery as a shared discovery.

Do not be discouraged if you have to edit what you hoped was a final draft. Take the writing where it leads you. Professional writers have to live with the same multiple editing and rewriting process. Such revision works even when it is unaided by anyone but the writer. To prove this, a teacher once wrote at the top of student papers that he hadn't even read, "Is this the best you can do?" Again and again, he returned the unread essays with the same comment to his students for revision. After several weeks of this, some students finally got brave enough to admit, "Yeah, this is the best we can do." Claiming that's what he was waiting for all along, the teacher finally read and graded the student papers. That was a cruel trick, but it worked. Draft three of those papers was better than draft two. The same is true of your writing. Because you put more into it, a later draft will be better than an earlier draft.

Writers sometimes complain that proofreading their own work does not work too well. This is true if you try to proofread too soon after you compose and certainly if you try to proofread *while* you are composing. Trying to pay two different kinds of attention at once will not work. If you have ever tried to write while the television set was on, you know how easily video dialogue can work its way into your paper. So, before you proofread, put your paper away for a while. When you come back to it, you will look at it in a fresher way, much as your eventual audience will. In proofreading you are standing in for that audience.

Some Proofreading Techniques

1. *Read your paper aloud.* Because you usually read aloud much more slowly than when you read silently, this will slow you down enough so that you can concentrate on each word or phrase.

2. *Read the paper backward.* This breaks the natural order, which is especially useful in catching misspellings.

3. *Use a mini–viewing window.* In an index card, cut a hole about this size:

Use it as a viewer to isolate individual words as you read through your writing. This will take a lot of time, but it is useful in giving you practice with the narrow tunnel vision it takes to catch typing, spelling, or transcription errors.

4. *Look for only one kind of error at a time.* Many writers fail at proofreading because they attempt too much at once. It is hard to catch capitalization, punctuation, spelling, and other errors all at once. Proofread several times, each time looking for a particular kind of error you tend to make: capitalization, spelling, commas, and so on.

Here is the second draft of the student paper we have been following:

Through Rain, Sleet, or Snow

At 5:30 every morning Mom leaves home for work. Her work day begins at 6:30 A.M. and is scheduled to end at 3:00. My Mom is a postal worker who delivers mail to dozens of households each day.

Once she gets to work she organizes large heavy sacks of mail to be delivered that day. When Mom leaves the station, it's already obvious the day will be a long one. It's really true that postal workers must deliver mail through rain, sleet, snow or scorching high temperatures. Pushing a cart full of mail for a countless number of households, my mom walks 10 miles a day. She could drive a jeep, but in most cases it's better to walk. The old jeeps often break down, and they easily get stuck in the snow and ice of winter or overheat in the high temperatures of summer.

Finally, after getting to the houses to deliver the mail, some of the people are screaming "Why is my mail so late? Where have you been? I should report you!" Most of the time their bark is worse than their bite, but this is not the case with the canine residents on her route. She has been chased, attacked and bitten several times by dogs whose owners ignore their pets' behavior. Even the teenagers in the area have to get in on the act. Some of them throw snowballs at her and bury her postal jeep in mountains of snow.

There is, however, a bright side to Mom's job. Most of the tots in the area help push her mail cart along the route. On cold days she's invited into many homes for hot coffee and the warmth of a fire. Mom's birthday is always remembered, and Christmas always brings a shower of cakes and pies. It's these nice experiences that always manage to carry her through the rough times.

It would be a comfort to report the student was all done, but there are still areas for improvement. For example, the title, the student decided, was not original. People are tired of hearing that rain, sleet, or snow do not keep postal workers from their appointed rounds. So she tried out several new titles:

It's All Worth It

Hard Work: Why My Mom Does It

A Superwoman at the Post Office

My Mom the Mailman

EXERCISE Choosing a Title

Circle one of the titles above and explain why you think it is the best of this batch of titles for the student essay.

_____

_____

Of course, more than one title might fit. The actual title the student chose is shown below.

The conclusion was also edited. The reference to clouds and silver linings was a cliché, the student decided, so she cut the first sentence of the last paragraph. She also did some proofreading to improve the capitalization. Should it be, for example, _my Mom_ or _my mom_? She also added several specific details.

After another round of editing here is what she came up with on her third draft:

My Mom the Mailman

At 5:30 every morning Mom leaves for work. Her work day, which begins at 6:30, is supposed to end at 3:00 but often drags on even later. My mom, a postal worker, each day delivers mail to hundreds of people.

Once she gets to work she faces huge, heavy sacks full of mail which must be sorted before delivery that day. When Mom leaves the station, it's already obvious her day will be a long one. Pushing a cart full of mail for scores of households, Mom walks ten miles a day and climbs countless stairs. She could drive a jeep, but in most cases it's simpler to walk because the old jeeps often break down and easily get stuck in the snow and ice of winter or overheat in the high temperatures of summer.

Finally, after getting to the houses to deliver the mail, she must calm down the complainers who scream: "Why is my mail so late? Where have you been? I should report you!" Most of the time their bark is worse than their bite, but this is not the case with the canine residents on her route. Several times she has been chased, attacked and bitten by dogs whose owners ignore their pets' behavior. Even a few teenagers in the area add to her delivery woes. Some of them throw snowballs at her or bury the postal jeep in mountains of snow.

There is, however, a bright side to Mom's job. Many of the tots in the area help push the mail cart along her route. On cold days she's often invited into homes for hot coffee or the soothing warmth of a fire. Mom's birthday is remembered by many of her customers, and Christmas brings a shower of homemade cakes and pies. Such cheering concern gets her out of the door every day in all weather at 5:30 A.M. ready to face the same mountain of mail, which brings her so many problems and some well-earned rewards.

Linda Williams

That is the final draft the student turned in. Had there been more time, she would have done at least another draft. Even though the student retained much of the structure she started with, there are many differences between this draft and the previous one.

EXERCISE STAR

Give one example each of substitution, taking out, addition and rearrangement that took place in the final draft over the previous draft (see pages 45–46).

Substitution

1. word or phrase from previous draft: _____

_____

2. substituted word or phrase in final draft _____

_____

Taking out

1. word or phrase from previous draft _____

_____

2. word or phrase taken out in final draft _____

_____

Adding

1. word or phrase from previous draft _____

_____

2. word or phrase added in final draft _____

_____

Rearranging

1. phrase or sentence as found in previous draft _____

_____

_____

2. phrase or sentence as rearranged in final draft _____

_____

_____

As you can see, this student put a lot of effort into working through the process of writing from prewriting through writing and rewriting. Her writing improved because what she had to say got clearer and more interesting. Writing for an audience is quite a job. You will be better able to handle that job if you do enough prewriting and rewriting.

Summary of the Writing Process

Finding a subject
Listing details
Organizing details

Writing

Editing
Rewriting

FLOWER: A Guide to the Writing Process

F = Find a subject—that is, limit or restrict a topic.

L = List images and details the subject brings to mind.

O = Organize, outline, or arrange those details you keep.

W = Write the first draft.

E = Edit your first draft by substituting, taking out, adding, and rearranging.

R = Rewrite the paper, incorporating all the changes you decided on in your editing. Proofread several times for specific errors or kinds of errors.

Note: Expect to do a lot of back-and-forth work in all six areas. Repeat the last two steps (ER) as often as necessary.

FLOWER is simplified. Although you will go through some prewriting, writing, and rewriting every time you write shared prose, the stages will seldom fall into a neat sequence without backtracking. Even if you are lucky enough to find a subject, many useful details, and an organization pattern, you still need more than one draft. That would expand FLOWER at least to: FLOWERER. And if it were not for deadlines, the process could go on indefinitely: FLOWERERERER . . . . .

You don't have to touch all the bases in every writing project. A very simple subject may come to you fully organized. Your writing process then might be graphed FWER. Sometimes, like a baseball runner, you have to go back to tag up between bases. On some occasions you might have this kind of writing experience. I found a subject and made a list, but then discovered I did not know enough about the subject, so I found a new subject, made a new list, organized it, and then started to write. Next, I added to my list some missing details before writing three drafts. In this case, FLOWER was stretched to FLFLOWERERER.

The letter-carrier essay we have been following turned out to be more straightforward. The student was lucky. The first subject she tried out generated a good enough list. When she went back to the list, she hit upon an organizing pattern that helped her revise the list and move on to writing. She then went through three drafts of writing, editing, and rewriting. Using the FLOWER method, her writing process could be graphed this way: FLOLWERERER.

Whatever form your writing process takes, whether it shrinks, repeats, or expands the six parts of the FLOWER method, it should take you from prewriting to writing and through rewriting.

From planning to production of a finished product, you have reviewed the writing process. Whether you use some or all of the six parts of that process as represented by the FLOWER method or you use some method of your own, you can see how and why it takes a writing process to get a written product.

WRITING ASSIGNMENT   "A Teacher Who Stands Out in My Mind"

Earlier, you brainstormed a list about a teacher or teachers (see page 27). Using the revised list and organizational plan you came up with, take that limited subject through the WER stages of writing (writing, editing, and rewriting). Your final product should be at least one paragraph.

WRITING ASSIGNMENT   Writing about Writing

Write a single paragraph or short essay in which you do one of the following:

1. Describe your own composing process. It can be totally different from FLOWER. Tell how and where you start and what works for *you*. Be specific. It might help to step the reader through a specific writing assignment you once did.
2. Explain how you learned to write—that is, who and/or what helped you learn to write.
3. Tell what you like or dislike most about the process of writing and why.

Whichever topic you pick, have a particular audience in mind. You might, for example, explain how you write to a younger brother or sister or to someone who is having trouble writing.

WRITING ASSIGNMENT   "How College Has Affected My Life"

Earlier you outlined, formally or informally, the topic "how going to college has affected my life" (see page 34). Revise the outline you created and write a paragraph or short essay on that topic. Provide plenty of specific details. You may wish to explain how it has affected you in one or two areas: financially, physically, emotionally, intellectually, socially, etc.

PART II

Writing Structures

3

The Sentence

Form and Sense

Sentences are the forms adopted by speakers and writers to make statements and requests or to ask questions. Every sentence is a word group that

contains a subject and a verb

and

makes a statement or request to which you can respond

or

poses a question to be answered.

Here are some simple sentences:

The cookie crumbled.
Is that a tarantula in the mailbox?
My roommate is weird.
The cafeteria is serving mystery meat again.

What about the cookie, roommate, cafeteria? They did or are doing something. Each sentence mentions some person or thing (subject) and asserts or questions some action or condition (verb). For now, remember that no matter how long a word group is, unless it details an action or a condition (that is, has a verb), it cannot be a sentence. (Verbs are discussed more fully in chapter 9.)

Sentences are often called "complete statements." That itself is a very incomplete statement. Take this sentence:

> Roxanne is going to Toronto.

There is an actor/agent—*Roxanne* (subject)—and an action is described—*is going* (verb). A listener or reader could agree or disagree about Roxanne's whereabouts, so we have a sentence, but how complete is it? Are you left with any questions? Roxanne who? you might ask. Obviously, whoever came up with this sentence would have added a last name if more than one Roxanne were around to confuse the audience. How is Roxanne going to Toronto? The composer of the sentence didn't think it important to mention whether she is going by train, plane, or dogsled. Yet we assume this sentence was complete enough for its particular audience. Let's just say all sentences are complete, but some sentences are more complete than others. Some sentences offer more detail than others. In this sense, how complete a sentence is depends upon how much information a writer assumes the reader knows and needs.

Sentences also have a sound that helps distinguish them. Here are two sentences, both complete:

> Dracula flashed his fangs.
> Dracula flashed his sharp fangs at his terrified victim.

Sentence 2 adds more detail and, in that sense, is a bit more complete.

Now read each sentence aloud, and notice how the final word is read each time.

In sentence 1, more than a pause sets off the word *fangs*. To signal the end of the sentence, a drop in pitch underscores its final word.

> Dracula flashed his
>
>   fangs.

In sentence 2, *victim*, not *fangs*, is underscored:

> Dracula flashed his sharp fangs at his terrified
>
>   victim.

Words that end sentences get a special emphasis (a change in pitch) that they receive nowhere else.

In sentences that are questions, the end word goes *up* in pitch, not down. Compare the sound of the following sentences.

The mail is here.   Is the mail here?

In each sentence the word *here* gets a change in pitch, either a drop or a rise, to signal the end of the sentence. This pitch change can help you recognize sentence patterns:

The mail is
        ↘
            here.

Is the mail
            ↗
        here?

Sentences not only end in a distinct way, but also have to act like sentences, that is, statements or questions with which you can agree or disagree:

Snakes slither.
The walls danced.
Santa's stomach shook.

Do snakes slither? Yes. Do walls dance? No. Does Santa's stomach shake? Yes. The fact that you can agree or disagree with these word groups is further evidence that they are sentences.
Try these word groups:

Because snakes slither
If you really want to find out
After three hours in the video arcade

You will have trouble giving a yes or no response to these word groups because their statements need to be concluded before they can stand alone as sentences. For example:

Because snakes slither, they scare me.

Now you have a statement with which you can agree or disagree.
Here are some words or phrases that often set up conditions which must be completed or explained:

after	ever since	when
as	every time	whenever
although	if	where
because	in order that	wherever
before	since	while
even if	that	
even though	though	

Whenever you use these words or phrases to signal conditions, *be sure to give the results of the conditions that these words announce*. It would not be logical to say to someone, "Because today is Friday," and stop there. Your audience would naturally expect some sort of "then what" statement.

Commonly known as subordinating conjunctions, these special words and phrases set up conditions to be completed. (See chapter 9, page 286, for more on subordinating conjunctions.) Conjunctions are connectors that prove very handy in bridging ideas. Subordinating conjunctions make what would be a stand-alone sentence subordinate to another sentence, one that finishes its meaning. To avoid fragments when using subordinating conjunctions, be sure all conditional statements are matched with what follows, the "then what happened."

<u>Because</u> it was nearly dawn, Dracula jumped into his coffin.
subordinating conjunction   *(then what happened)*
(conditional statement)

Dracula jumped into his coffin <u>because</u> it was nearly dawn.
(what happened)   *subordinating conjunction*
                                        (conditional statement)

Note: No comma is needed when the conditional statement *ends* a sentence.

EXERCISE   Conditional Statements

Underline the conditional statements (those introduced by a subordinating conjunction). Add a comma after those that come before "then what" statements. For example:

<u>Because my sister has a cabin on the Bay of Fundy</u>, we go to Canada every summer.

If the conditional statement comes at the end of the sentence, do not add a comma. For instance:

People often look uncomfortable <u>whenever I tell them I teach English.</u>

If the word group needs a "then what" statement to form a grammatical sentence, write in a suitable one. For example:

<u>Even though books for children may look simple</u>, *they are quite difficult to write.*

1. Because the ice cream was dripping on her shoes.

2. Although porpoises communicate they have no written language.

_____

3. After watching thirty cartoons.

_____

4. Everyone stared at me since I was so late to class.

_____

5. Even though Anthony was late he strolled in smiling.

_____

6. Whenever I'm in Washington, D.C. I always head for my favorite Ethiopian restaurant.

_____

7. Sit down and wait while I finish burping the baby.

_____

8. If you like strange food.

_____

9. Wanda got over her fear of writing because she kept a journal.

_____

10. If you go to Monterey don't miss the sea otters.

_____

_____

Sentences have to look, sound, and act like sentences. To judge whether or not a group of words is a sentence, use the following tests:

Test 1: The LOOK

Check for a subject and a verb. Without a verb, there can be no sentence. (For a review of verbs, see chapter 9.)

Subject warning: A subject can be implied. "Stop!" means "(You) stop!" A single word can be a sentence if that word is a verb that suggests or implies a subject by addressing it directly:

Merge. = You merge!
Halt! = You halt!
Smile! = You smile!

Verb Warning: Not every word ending in *ing* is a verb. "The fans tearing down the goalposts" is *not* a sentence. "The fans were tearing down the goalposts" *is* a sentence. A word ending in *ing* will not function as a verb without another helping verb, such as *has, have, is, was.* The helping verb plus the *ing* word form a verb phrase that can function as a verb in a sentence.

Compare the following:

Miranda living on roots and berries (not a sentence)
subject   (no verb)

Miranda was living on roots and berries. (sentence)
subject   (verb phrase)

Miranda has been living on roots and berries. (sentence)
subject   (verb phrase)

Without a verb, there can be no sentence.

Test 2: The SOUND

If a word group has a subject (stated or implied) plus a verb, then make sure it sounds like a sentence.

The volcano erupted

The above group of words passes test 1. Test 2 is the pause and drop or rise in pitch expected at the end of sentences.

The volcano

erupted.

What about these groups of words?

The volcano erupting
The volcano was erupting

The first example lacks the drop in pitch of the statement sentence or the rise in pitch of the question sentence, so this word group is not a sentence. The second example ends with the drop in pitch expected of a statement sentence.

Test 3: The SENSE

The final test to determine whether a word group is a sentence is a simple head-shake. If you can shake your head yes or no at a group of words, they must be making sentence sense. If you can't shake your head yes or no at a word group (agree or disagree with it), it is not a sentence. Try this group of words:

> Because a grasshopper hopped into the fruit punch

These words pass test 1 (LOOK) because there is a subject *(grasshopper)* and a verb *(hopped),* but they fail test 2 (SOUND); *fruit punch* does not get the expected drop in pitch. It also fails the final test (SENSE). Before you could agree or disagree, you would have to know what happened because a grasshopper hopped into the fruit punch.

In direct response to a question, the fragment above would make sense. For example:

> Why aren't you drinking your fruit punch? Because there is a grasshopper in it.

Except in such question-answer formats, a word group with a subordinating conjunction will be a fragment unless it includes a "then what happened" statement. For example:

> Because a grasshopper hopped into the fruit punch, no one drank any.

EXERCISE   The Three Tests for a Sentence

Circle all the tests that the following word groups pass. Only those word groups which pass all three tests are sentences. For example:

> Whenever a teacher scratches his fingernails on a blackboard.
> (Look)   Sound   Sense

1. The teacher was scratching his fingernails on the blackboard.

    Look   Sound   Sense

2. The teacher scratching his fingernails on a blackboard.

    Look   Sound   Sense

3. For example, fingernails scratching on a blackboard.

    Look   Sound   Sense

4. Whenever the teacher scratches his fingernails on a blackboard, the students cringe.

    Look   Sound   Sense

5. I cringe when I hear fingernails scratching on a blackboard.

    Look   Sound   Sense

Make complete sentences out of the word groups above that fail one or more sentence tests. Give the number of the word groups you are correcting.

_____

_____

_____

_____

_____

_____

You can know the look, sound, and sense of a sentence and still have some problems forming sentences. Why? When you concentrate as you should on the sense of what you are writing, structural errors sometimes creep in. There are three major violations of sentence form to watch for: the fragment, the comma splice, and the run-on sentence.

Sentence Violation 1: The Fragment

The fragment is a word group that lacks some sentence element, either a subject or verb or both. Or the word group might have a subject and a verb, but the sentence composer made a conditional statement and forgot to tell "then what happened."

As you have seen earlier in this chapter, failing to follow conditional words to the "then what" creates many fragments. For example:

> Since there was a blizzard (fragment)
> *subordinating*
> *conjunction*

> Since there was a blizzard, classes were canceled. (sentence)

Other kinds of fragments to watch out for are explained below.

Fragment Warning: ing words. As you saw earlier in this chapter, words that end in *ing* can also lead to fragment trouble:

> Driving on the freeway for two hours every day

The group of words above is not a sentence because *driving* is not used as a verb and there is no other word doing the work of the verb.

Cures for *ing* fragments: Attach the fragment to an adjoining sentence:

Driving on the freeway for two hours every day, she felt trapped.

Another cure for this kind of fragment is to change the verb form.

The students squirming in their seats (fragment)

becomes

The students were squirming in their seats. (sentence)

or

The students squirmed in their seats. (sentence)

Fragment Warning: who, which, where, that. Although they are pronouns, the words *who, which, where,* and *that* also signal clauses that cannot stand by themselves.

The preacher who lived in Rangoon (fragment)
The creature, which lurked in the black lagoon (fragment)
The black lagoon where the creature lurked (fragment)
The creature that lurked in the black lagoon (fragment)

Cures for *who, which, where, that* fragments:
1. Add another verb to the *who, which, where,* or *that* clause:

The creature that lurked in the black lagoon had bad breath.
     subject   *verb*

2. Remove *who, which, where,* or *that:*

The creature lurked in the black lagoon.
     subject   verb

Fragment Warning: explainers. Sentences may begin with explanatory words or phrases, such as *for example* and *that is,* but they must include a subject and a verb.

For example, the creature from the black lagoon (fragment)

Cure for explainer fragments: Add a verb or a subject and a verb.

For example, the creature from the black lagoon was one of the first
             subject   *verb*

3-D movie monsters. (sentence)

Like the creature from the black lagoon (fragment)
Like the creature from the black lagoon, Godzilla has bad breath.
(sentence)   *subject   verb*

Special Warning on Explainers: such as. There are very few words or phrases you could not use at the beginning of a sentence. Some students, for example, think it is wrong to begin a sentence with *and* or *but.* That rule does not hold up. Here is one that does: Never begin a sentence with *such as.*

> Such as the creature from the black lagoon (fragment)

Cure for fragments with *such as:* Put *such as* in the previous sentence.

> There are many memorable movie monsters, such as the creature from the black lagoon. (sentence)

Such as introduces a specific example, so attach it to whatever sentence could use that example.

In summary, there are many kinds and causes of fragments. Some are highlighted above. A fragment is simply any word group that fails one or more of the three tests for the sentence:

The LOOK
The SOUND
The SENSE

EXERCISE   Recognizing Sentences

Circle the *one* complete sentence in each group.

1. gambling in casinos where it is legal.
2. legal gambling in casinos.
3. legal gambling which takes place in casinos.
4. gambling is legal in some casinos.
5. although gambling is legal in some casinos.

6. The sweltering heat of the jungle.
7. The jungle where it swelters.
8. The jungle swelters.
9. That sweltering heat of the jungle.
10. To endure the sweltering heat of the jungle.

11. Starting a car in cold weather.
12. Starting a car when the weather is cold.
13. When you are starting a car in cold weather.
14. The car which is hard to start in cold weather.
15. Starting a car in cold weather takes patience.

16. Attending college involves increased costs.
17. The increasing costs of attending college.
18. Attending colleges where costs are increasing.

19. If the cost of attending college keeps increasing.
20. Whenever the cost of attending college increases.

EXERCISE   Recognizing Fragments

Use the label **F** for those word groups below that are fragments (those that fail one or more of the three tests for sentences: LOOK, SOUND, SENSE). Use the label **S** for those word groups below that are sentences (those that pass all three tests for sentences).

_____1. Meanwhile, back at the ranch.
_____2. Although Ewoks look harmless.
_____3. The pie crust which tasted like wet cardboard.
_____4. That time when the dog attacked the Christmas tree.
_____5. Ripping open the bag with my teeth.
_____6. Ever since we planted the corn in the rattlesnake patch.
_____7. He was so boring that he put himself to sleep.
_____8. For instance, music that is so loud it hurts your ears.
_____9. Although the air conditioning was turned on.
_____10. Smile.

EXERCISE   Repairing Fragments

After considering the following examples, make sentences of the fragments below.

> Mexican restaurants opening up all over town (fragment)
> Mexican restaurants *are* opening up all over town. (fragment repair)

> Wearing a polka-dot tie with a plaid shirt (fragment)
> Wearing a polka-dot tie with a plaid shirt, *Henry looked like a clown.* (fragment repair)

> The waiter who was dressed like a chicken (fragment)
> The waiter who was dressed like a chicken *felt foolish.* (fragment repair)

Notice that you often do not have to rewrite the fragment, but merely supply a missing word, phrase, or clause. You may also have to change the punctuation.

1. A walrus which was in the back seat of the station wagon.

   _____

2. Wishing her an ordinary day.

   _____

3. After being told by ten different people to "have a nice day."

   _____

4. Struggling to open the childproof aspirin bottle.

_____

5. Although wheat germ sounds nasty.

_____

6. The alligator that was crawling in our backyard.

_____

7. Ever since the basement flooded.

_____

8. Because the television set was broken.

_____

9. Picking up the pieces of broken glass.

_____

10. The peanuts which they sell at the zoo.

_____
_____

EXERCISE   Repairing Fragments

Rewrite the fragments listed below as complete sentences.

1. The way that each pattern is delicately carved.

_____
_____

2. Such as reduced fatigue and a more relaxed state.

_____
_____

3. Which creates an atmosphere that stimulates relaxation.

_____
_____

4. Depending on how much you want to play.

_____
_____

5. For example, when I'm in the mood to relax.

_____

_____

Sentence Violation 2: The Comma Splice

Comma splices are two or more sentences separated only by commas. Extremely short sentences may be separated in this way and will still be correct:

> Snow fell, icicles formed.

With the exception of such very short sentences, a comma alone should not be used to join sentences:

> The semester was finally over, students and teachers hurried home to celebrate. (comma splice)

If you shouldn't use a comma by itself to separate sentences, what should you use?

Cure for comma splices: Separate the sentences with a period or a semicolon.

> The semester was finally over. Students and teachers hurried home to celebrate. (period)

> The semester was finally over; students and teachers hurried home to celebrate. (semicolon)

Semicolon warning: Do not use semicolons between sentences that are not closely related:

> I raise peacocks; I am a mechanic.(incorrect)
> He is my psychology teacher; he is not good at racquetball.(incorrect)

Use semicolons if the sentences are *closely related:*

> I raise peacocks; they are splendid birds.
> My biology teacher is entertaining; her lectures are quite funny.

Cure for comma splices: coordinating conjunctions. Without changing the punctuation, you can fix a comma splice by adding one of the special connecting words called coordinating conjunctions:

and	but	or
yet	so	for
		nor

The semester was finally over, <u>and</u> the students hurried home to celebrate.   *coordinating*
                                              conjunction

For more on coordinating conjunctions, see chapter 9.

EXERCISE Comma Splices

Correct the comma splices below either by changing the comma to a period or a semicolon or by adding a coordinating conjunction. If you use a coordinating conjunction, make certain that the one you pick fits.

He knew the Bible well, he was always quoting it. (comma splice)
He knew the Bible well; he was always quoting it. (comma splice fixed with a semicolon)
He knew the Bible well. He was always quoting it. (comma splice fixed with a period)
He knew the Bible well, and he was always quoting it. (comma splice fixed with appropriate coordinating conjunction)
He knew the Bible well, but he was always quoting it. (comma splice fixed with inappropriate coordinating conjunction)

Do not rewrite the sentences; just insert your corrections as indicated above. Make sure you add a capital letter to begin a new sentence after a period.

1. Dwayne never saw a green milkshake, he never hoped to see one.

2. John can sing "America the Beautiful" at the breakfast table, his wife

   won't let him.

3. Sally smashed the wineglass, she loved to hear the sound of tinkling glass.

4. Everyone in the restaurant stared at him, he felt like Boy George at an

   American Legion convention.

5. The cafeteria food is starchy, carbohydrate freaks just love it.

6. I really enjoyed the horror movie, I understood it better the second time.

7. My family is anxious, they don't understand college life.

8. This is the story of a man called Charley, it takes place in Boston.

9. My family loves my cooking, besides it's not something I mind doing.

10. Classes were over at three, then we went off to party.

Cure for comma splices: subordinating conjunctions. Another way to cure a comma splice is to use a different kind of conjunction: a subordinating conjunction. For example:

His feet are on the ground, his head is in the clouds. (comma splice)
<u>Although</u> his feet are on the ground, his head is in the clouds.
subordinating
conjunction
(comma splice corrected)

Note the subordinating conjunction can introduce either clause:

His feet are on the ground although his head is in the clouds.

EXERCISE   Correcting Comma Splices with Subordinating Conjunctions

Correct each of the following comma splices by adding a subordinating conjunction taken from the following list:

if	when	even though
although	because	because
since	as	until
while	whenever	before

You may add the subordinating conjunction to either of the two sentences separated by a comma. In some cases you will have to cross out the comma.

1. The dog howled, somebody stepped on its tail.

2. No one else wanted to go to the zoo, I talked them into it.

3. The salesclerks were too pushy, they didn't make many sales.

4. I was broke, I decided to go out to the movies anyway.

5. He was on a diet, he covered his eyes when he passed a bakery.

Sentence Violation 3: Run-on Sentences

Run-on sentences (sometimes called fused sentences) are very much like comma splices. They are two sentences run together, not with the wrong punctuation (the comma), but with *no* punctuation between them. For example:

The little red hen baked her bread she shared it with no one.

Cure for run-on sentences: Break up the logjammed sentences. How? As with the comma splice, use a period, a semicolon, or a conjunction.

The little red hen baked her bread. She shared it with no one. (period)
The little red hen baked her bread; she shared it with no one.
(semicolon)
The little red hen baked her bread, but she shared it with no one.
(coordinating conjunction)
When the little red hen baked her bread, she shared it with no one.
(subordinating conjunction)

EXERCISE   Run-on Sentences

Correct any run-on sentences you find below. Use periods, semicolons, or conjunctions. When you use coordinating conjunctions, include a comma. When you use subordinating conjunctions, include a comma only when such conjunctions are added to the *first* of the two clauses. Vary the corrections that you use. Label "OK" those sentences which are not run-ons. Do not rewrite entire sentences.

1. I am glad she won I am sure she deserved it.

2. Two men came up to the car and offered me their help to get it started.

3. The recovery was terrible excruciating pain followed for the next four

    weeks.

4. Put down the jukebox you know you can't carry a tune.

5. Before I joined the program I was 200 pounds now I'm 165.

6. I feel the movie was a waste of time I could have had more fun watching

    test patterns on TV.

7. The book is excellent it helped me a lot.

8. It is not easy to be lazy it takes a lot of practice.

9. I usually pass on the first pitch the second pitch I usually take.

10. The movie was funny however it could have been longer.

Variety

To write effective sentences you have to do more than avoid major errors like fragments or run-ons. Even correct sentences can have flaws. One common fault is to have too many sentences, especially short sentences, beginning the same way.

Correction Table for Major Sentence Errors

Sentence Fault	Abbreviation	Representation	Remedies
Fragment	frag	—Sentence (something less than a sentence)	Attach to next/previous sentence Add missing verb/ subject Add "then what"
Comma Splice	cs	Sentence 1, Sentence 2	Keep comma and add coordinating conjunction Add subordinating conjunction* Remove comma and add period Remove comma and add semicolon (if sentences are related)
Run-on Sentences	ro	Sentence 1, Sentence 2	Same as for comma splice

*Comma is kept only when the subordinating conjunction is added to the *first* of the two sentences.

Read this passage:

It was Monday. It was Monday evening. The President entered the East Room of the White House to speak to the reporters. He began with a brief announcement. It was about income-tax reform. He answered dozens of questions. An hour passed. The press conference ended.

That passage was painful to read, not because the sentences are fragments or mispunctuated, but because many of the sentences are short and begin the same way.

Here's one possible revision:

On Monday evening the President opened his White House press conference in the East Room with a brief statement about income-tax reform. He then answered dozens of questions posed by the reporters. After an hour, the press conference ended.

Although the revision still lacks some detail (what questions were answered, how well, etc.), the three sentences pack more interest than the eight sentences that string out every detail separately. Putting more details into each sentence helps you carry more information to the reader. This helps create more interesting sentences.

Sentences have a beginning, a middle, and an end. This gives writers many options for rearranging sentence elements. The subject and verb can, for example, be delayed by details built up *at the beginning of the sentence:*

On Monday evening the President held a press conference.
    details   *subject   verb*

Or details can be inserted *between* subject and verb:

The President   on Monday evening, held a press conference.
       subject   *details*   *verb*

Or details can be added *after* the subject and verb:

The President held a press conference on Monday evening.
       subject   *verb*   *details*

All three sentences are correct. It is up to the writer to arrange elements within a sentence to achieve particular effects. Move the sentence parts around until you get the effect you want.

Here are three sentences, all with the same words, but rearranged:

Maybe I will take you to lunch.
I will, maybe, take you to lunch.
I will take you to lunch, maybe.

To stress that the offer is not firm, the first and third sentences work well because they emphasize the word *maybe* by putting it up front or last. The second sentence, which tucks *maybe* in the middle of the sentence, makes that qualifying word less obvious.

EXERCISE   Rearranging Sentence Elements

The following sentences need rearranging so that important words and ideas come at the end, not in the middle. Rewrite them so that they end more emphatically. For example:

I am going to Africa if I save enough for air fare.
Rewritten: If I save enough for air fare, I am going to Africa.

I will major in belly dancing probably.   ·
Rewritten: I will probably major in belly dancing.

1. I don't mind shoveling snow most of the time.

   _____

2. You can find Henrietta at the computer terminal usually.

   _____

3. I avoid small, useless dogs as a general rule.

   _____

4. The sheepdog slobbers sometimes.

   _____

5. There can be no peace without justice, at least in theory.

   _____

6. I'll have to change my study habits, I guess.

_____

7. Detective stories are fine escape reading at times.

_____

8. Your Superman costume will be ready at noon, probably.

_____

9. I forget to put film in my camera before taking pictures on many occasions.

_____

_____

10. Burying dead parrots in tuxedos is outrageous, I believe.

_____

_____

Standard and Periodic Sentences

Arrangement depends upon a writer's intention. Adding modifiers *after* the subject and verb is the most common order:

Dinner was served on the patio, which was lit with dozens of lights.
subject   *verb*   *details*

Such an arrangement is called the standard sentence. Reverse that order and you get the periodic sentence.

On the patio, which was lit with dozens of lights, dinner was served.
details   *subject*   *verb*

Since periodic sentences keep the reader in temporary suspense, they help maintain audience attention. (You have just read just such a sentence. Reread it and see.) Periodic sentences make for harder reading, however, because the reader must store a lot of details before getting to the subject and verb to which those details are tied. Standard sentences are easier to read because the subject and verb on which the reader pins meaning are provided first. Here, for example, is the first sentence of this paragraph rewritten as a standard sentence:

Periodic sentences help maintain audience attention since they keep the reader in temporary suspense.

Compare that sentence with the first sentence of the paragraph above. It should be obvious which sentence is easier to process in your mind and therefore to read.

Sentence Parallelism

Another way to help readers string together meaning is to use parallelism.

Here's a very familiar periodic sentence:

> Over the river and through the woods to Grandmother's house we go.

What makes this sentence so readable (and memorable) is not simply the suspense element. You do read on to find out how the sentence will end, but you don't get lost along the way because of the way the sentence elements before the subject and verb were grouped. They repeat the same grammatical construction:

> Over the river   and
> through the woods
> to Grandmother's house   we go.

In a parallel construction, some sentence elements have been placed in similar grammatical forms. In the sentence above, parallelism appears in a string of prepositional phrases:

Preposition	Object of Preposition
Over	the river
through	the woods
to	Grandmother's house

For parallelism, you could use a a string of verbs, nouns, adjectives, even whole phrases or clauses. Here are some more examples of parallelism within a single sentence:

> Scratching his head,
> straightening his tie, and
> clearing his throat,   the nervous teacher started his lecture.

> The jet soared,
>   banked,   and
>   dived.

> To sleep,
> to study,   and
> to party   were Zena's weekend goals.

> "When there was no fatback to go with the beans,
>   no socks to go with the shoes,
>   no hope to go with tomorrow,
>   she'd smile and say:
> 'We ain't poor,
> We're just broke.'" (Dick Gregory)

Parallelism can also mean the deliberate repetition of the same phrase or sentence. Martin Luther King, Jr.'s most famous speech was the one in which he repeatedly thundered: "I have a dream." John F.

Kennedy used that device in his much-remembered speech at the Berlin Wall in which he came back again and again to the sentence: "Let them come to Berlin." Here's an example of repeated-word parallelism from the article "On Keeping a Journal," which you read in chapter 1:

> By keeping notebooks, you improve your writing ability. . . .
> By keeping notebooks, you discover patterns in yourself. . . .
> By keeping notebooks, you heighten some moments and give substance to others. . . .
> And by keeping notebooks while still in college, you chart a terrain. . . .

Tips on Parallelism

Parallelism does not mean just any repetition; it means repetition for an effect. A string of sentences that all begin with the word *the* would not automatically suggest deliberate parallelism.

Once you start a string of parallel items, do not break the chain:

> I like soccer, football, and billiards. (parallel)
> I like soccer, football, and playing billiards. (not parallel)
> To play soccer, football, or billiards is my idea of fun. (parallel)
> My idea of fun is soccer, football, or to play billiards. (not parallel)

EXERCISE   Parallelism

Label P those sentences which maintain their parallelism, and label NP those which fail to maintain parallelism.

_____1. The dumb husband, the messy kid, and the smart wife are stock characters on many TV commercials.

_____2. On summer jobs I have worked as a cashier, an usher, and I baby-sat.

_____3. Loosening his tie, unbuttoning his coat, and his napkin grabbed, he was ready for dinner.

_____4. She put a record on the stereo and a log on the fire.

_____5. With much talent and practice and hoping to succeed, she entered the competition.

_____6. Block after block, mile after mile, they ran.

_____7. Closing their books and their pens capped, the students signaled that the class was over.

_____8. Hips shaking, fingers snapping, with heads that bobbed, the dancers were lost in another world.

_____9. Eggs that are poached, a toasted bagel, and orange juice are what I like for breakfast.

_____10. If you like wooden acting, contrived situations, and cardboard characters, you'll love the new movie.

WRITING ASSIGNMENT   Parallel Sentences

Compose three sentences that use parallelism. You may, if you wish, rewrite some sentences you have already written for another writing assignment.

1. _____

_____

_____

2. _____

_____

_____

3. _____

_____

_____

Active and Passive Voice

Rearrangement might also mean shifting the focus of a sentence. Compare these two sentences:

> The witches called a strike.
> A strike was called by the witches.

Both sentences give their subjects and verbs up front, so they are both standard sentences. The first sentence is in the active voice; the second sentence is in the passive voice. Active-voice sentences show a subject acting. Passive-voice sentences, which show a subject which is acted upon, use (1) some form of the verb *to be*, (2) a verb's past participle,* and (3) often, but not always, the word *by*.

Now compare these sentences.

> The referee called a time-out. (active)
> A time-out was called by the referee. (passive)
> A time-out was called. (passive)

Passive-voice sentences are usually wordier and weaker than active-voice sentences. Compare:

---

*The third form of the verb as listed in a dictionary. See chapter 9, page 265.

The actors were hit by giant tomatoes. (passive)
Giant tomatoes hit the actors. (active)

Because they are more direct and easier to read, active sentences are usually preferred over passive sentences. Therefore, most of the time you will compose more sentences in the active voice.

For example, if you were driving the wrong way on an expressway ramp, which of these two signs would be more effective?

The wrong way has been driven by you.
You are driving the wrong way.

It should be obvious that the second sign, the one in the active voice, is more direct. As a matter of fact, the state of California uses a version of it: *Go Back! You are driving the wrong way.* That's direct and emphatic, something hard to achieve in the passive voice. So avoid the passive voice except in the following cases:

1. Use the passive voice when you want to draw attention *away* from the subject:

An error has been made in your account by our billing department. (passive)

Compare that with:

Our billing department made an error in your account. (active)
This sleazy restaurant was picked by me. (passive)
I picked this sleazy restaurant. (active)

2. Use the passive voice when the actor is unknown:

My teddy bear has been stolen.
Chuckles the clown was kidnapped yesterday.

EXERCISE   Active and Passive Voice

Convert the sentences below from the active to the passive voice or vice versa. For example:

Snow White was found by the seven dwarfs. (passive voice)
The seven dwarfs found Snow White. (active voice)

Notice that you have to get the noun that follows the word *by* to be the subject of the sentence and to change the verb form. Where *by* and its accompanying noun is implied, you will have to supply a subject.

Our tuition bills are issued every month. (passive voice)
The college issues our tuition bills every month. (active voice)

1. A concert was sponsored by the fraternity.

2. Someone in a kangaroo suit delivered the pizza.

_____

3. The computers in our dorms are used by many students.

_____

4. A meeting was called by the heffalumps.

_____

5. The billy goats were bothered by a troll.

_____

Simple, Compound, and Complex Sentences

Besides choosing between active and passive voice and between standard and periodic sentences, writers also have several major kinds of sentence constructions to pick from: *simple, compound,* and *complex*.

Simple Sentences

All sentences have at least one clause. A clause is any word group that has a subject and a verb. A simple sentence has only one clause.

> The dog howled. (simple sentence)
> subject   verb
>
> CLAUSE 1

The simple sentence can also have modifying details but only within the same main clause. For example:

> The mangy old dog howled at the moon every night.
> subject   verb

Compound Sentences

Adding a coordinating conjunction plus another independent clause to a simple sentence creates a compound sentence:

> The dog howled at the moon, and the neighbors complained.
> S1   V1   coordinating   S2   V2
>   conjunction
>
> CLAUSE 1   CLAUSE 2

Adding a linking word to create a *compound subject* or *compound verb* does *not* make a sentence compound:

> The dog and its owner howled at the moon. (simple sentence)
> S1   S2   V

The dog yawned and howled at the moon. (simple sentence)
S   V1   V2

The dog yawned, and it howled at the moon. (compound sentence)
S1   V1   S2 V2

Complex Sentences

A complex sentence also has two clauses, but one of them is introduced by a subordinating conjunction.

When the hound dog howled, the neighbors complained. (complex sentence)
subordinating clause (dependent)   *independent clause*

The neighbors complained when the hound dog howled. (complex sentence)
independent clause   *subordinating clause (dependent)*

Any of the subordinating conjunctions can signal a subordinate or dependent clause.

although	when	as
because	whenever	after
if	since	before
while	even though	until

(A fuller list appears on the inside back cover.)

In addition, the following pronouns can introduce subordinating (dependent) clauses.

that	who
what	whoever
whatever	which

For example:

Whatever Lola wants, Lola gets.
dependent clause   *independent clause*

To know how to classify sentences as simple, compound, or complex is useful, but there is no formula to tell you how many sentences of a particular type to use. Too many simple sentences create an annoying "See Dick run" sameness. Too many complex sentences complicate the reader's job. A good mix of sentences is what you should be after.

EXERCISE   Simple, Compound, and Complex Sentences

Label the following sentences **S** for simple sentence, **Cd** for compound sentence, or **Cx** for complex sentence.

_____1. Jogging is addictive, but it is a positive addiction.

_____2. Because the bananas were bruised, we didn't buy any.

_____3. Some TV and radio commercials are clever.

_____4. My favorite mythological creatures are Pegasus and Fafnir.

_____5. Some TV commercials are clever, but many are crude.

_____6. Some modern music sounds as if it were sung by a bunch of demented birds.

_____7. Cold pizza may not be your idea of breakfast food, but I like it.

_____8. The snowy owl stared at us and hooted.

_____9. Whales and porpoises can be spotted off the coast of New England in the summer and early fall.

_____10. My friend, who is very vain, can't pass a mirror without flashing an approving smile.

EXERCISE   Sentence Combining for Simple Sentences

Combine each group of sentences below to create a single simple sentence. For example:

> The movie was crude.
> The movie was disgusting.
> The movie was well attended.
>
> *Combined:* The crude, disgusting movie was well attended.

1. The movie is from Brazil.
   The movie will be shown in the art museum.
   The movie will be shown at 7:00 P.M.

   _____

   _____

2. Fred fed the pigeons.
   The pigeons were in the park.
   He fed the pigeons peanut butter.
   The peanut butter was poisoned.

   _____

   _____

3. The teacher entered the names of students.
   He entered them in his grade book.
   He entered them carefully.

   _____

   _____

4. The photograph was old.
   The photograph was faded.
   The photograph held memories.
   The photograph held many memories.

   _____

   _____

5. She ripped the box open.
   She ripped it eagerly.
   It was a Crackerjack box.
   It was to find something.
   It was to find the prize.

   _____

   _____

EXERCISE   Sentence Combining for Compound Sentences

Combine the pairs of sentences below to make a compound sentence. For example:

> Some people think squirrels are cute.
> To me they are cute rats.
>
> *Combined:* Some people find squirrels cute, but to me they are cute rats.

Be sure to use appropriate linking words. *And,* for example, would not fit in the above compound sentence.

1. Ruth sat in the cockpit.
   She stared at several of the gauges.

   _____

   _____

2. *Huckleberry Finn* was written for boys and girls.
   Today many readers see it as an adult novel.

   _____

   _____

3. He knew a lot about computer games.
   He knew little about computers.

   _____

   _____

4. Bread baking is not difficult.
   It is rewarding.

_____

_____

5. Don't stick your finger in the food processor.
   It won't be your finger for long.

_____

_____

EXERCISE   Sentence Combining for Complex Sentences

Combine all the details given in each example to make a complex sentence. For example:

> He had a ring around his collar
> He didn't wash his neck.
>
> *Combined:* He had a ring around his collar *because* he didn't wash his neck.
> *Because* he didn't wash his neck, he had a ring around his collar.
>
> The debating society has picked a mascot. It is a unicorn.
>
> *Combined:* The mascot that the debating society has picked is a unicorn.

1. It was Wednesday.
   The doctor was not in.

_____

2. Pigeons spread disease.
   I still like to see them around.

_____

3. Pigeons spread disease.
   That's why I call them rats with wings.

_____

4. Rosey Grier is a former football player.
   He does needlepoint.

_____

_____

5. The cat got bubble gum in its long, mangy hair.
   I spent all evening getting it out.

_____

_____

_____

     The exercises that follow give you practice in sentence recognition and rearrangement. They should help you detect major sentence errors, such as comma splices, run-on sentences, or fragments. More importantly, they should help you decide what to do about such errors. Revision strategies will be demonstrated to make you a more skillful composer of the writer's main unit of expression—the sentence.

EXERCISE   Comma Splices

Many of the sentences below have comma splices. This means that a comma is used between sentences without any joining words. Correct the comma splices you find by adding either (1) a coordinating conjunction to the box *above* the comma, or (2) punctuation to replace the comma in the brackets *below*. For example:

[   ]

Learning to drive isn't easy, it takes determination.

[.]

or

[   ]

Learning to drive isn't easy, it takes determination.

[;]

or

[and   ]

Learning to drive isn't easy, it takes determination.

[ ]

If you find that a numbered item contains no comma splice, leave both boxes blank. This signifies that the comma is used correctly.

[   ]

Because it takes determination, learning to drive is not easy.

[ ]

[   ]

1. The temperature is 30 below zero, I'm staying inside.

[ ]

[   ]

2. When Gladys directs our choir, she looks mean.

[ ]

[   ]

3. Susan starts off with a word of encouragement, then she has us

[ ]

warm up before practice.

[   ]

4. Learning to drive is hard, therefore it takes determination.

[ ]

[   ]

5. Otis is a cyberphobe, someone afraid of computers.

[ ]

[   ]

6. The perfect job meets your expectations, and it requires what you

[ ]

are willing to give.

[   ]

7. The meal was a lot better than I expected, I shall never

[ ]

underestimate my husband again.

[   ]

8. I knew my husband could handle the cleaning, it was his cooking

[ ]

that I was afraid of.

[   ]

9. Gloria jogged every day without fail, she never put it off for

[ ]

anything.

[   ]

10. The project may look complicated, it's very clear to me.

[ ]

EXERCISE   Follow-up Work on Comma Splices

Take any five comma splices from the preceding exercise and correct them by using any *subordinating conjunction (although, because, if,* etc.)* or any of these pronouns which can introduce subordinate clauses.

that   whatever
which   who
what   whoever

1. _____

   _____

2. _____

   _____

3. _____

   _____

4. _____

   _____

5. _____

   _____

EXERCISE   Sentence Faults

Label the following **CS** for comma splice, **RO** for run-on or fused sentence, **F** for fragment, or **S** for complete sentence.

_____1. They are working on something important, a cure for cancer.
_____2. All the houses are very similar it seems as though they were built by the same architect.
_____3. My neighbors are nice people, we are all concerned about the environment of our block.
_____4. Cars passing, horns blowing, and tires screeching.
_____5. While music blasts until 3:00 A.M.
_____6. Students laughing and talking at the tops of their voices.
_____7. I seldom see them because they are either getting over something or coming down with something.
_____8. I don't know why, here the summer is different.

*See the inside back cover for a more complete list.

_____9. Making my first mistake, which was feeding the dog from the · table.

_____10. The elephant standing on the Volkswagen.

_____11. My living room is clean and comfortable that's why it's my special room.

_____12. Such as how many essays the teacher expected.

_____13. For example, the way you comb your hair.

_____14. Everything was so convenient the store wasn't far.

_____15. She's checking out the car, she doesn't notice the oil leak.

_____16. He could save a lot of people, many people die of dandruff every year.

_____17. I know I can write because I have written many essays.

_____18. Bright curtains trim the windows wood cabinets and shelves elbow each other for space.

_____19. Hoping that the startling news will improve international relations.

_____20. If it is a long trip to Bloomington.

EXERCISE Follow-up Work on Sentence Faults

1. Take any comma splice from the preceding exercise and rewrite it with correct punctuation.

Sentence #_____: _____

_____

2. Do the same for any run-on sentence.

Sentence #_____: _____

_____

3. Add an appropriate coordinating conjunction to any comma splice from the preceding exercise.

Sentence #_____: _____

_____

4. Add an appropriate coordinating conjunction (with a comma in front of it) to any run-on sentence from the preceding exercise.

Sentence #_____: _____

_____

_____

5. Add a "then what happened" to any one of the fragments from the preceding exercise that uses a subordinating conjunction.

Sentence #_____: _____

_____

_____

6. Change the verb form or add a helping verb to any fragment from the preceding exercise that needs such a correction. (You may also have to add a missing subject, depending on the fragment you pick.)

Sentence #_____: _____

_____

_____

7. Remove the subordinating conjunction from any fragment that uses such a word. Write the remaining words below.

Sentence #_____: _____

_____

_____

Is the result a complete sentence?   Answer Yes or No _____
8. Using any method you wish (rewriting, adding punctuation), correct any comma splice that you have not already corrected.

Sentence #_____: _____

_____

_____

9. Do the same for any run-on sentence from the preceding exercise. Do not use one you have already corrected.

Sentence #_____: _____

_____

_____

10. Do the same for any fragment from the preceding exercise. Do not
    use one you have already corrected.

Sentence #_____: _____

_____

EXERCISE   Comma Splices and Run-on Sentences

Label the following sentences **CS** for comma splice, **RO** for run-on sentence, or **OK** if the sentence contains no such error.

_____1. I only had one dog, but it was a three-dog night.
_____2. I trudged through hip-high snowdrifts, finally I made my way
         to the mailbox.
_____3. It was frozen shut, so I had to track my way home with my
         unmailed letter.
_____4. It wasn't her usual voice, it seemed there was some sort of
         panic.
_____5. Your body stays nice and cool you don't feel like you have
         been exercising for an hour.
_____6. My house was so cold that I wore gloves indoors.
_____7. The essay was finished, now it was finally ready to turn in.
_____8. The second chapter could have been more detailed, more exer-
         cises are needed.
_____9. The growth of the plants is very rapid during this period they
         need a lot of attention.
_____10. My father took me to Mississippi with him, it was in 1982.

EXERCISE   Sentence Improvement

Go over some of your writing and pick out five sentences that would benefit from revision. Rearrange or completely rewrite them. Be sure to work
on sentences you composed yourself.

1. Original sentence before revision:

_____

_____

_____

Rearranged or rewritten sentence:

_____

_____

_____

2. Original sentence before revision:

_____

_____

_____

Rearranged or rewritten sentence:

_____

_____

_____

3. Original sentence before revision:

_____

_____

_____

Rearranged or rewritten sentence:

_____

_____

_____

4. Original sentence before revision:

_____

_____

_____

Rearranged or rewritten sentence:

_____

_____

_____

5. Original sentence before revisions:

_____

_____

_____

Rearranged or rewritten sentence:

_____

_____

_____

_____

EXERCISE   Sentence Variety

Look in a newspaper or magazine for a periodic sentence, a sentence that shows parallelism, and a sentence in the passive voice. Write them below. Then rewrite the passive-voice sentence to convert it to the active voice.

periodic sentence: _____

_____

_____

_____

sentence showing parallelism: _____

_____

_____

_____

passive-voice sentence: _____

_____

_____

_____

rewritten in active voice:

_____

_____

_____

_____

WRITING ASSIGNMENT   FLOWER

Choose one of the following topics and take it through all the remaining stages of writing: listing, organizing, writing, editing, and rewriting.

1. What one adjective would best describe you? Explain.
2. I would rather have a horrible toothache than _____(for example: fly in an airplane, listen to annoying commercials, etc.).
3. There ought to be a law against _____.
4. If I ran this school, the first change that I would make would be _____.
5. Explain the bargain that wasn't.
6. Describe Thanksgiving from the viewpoint of the turkey or Halloween from the viewpoint of the pumpkin.
7. Prove or disprove this bit of street wisdom: "You play, you pay."
8. Prove or disprove this Greek proverb: "Pain is gain."
9. Make up and explain six rules for any activity (for example, dieting, working in a photographic darkroom, studying).
10. What person or what event (past or present) would you like to make disappear?

4

The Paragraph

A paragraph is simply a grouping of related sentences. White space is the visual cue that signals the beginning and end of a paragraph. When you indent, you are signaling the start of a paragraph, and when you leave space after a sentence beyond the normal spacing between sentences, you are signaling the end of a paragraph.

A paragraph looks like this:

Sentence 1
(indent)_____

                              Sentence 2
_____. _____

_____

        Sentences 3, 4, etc.
_____. _____

_____

_____. (space)

When to Paragraph

There are no tight rules on paragraph length. The typical paragraph will have several sentences, but some special-purpose paragraphs might contain only a single sentence. During the composing process, some paragraphs will suggest themselves. Moving from one group of related sentences to another is one cue to start a new paragraph. Other paragraphs will get carved out later when, with an audience in mind, you edit. You can therefore wait to create many paragraphs during the editing and rewriting process.

The Why of Paragraphs

Groups of sentences surrounded by white space, paragraphs do more than give the reader a place to rest. They offer writers a place to collect and connect their ideas and guide readers to comprehend those ideas.

Paragraph Basics

Unity

There are some basic qualities that readers expect from paragraphs. The first of these is unity, or oneness. This means a paragraph will center on and not drift from *one* central topic. For openers, the reader will expect, early in the paragraph, if not in the first sentence, a general statement of what the paragraph will cover. This is a topic sentence— that is, a sentence that expresses the topic and the point of view you will support throughout the paragraph. For example, if you were writing about your least favorite day of the week, you might, early on, tell the reader, "I hate Mondays." Mondays is what you will cover in the paragraph, and "I hate" is your point of view (how you feel about the topic). The topic sentence announces what the paragraph will be about. Other sentences in the paragraph support with details what that topic sentence promises to cover. In this case, you could bring up how hard it is to get back to work after a weekend off, how you hate getting up early, facing early-morning classes, and so on. It is not likely that within that paragraph you would shift to saying Mondays are not really so bad. This would violate the central point of the paragraph, the topic sentence you are trying to prove. You can, of course, modify your topic sentence if you find your details support such a change.

Tips on the Topic Sentence

To get and keep paragraph unity, provide a clear topic sentence and don't digress from it. Stick to the point you are trying to demonstrate or prove. A topic sentence can be left out only if your paragraph topic is completely understandable without it. We will have some examples of that kind of paragraph to show you later. For now, view a topic sentence as essential.

Because the topic sentence is a promise or commitment to a reader, it tells you what the entire paragraph will be or has been about. The topic sentence will therefore be the most general, least specific sentence in a paragraph. The remaining sentences deliver on the topic sentence's promise by supporting it with specific details.

EXERCISE Recognizing Topic Sentences

Find the topic sentence in the following paragraphs.

I

(1) Gospel music is the music I most admire. (2) I listen to it every day. (3) It relaxes me when I'm feeling tense. (4) When I'm alone, it's like a company keeper that makes me know that God is with me. (5) When I'm sad, gospel music lifts my spirits with songs like "Love Will Hold You," "Peace Be with You," "Joy in my Soul," and "Happiness Forever," which all speak of making this world a better place to live in. (6) I really believe it is lyrics like these that make gospel music so popular.

By number only, indicate the topic sentence of the paragraph above—that is, the central point the writer is trying to demonstrate. Note that the numbers come *before*, not after, the sentences they label. Circle one number:

1   2   3   4   5   6

II

(1) Whenever I get annoyed, it's usually when I am in public places. (2) For instance, when I go to the library to study, I always seem to run into a couple of people who bump into each other and start a conversation. (3) As they continue talking, they fail to realize that they are getting louder and disturbing others around them, including me. (4) Another regular annoyance is a radio blasting away on a bus. (5) I usually have to move to the front of the bus to give my eardrums a little relief. (6) I should not have to pay to ride the bus and have to put up with such a noisy assault. (7) Last on my list of annoyances are the line crashers. (8) Whether it's a line for a movie, a rock concert, an amusement park ride, or even a restroom, I really get irritated whenever

people suddenly walk up, see a person they know, and stand there talking until they've become part of the front of the line.

Aubry J. White

By number only, indicate the topic sentence of the paragraph above—that is, the central point the writer is trying to demonstrate. Note that the numbers come *before* the sentences they label. Circle one number:

1   2   3   4   5   6   7   8

III

(1) Every year since Bob was nine he has gone to all the major league baseball games that have been played in Detroit. (2) Bob is truly a baseball fan. (3) In his spare time he coaches a Little League team in our neighborhood. (4) Bob is also president of a local Reggie Jackson fan club. (5) When Bob was younger he collected over two hundred thousand baseball cards. (6) His bedroom walls look as if they have layers and layers of cardboard on them because of all the posters of the various teams and the newspaper clippings he has collected.

By number only, indicate the topic sentence of the paragraph above—that is, the central point the writer is trying to demonstrate. Note that the numbers come *before* the sentences they label. Circle one number:

1   2   3   4   5   6

Support

Although a topic sentence is extremely important and most of the time essential to paragraph meaning, it will not by itself prove a point to an audience. The topic sentence commits you to explaining or defending a topic and a point of view. Support delivers what the topic sentence promises. The reader will expect to know what you base your view on. To meet that expectation, be specific with paragraph support. "Be more specific" is advice that writing teachers have been preaching for centuries. It means to provide enough concrete details or examples to support what you are writing about.

Support your assertions in every paragraph by providing proof, illustration, and/or examples:

Proof—facts, reasons, statistics, evidence, or data: This does not mean absolute proof in the legal sense. It means convincing reasons and facts to support the points you make.

Illustration—description, details, or stories: These elements are called illustration because they show or illustrate a point. Showing is often superior to telling. It is easy to grasp or remember what is described or put into story form.

Examples—examples or explanations: Providing examples is another effective way of showing the reader what you are talking about. You may use several examples or one very detailed one.

Proof + Illustration + Examples = PIE. PIE is a handy reminder to provide proof, illustration, and/or examples in every paragraph. You won't need all three kinds of support in every paragraph, but you should know the kinds of support to use. PIE will not make your writing job easy as pie; it will remind you of the need not just to tell the reader but also to show the reader.

Here are three sample paragraphs, all on the same topic. Although paragraphs can use a variety of support, each paragraph makes primary use of one of the three kinds of paragraph support: proof, illustration, and examples.

Proof

Over *fourteen million people* in the United States wear contact lenses. Last year alone, *two million new users* started wearing these vision-corrective devices. Although the contact lens has been around for over *thirty years*, it is only in the last *ten years* or so, with the introduction of the soft contact lens, that wearing contact lenses in this country has become so popular with Americans with vision problems.

statistics

facts

Illustration

The so-called soft contact lenses are water-absorbent and work *by creating suction on the surface of the eye.* Because they can *shape themselves to the eye,* they are less likely to cause eye irritation than hard lenses. They do, however, require regular maintenance and cleaning. Contact lens owners have to use special eye drops to lubricate the lenses and cleaning solutions to disinfect them. Without such regular cleaning, seeing through them would be *like trying to see through an ice cube.*

shows how they work

shows what would happen

Examples or Explanation

The first contact lenses were hard in a double sense. Made of a rigid plastic, *they shut out oxygen, which caused much discomfort, making them hard to adjust to. They also tended to pop out without warning.* By contrast, today's soft contact lenses, *being porous and water-absorbent, are lighter and easier to wear, and they almost never pop out accidentally.*

examples of difficulties

examples of advantages

EXERCISE   Unity and Support

Read each of the following paragraphs and answer the questions listed after them.

I

<u>Television is a great source for learning English.</u> Television has taught me proper grammar and diction and improved my vocabulary immensely. Watching Blake Carrington deliver a speech at the annual board of director's meeting on the nighttime soap opera *Dynasty*, I learned some public speaking techniques, proper pronunciation of some familiar old words, and correct context usage of some new ones. Soap operas don't do much for my spelling or the punctuation errors I sometimes have problems with. Without a dictionary my spelling ability goes out the window, and punctuation becomes a trial for me.

1. Is there any point where the author digresses—that is, drifts from the underlined topic sentence?

   yes   no

   If yes, draw a line through the part of the paragraph which is a digression from the main topic.

2. What kind of support is used? Circle as many as apply.

   proof   illustration   example

3. Is there enough support to prove the author's main point?

   yes   no

II

After working all day, I like to come home in the evening and sit back and relax as I turn on my stereo. <u>The disk jockey lets you know that you're listening to WGCI, 107.5 FM, the best radio station in Chicago.</u> You don't just listen to the music, you become part of it. WGCI always seems to know what music I like to hear and at the right time. Just when I think that they've outdone themselves with some nice jazz by George Benson, Al Jarreau, or Grover Washington, they turn around and give you a double dose of a nice love ballad by Rolls Royce, the Dramatics, or Marvin Gaye. Love ballads always move me more than any other form of music. I can relate my everyday life to the words being sung. It seems as though everything that happens to me, has happened to someone else already, and someone is singing about it now. If you sit back and consider it, most music carries a message. It's up to you, the listener, to find that message that the composer is trying to express.

Jesse E. W. Hill III

1. Is there any point where the author digresses—that is, drifts from the underlined topic sentence?

   yes   no

   If yes, draw a line through the part of the paragraph which is a digression from the main topic.
2. What kind of support is used? Circle as many as apply.

   proof   illustration   example

3. Is there enough support to prove the author's main point?

   yes   no

III

In Mississippi, where I grew up, we children had a favorite adventure place. This was Big Oak, a woody area far away from home and out of sight of the road. There we had our picnics, built tree houses, and played our games. Here as well was our secret blackberry patch. We would pick berries during the summer. In the fall we would gather hickory nuts from the trees that grew in the woody area. It, too, was forbidden territory, but no child in our neighborhood missed picking the berries or gathering nuts in the fall. However, no parents could be fooled when they heard the cracking of nuts or saw our berry-stained lips and hands.

1. Is this paragraph unified around one central topic sentence?

   yes   no

   Circle one choice. If *yes*, underline the topic sentence.
2. What kind of support is used? Circle as many as apply.

   proof   illustration   example

3. Is there enough support to prove the author's main point?

   yes   no

Arrangement

Besides having a point that is well supported, paragraphs must be arranged in some consistent way. There are many ways to arrange the topic sentence and the supporting details that back it up. You could begin with a general statement that you wish to prove, like "I hate Mondays," and then add several sentences that detail your specific support. This is the most common paragraph arrangement.

Topic sentence up front   I hate Mondays.

                                                    ↓

                             supporting sentences: PIE

Turning that format upside down is just as logical:

Topic sentence last   supporting sentences: PIE

I hate Mondays.

You can even have it both ways, beginning and ending a paragraph with a topic sentence.

Topic sentence repeated   I hate Mondays.

supporting sentences: PIE

I hate Mondays.

Sometimes you might want to classify your topic sentence before presenting it—that is, to first show how the topic sentence fits into a more general category:

Topic sentence delayed   Pet Peeves

I hate Mondays.

supporting sentences: PIE

In other words, after a more general topic, you present a restricted topic, which you then support with proof, illustration and/or examples.

Here is another arrangement, one that is less common in student writing:

Topic sentence implied (not stated) $\rightarrow$ supporting sentences: PIE

Only if it is absolutely clear what your main point is can you skip giving the reader a topic sentence. If a student writer, for example, were complaining about loud gum-chewers, people who play loud music, and snooty waiters, it would be obvious he or she was writing about pet peeves. In such a case, the writer could get by without a stated topic sentence. Where the topic sentence is not so obvious—that is, most of the time in student writing—it must be stated rather than implied.

Although it is not necessary to memorize the various placements for the topic sentence, here is a handy way to remember that you have several options for where to position the topic sentence in each paragraph:

L   U   R   I   D

L = Last
U = Up front

R = Repeated
I = Implied
D = Delayed

Paragraph Patterns

There are many paragraph patterns. These patterns show not just where to place topic sentences but also how to arrange the supporting sentences. Here are some common patterns of arrangement for paragraphs.

Topic–Restriction–Illustration (TRI)

Many paragraphs start by announcing a topic, then restrict the topic in some way. This is the topic–restriction–illustration pattern, which is the most popular way to develop a paragraph. Here is an example:

[T] <u>When it comes to music, give me Frank Sinatra because his unique style of singing is always a pleasure to hear.</u> [R] His remarkable phrasing plus his musical arrangements are compelling. [I] I have just about every record he has ever recorded, and I never cease to appreciate his music. [I] When you hear him sing songs like "Laura" or "Only the Lonely," you can understand why he's known as the master storyteller.

Clarence Nolan

The TRI paragraph proceeds from an announced topic through restrictions and illustrations or examples. The first announced topic will not always be the topic sentence of the paragraph. In this case, it is. In many cases, one of the restricted sentences functions as the topic sentence. In the examples that follow, all topic sentences are underlined. Note the funnel-like shape of a TRI paragraph:

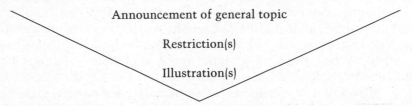

Announcement of general topic

Restriction(s)

Illustration(s)

Any number of restrictions and illustrations may be used in any order in the TRI pattern paragraph. For example:

[T] <u>I believe that some of Sinatra's songs do somehow relate to his life.</u> [I] For instance, when I hear him sing "Here's That Rainy Day," it gives me the impression that he's seen troubled times. [I] I also feel this way when he sings "A Man Alone," for he describes loneliness so exactly you can almost feel it. [R] The message of what he's singing about comes out loud and clear.

Clarence Nolan

A TRI paragraph is any paragraph that starts out with a general topic which is then restricted and/or illustrated in any way. Thus the TIIR paragraph above would fit the overall TRI pattern, as would other variations, such as TRRR or TRII. For convenience, they would all be labeled simply TRI paragraphs.

Another variation on TRI includes a switch in topic:

[T] There are several singers with noted styles, such as Tony Bennett, Johnny Mathis, and George Benson. [S] Frank Sinatra, however, sets the tone for what singing should be. [R] He is a singer's singer. [I] His song "Young at Heart," recorded many years ago, still sounds fresh in today's times of hard rock and reggae music.

topic switch

Clarence Nolan

The reader is, at first, led to believe the paragraph will be about one or more of the singers mentioned. The second sentence uses "however," a turnaround transition, to switch the topic. TRI here becomes TSRI.

A common variation of the TRI pattern is to repeat a topic idea at the end of the paragraph. TRI becomes TRIT:

[T] Sometimes people may feel in need of a quick vacation. [R] They have a need to get away from it all, family and friends included. [R] Everything seems to be coming down on them too fast or too hard. [R] I have found that if you can't get away for a couple of days, then make it a couple of hours and take a long, long ride. [I] Make sure you have a dependable car, a full tank of gas, four good tires, and some money. [T] With these necessities, you can easily fulfill your need for a quick minivacation just about anytime.

Most paragraphs move from general statements to more specific ones. That is, they use deductive order. They therefore usually follow the TRI pattern. Paragraphs that are inductive (moving from specifics to a generalization) invert that pattern to IRT:

[I] "4000 People Show Up for 200 Jobs" was the headline of the article in the *Chicago Sun-Times.* [R] My brother, my cousin, and I were part of the four thousand. [R] The jobs were at the Kool-Aid Division of the General Foods Corporation at 7400 South Rockwell in Chicago. [R] Believe it or not, we actually spent the night out there. [R] We arrived at 11:30 P.M. Friday in order to be part of the first two hundred to receive applications when they were passed out at eight Saturday morning. [T] Our ordeal in quest of a job had just begun.

The IRT paragraph pattern has an inverted funnel shape:

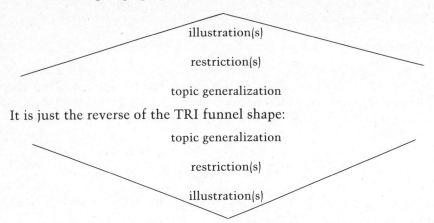

illustration(s)

restriction(s)

topic generalization

It is just the reverse of the TRI funnel shape:

topic generalization

restriction(s)

illustration(s)

There are two more common paragraph patterns: question–answer and problem–solution.

Question–Answer (QA)

The QA type of paragraph is shaped by an opening question, which is then answered:

[Q] Who would think that a puny, wiry-haired man with indented jowls, slew feet, and a very gravelly voice could hold my attention in drama class? [A] <u>Well, outside of his having comic features, Mr. Robert Waldren, my dramatics instructor from my sophomore through my senior year, was a "dynamite" instructor.</u> He taught me how to create a character, write a monologue, and portray a character that could captivate an audience.

Problem–Solution (PS)

In the PS pattern the writer first poses a problem, then offers a solution.

[P] <u>The low-calorie pound cake I made for my dieting family was monstrous.</u> Once we cut into the golden brown crust, we saw the inside, which was heavy and gummy. [S] In the future, I'll choose a light cake flour that has been sifted several times. Less butter will be mixed in, along with the imitation sweetener. Then I'll beat it in the mixer until it's light and fluffy and cook it slowly in a 300-degree oven for about an hour. If that doesn't work, my family says, goodbye, diet.

Jewelean Williams

Answers and solutions are usually more detailed and more specific than questions and problems. The problem–solution and question–answer paragraphs are therefore specialized variations of the TRI pattern we started with.

Summary of Paragraph Arrangement Patterns

Position of Topic Sentence	Paragraph Pattern
Last	IRT
Up front	TRI or QA or PS
Repeated	TRIT
Implied	RRR or III or RI
Delayed	TSRI

EXERCISE   Paragraph Arrangement

For placement of topic sentence,

L   stands for topic sentence last.

U   stands for topic sentence up front.

R   stands for topic sentence repeated.

I   stands for implied topic sentence.

D   stands for delayed topic sentence.

For paragraph patterns, the abbreviations are:

QA—question–answer
PS—problem–solution
TRI—topic–restriction–illustration
TRIT—topic–restriction–illustration–topic
TSR—topic–switch in topic–restriction
IRT—illustration–restriction–topic
RRR—restriction–restriction–restriction [no topic sentence]

I

After much inner struggle, I decided to go back to school. But there are some disadvantages to going to college twenty years after high school. Some of the disadvantages are my poor study habits, the inability to concentrate and retain the materials I am studying, and the fear of failing.

The paragraph above uses what type of topic sentence pattern? Circle one letter only.

L   U   R   I   D

What paragraph pattern is used? Circle one.

TRI   TSR   PS

II

Have you ever been a cashier? Well, I have, and it is not very easy work. I was employed at Newman's Drug Store, where I did everything waiting on customers to pricing and putting stock on the shelves. Even though I only worked five hours a day, it seemed like eight because the work was so tiresome. Pharmacy counter, candy counter, cosmetics counter, cigarette counter, I have worked all of them at Newman's Drug Store.

Donna Smith

The paragraph above uses what type of topic sentence pattern? Circle one letter only.

L　　U　　R　　I　　D

What paragraph pattern is used? Circle one.

TRI　　TSR　　PS

III

The chewing dog is the guard dog, the animal who protects property and person. He may permit neighbor children to play with the master's kids but will bite an adult neighbor who should stray into the yard. The chewing dog is usually large and has an even personality— always evil. The chewing dog's tricks range from lunging at the throat of a threatening stranger to treeing the meter reader with a surly growl. This dog usually has a name like Tiger or Killer.

The paragraph above uses what type of topic sentence pattern? Circle one letter only.

L　　U　　R　　I　　D

What paragraph pattern is used? Circle one.

IRT　　PS　　TRI

IV

College has created a strain on my personal life. Since my family is accustomed to my spending my spare time with them, it gets a little tough for them to understand that I now need my own time for studying. On school nights I don't make dinner because I just don't have the time. The entire day seems rushed when it ends with evening classes. I can no longer watch my favorite nighttime soap opera or *Monday Night Football.* My bedtime has been shifted from ten to midnight. As you can see, going to college has made my personal life hectic.

The paragraph above uses what type of topic sentence pattern? Circle one letter only.

L　　U　　R　　I　　D

What paragraph pattern was used? Circle one.

TRIT　　TRI　　PS　　IRT

V

The snipe has a long, flexible, and smooth, soft bill which is extremely sensitive. The eyes of this game bird are large and placed far back. While the male and female are alike in plumage, the female is rather larger and plumper than the male. Blackish brown, blended with pale brown, and a rich buff are the colors of this fragile bird.

The paragraph above uses what type of topic sentence pattern? Circle one letter only.

L U R I D

What paragraph pattern was used? Circle one.

TRI TRIT RRR PS

Summary of Paragraph Basics: Unity, Support, and Arrangement

Paragraphs deserve care. Whether they are created while writing or discovered while editing and revising, they need unity, support, and arrangment. That's USA for short. Use this abbreviation as a memory aid for the qualities expected in paragraphs.

USA
U = UNITY
S = SUPPORT
A = ARRANGEMENT

Unity

Unity may seem obvious, but do not take it for granted. Read the following paragraph by a student who did just that.

The choir director Gladys Bennett is a very bright person. When Gladys starts off choir rehearsal, she begins with a prayer. After prayer Gladys will have us warm up on some songs before we have choir rehearsal. Gladys is a very good director. I really like how she directs the choir. When she directs the choir, her arms are swinging left and right. Her face looks mean. By giving us dirty looks, she lets you know she wants you to sing loud. If a song doesn't sound right to her, we will sing it over until we get it right, no matter how long that takes. Only then will she say we can go home.

The central point of this paragraph is one of the following:

1. The choir director is a very bright person.
2. Gladys is a very good choir director.
3. The author likes the way Gladys directs the choir.
4. Gladys looks animated when she directs the choir.
5. What a typical choir rehearsal with Gladys is like.

Any of the above could be the topic sentence of a paragraph, but because all of the above are stated or implied in a single paragraph, that paragraph lacks unity. The student did not decide what *one* central idea about the choir director she wanted to explain.

Support

The paragraph does support some of the topic sentences listed above, but there is a little bit of this and a little bit of that instead of plenty of support for one topic sentence. Once the student decides which *one* of the statements about her choir director she wants to deal with, her paragraph will be easier to support.

Once the paragraph is unified, it will be easier to write and to read. If, for example, the aim is to show that Gladys is an excellent choir director, the writer might offer this kind of support:

Proof: Reasons the student likes her choir director
Illustration: A description of how Gladys directs the choir or what her typical choir rehearsal is like
Examples: Some specifics that make Gladys an effective choir director

This example shows that having a limited subject is not enough. You must nail down your attitude (your point of view) toward that subject and stick with it. Then you can line up and arrange supporting details around a topic sentence.

Arrangement

Fitting Sentences Together within Paragraphs

To help arrange supporting details and sentences within paragraphs, use transitions. These handy words or phrases signal the way paragraph elements fit together and thus move the reader along smoothly by providing helpful cues to where the writer is headed.

Here are some typical transitions or signal words, grouped by how they work within paragraphs:

1. *Stringers.* Stringers alert a reader that there is more information to come on the same level that has been set up. Some stringers sequence the reader *forward:*

first	also
next	moreover
second	once
then	after
and	in addition to

Some stringers *reverse* a direction set up earlier:

but	however
yet	on the contrary
nevertheless	before
earlier	on the other hand

2. *Explainers.* Explainers are words or phrases that direct a reader to specific reasons or examples. Some explainers are:

for example	that is
specifically	because
to illustrate	since
such as	

3. *Enders.* Enders summarize or conclude. They can bring the reader back to the level of the topic sentence. Some common enders are:

to conclude	finally
therefore	in summary
so	to summarize
thus	to sum up

Transitions are a writer's directional signals to move readers along from point to point. They are not always required, but they can be quite useful in leading an audience to where a writer is headed. Signal your turns. You do, however, have to use appropriate transitions. Although transitions can often substitute for one another, make sure those you choose fit your purpose. We are all tired, for example, of speakers who say "in conclusion" but keep talking at length.

EXERCISE Transitions

Circle the transitions that fit each example. More than one example may be correct.

1. The campus store offers forty-four different kinds of ice cream,
   for
   but
   yet   plain old vanilla is still the best seller.

2. You're a good employee, but
                    , so
                    ; however,   we have to lay you off.

3. The popcorn was delicious; however,
                    , and
                    , but   it was too salty.

In the next sentences insert any appropriate transition.

4. First open the carton carefully; _____read the directions.

5. The ice is thin, _____stay off.

6. There were many kinds of dinosaurs, _____stegosaurus,

    allosaurus, and brontosaurus.

7. The shop sold many stuffed unicorns, _____I can't stand them.

8. The time lord was scared _____she was meeting her first dragon.

9. The dog went for the letter carrier's leg, _____it would rather

    have had a steak.

10. The record club keeps sending me records I don't want _____ I

    keep forgetting to cancel each month's order.

EXERCISE   Kinds of Transitions

Some of the transitional devices in the following paragraph are indicated
with CAPITAL letters. Your job is to indicate what kind of transitions they
are. Using the space *above* the CAPITALS, label the transitions or signal
words as follows:

> **Ex** for explainers that move to reasons or examples
> **St+** for stringers that sequence the reader forward
> **St−** for stringers that reverse a direction set up earlier
> **En** for enders which conclude or summarize

> Many people associate books for children with childishness, BUT
> there is often a great deal of literary care in even the simplest books for
> the young. FOR EXAMPLE, Maurice Sendak, author-illustrator of
> *Where the Wild Things Are*, admits he takes more than a year to write a
> one-hundred-word picture book, AND many writers for adults, SUCH
> AS Dickens, Twain, and Ruskin, have also written juvenile books. SO
> so-called nursery trifles can be a serious and careful literature.
> THEREFORE, the next time you pick up a book for children, take a

second look, BECAUSE you might find much creative and careful

writing.

In addition to transitions, there are three more ways to link elements within a paragraph: (1) *repetition,* (2) *synonyms,* and (3) *pronouns.*

When you use transitions, repeat key words or phrases, provide alternate words (synonyms), or use pronouns, you are helping paragraph parts fit together.

Here is the paragraph shown in the exercise above with its linking elements labeled for you. The transitions are again printed in CAPITALS.

Many people associate books for children with childishness, BUT there is

often a great deal of literary care in even the simplest books for the young.
                                                              synonym
FOR EXAMPLE, Maurice Sendak, author-illustrator of *Where the Wild*

Things Are, admits he takes more than a year to write a one-hundred-word
                        pronoun
picture book, AND many writers for adults, SUCH AS Dickens, Twain, and

Ruskin, have also written juvenile books. SO so-called nursery trifles can be a
                          synonym   *synonym*
serious and careful literature. THEREFORE, the next time you pick up a book
                                                                pronoun
for children, take a second look, BECAUSE you might find much creative and
repetition   *pronoun*
careful writing.

Don't neglect the four ways of linking elements within paragraphs: *repetition, synonyms, pronouns,* and *transitions.* Here's a student paragraph that did just that.

> The making of eggs is not a difficult task to master. You just follow the instructions properly to prepare the eggs properly. A <u>mixing</u> bowl and <u>mixing</u> spoon will be required to <u>mix</u> the eggs and ingredients together. The ingredients, consisting of eggs, salt, pepper, and milk, will be placed into a <u>mixing</u> bowl and <u>mixed</u> with a <u>mixing</u> spoon until thoroughly <u>mixed</u> together. A frying pan and heat will be needed to cook this combination of ingredients into the scrambled egg dish you desire. If you follow the recipe properly, your scrambled eggs will be a tasty success.

Doesn't the constant repetition of *mixed* and *mixing* make your skin crawl? Synonyms, pronouns, and transitions are much needed in this or any other paragraph.

EXERCISE Linking Elements within a Paragraph

Here is a student paragraph that does make much use of devices to link elements within a paragraph. Read it and then finish labeling every one you can find. Note that transitions and other aids to fitting paragraph parts together can appear anywhere in a sentence, not just at the beginning.

Use these abbreviations:

P = Pronoun
R = Repetition
T = Transition
S = Synonym

The first four sentences have been done for you.

>   P   P   T   P   P
> I'll never forget my first time at sea. At first, I didn't think I would be
>   P   S
> called a "boot." This is like being put down as a "freshy" when you
>   P
> first go to high school. I was new to the ways of a fleet sailor. However,
> I had been out of boot camp for more than two months, so I didn't
> expect to be a "boot." After all, I had been in the navy for almost six
> months. When I told the fleet sailors this, they only laughed. They had
> different rules for becoming one of the guys. For one, you had to have
> your sea legs, and these you only got at sea. One close friend tried to
> explain what it would be like. He told me being on a ship was like
> riding a roller coaster. But I love roller coasters, I told him, so I expected
> nothing more terrifying than the Silver Streak, my favorite amusement
> park ride.

    Kenneth C. Hardy

Note: Since pronouns are very common and often repeated, label all pronouns P and save the R marking for repetition of words or phrases other than pronouns.

EXERCISE Transitions

Write down any three transitional words or phrases used in the paragraph you just read. Then label them stringers, explainers, or enders.

Transition	Kind of Transition
1. _____	_____
2. _____	_____
3. _____	_____

We have reviewed paragraph unity, support, and arrangement and shown how pronouns, repetition, synonyms, and transitions help paragraph parts fit together. Now it is time to work on whole paragraphs.

EXERCISE   Scrambled Paragraph

Read the following scrambled paragraph. Using the numbers that come before each sentence, rearrange the sentences so that they would make sense in a single paragraph. The first sentence has been listed for you.

Computers: The State of the Art Headache

(1) If the file can be found, the computer then decides to change certain key functions; for example, the backspace key now deletes a whole paragraph instead of a single character.

(2) Computers seem to know just when an ill-timed malfunction would be most annoying.

(3) After you correct any or all of these mechanical headaches, everything may be in order, but watch out—the middle page, swallowed up somewhere by the computer, is now missing.

(4) Once that is corrected and everything is finished and ready to be printed, the printer suddenly believes that a page should consist of only seven lines of type or that Japanese characters should replace the English alphabet.

(5) A tiny speck of dust shows up on the disk, and the whole file seems to disappear.

(6) The night before a paper is due, the disk drive decides to get temperamental.

Jordan Graham

The correct order of the sentences for the paragraph above is:

2 ____ ____ ____ ____ ____

Sentence Combining

There is a great exercise to give you practice fitting sentences together in paragraphs. It goes like this. You will be given a series of sentences that belong in a single paragraph, but all the details have been strung out. Your job is to combine the details of several sentences into one and come up with a paragraph that contains all the given details but in a more concise and interesting manner. The first example of sentence combining will be done for you.

It was during World War I.
It was an interlude.
It was incredible.
It was Christmas eve.
There was a small band of soldiers.
German soldiers were facing English soldiers.
English soldiers were facing German soldiers.
They were in bunkers.
They were dug in.
From one side came an officer.
He was waving a flag.
It was small.
It was white.
The shooting stopped.
A truce was agreed on.
It was a temporary truce.
The German soldiers had some beer.
The British soldiers had some wine.
They shared what they had to drink.
They shared the food rations.
They sang Christmas carols.
They sang Christmas carols together.
After a few hours, the celebration stopped.
They wished each other Merry Christmas.
They said goodbye.
They went back to their bunkers.
It was midnight.
It was December 25.
Both sides resumed fire.

Strung out like that, the sentences are painfully boring. Here is one way they could be set in a single paragraph:

During World War I an incredible interlude happened between one small band of British and German soldiers. It was Christmas Eve, and the two sides, dug in in bunkers, had been firing at each other for days. Suddenly a small white flag appeared. A temporary holiday truce was quickly agreed upon. Sharing their wine and food rations, soldiers from both sides joined in singing Christmas carols. The celebration lasted for a few hours. At midnight the officers and soldiers wished each other Merry Christmas. They went back to their original positions in their bunkers. Both sides resumed fire.

That was just one way of combining the sentences into a single paragraph. There are many ways of combining details. Note that you often have to take the details from three or more of the strung-out sentences to create one detailed sentence.

EXERCISE Sentence Combining

Now it is your turn. Read the following sentences. Combine the essential details into sentences that make up a single unified, structured, and arranged paragraph. Details from several sentences may be combined into a single sentence. You will have to cut down on much of the deliberate repetition.

Bernie had a lot of experience with games.
The games were video games.
He played them in an arcade.
He played them all.
He played primitive games like TV Tennis.
He played more complex ones like Tron.
He could not stay away from arcades.
Every time he saw one, he stopped in to spend some money.
His favorite game was Defender.
Defender is played with sharp reflexes.
Defender has a screen.
It is a large screen.
It gives a clear view of what you are doing.
Defender gives you three attack spacecraft.
The object is to destroy them before they destroy you.
Sometimes Bernie got mad.
Sometimes he made the wrong move.
Sometimes he got a low score.
Bernie kept on playing.
To Bernie, Defender was the best video game of them all.

Do several versions of your sentence combining until you come up with a paragraph that contains all the information and that flows well. If you experiment enough with it, sentence combining does work. By providing the data for a paragraph, it lets you concentrate on transitions and other devices to link sentences and sentence parts. Sentence combining works by taking care of unity and support for you. This frees you to work on arrangement.

Compare your final version of the combined sentences with those of your classmates. There will be many variations, some better than others, but there will be *no one single correct way* to link the paragraph elements. You should find many legitimate ways the sentences can be combined and arranged into a paragraph.

Another sentence combining exercise follows.

EXERCISE Sentence Combining

Read the following sentences. Combine the essential details into sentences that make up a single unified, structured, and arranged paragraph. Many details can be packed in a single sentence. You will have to cut down on much of the deliberate repetition.

It was November 10, 1975.
There was an ore carrier.
It was 729 feet long.
It was called the *Edmund Fitzgerald.*
There was a storm.
The ship was hit by winds.
The winds gusted to 58 knots.
Waves reached 25 feet or more.
The ship was snapped in two.
The ship sank.
It sank near the U.S.–Canadian border.
It was not far from Whitefish Bay.
Today, the ship lies at the bottom of a lake.
It lies 530 feet below the surface.
The lake is Lake Superior.
Lake Superior is the largest of the Great Lakes.
Lake Superior is the deepest of the Great Lakes.
There were no survivors.
There was an inquiry.
It was conducted by the U.S. Coast Guard.
They investigated all aspects of this terrible accident.
They could not conclude why the ship sank.
There were no witnesses.
None of the bodies has ever been recovered.
The incident was commemorated in a ballad.
The ballad is by a folk singer.
The folk singer is Gordon Lightfoot.
Lightfoot is a Canadian.

Remember, there is no single one correct way to link the paragraph elements. Do not feel bound to keep the details in the order in which they are presented.

Some informal paragraph arrangements were suggested in the section on prewriting in chapter 2. Remember SCALE? It should not surprise you that what helped you organize the rough details you brainstormed can help you organize a paragraph. The next exercise asks you to apply some of these familiar arrangement patterns to paragraphs.

EXERCISE Paragraph Organization

Label the following paragraphs **S, C, A, L,** or **E** for Spatial, Chronological, Affirmative or Negative, Logical, or Emphatic order. If more than one kind of organization is used, use more than one letter to label each paragraph. See chapter 2, pages 25–26, for a review of these organizational patterns.

I

I have taken it upon myself to reveal the not so joyous events of the Christmas season. Take those beautiful mounds of snow which line city streets. How wonderful is all that snow when you're digging your car out of three feet of it? Seeing all the lovely twinkling lights just makes you melt inside. But when the electric bill comes in January, no one wants to see it. Sweet Aunt Martha went to all the trouble of making a huge Christmas dinner. Who's going to be the one to tell her she's not that great a cook? And who wants to help with all the dishes? You can't forget how nice it is to shop for gifts. After spending three weeks searching for a perfect shade of green in a silk blouse for Cousin Ann, all she gives you is a tacky card saying "Season's Greetings, P.S. Mail my gift." Is it still better to give than to receive? With all these things to look forward to, who wants to celebrate Christmas anyway?

Lillian Williams

The paragraph above uses what kind of organization? Circle the letter or letters that apply.

S   C   A   L   E

II

My worst job interview was the second part of an interview as an overhead crane operator. The first part tested general information, such as safety regulations and capabilities of the crane. I had reviewed this prior to the interview and successfully passed this phase. Next came the practical second part. I had never actually operated an overhead crane, only read a manual which explained the operating levers. The interviewer led me to a ladder under the crane cab. It was fifty feet high. Cautiously, I climbed up the ladder and into the crane cab. The three strange levers used to operate the crane were there. From the moment I turned a lever to move the crane to the left, I was doomed. The hook began to swing violently, I hit the brakes and the hook swung completely out of control. People working on the ground shouted and ran to avoid the menacing hook. Angrily, the interviewer screamed at me. He ordered me to stay in the cab until the hook stopped swaying and then come down. Coming down the ladder, I felt like an ashamed "klutz." My head down, I slunk away from the humiliation of my worst job interview.

Louis Marchman

The paragraph above uses what kind of organization? Circle the letter or letters that apply.

S   C   A   L   E

III

One only has to look at Socrates to determine that he is weird. He usually wears a multicolored knit cap even in summer. Socrates has a pony tail in his long white hair and sports a long white scraggly beard. Red are his eyes as well as his nose. He is about five feet and weighs about two hundred pounds. Socrates' arms and legs look almost too small for his already too-small body. His voice is almost like that of a chipmunk. He usually stands on a corner talking to anyone and everyone, especially himself. You can spot Socrates from three blocks away. All you have to look for is somebody with his head moving slowly from side to side, walking very slowly and waddling like a penguin.

Hilario Perez

The paragraph above uses what kind of organization? Circle the letter or letters that apply.

S   C   A   L   E

IV

Because of the solid blue curtains that blanket the window, the room was dark. The bricks under the curtains were cold-looking, but as I drew the curtains back, the bricks began to look warm. Outside the window, the view was heaven. The bright, clear sky and the energetic blowing of the wind made the trees sway like Hawaiian dancers.

The paragraph above uses what kind of organization? Circle the letter or letters that apply.

S   C   A   L   E

V

The business world has become the computer world. Because my employer (Illinois Bell Telephone) uses computers in every phase of its operations, our everyday language at work has been changed greatly. We find ourselves referring to many aspects of our jobs by initials only. My job title, for example, is COT (central office technician). I work in the TCC (Toll Control Center), which is a segment of the SCC (Switching Control Center), which is a department of the IBT (Illinois Bell Telephone). As a COT I work with the TIRKS (Trunk Integrated Record System) computer. TIRKS issues orders to all SCC and TCC offices in the Bell System, and we have the responsibility of getting the work completed. The equipment used on these orders is CX (carrier), PBX

(Public Branch Exchange), and ES (Electronic Switching). Our TIRKS computer talks to other computers. Some of these are OSCARS (Order Status Control and Reporting Systems), COCS (Circuit Order Control Systems), WORD (Work Order Record Details), and DDS (Digital Data Systems). We call this language computer talk. When we converse in the office we understand the meaning behind our jargon. Outsiders listening in might become confused unless they are familiar with our brand of computer lingo.

Ora Walton

The paragraph above uses what kind of organization? Circle the letter or letters that apply.

S   C   A   L   E

VI

The drill instructor assumed his position in front of the platoon. "Right face," sounded the drill instructor with authority. Just like a well-honed machine, we all pivoted in unison. As we marched off the parade field, we passed the new recruits coming in to begin processing. Immediately the sound of our heels hitting the ground seemed to increase threefold. The look of pride and admiration showing on their faces as we marched by let us know that we were finally Marines.

Will T. Roberts

The paragraph above uses what kind of organization? Circle the letter or letters that apply.

S   C   A   L   E

EXERCISE   Paragraph Arrangement

Underline the topic sentence or sentences in each of the six paragraphs you just read. Also indicate below in questions 1–6 what arrangement pattern was used for the topic sentence, using the label **L, U, R, I,** or **D.** The first paragraph has been done for you.

1. Paragraph 1: Arrangement Pattern   R

2. Paragraph 2: Arrangement Pattern _____

3. Paragraph 3: Arrangement Pattern _____

4. Paragraph 4: Arrangement Pattern _____

5. Paragraph 5: Arrangement Pattern _____

6. Paragraph 6: Arrangement Pattern _____

7. List by number a paragraph that shows the TRI pattern (topic-restriction–illustration) _____

8. List by number a paragraph that shows the TRIT pattern (topic–restriction–illustration–topic) _____

9. List by number a paragraph that shows the IRT pattern (illustration–restriction–topic) _____

WRITING ASSIGNMENT   Paragraphs

Choose any writing topic below as directed by your instructor. Include with your final draft evidence that your writing has gone through the FLOWER stages (lists, outlines, drafts, etc.).

1. Try These for Openers
   Compose a paragraph that uses any one of the topic sentences below. Use the topic sentence anywhere it fits within your paragraph:

   a. It was an unfortunate day for _____. (Insert the name of a person, or an activity, such as tennis or a picnic.)
   b. Things were quite normal until . . . .
   c. Finally, it was my turn.

2. What Bugs You?
   Compose a paragraph on the topic "pet peeves" (annoyances in your life). You may write about a single annoyance or several.

3. Are You Hooked?
   Jogging has been defined as a "positive addiction." Explain a positive (or a negative) addiction you have to a food, hobby, sport, or the like.

5

Kinds of Paragraphs

The kind of paragraph you select to write stems from your special aim or purpose in writing. When you write, you are doing one of the following:

Describing something
Explaining something
Arguing in favor of something
Telling a story

In order, these four aims of the writer are:

Description
Explanation
Argumentation
Narration

Getting at your special aim or purpose in writing will help suggest how to approach that topic. If your paragraph topic was video games, you would do well to come up with a more specific aim:

Describe one video game or games.   (description)
Tell how to get a high score on one game.   (explanation)

Show why a particular game is the best available.   (argument)
Tell the story of how you won a video tournament.   (narration)

Getting at your specific aim during prewriting will save you from loose, unfocused paragraphs. Some topics will naturally suggest the aim you have in mind, but do not automatically lock onto an aim. If you were doing a paper about a skyscraper, like the Sears Tower in Chicago, description might seem the most natural approach. You might want to describe this, the world's tallest office building, to someone who has never seen it. You could just as well write about how the building is used (explanation) or show that the building is impressive (argument) or tell how the building was constructed (narration). Whatever you have to write about (the swimming team, koala bears, St. Patrick's Day, capital punishment), these four aims will help focus your writing and suggest ways to develop it.

To help keep these aims in mind, put them in this order: Description, Explanation, Argumentation, Narration. Taken in that order, the first letter of each aim spells **DEAN.** That memory marker will keep you aware of the four aims or purposes of writing.

The exercise that follows will demonstrate that you already know how to recognize the four aims of the writer.

EXERCISE DEAN

Label the aim of each of the six paragraphs on pages 113–115 by using one of these letters:

D = (description)
E = (explanation)
A = (argumentation)
N = (narration)

The first paragraph has already been done for you.

Paragraph I   _A_

Paragraph II   ____

Paragraph III   ____

Paragraph IV   ____

Paragraph V   ____

Paragraph VI   ____

Narration

Narration is the one aim that students most often forget to include when they are asked to analyze why they write. This is probably because narration—or storytelling, as it is more popularly called—is so natural it is taken for granted. Storytelling is our most common communication mode. Narration, or storytelling if you prefer, is simply telling what happened and to whom. Stories are how we make sense of our experiences for ourselves and for others.

To tell what happened, you need some chronological arrangement so that your audience will not get lost. Although such an order occurs automatically to the storyteller, that does not make storytelling easy. An audience expects more than a timetable from the storyteller. The art of storytelling is knowing what to include, knowing what to leave out, and not getting lost on the way.

How Not to Tell a Story

1. *Don't try to tell everything.* Some people tell stories poorly because they have not discriminated between what is important and what is not. You have all heard storytellers who tell too much, such as what they had for breakfast when their story deals with what happened at midnight.

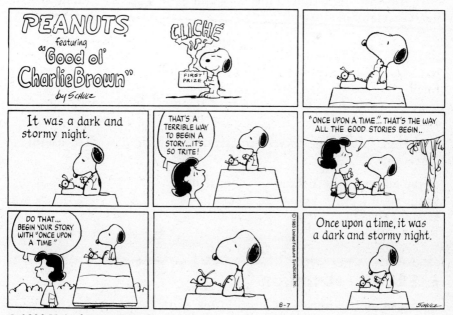

© 1983 United Feature Syndicate, Inc.

2. *Don't interrupt yourself.* This makes a story hard to take in. We all get impatient with storytellers who tell us, "I forgot to tell you that the story takes place in Maine," or "I should have told you the hero's name is Elbert." Such afterthoughts make the reader do too much work keeping track of *your* story line.

3. *Don't overuse some transitional phrases when you move from event to event: then . . . then . . . then*, for example. Avoid stock or clichéd beginnings. "Once upon a time" is fine for a fairy tale that relies on a traditional formula to suggest a timeless setting. Your narratives can be more definite than that.

How to Tell a Story

1. *Plan what you will include and in what order.* Rambling narratives are hard on readers. Without leaving out important detail, cut what is not essential.

2. *Use an easy-to-follow chronological order.* You may use a strict chronological order, or you may go backward in time instead of forward. Whether you use conventional time order or flashback, using a chronological approach does not mean you have to tell what happened minute by minute. It does mean that you will sequence the reader through events using varied and appropriate transitions. There are many such transitions. Try not to overuse any of them. *Then*, as we noted above, is an especially overworked transition.

Here are some *time* transitions that are useful in all kinds of writing, especially in storytelling:

first	then	while
second	meanwhile	when
last	at the same time	after a while
finally	now	later
next	at that time	much later
one day	after	

Here are some *place* transitions, which are also useful in narration:

to the left	behind	alongside
to the right	below	next to
straight ahead	here	near
across from	there	

EXERCISE Narration

Underline all the transitions used in the narrative paragraphs below to sequence the reader from event to event or from place to place. In paragraph I, the first of these has been done for you.

I

The familiar sound of the drill instructor's voice boomed throughout the barracks. <u>Immediately</u>, everyone is awake. On this day, there isn't the anxiety normally experienced upon waking; today, August 26, 1984, is graduation day. I feel more relaxed and eager to get dressed than I had ever felt since passing under the arches of Camp Pendleton, California. All at once, everyone is busy getting dressed. The day before, we had spent all of three hours checking to see that our uniforms were perfect. Moving past my squad to make sure everyone is dressed properly, I check to make sure their brass and shoes gleam with a mirrorlike finish. Now we are ready for our final hour of boot camp.

II

Sitting in the doctor's office waiting for my name to be called, I find that I'm biting my fingers. After eating away all my fingernails, I find the fingers are all that are left. "Mrs. Williams, your test was positive. Your baby will arrive in April." I'm so excited I really can't speak. After ten minutes of watching my husband thanking the doctor and shaking his arm out of the socket, we say our goodbyes and leave for home.

Circle one letter to indicate the kind of organization used in these paragraphs.

S   C   A   L   E

WRITING ASSIGNMENT   Narrative Paragraphs

Using story form, write a paragraph that uses any one of the following paragraph starters.

1. It was a perfect day for Lefty.
2. I knew my day would not go well when . . .
3. Out of nowhere it came.
4. It was hardly what we expected.
5. Her problem was most unusual.

Argumentation

In argumentation you take a stand, either for or against a certain position. For example, you may be in favor of (pro) building a new football stadium at your school or you may be opposed to (con) such a project. Obviously, you can only have an argument about a topic that is still open. Once the stadium is built, you can no longer argue whether or not it should be built. You can, of course, still argue whether it was too expensive or offers enough seating, and so forth.

Argument differs from persuasion. Trying to get someone to do something is persuasion, not argument. You argue for or against something; you persuade someone to take or not to take a course of action. Argument is set up to convince an audience that the speaker's or writer's view is right. Persuasion attempts to get an audience to do or not do something.

Tips on Argumentation

1. *Don't just state your opinions.* Back them up. Readers need to know not just what you believe, but why you believe as you do, before they possibly can agree with you.

2. *However strongly you feel about the rightness of your side of an argument, do not engage in name calling.* For example, "Only the lily-livered are opposed to capital punishment."

3. *Answer the objections of those who hold opposite views.* If there were no opposite side, there would be no argument.

4. *Back up your argument with facts, examples, and so on.* I once received two essays from students in the same class about their hometown, St. Joseph, Michigan. One student maintained it was a terrible place in which to grow up; the other student portrayed it as a great town for a youngster to live in. Because they each gave enough information and arranged it well, they both proved their case. Which student was right? They both presented convincing details for their different points of view. Remember, the reader does not expect court-of-law arguments, only a demonstration of why you hold a certain point of view.

EXERCISE Argumentation

Read the following argumentative paragraphs. Then answer the questions that follow.

I

Jean-Paul Sartre, who defined hell as other people, is a narrow-minded idiot. If he would have said "Hell is certain people," I could accept his definition. Certain people are very evil and could easily be identified as hell. Sartre's definition is too sweeping. Hell cannot be defined as other people.

II

I feel that having to wear high school uniforms is very unjust. My mother lets me choose my own apparel. Why can't the school trust my opinion on what to wear? Whatever their reasons, I will never agree to wear a school uniform.

III

I dislike wearing a school uniform. First of all, it is unfashionable. I don't like to have to look dowdy for the sake of uniformity. Second, five whole days in a uniform can be unbearable because the material chosen is winter weight. For heaven's sake, who likes burning up in navy blue wool when the temperature is 85 degrees or more? Not only was I uncomfortable, but I also had to endure the jeers of public school students when they caught me in my regulation wool jumper. I can't think of a single reason for subjecting students to uncomfortable and unfashionable uniforms. I will never wear one again.

Answer the following questions by supplying a paragraph number or by circling the letter in front of the best answer of those provided.

1. Which paragraph do you think does the best job of proving its case? _____
2. Which paragraph engages in name calling? _____
3. Which paragraph or paragraphs need more detailed reasons or explanations? _____
4. Paragraph III
    a. engages in name calling.
    b. fails to provide enough reasons or explanations.
    c. fails to meet the objections of those who hold an opposite view.
    d. does none of the above.
5. How many specific reasons are used to support the argument against school uniforms in paragraph III? _____

WRITING ASSIGNMENT   Argumentative Paragraphs

Write a paragraph on either of the following subjects.

1. Pretend you are a school official. Write a reply to the student who wrote against school uniforms. Try to convince her of the reasons your school wants its students to wear uniforms.
2. Defend or refute Jean-Paul Sartre's observation that "hell is other people."

Description

Simply telling what something is like, description should be easy to follow without omitting significant details. There are many ways to organize description. For example, if you were describing the Statue of Liberty, you might begin with the torch and move down, ending with the base of the statue. You could as well begin from the inside of the statue and proceed to its outer copper skin. Here are some typical patterns used in descriptive writing:

Horizontal (left to right, right to left)
Vertical (top to bottom, bottom to top)
Circular (clockwise, counterclockwise)
Inward (outside–in)

Outward (inside–out)
Zooming (near to far)
Zeroing in (far to near)

Besides such spatial organization, a paragraph may also be arranged around one dominant impression or idea. Such a logical order makes sense if you want to make one major impression stand out in the subject described—for example, the idea that, from close up, the Statue of Liberty looks grotesque.

Tips on Description

1. *Avoid vague words such as* nice, good, *and the like.* Telling a reader that an object looks nice offers little detail to build on. Instead, use more exact words that help the reader see the object as you see it. A student who was describing how much red pepper she put into her soup used the vivid phrase "blood-red." That was a lot more effective than simply stating that the soup was "very red."

2. *Follow an organizational plan* so that the reader won't get lost in a cluster of details. You need not formally announce the plan you decide on, but the reader should always have a sense of where you are and where you are headed.

EXERCISE Description

Read the following paragraphs and answer the questions that follow.

I

What strikes one first about Mrs. Lane is her physical appearance. One might be led to believe she's a Marine, her career now over, her once bulging muscles turned to pound after pound of useless fat. Her hands are now puffed so that one cannot distinguish fingernails from phalanges; her facial features are now rounded and pudgy; her flabby forearms resemble oversize hanging earlobes. Once black, her curly hair is now sparse and gray, resembling a worn Brillo pad, with steely bushy eyebrows to match. Together these deteriorated features form the image of a once-fit coach who preaches fitness but who has now let herself go to pot.

Aaron Bator

1. The above description is arranged

   a. spatially   **b.** logically

2. What kind of spatial order (vertical, circular, etc.) or dominant impression was used to organize the student paragraph above?

3. List two vivid words or phrases used to describe Mrs. Lane.

_____   _____

II
Her long blond hair is piled high atop her head. Fixing you with a stare, her alert eyes expect attention, but her drawn cheeks and frown scare you away. Holding her neck stiffly at attention, she sits ramrod-straight even on a lawn chair.

1. The above description is arranged

    a. spatially   **b.** logically

2. What kind of spatial order (horizontal, vertical, circular, etc.) or dominant impression was used to organize the student paragraph above?

_____

III
Outside the window right below me I can see the preschoolers from the day-care center digging in the sand or climbing all over the jungle gym. Beyond their fenced enclosure are clumps of protective trees which sway in the wind like Hawaiian dancers. Further back are prairie grasses where an occasional pheasant hides out. Nature stops here. Beyond are railroad tracks and abandoned boxcars going nowhere, and, this being a clear day, I can just make out in the distance the Sears Tower and the Hancock Building, the gray giants of Chicago's skyline. From my classroom window they look like toy building blocks, small and insignificant.

1. The above description is arranged

    a. spatially   **b.** logically

2. What kind of spatial order (vertical, circular, etc.) or dominant impression was used to organize the student paragraph above?

WRITING ASSIGNMENT Descriptive Paragraphs

Roberta Flack learned to play music on a junkyard piano. That piano, such as it was, remained very special to her. Describe, in one paragraph, an object that was or is special to you: your first bicycle, your first typewriter, the first book you ever read, etc. Assume your audience has never seen the object you are describing.

Explanation

There are many special ways to explain a subject. They include using examples, describing a process, comparing and contrasting, classifying and dividing, defining, and giving reasons and results.

Examples

Giving examples is one of the most common kinds of explanatory writing. Examples are effective in suggesting the many forms a subject can take. Of course, all kinds of paragraphs can offer examples, but an example paragraph supports its topic by relying heavily or exclusively on examples.

Tips on Using Examples

1. *Use several examples or give plenty of details for a single extended example.* An extended example is one you focus on at length. If you use a single example, cover it thoroughly. To bring a subject home to a reader, provide either plenty of examples or a great deal of details on a single example.

2. *Choose examples that suggest the entire range of your subject.* For example, if you were listing only three kinds of video games, you would not pick two from the same category, such as two maze games or two space-invader games. In their illustrated examples, TV commercials are often quite calculated. Three women might be shown smiling at a box of laundry detergent. To suggest that women all over are praising the touted product, no two will be from the same section of the country. One may be from Georgia, one from New York, and one from California. Examples, therefore, are stand-ins for whole groups and categories. Since, in a short paper, you won't have room for an exhaustive list of examples, pick carefully the few that you do use. They should be representative of the entire subject.

Here is an example of a paragraph that relies on a few well-chosen examples. The student writer is explaining the kinds of things her father did for her while she was growing up.

He taught me how to climb trees, catch frogs and snails, ride a bike, play baseball and basketball, build tree houses, respect authority and my elders, be polite, be on time, and above all respect my family by never doing anything to shame them. He carried me to the hospital when I broke my arm and defended me when big kids picked on me. When I smashed my fingers in a door, he stuck my hand in a carton of ice cream because we were out of ice. When I had a cold he would break up the capsules in a big glass of water so I could drink the floating colored pieces instead of a big pill. He cried with me when my assorted pets died and helped me bury them in the backyard.

Note what helps tie together these well-chosen examples: parallelism. The repetition of *he* and *when* add structure to the assorted examples.

EXERCISE   Example Paragraphs

Read the following paragraphs and answer the questions that follow.

I

Most people associate the word *hell* with death, damnation, and the devil. But, in my opinion, you don't have to die to experience "hell." Here are a few of my examples of a living hell: You lend your favorite silk blouse to your best friend but get it back after her German shepherd chewed it up. A 250-pound woman comes into the clothing store where you work and insists that you stuff her into a size 12. Elbowing his way past you on a city bus, a 200-pound thug repeatedly stomps on you. After you loan your boyfriend 500 dollars, he leaves town with a woman who was supposed to be your best friend. If time and paper allowed, the list could go on and on. So the next time I'm told to go to hell, I'll simply reply that I've already been there.

Jeannine Sharpe

1. How many specific examples are provided?   _____
2. Are they sufficient to prove the writer's point?   _____
3. What arrangement was used to structure the examples?

   a. chronological
   b. emphatic
   c. spatial
   d. logical

II

The small town in Mississippi where I grew up always gave me something exciting to do. The real adventure was in those places where we children secretly prowled. Valley Creek was one of our favorite haunts. Just down the gravel road around the curve, where a shaky old bridge spanned a creek about six feet wide, and where willow trees cast their shade, days would go by without any intruders. We regarded the area as our private turf. Nothing was more fun than our sneaking away from home to gather near the creek. Our parents were afraid of Valley Creek because of the snakes crawling across the road or lurking in the creek. But that only added to our adventure as we swam in the creek, fished for minnows, and tried to capture enormous frogs.

1. How many specific examples are provided?   _____
2. Is it or are they sufficient to prove the writer's point?

   yes   no

Explain what kinds of examples should have been included, or explain why you think the example(s) are sufficient.

_____

_____

3. What arrangement was used to structure the paragraph?

   a. chronological   **c.** spatial
   b. emphatic   **d.** logical

4. What paragraph pattern was used?

   a. TRI   **b.** IRT   **c.** PS

III

As I was reading _Good Housekeeping_ magazine, I came across an article about saving energy on anything you own in your home. I learned a lot. For instance: I didn't know that some fluorescent bulbs are designed to fit ordinary light sockets. They may cost more, but they give as much light as an ordinary bulb at less than half of the energy cost, and they last much longer.

1. How many specific examples are provided? _____
2. Is it or are they sufficient to prove the writer's point?

   yes   no

Explain what kinds of examples should have been included, or explain why you think the example(s) are sufficient.

_____

_____

3. What paragraph pattern was used?

   a. TRI   **b.** IRT   **c.** PS

IV

What I enjoy doing most is eating. Nothing could be more pleasurable than my favorite meal. My mind and my body are truly inspired by the anticipation of shrimp or lobster prepared and served right before my eyes. In a more common setting, fries and a burger could have the same effect on me. I like everything from applesauce to zucchini. I eat vegetables, fruits, lean meat, and seafoods willingly, but that's not enough. I love and crave fatty foods, such as bacon and other forms of pork, and all pastries, the gooier the better.

Loraine Renfroe

1. How many specific examples are provided? _____
2. Are they sufficient to prove the writer's point?

   yes   no

Explain what kind of examples should have been included, or explain why you think the examples are sufficient.

_____

_____

3. What arrangement was used to structure the paragraph?

   a. chronological   **c.** spatial
   b. emphatic   **d.** logical

Process

Effective as they are, examples are sometimes not enough to explain a subject, especially a dynamic one. If you are detailing the features of a new video game, examples would work well. If, however, you tried to explain how to score high on a particular video game, you would need more than some examples. Explaining a process is more complicated than merely explaining by example. That is simply because a process functions through the interaction of many elements. Your job in process explanation is to find those elements, illustrate them clearly, and show how they fit together.

In explaining a process you are giving either information or directions. That simply means you are informing readers how a certain process works or telling them how to take part in a certain process. The difference is focus. For example, a paragraph that explains what security measures are usually taken at a rock concert would be informational; a paragraph telling *how to* maintain crowd control at a rock concert is directional. In other words, a "how to" paragraph is directional. A paragraph that explains a process or event but does not tell the reader how to do something is informational.

Tips on Process Paragraphs

1. *Make a list before you start to write.* This will help you plan a sequence that is easy to follow without backtracking. The end of a recipe, for instance, is hardly the place to tell someone to preheat the oven. Follow your own directions and step through them. For example, do you pass four or five stoplights before turning right? When do you start counting stoplights?

2. *Be clear and exact.* Make sure nothing is left for the reader to puzzle over. If you are explaining how to develop film, don't assume the reader knows how to open a film canister in the dark. Telling a reader to use a thermometer during the film-developing process won't help unless you spell out the need for a thermometer and what kind to use.

© 1984 United Feature Syndicate, Inc.

3. *Spell out where your directions have to be followed exactly and where there is an acceptable range of variables.* For example, although it may be best to develop film at 68°F for seven minutes, can the film be developed at 70°F?

EXERCISE   Process Paragraphs

Read the following paragraphs and answer the questions that follow.

I

I tried every way I knew to quit smoking. I tried cutting down to only four cigarettes. I even tried quitting "cold turkey." Nothing worked. Finally, I decided to go to a hypnotist. The hypnotism was a simple two-hour process. First of all, you receive counseling to discuss the negative effects of smoking, such as how smoking can kill white blood cells and cause poor blood circulation. This counseling session lasts about forty-five minutes. Next, the hypnotist spends about a half hour to get you relaxed and in a sleepy state while you constantly stare at a flickering light. Then, the hypnotist will devote a good hour trying to get your subconscious to let go of the habit of smoking. Finally, the hypnotist will bring you out of the hypnotic trance by counting one to ten. When the session is over, you should feel you have received that extra something needed to quit smoking. I did. That was nine months ago, and I have not smoked a cigarette since.

1. This paragraph uses what kind of explanation?

   a. informational **b.** directional

2. How many steps are involved in the process explained above? _____

3. Are they sufficient to prove the writer's point?

   yes no

4. What arrangement was used to structure the examples?

   a. chronological **c.** spatial
   b. emphatic **d.** logical

II

To avoid writing you must first overload yourself with a lot of unnecessary tasks. I'm referring to tasks that you do which could really wait until a later date. For instance, try ironing two weeks' worth of clothes in one day. Then, even though it's a routine hamburger-and-fries night, fix a full-course meal instead. After dinner is done and the kitchen is spotless, sit down to catch that television special featuring Kool and the Gang, even though it will be shown three more times this month. You might get busy and miss it. After an hour of hip shaking, finger popping, and singing along, run the vacuum cleaner, dust the tables, and wash the mirrors. That way, you won't have to do these chores tomorrow. Then invite some friends over to chat while you rearrange all the books on your shelves. After your company is gone, do your hair and your nails. Oops, don't forget to do your toes. It should be time for bed now. Good night.

Sharon J. Green

1. This paragraph uses what kind of explanation?

   a. informational **b.** directional

2. How many steps are involved in the process explained above? _____

3. Are they sufficient to prove the writer's point?

   yes no

4. What arrangement was used to structure the examples?

   a. chronological **c.** spatial
   b. emphatic **d.** logical

5. Explain in what way you find this paragraph different from the typical process explanation.

   _____

   _____

_____

_____

III

It's 5:30 A.M. and time to get up for school. I can tell by the ringing
of the alarm clock that I set the night before. As every morning, I'll lie
here for an extra three minutes just to clear the sleep from my eyes.
After I've gotten through this worst part of the morning by just
touching feet to floor, the rest will be easy. As I stumble to the clothes
closet, I find the decision of what to wear today is not a hard one to
make. It's rainy and cold outside, so I'll lay out something warm. After I
take a shower, I brush my teeth and comb my hair. I am now ready for
the long bus ride to school.

1. This paragraph uses what kind of explanation?

    a. informational   **b.** directional

2. How many steps do you find in the process that is
   explained? _____
3. Are they sufficient to prove the writer's point?

   yes   no

4. List an important step left out: _____

   _____

5. What arrangement was used to structure the examples?

    a. chronological   **c.** spatial
    b. emphatic   **d.** logical

WRITING ASSIGNMENT   Writing Example or Process Paragraphs

In one or two paragraphs write on any one of the following topics:

Explaining by Examples

1. Projects you never finished
2. The price of being late
3. People who never would be missed

Explaining a Process (Informational or Directional)

1. Washing a dog or how to wash a dog
2. Wasting a weekend or how to waste a weekend
3. Making a pizza or how to make a pizza
4. Passing a particular course or how to pass a particular course

Comparison and Contrast

Sometimes you can best explain something by comparing or contrasting it to something else. The writer using this method is like a jeweler who uses black velvet to display jewels. Thus highlighted, the brilliance of gems is set off (contrast). Putting two diamonds next to each other also makes precise evaluation possible (comparison). Likewise, in writing, you can explain an idea or concept by finding something with which to contrast or compare it. For example, you might explain how a human brain is and is not like a machine. That would result in a comparison-and-contrast paragraph (or longer writing passage). This kind of paragraph shows the similarities and/or differences between any two objects or persons.

There are two basic ways to structure a comparison–contrast paper: in chunks or slices. Using chunks means that you tell all about one subject and then all about another.

Chunks
All about
Subject A: Sentence 1
Sentence 2
Sentence 3, etc.
All about
Subject B: Sentence 4 (or new paragraph)
Sentence 5
Sentence 6, etc.

If you were comparing two video games, using the chunk (or block) method, you might write first about one video game, Centipede, before describing another video game, Ms. Pac-Man.

Another way to handle comparison and contrast is to use smaller slices of prose, rather than whole chunks. The slice version of comparison–contrast looks like this:

Slices
Subject A: Sentence 1   Subject B: Sentence 2
Subject A: Sentence 3   Subject B: Sentence 4
Subject A: Sentence 5   Subject B: Sentence 6, etc.

In the slice method, there is a constant back-and-forthness, much as in a tennis match. The writer moves from a particular point about one subject to a similar or contrasting point about another subject. For example, you might move from describing the playing screen of one video game to the playing screen of another. Then you could deal with another facet of each game, such as how points are scored. The shift from one subject to another may even take place *within* sentences:

Sentence 1: Subject A/Subject B
Sentence 2: Subject A/Subject B
Sentence 3: Subject A/Subject B, etc.

Both forms of comparison–contrast are useful. Because the slice method shows point by point what each similarity or contrast consists of, the result is easier to read. But it is harder to write because you have to provide many transitions so that the reader will know when you are shifting from subject A to subject B. The slice (or side-by-side) method is especially useful if the subjects you are comparing and contrasting are not too complicated.

For complex subjects, the chunk method is a better choice. In the chunk method you finish subject A before moving to subject B. The reader, in this method, is expected to find or remember what you said about subject A while reading about subject B. In short, the slice method is harder to write but easier to read. The chunk method is easier to write but harder to read. Try both forms out on a particular subject. If your comparison–contrast does not need point-by-point scrutiny, use the chunk method. Otherwise, use the slice method.

Whichever method of comparison and contrast you use, you also have an option to stress similarities or differences. If you only deal with similarities, your paragraph is, strictly speaking, a comparison. Likewise, if you only treat differences, you are writing a contrast paragraph. If you decide to treat similarities and differences, your paragraph will look something like this in the slice (or side-by-side) method:

Similarities

Sentence 1: Subject A+/Subject B+

Sentence 2: Subject A+/Subject B+

Sentence 3: Subject A+/Subject B+

Differences

Sentence 4: Subject A−/Subject B−

Sentence 5: Subject A−/Subject B−

Sentence 6: Subject A−/Subject B−

In the chunk (or block) method, the arrangement would look like this:

Similarities

Subject A+ and Subject B+: Sentence 1

Subject A+ and Subject B+: Sentence 2

Subject A+ and Subject B+: Sentence 3

Differences

Subject A and Subject B: Sentence 1 (of new paragraph)

Subject A and Subject B: Sentence 2

Subject A and Subject B: Sentence 3

You can, of course, treat differences first. That would result in a pattern which reverses that presented above.

Whether you use the chunk or slice method and whether you present similarities or differences, you will need transition words or phrases. Here are several you might find useful:

For Showing Differences

on the other hand	yet
but	however
even though	by contrast
nevertheless	

For Showing Similarities

and	at the same time
also	in the same way
another	like
similarly	as well
both	

Here are some effective comparison-and-contrast paragraphs by a professional writer:

I have always distrusted sequels. Well, not sequels per se. The Arabian Nights, which I love, consists of Scheherazade's original midnight story plus one thousand sequels. *Huckleberry Finn*, the best book Mark Twain ever wrote, is the sequel to *Tom Sawyer*. Tolkien wrote *The Lord of the Rings* as the sequel to his book about hobbits.

What I distrust are sequels that advertise themselves as such by their titles. This phenomenon is most common in the world of children's books. An author will do one really nice book—say, the adventures of a little Ohio farm girl named Karen and her still smaller brother, Kurt. Then over the next decade fourteen more books appear, and they are successively called *Kurt and Karen Meet a Friend, Kurt and Karen Go to Chicago, Kurt and Karen's Giant Mystery Book,* and so on. Some may be good, some are sure to be worthless; all are trying to cash in on the success of the first volume. Each clutches a piece of the original title for that purpose. It's a low, contemptible practice, like the "son of" titles that used to be common in movies a generation ago, or the Roman-numeral titles that flourish now. (The only movies worth seeing, in which the final element of the title is a Roman numeral, are called things like *Henry V* and *Richard II*—and there it wasn't even Shakespeare, let alone the film producer, who put on the numeral; the Plantagenets came that way.)*

WRITING ASSIGNMENT   Comparison and Contrast Paragraphs

In two or more paragraphs, compare and contrast a sequel (book, movie, etc.) with its original. Show which work you prefer.

EXERCISE   Comparison and Contrast

Read the following comparison-and-contrast paragraphs, and answer the questions that follow them.

I

     The analog computer carries out calculations by making measurements. Dealing with continuous quantities, it can translate physical conditions, such as temperature, pressure, and voltage, into mechanical or electrical quantities. Its chief function is in structural design calculations. Analog computers are also used to make scientific computations, solve scientific problems, and control manufacturing processes. The more popular digital computer deals strictly with numbers and operates on the binary number system. Its absolute precision makes it best suited to business problems where a large storage capacity for information is needed.

Which method of comparison and contrast does this paragraph use?

a. chunk (block)   **b.** slices (side by side)

II

     I have found that either a motorcycle or a moped will best suit my need for an inexpensive and convenient means of transportation. To find out which is better suited to me, I have analyzed each vehicle. The first problem to consider is cost, including the initial investment, insurance, and gas. The lowest starting price for a new motorcycle I can find is around $495, which I definitely cannot afford right now. On the other hand, I find that new mopeds, priced at around $320, are closer to what I can afford. Since drivers of motorcycles in my state are required to carry liability insurance, I would have to pay an additional $50 a year if I bought a motorcycle. Mopeds can be driven without liability insurance. I will also have to pay for my own gas. Motorcycles average 50 to 75 mpg, but a moped can get 100–200 mpg. Furthermore, I can ride the moped on the university bicycle paths. For getting to and from

---

*Noel Perrin, *Second Person Rural: More Essays of a Sometime Farmer* (New York: Penguin Books, 1981), Preface.

classes easily, the moped would definitely be more convenient than the motorcycle. Another convenience of the moped is that I would not need a special license, other than the automobile license I now hold. After comparing the motorcycle and the moped, I find that the moped better suits my needs. I would advise any student in my position to buy one instead of a motorcycle.

Elizabeth Purches

1. The above paragraph uses what comparison-and-contrast method?

   a. chunk (block)   **b.** slice (side by side)

2. On what specific features are the motorcycle and moped compared?

   _____

   _____

3. Circle three transitional words or phrases used in this paragraph.

WRITING ASSIGNMENT   Comparison and Contrast Paragraphs

Choose *one* of the exercises below.

1. Rewrite either of the two paragraphs from the preceding exercise on comparison and contrast. If the paragraph was arranged in the chunk form of comparison and contrast, rewrite it in slices; if the paragraph was arranged in slices, rewrite it in the chunk form.
2. In one or two paragraphs, compare and contrast any one of these topics.

   a. Thin-crust and thick-crust pizza
   b. A three-speed and a ten-speed bicycle
   c. Crocheting and knitting
   d. Two different models of computers
   e. Two commercials
   f. Two fast-food restaurants
   g. Two bosses you have worked under
   h. Two department stores

Classification and Division

Classification and division are two more ways of explaining a complex topic. Literally, classification means showing in what *class* of objects a collective term belongs. For example, two classifications of video games are bottom-movement games and upward-movement games. In bottom-movement games, such as space-invader games, targets descend, but playing movements are confined to the bottom of the screen. Upward-movement games allow simulated moves from the bottom of the screen toward some goal at the screen top. Classification, then, means the creation of groupings based on logical characteristics. If you have ever sorted mail or laundry, you know something about the grouping or categorizing process called classification.

Division also groups characteristics, but instead shows what parts make up a *single* entity. A video game, for example, could be divided into significant parts: simulation screen, buttons and levers that control movement, and instructions on how to operate them.

Classification and division are often linked. A writer might classify a video game as a maze game, but then go on to describe the special features found in a particular maze game like Ms. Pac-Man. To help distinguish these two writing forms, think of classification as an *upward* movement. When you classify, you are placing something in a more general category, or *class.* For example, you might explain the video game Burger Time by describing it as an obstacle game. Division is a *downward* movement. That is, it divides a subject into more particular parts. For example, the video game Burger Time could be explained by dividing it into its two major display features: (1) the player who takes on the role of a chef and (2) the obstacles attacking the chef: pickles, lettuce, hamburger buns, and so on.

Suggestions for Classification and Division

1. *For classification use a term that has a plural meaning: furniture, college freshmen, English teachers.* The term to be classified need not be a plural word so long as it denotes a plural *concept.* For example, because there are many varieties of it, the word *weather* is plural (or collective) in meaning. For division pick a term that is singular: *camera, light bulb, computer.* There are many ways to classify computers: by type, brand, price, and so forth. For division you would discuss the features of one computer or one kind of computer.

2. *Make your classifications and divisions clear.* The reader will accept your categories if you make it clear what they are based on. You could, for example, classify video games into those that you enjoy playing and those you don't, but you would have to explain your basis for that subjective classification.

3. *Make your classifications and divisions complete.* If you classify video games into those that simulate violence and those that do not, you would need some additional classifications or subclassifications. The violence might be simulated fantasy (as in a chef being attacked by a pickle in Burger Time) or a real-life situation (as in video games that show cars running down pedestrians). Another important classification of violent games is whether the game player is the aggressor or the victim of the simulated violence.

<hr>

EXERCISE   Classification and Division

Read the following student paragraphs on classification and division, and answer the questions that follow.

I

I would like to tell about some of the people I know. Most of them are my very good friends, and the others are "Beautiful weather isn't it, How do you feel, and Good to see you again" kinds of friends. I have different types of friends. Some of them are conservative, some are forever wild, some are clowns that keep me laughing all the time, some are hip like "What's happening, Dig it, and Check you later," and some are actually weird.

Cheryl Turner

1. Do any of the classifications listed above overlap? If yes, list two that do.

   yes   no

   _____

   _____

2. One defect of the paragraph is that there is more than one basis for classifying friends. List two of these below:

   _____

   _____

   (Do not list the categories, just what you think the student based those categories on.)

3. Is the first classification—very good friends and "beautiful-weather-isn't-it" friends—a useful classification?

   yes · no

   Explain your answer below:

   _____

   _____

   _____

   _____

II

There are two major kinds of Oriental self-defense. One category is the defense which requires a person to have skillful knowledge of one or more Oriental weapons. *Kyudo* (zen archery), *kendo* (swords), *bokken* (wooden staffs), and *sais* (hooked knives) are examples of armed self-defense styles. These martial art forms are very effective in deterring aggression. The other major category of self-defense includes the unarmed methods of *judo, aikido, jujitsu,* and *karate.* These defense methods require skillful and fluid body dexterity to foil an opponent.

Lee Hines

1. What is the one basis of classification used above?

_____

2. The kind of self-defense that uses weapons is divided on what basis?

_____

3. While the paragraph does classify and divide, it is also an example of comparison and contrast. Which kind?

    a. chunk (block)   **b.** slice (side by side)

4. Circle the transitional words or phrases that introduce the two major kinds of Oriental self-defense.

WRITING ASSIGNMENT   Classification or Division Paragraphs

Choose any one of these classification or division writing exercises and develop it in one or two paragraphs.

Classification Writing Exercises

1. Go out to one parking lot at your school and classify the cars parked there.
2. Classify three or more kinds of video games you are familiar with.
3. Classify three or more TV or radio commercials you are familiar with.
4. Classify the objects you keep in your purse, backpack, briefcase, desk, etc.

Division Writing Exercises

1. Discuss the logical divisions of a computer you are familiar with.
2. Make up your own divisions for a magazine or newspaper you are familiar with.
3. Discuss the components of one particular video game.

Definition

Definition in many ways is a combination of classification and division. When you set out to define a term or topic, you usually first classify it and then separate that topic from other members of its class. If you tell someone a video game is one played on a screen, that's a classification. In many cases, that may be all you need, but classification by itself is not a literal definition. A literal definition spells out the thing being defined and no other. A definition of a video game would have to specify what kind of screen and how the screen is activated. Is the screen a home television set, or is it part of a commercial video game found in an arcade?

Precise definition is not easy. The dictionary is, of course, a help, but even it often has to hedge. It might define a brick as a form of baked clay in oblong form usually used for architectural purposes. The qualifying word *usually* allows for exceptions, such as using a brick for a doorstop.

Luckily, readers do not always require an exact definition. They are often quite content with a working definition or merely want to know which one you are operating under. Besides, in writing you often want to go into a definition at length. The result is an extended definition that is a paragraph or more long. This gives you a chance not just to define but also to illustrate what you mean by your definition.

Tips on Definition

1. *Don't use a synonym as a complete definition.* You will wind up with a classification at best. Telling someone a squirrel is a rodent does not define; it merely classifies. You can, of course, begin with a synonym, but then you must show significant differences to distinguish the term defined (squirrel) from other members of the rodent family (rat, mouse, etc.).

2. *Don't use the term to be defined in the definition.* "Patriotism is being patriotic" runs a reader in a semantic circle.

3. *Don't quote a dictionary* unless you think the definition is not well known or the quotation is really needed to clarify a term that is not readily understood. Why tell readers what you think they already know?

4. *If there are many meanings of a topic you are discussing, indicate which one you are using or offer your own definition.* Explain what a particular term means to you. This will probably not be a true literal definition, but in many cases you may not need such an exact definition.

5. *Don't make your definition too broad.* For example, if you say a library is a place where books are kept, you'd better include the books under your bed as a library. If the definition allows some examples you didn't intend, revise it. Likewise, if the definition excludes some legitimate examples, revise it. A definition of a library as a building in which books are kept is flawed in this way. Libraries often stock records and other nonbook resources.

EXERCISE   Definition

Read the examples and answer the questions that follow.

I

A ballpoint pen is a writing implement that allows ink to flow onto paper or other materials in a controlled manner.

1. What kind of definition is given above?

    a. extended   **b.** dictionary or literal   **c.** informal

2. Does the definition fit a ballpoint pen and no other writing implement?

    yes   no

    If no, name another writing implement that the definition would fit:

    _____

II

A ballpoint pen is a writing implement which is made in a cylindrical shape.

3. The example above is

    a. an extended definition   **c.** a classification
    b. a dictionary or formal definition   **d.** none of the above

III

The ballpoint pen is a cylindrical writing implement with a hard, tiny ball as its writing tip. The ball, which is usually made of tungsten carbide, is held in a socket below the tube leading from the ink supply. The ink supply is held in a plastic or metal reservoir centered in the body of the pen. As the pen moves across the paper, the ball rotates and thus transfers the ink from the ball to the paper.

4. The definition above is

    a. a classification   **c.** a dictionary or real definition
    b. an extended definition   **d.** none of the above

IV

Founded in 1956 by Christopher Moore, the Chicago Children's Choir is a musical training and performing group that serves over 400 young people of grammar school and high school age. Ethnically and racially diverse, they are drawn from many Chicago neighborhoods and suburbs. They sing every kind of choral music from Buxtehude to Ray Charles. In many languages (Latin, French, even Igbo), they regularly perform in concert in many parts of the United States and Canada.

5. The example above is

    a. an extended definition   **c.** a classification
    b. a dictionary or formal definition   **d.** none of the above

---

WRITING ASSIGNMENT   Definition Paragraphs

Choose any *one* definition exercise listed below.

1. Write your own definition of one of the following: an A essay, an F essay, a perfect vacation, a perfect morning.
2. Take a simple object (stapler, gourd, pencil, etc.) and, without using a dictionary, try to write a literal and precise definition of it. Then look the term up in a dictionary. Copy it after your definition. Write a follow-up paragraph in which you discuss the differences between your own definition and the one you found in the dictionary.
3. Look up the definition for an object (brick, lemon, basket, light bulb, etc.) in three different dictionaries. Then write a paragraph that discusses the differences you found in the definitions. Finally, using the best features of each definition, make up a composite definition. (Hint: This assignment is easier if you find a term that has only one or two meanings listed in the dictionary. Do not choose a word such as *spring*, which has many, many different meanings.)

Reasons and Results

The last kind of explanation is giving reasons and results. Paragraphs that focus on reasons or results show what caused something or what effects will result or have resulted from something. If, for example, you explain what makes you an expert on a particular video game, you are providing reasons or causes. If you explain what happened when you won a video game tournament, you are focusing on results or effects.

Tips on Reasons and Results

    1. *Give all the important reasons you can find.* Often a single reason for an event will not be enough to account for it. Telling the reader you won a tournament because you were lucky is not enough. Give sufficient reasons to explain what happened or to predict what will happen.

    2. *Not only must there be enough reasons, the reasons given must be closely associated with the results you are discussing.* Also show how a series of reasons are linked to explain an effect. Saying that video games are popular because of advertising is not a sufficient cause. You might show that reason as one cause in a whole series which explains the popularity of video games.

Here is a paragraph from a professional writer who offers almost a dozen reasons for her decision not to go back to wearing skirts or dresses.

Then why do I persist in not wearing skirts? Because I don't like this artificial gender distinction. Because I don't wish to start shaving my legs again. Because I don't want to return to the expense and aggravation of nylons. Because I will not reacquaint myself with the discomfort of feminine shoes. Because I'm at peace with the freedom and comfort of trousers. Because it costs a lot less to wear nothing but pants. Because I remember how cold I used to feel in the winter wearing a short skirt and sheer stockings. Because I can still call to mind the ugly look of splattered rain water on the back of my exposed legs. Because I recall the anguish of an unraveled hem. Because I remember resenting the enormous amount of thinking time I used to pour into superficial upkeep concerns, and because the nature of feminine dressing is superficial in essence—even my objections seem superficial as I write them down. But that is the point. To care about feminine fashion, and do it well, is to be obsessively involved in inconsequential details on a serious basis. There is no relief. To not be involved is to risk looking eccentric and peculiar, or sloppy and uncared for, or mannish and manhating, or all of the above.*

Note how parallelism (the repetition of the word *because*) helps tie together the various reasons the author offers.

EXERCISE   Reasons and Results

Read the following paragraphs, and answer the questions that follow.

Chico the Playboy

Chico, my brother, has always considered himself a playboy. Could the reason for this lie in the fact that he was constantly beseeched by female companions? Our home phone would ring continually with an excited feminine voice on the other end. Or was it just because he looked in the mirror and admired what he saw? To the young mind of his day he did seem impressive with all the credentials he wore proudly as class president, a basketball player, and the star of the football team. His name was glorified in the school and city newspapers. What girl could possibly resist Chico, our high school's prime playboy?

Bertha Jackson

Flying Bloodsucker

The mosquito, an uninvited guest, is annoying as it buzzes around you while you fan it away. You swat and spray to rid yourself of this pesty visitor. When you feel the sting of its hurtful bite, you smack at it while

---

*Susan Brownmiller, *Femininity* (New York: Linden Press, 1984), p. 81. Copyright © 1984 by Susan Brownmiller. Reprinted by permission of Linden Press, a division of Simon & Schuster, Inc.

the mosquito sucks your blood and then dies from your blow. Why does it come and spoil your fun and eventually cause its own death? I guess it's nature's way of reminding us that life holds challenges and risks.

Love All

"Can't you control the ball any better?" he complained. My immediate reaction was to smash the next ball as if it were his face. Red-faced and breathing hard, my good-looking opponent smirked at me across the tennis net. He seemed to enjoy instilling a sense of inadequacy in me. Raising my arm above my head, I held back and watched my return plink across the net. I had to hold myself back because this temperamental, energetic player was not just an opponent, but my boyfriend, whom I had been trying to coax into a tennis game for weeks. I was torn between anger and acceptance. His frequent complaints made me feel incapable of performing well. I felt it was wrong of him to place me under a magnifying glass, but I knew he was treating me as an equal in many ways outside of tennis. Because of our friendship, our interactions have become more than squabbles over a tennis game. A simple tennis game with your boyfriend can turn into frustration.

Miranda Bator

1. Which paragraph above does not give sufficient reasons? Circle one choice.

   a. "Chico the Playboy"   **b.** "Flying Bloodsucker"   **c.** "Love All"

2. Which paragraph suggests the most reasons to explain a result? Circle one choice.

   a. "Chico the Playboy"   **b.** "Flying Bloodsucker"   **c.** "Love All"

3. The third paragraph, "Love All," gives only one reason for a result, yet it is sufficient. Why? Explain:

   _____

   _____

   _____

4. Which paragraph has the most interesting beginning? Explain your choice.

   _____

   _____

   _____

WRITING ASSIGNMENT   Reasons and Results

Write on any one of the following topics in paragraph form.

1. Why you do or do not like horror movies
2. Why you do or do not watch "soap operas"
3. The results of cramming for a particular exam
4. The results when you once stayed up late to write a particular paper or to study for an exam
5. The reasons you saw a particular movie more than once
6. Why you read any one of these: newspaper comics, science fiction, fantasy, or horoscopes
7. Why you gave up _____ (coffee, smoking, alcohol, etc.)

Summary of the Four Aims in Writing

Description—what something looks like
Explanation—what usually happens or how to make something happen
Argument—what will or will not or should or should not happen
Narration—what happened and to whom

As you may have noticed, there is some connection between the four aims of writing and the various way of organizing what you write. Narration, for example, would get nowhere without chronological order. Description relies on some form of spatial order. The accompanying table shows how **SCALE** fits in with the four aims of writing and the specialized paragraph forms.

Summary of Writing Aims

Aim	Kind of Paragraph	Organization
Description	descriptive	spatial logical
Explanation	examples explaining a process comparison and contrast classification and division definition reasons and results	logical emphatic chronological
Argumentation	argumentative	logical emphatic
Narration	narrative	chronological spatial

Notice that there is much overlap. Chronological order, which is indispensable to narration, is also useful in explaining a process. Spatial order is essential to description, but a storyteller would need that order as well. Likewise, you may be using reasons and results to explain a conclusion or to argue it. Explanation, the most common reason for writing a paragraph, suggests the most specialized paragraph forms. And the kinds of paragraph are not always locked into a certain order. You could, for example, use a chronological, emphatic, or logical order in a paragraph that uses examples. While the aim of this chapter has been to explain various kinds of paragraphs, there is, as I have shown, much interconnectedness between the writer's aim, the organizational pattern, and the special kinds of paragraphs.

How the special kinds of paragraphs are used in connection with one another will be explained in chapter 7.

EXERCISE The Four Aims of Writing

In questions 1–10, label the following examples D for description, E for explanation, A for argument, or N for narration. For example:

Instructions for assembling a bicycle <u>E</u>

1. Directions for how to get to a restaurant _____

2. A letter to a college asking for admission information _____

3. Why capital punishment should be abolished _____

4. Where to find student housing in Greece _____

5. The view from your bedroom window _____

6. How to win at racquetball _____

7. A guided tour _____

8. An account of the first Thanksgiving _____

9. A joke _____

10. Why you should have a computer in your home _____

11. Of those examples you labeled explanations, list by number those

that explain a process or event. _____

12. Which of the explanations of a process or event are directional (tell

how to do something)? List them by number only. _____

Photograph by Robert Bator

WRITING ASSIGNMENT Description, Explanation, Argumentation, or Narration

Using the photograph reproduced above, write a paragraph which is one of the following:

1. A description of this scene or of the person who posted the sign that threatens would-be trespassers with jail: "ANY COUT BACK HERE WILL BE PUT IN JILL AT WONTS."
2. An explanation of why the photograph was taken or of what activity or business goes on behind that sign.
3. An argument that deals with the reasons for the rather creative spelling on the sign or why the sign had to be put up.
4. A story that uses as its setting the scene in the photograph.

ADDITIONAL PARAGRAPH WRITING ASSIGNMENTS

Choose any writing topics below as directed by your instructor. Include with your final draft evidence that your writing has gone through the FLOWER stages (lists, outlines, rough drafts, etc.).

1. *Out of Film Again*
   Describe a photograph you wish you had taken, and explain why.

2. *Something Weird*
   Describe or explain some object, place, or person you find weird.

3. *Let's Hear It for the Dictionary*
   Explain some useful words you just learned.

4. *What's in Your Name?*
   Explain why you like or dislike your name or names.

5. *Don't Call Us. . . .*
   Describe or explain an interview you took part in.

6. *Can You?*
   Describe the taste of chocolate or vanilla.

7. *Were You Ever Taken?*
   Explain how you were once cheated or gypped.

8. *Do You Ever Talk to Yourself?*
   Explain the best or worst advice you ever gave yourself and the
   results of that advice.

9. *Do You Hear Anything?*
   Explain the music you like to surround yourself with.
   Be specific, and explain why you like a particular musical form,
   style, or instrument.

10. *Are You a Law Breaker?*
    Saint Augustine and Martin Luther King, Jr., among others, have
    maintained that an unjust law is no law at all. Have you ever bro-
    ken a law or rule you considered unfair or unjust? Explain with one
    or more examples.

11. *Move Over, Mr. Webster*
    Without consulting a dictionary, give your own extended defini-
    tion of any of the following:

    a. reckless driving
    b. a "wimp"
    c. patriotism
    d. school spirit
    e. some enchanted evening
    f. gross behavior

12. *Think Positive*
    Explain what is good about some recent writing of yours.

6

The Essay

Whether their teachers ask for an essay, a theme, or a composition, students are often uncertain about this writing structure. Sentences are standard communication forms, and paragraphs are familiar groupings for those sentences. But whenever students in a new class are asked to write their first essays, after the groans come these questions:

How many pages?
How many paragraphs?
How long do you want it?

Even the students who are not brave enough to ask also want to be reassured about the essay's boundaries.

It is not a question of how long teachers want it but how long it takes to cover a particular subject adequately. That's what I (and many other writing teachers) tell students about paragraph length. For example, an essay on how to wash a car would probably not run as long as an essay on how to convince the legislature not to raise tuition at the state university.

Understandably, my students are not satisfied with that rubber-band answer, so when they back me into the blackboard, I often give them this simple pronouncement:

Essays should be several paragraphs long.

Several paragraphs means more than two. If you are not writing skimpy paragraphs (and you shouldn't be), that translates into an essay of at least two pages. Many texts suggest a four- or five-paragraph composition as a model. That's fine. Sometimes you can get by with three paragraphs, and sometimes you will have to go on to six or more. Your teacher may expect a minimum number of paragraphs (usually five) or x number of words. Five hundred words is the usual target number. That does not mean a teacher will turn down 510 words or 499. By requiring a specific number of words or paragraphs, teachers are trying to rescue students from skimpy, underdeveloped essays.

To write an essay is to go on a literary excursion. Go where and as far as your essay topic takes you. Do so, and you will be able to come up with the makings of an essay, several ample paragraphs that belong together. You saw an example of such an excursion in chapter 2 in the evolution of the essay "My Mom the Mailman."

Here is another example of how a student moved from finding a subject to writing the final draft of an essay.

Finding a Subject

This was easy. The student began with this assigned subject: How going to college has affected me.

Listing Details

Following the FLOWER format, she first made up a list of what came to mind on that topic. Here is her first list:

1. Money: increased expenses
2. Husband bothered
3. No dinner on school nights
4. Can't watch nighttime soaps
5. Decreased spare time because of increased study
6. Less sleeping time at night
7. Irritable at midterm and final time
8. Days seem rushed

This first list was not only incomplete, it lacked specifics. For example, why does the student put up with all these inconveniences and hardships? Also, what are the actual costs of college? Going back to the list, the student added more entries as well as more specifics on the ones she started with. Here is the revised list:

1. Increased expenses
2. Books
3. Transportation
4. Tuition

 5. Supplies
 6. Husband feels neglected when I study at home
 7. Can't cook dinner for family on school nights
 8. Decreased spare time due to increased study time
 9. Less sleeping time at night
10. Irritable at midterm and during final exams
11. Can't watch *Dynasty*
12. No more *Monday Night Football* on TV
13. More gas for the car to drive to school
14. Bedtime moved from ten to midnight
15. Plan to become a systems analyst
16. Someone paid to think
17. I'm good at math
18. The movie *Tron* motivated me
19. Family and friends distract me
20. The TV is too loud at home

Toward the end of this expanded and revised list the student added some positive reasons for going to college. Throughout the list she has added more detail, such as which particular television program she no longer gets to watch. Many but not all of the details are now clustered in logical groupings (the costs of going to school, the benefits, etc.). Some of these groupings suggest a possible arrangement, so the student moves to the next stage of her writing.

Organizing

Here are some of the logical groupings the writer used to put order in her random list:

How College Has Affected Me

  I. College Expenses
 II. Effects of College on My Personal Life
III. Why I Put Up with These

Under these headings she grouped details. For example, the costs of commuting and of books and supplies fit under expenses. Her organizational plan not only suggested an order, but it also showed she needed more specifics, such as how much she paid for books, tuition, and so on. After adding some of these missing details, she started on a first draft.

Writing

Here is the student's first draft, which grew out of the revised and organized list.

I never knew how expensive college can be until I received a letter stating ineligible for financial aid. College is expensive. The money spent on books, supplies, transportation take a large bite out of my salary. Some colleges cost 20 to 300 dollars a semester hour depending on if the institution is a private or public one. Books can run at least $40 with some classes requiring 2 or 3 books. The extra gas used or the extra bus fare can add up to $25 a month or more. With funding cut, my biggest fear is if I can afford to return to school next semester.

College has created a strain on my personal life. My family is used to me spending my spare time with them. It gets a little tough for them to understand that I now need that time studying. I can no longer watch Dynasty or Monday Night Football. My bedtime has been shifted from ten to midnight. I don't have time to make dinner anymore on school nights. I don't make dinner on school nights, because I just don't have the time. The entire day seems rushed when it has to end with classes. The frustration of this hectic living can hit me all at once and I just have to take a break.

At the end of my college career I want to be a systems analyst. Computers are exciting. I don't think I have any problems in this field of study.

Notice that the three major divisions of her plan led the student to create three paragraphs. Putting this rough draft away for a while, the student came back to it for the last two stages of FLOWER.

Editing and Rewriting

The biggest need the student discovered was for some way to draw the reader into reading about her experiences. She therefore added an introductory paragraph and a title. She also worked on cutting down wordiness, rearranging the order of sentences, and adding transitions. Her writing, editing, and rewriting continued for two more drafts. Her last draft follows.

College: Dream and Reality

As children most of us are told that college is an important route to a successful life. We are told about all the benefits a college degree promises. We are told to anticipate the joy graduation day will bring. But what we're not told about are the costs of college, not just the obvious financial costs, but also the incalculable personal costs.

College is expensive. Some colleges charge hundreds of dollars per credit hour. Even though I attend a public community college, my semester tuition bills are several hundred dollars more than in the good old days when our city colleges were free. Add to that the cost of books. This semester's books ran $15 to $30 each, and in two classes we used more than one text. The bus fare or extra gas for my car adds up to $30 a month or more. With government funding cut, I'm not only aware of these day-to-day college expenses, but I fear not being able to afford to return next semester.

College has created a strain on my personal life as well. Since my family is accustomed to my spending my spare time with them, it is difficult for them to understand that I now need that precious time for studying. How do you convince your eight-year-old son that your calculus exam demands your attendance on the night of the school play? Time constraints also mean I can't make dinner on school nights. When it has to end with classes, my entire day seems rushed. I have to do without *Monday Night Football* and *Dynasty*, my favorite prime-time soap opera. My bedtime has been pushed from ten P.M. to midnight.

So why do I put up with all these financial and emotional headaches? I'm learning a lot. If I'm getting a workout, so are my brain cells. I may not know what happened with the Redskins and the Broncos, but I'm learning a lot about the Civil War and PASCAL. At the end of my college career, I expect to be a computer systems analyst. Maybe then I'll be able to take advantage of the rest of the benefits of a college education. Maybe then I'll experience that excitement and joy of graduation day. In the meantime, I'll just take two aspirin for my pains and give it the old college try in the morning.

Linda Williams

Essays, you can see, require a lot of planning. That is what prompts all those questions about length, number of paragraphs, and the like. Students want to know what is required. Having had several English teachers, they know that while there is consensus on what an essay is, specific requirements in length and format may differ. (See chapter 11 for recommendations on manuscript format.) Your teacher will, no doubt, provide additional specifics on a recommended length and format for your essays.

The Parts of the Essay

Writing an essay is not a matter of counting words or paragraphs. Writers must plan and shape the essay to guide the reader. Not merely a number of paragraphs, essays are grouped and arranged paragraphs with these components:

1. An introduction
2. Body paragraphs
3. A conclusion

Since the introduction and conclusion are expressed in separate paragraphs, it would take a bare minimum of three paragraphs for an essay. But that would hardly give much room for the main part of the essay. To ensure that the body of the essay will be amply developed, many grammar texts stress the model four- or five-paragraph essay:

The Four-Paragraph Essay	The Five-Paragraph Essay
Paragraph 1—introduction	Paragraph 1—introduction
Paragraphs 2, 3—body	Paragraphs 2, 3, 4—body
Paragraph 4—conclusion	Paragraph 5—conclusion

This does not mean an essay could not be completed in three or go on to six or more paragraphs. Since it is unlikely a short essay would need more than a single paragraph as introduction and one for a conclusion, essays of more than five paragraphs would require only additional body paragraphs.

Here, with its major parts labeled for you, is the student essay you read earlier in this chapter.

College: Dream and Reality

As children most of us are told that college is an   *Introduction*
important route to a successful life. We are told about all the
benefits a college degree promises. We are told to anticipate
the joy graduation day will bring. But what we're not told
about are the costs of college, not just the obvious financial
costs, but also the incalculable personal costs.

College is expensive. Some colleges charge hundreds of   *Body*
dollars per credit hour. Even though I attend a public   *Paragraphs*
community college, my semester tuition bills are several
hundred dollars more than in the good old days when our city
colleges were free. Add to that the cost of books. This
semester's books ran $15 to $30 each, and in two classes we
used more than one text. The bus fare or extra gas for my car
adds up to $30 a month or more. With government funding
cut, I'm not only aware of these day-to-day college expenses,
but I fear not being able to afford to return next semester.

College has created a strain on my personal life as well.
Since my family is accustomed to my spending my spare time
with them, it is difficult for them to understand that I now
need that precious time for studying. How do you convince
your eight-year-old son that your calculus exam demands your
attendance on the night of the school play? Time constraints
also mean I can't make dinner on school nights. When it has to
end with classes, my entire day seems rushed. I have to do
without *Monday Night Football* and *Dynasty*, my favorite
prime-time soap opera. My bedtime has been pushed from ten
P.M. to midnight.

So why do I put up with all these financial and emotional   *Conclusion*
headaches? I'm learning a lot. If I'm getting a workout, so are
my brain cells. I may not know what happened with the
Redskins and the Broncos, but I'm learning a lot about the
Civil War and PASCAL. At the end of my college career, I
expect to be a computer systems analyst. Maybe then I'll be
able to take advantage of the rest of the benefits of a college
education. Maybe then I'll experience that excitement and joy
of graduation day. In the meantime, I'll just take two aspirin
for my pains and give it the old college try in the morning.

The Introduction

Writers have to coax their readers into reading and set them up for the
main part of the essay, the body paragraphs. That's what an introduction does. It introduces your subject and tells the reader where you are

headed. Your observation, experience, or research put you well ahead of the reader who may not know your subject well or at all. Your hobby or vacation may not immediately interest such a reader who has never raised a guppy, read *Huckleberry Finn*, or driven California's Highway 1. You have to back off to find how to introduce the essay topic you have developed. Since you must plan an introduction for the sake of your readers, how can you begin?

First, here is how *not* to begin:

1. *Don't play "little me."* That is, don't start off by apologizing or denying your expertise ("I don't know much about wind surfing"). Essays are not necessarily written by experts. Observation and interest alone can qualify you to give a topic your attention.

2. *Don't use an overworked formula* like "Once upon a time" or "The dictionary defines. . . ." Pity your audience. What you the reader would tire of, you the writer should not count on.

3. *Don't begin with a flat announcement*, such as, "Here is the answer to question 3," or "This is my report on the French Revolution." Ask yourself, would you want to sit down and read the answer to question 3? Be clear but not so obvious.

How to Introduce an Essay. There are many kinds of introductions. Remember, your job is to buttonhole the readers, that is, grab them by the lapels and make them want to read on. Only if the introduction makes the reader stay will you be able to convince, persuade, describe, or explain. Your job or hobby, although immensely important to you, may not immediately interest your readers. Flag down that audience to get their attention and hold it so they will want to read on.

How? Here are some varied ways to begin. Scan the list to see what might suit a particular topic. More than one may be suitable.

1. *Illustration or example:* These should be striking. A description of some elderly persons rummaging through a garbage can for food might launch an essay on urban hunger. A newspaper reporter used this graphic illustration to begin an article. Keep the examples specific. For example, the current price of your textbooks or your latest tuition bill could be cited to show how inflation has affected you.

2. *Quotations:* Be careful here. Readers get used to seeing the same quotations constantly served up. For example, "O death, where is thy sting?" has lost much of its sting. To flag a reader's attention with a quotation, make sure it fits and has not been overused. Here's one a student used to begin a paper: "'Hell is other people,' Jean-Paul Sartre wrote, and was he ever right."

3. *Statistics:* Cite statistics only if they are impressive or surprising. Telling readers that sorghum is 2 percent of the crops in Zimbabwe won't make them blink. Pointing out, as one magazine did, that there are over 30 million bird watchers in the United States did earn attention for an introduction.

4. *Anecdote:* This is a brief story with a point that fits your essay without requiring extensive explanation. For example, an essay on math anxiety might begin with the tale of how a streetcar conductor once bawled out Albert Einstein for lacking the simple math sense to count his fare properly. Anecdotes are drawn from your prewriting: reading, observation, and experience. Keep them brief or you will wind up with a top-heavy introduction.

5. *Comparison or contrast:* Use this to clarify or explain, but make sure it is striking. For example, "My gym teacher is Conan the Barbarian" would be more eyebrow-lifting than "My gym teacher is a tyrant." The comparison or contrast should fit and be apparent or easily explained.

6. *Question:* Even obvious questions are better than flat statements. "How do you cook a porcupine?" is more effective than "Here is how to cook a porcupine." Questions, even about topics that may not interest you, do work— for example, "How many toothpicks were manufactured last year?" or "How much sand is there in Iran?"

7. *A surprising or unexpected statement:* "Tinker Bell deserved to die." "Jogging is bad for your health." Notice how such statements command your attention and make you want to read on.

8. *A change of direction:* After an initial clause or one or two sentences, turn the reader around to a different point of view. For example, the student essay you read which detailed the problems of going to college began instead with the rewards a college education promises. Here's another turnaround introduction: "*Playboy* is an extremely popular men's magazine, but it turns me off."

EXERCISE   Introductions

Choose by letter the statement that best describes each of the introductions or the first sentence of the introductions below. Answer by circling one letter only.

1. Ninety percent of all U.S. high school graduates fail to study even one foreign language. This is an educational shame. Something must be done about it soon.

   a. change of direction   **b.** statistics   **c.** anecdote

2. How many bagels are consumed every day?

   a. quotation   **b.** statistics   **c.** question

3. Gore Vidal complains that television is "moving wallpaper." Looking at the new prime-time shows this year, I agree with him wholeheartedly.

   a. fresh quotation   **b.** flat announcement   **c.** overused quotation

4. Men are supposed to be handy. I can't even change my own type-writer ribbon.

   a. anecdote.   **b.** surprising statement   **c.** change of direction

5. "Rome wasn't built in a day."

   a. anecdote   **b.** fresh quotation   **c.** worn-out quotation

6. I don't know where to begin.

   a. playing "little me"   **b.** anecdote   **c.** example

7. My topic is helium.

   a. example   **b.** playing "little me"   **c.** flat announcement

8. Writing a sentence is like packing a suitcase: everything should be in the right place with nothing left out.

   a. flat announcement   **b.** overworked formula   **c.** comparison

9. In 1983 the average annual pay of male college graduates aged 24–35 was $22,375. Women graduates in the same age bracket earned $15,888 annually.

   a. anecdote   **b.** statistics   **c.** quotation

10. Sophia Loren was once the victim of a burglary. While she was bemoaning the loss of her jewels, a famous movie director advised her never to shed tears over something that can't cry over you.

    a. anecdote   **b.** statistics   **c.** quotation

Besides getting a reader's attention, an introduction should direct that reader to the main point of an essay. Here is an introduction that quite clearly does both.

How would you like to swing with four people of the opposite sex all at one time? Sounds anything but square, right? No, not when you're considering America's most popular folk dance, the modern square dance. You must, however, include the other three of the same sex that it takes to fill the square, four couples being the basic unit of the dance. **Modern square dancing has created major changes from old-time barn dancing.** Three of the major changes that have taken place are in the type of music played, the places dances are held, and the sophistication of the callers.

Question

Main Idea

The sample introduction above begins with a surprising, even provocative question. Then it moves to its limited subject—modern square dancing. And it ends by highlighting three areas of change that mark the evolution of that dance form: the form of the music, the setting, and the callers. This sets up the body of the essay, in this case three body paragraphs, one each for the three areas of change outlined.

As with many introductions, there is a funnel shape:

Attention getter (question about swinging)
Restriction (square dancing)
Main Idea

The sample introduction does what any good introduction should:

1. It gets your attention.
2. It directs you to the essay's main idea.

WRITING ASSIGNMENT   Introductions

This is your chance to play editor. The following student essay on automobile advertising lacks an introduction. Read the essay. Then write an introduction (no more than a paragaph) that would be suitable for this essay.

Televised automobile commercials sometimes feature awesome natural scenery, such as mountains, the ocean, or vast open spaces. A Chevrolet advertisement shows a car in a background of huge, snowcapped Colorado mountains. A single car in this setting depicts solitude and independence. Here it is, this one car amid the huge vastness of nature. This type of ad is very effective. The beauty of the backdrop cannot help but add to the beauty of the car.

Another form of setting takes us to the world of practicality. Volvo uses the stereotyped suburban setting of a typical family, manicured green lawn, white house framed by oak and maple trees, and, of course, while the kids are scampering around the car, Mom is removing three thousand dollars' worth of groceries from the inside of a twenty-thousand-dollar car. For the average family, this advertisement might be the picture of contentment, security, and happy family living. What about the car? It just naturally fits into place. If you want this type of situation, you must have this type of car. Any further explanation is unnecessary.

The most entertaining setting used in automobile commercials is the one which leads to the question, "How did they do that?" This one is seldom used, probably because it comes at a very high cost. Imagine an underwater coral garden, beautifully colored tropical fish swimming lazily about with seaweed swaying gently in the current. Out of the blue comes an International Jeep, big as life, rambling down the way, scattering fish and crunching coral which took hundreds of years to grow. Amazing! As a matter of fact, it's as amazing as a Chevy Caprice perched atop a bleached, barren, fifteen-square-foot Montana butte. Of course, there is hardly room for the car and no access roads can be seen. Or have you seen the commercial in which they drop a jeep by parachute over a canyon and show it hanging in the air and then miraculously land without a thud or a scratch. Now how did they do that?

By presenting these types of settings, automobile manufacturers gain a major advantage over the public. Providing scenic fantasies, they get the readers interested without telling them much about the car. The more you don't know about the car, the better. After all, if a car can be driven underwater, atop mountains, and to the grocery store, it must be good. Whether or not you ever use the car for these purposes is insignificant because you the viewer have seen proof that it can be done. I doubt if anyone actually believes these fantasies, but stop and think: the next time you go to purchase a car, some portion of the money you will pay will not go for the car. You will be contributing to your and the manufacturers' next advertising fairy tale.

The Conclusion

The body of an essay presents less of a problem for students than beginnings and endings. Besides uncertainty about how to begin, students are often stumped about how to end an essay. They sometimes need help in knowing how to conclude an essay or are not sure when they have a good conclusion.

Here are some pointers for concluding an essay. First, here is how *not* to end an essay:

1. *Don't just stop.* Good essays conclude, not stop. The conclusion is a chance to polish an impression you created. It signals the end but also gives you one more chance to alert the reader of your main idea, the pleasures of volleyball, the joy of raising guppies, whatever your topic is.

2. *Don't use tag formulas,* such as "in conclusion" or "to conclude" or "The End." These are overworked, unnecessary reminders. If you have really concluded, the reader will see so by the white space at the end of the essay or the fact that there are no more pages to turn. A well-finished piece of writing will not leave the reader expecting another paragraph or even another sentence. In a movie theater we do not require the words "The End" to know that a well-directed film is over. Likewise, in a well-written essay the final paragraph signals that the essay is finished, not a tag ending like "in conclusion" or "The End."

3. *Don't "fondwish."* That is, do not end your essay with a magic wand. For example, a paper on the abundance of junk food in supermarkets could not end realistically with a prediction that soft drinks will soon vanish from the American diet.

4. *Don't introduce a new topic.* You won't have enough space at

the end of a short paper to provide enough details to flesh out a brand-new topic. The ending is the last impression you will make on a reader. Don't weaken it by going off in a new direction you can't cover adequately.

How to Conclude an Essay. So much for negative advice on how to end an essay. Now some positive suggestions for how to conclude:

1. *Restate some major point or the main idea of your paper.* For example, "Truly, my dorm is a zoo."
2. *Offer a believable solution to the problems outlined in your paper or predict what is likely to happen.* For example, "Every college student should take a course in computer literacy," or "By the year 2000 Nevada will have doubled its present population."
3. *Return to some point made in your introduction.* This gives a finished quality to your writing. Because you end where you have begun, the reader can easily sense you are finished. For example, a paper that began with admitting your fear of computers could end by repeating that point.
4. *Draw a conclusion.* Some essays, especially narrative and descriptive essays, do not state a thesis early on but build to a point. Simply state that point, such as "I'll never ride a motorcycle again."
5. *Summarize the major areas covered in the body of your paper.* An essay on why children should not be spanked ended with this summary: "Three outcomes result from spanking: conforming behavior, reforming behavior, or behavior that backfires on the parent." Keep such summaries brief and don't simply repeat an earlier statement word for word.

Earlier, you were shown an introduction to a student paper on modern square dancing. I suggested how that essay would be developed. Here is how it was concluded.

If you're interested in swinging, do-si-do-ing, and promenading, you'll find these and many more in the challenging folk art of the square dance. Both barn and modern square dancing capture the spirit along with the step. But modern square dancing, this spirit now tamed and its step smoothed, has moved far from the barn.

Notice that this conclusion comes full circle to the key introductory word, *swinging.* Then it briefly summarizes the three changes previewed in the introduction: the changes in the kind of music, the callers, and the location, which distinguish modern square dancing from barn dancing.

To summarize, conclusions can either point **BACK** by repeating a key idea (**repetition**) or summarizing major points (**summary**) or point

FORWARD by concluding what will be done (**prediction**) or what should be done (**drawing a conclusion**).

EXERCISE Conclusions

Classify these sample conclusions by circling the letter before each correct answer.

1. That's why I gave my car away.

    a. summary   **c.** tag formula
    b. drawing a conclusion   **d.** prediction

2. By the year 2000 Mexico City will have 20 million inhabitants.

    a. summary   **c.** "fondwish"
    b. tag formula   **d.** prediction

3. In conclusion, I am opposed to another tuition increase.

    a. tag formula   **c.** prediction
    b. "fondwish"   **d.** summary

4. Changing your diet will help prevent heart disease.

    a. tag formula   **c.** prediction
    b. "fondwish"   **d.** summary

5. As you can see, developing your own color slides is difficult, expensive, and time-consuming.

    a. tag formula   **b.** summary   **c.** "fondwish"

The Body of the Essay

I am discussing the body of the essay last because student writers express more concern about how to start and end an essay than about what to say. The body of an essay should be the easiest part to compose, especially if you do enough prewriting.

Why? The middle or body of the essay is where you express your major ideas. If you are writing about something you know or have researched well, you should have no trouble getting to the middle of the essay. Writing about something you know well should make the middle seem almost to take care of itself.

The body of the essay is your chance to present support for your main idea. When composing body paragraphs, "tell 'em where you got it." That is, provide many examples and details for the reader to follow. It is not enough to state opinions or generalizations. Back these up with reasons or data so the reader will know what you are talking about and can form a basis for accepting what you are saying. Remember proof, illustration, and example from the chapter on paragraphs? These are just as important in the body paragraphs of an essay.

A well-supported paragraph does not simply provide details and reasons. The proof, illustration, and examples provided must be concrete and specific. An audience often has to grasp a subject entirely from what details you provide. Don't take those details for granted. Your readers who need them won't be able to, as the following newspaper article clearly demonstrates.

Kraut Barrel Adds Taste to Writing

This is the case of the missing sauerkraut barrel. I hope you can help me solve it.

First, some background.

A sometime moonlighter, I earn my mad money by teaching adults how to write.

Chiefly, I help them unlearn most of what they've learned. In this society, a lot of life is lost in living and learning.

Take, for example, one of my most recent students.

We'll call him Art, because that's not his name.

Art is a highly trained, competent technocrat.

He holds a responsible job with a major corporation. He's also a nice guy.

If he gives himself a chance, Art could learn how to write. But to do this, he will have to remember a lot of what he has forgotten and forget a lot of what he has remembered.

The sauerkraut barrel is a case in point.

Not long ago, I asked the members of my class to write a description of their childhood home, their present home and their dream home.

A West Sider, Art grew up in an apartment over his father's butcher shop. In his paper, Art alluded to the butcher shop, but for his readers the place never came alive.

I pressed Art for details.

"Was there sawdust on the floor?" I asked.

"Sure," he replied, as if all the shoppers who buy their meat in antiseptic supermarkets had once shuffled through the sawdust of an honest-to-God butcher shop.

"Tell me more about that place," I persisted.

"Well, there was the sauerkraut barrel," Art recalled.

"The sauerkraut barrel!" I shouted.

"Why did you ever leave that out? And I'll bet you had a dill pickle barrel too, and savory sausages hanging from the ceiling."

"Of course," said Art.

By then, even Art was getting interested in his own story. As he added details about the arctic air blasting his face as he opened the cooler and the smells that drifted upstairs to his bedroom, the whole class got the picture of a place full of evocative sights and sounds and smells.

After that, I never missed a chance in class to proclaim the gospel once articulated by a leading architect: "God is in the details!"

As I think of all the students I have known in recent years I realize Art is not the exception. He is the rule.

Good people. Bright people. Competent people.

But people who repress the best parts of themselves and live in a world of bloodless abstractions.

Why?

What made Art forget about the sauerkraut barrel until the information was pried out of him?

Is it because our schools have begun to specialize in processing Velveeta cheese and mass-producing "classic chablis"?

Is it because our corporations are imposing on all their executives bland diets?

Is it because our churches are filling their communion cups and chalices with Welch's grape juice?

I don't know what's doing it.

But I'm prepared to give my life, if necessary, to slay what William Butler Yeats called "the dragon of the abstract."

Like Wallace Stevens, I believe "The greatest poverty is not to live / in a physical world."

That's why all my future students will get large doses of Theodore Roethke's poetry.

Roethke's writing was "drenched in particulars." And it was "silo-rich." Wisely, he stayed close to "the compost heap of life" that enriched the soil in which his language grew.

Early on, Roethke made a decision that contributed immeasurably to his success as a poet. He chose as his father a man who operated a greenhouse.

For a writer, that's the next best thing to having a father who ran a West Side butcher shop complete with sawdust on the floor and—you guessed it—an unforgettable sauerkraut barrel.*

Roy Larson

In this article Roy Larson not only calls for writing "drenched in particulars," he provides plenty of his own, and he demonstrates the need for "evocative" writing—that is, writing that evokes or calls up memories, feelings, and images. Using proof, illustration, and examples, your job as a writer is not only to tell but to *show* the reader, who needs to feel the sawdust and taste the sauerkraut.

(Note: because the article originally was printed in narrow newspaper columns, its paragraphs are much shorter than they would be in typical essay format.)

The body paragraphs must deliver on the promises made in the introduction. Body paragraphs carry the burden of support for the essay's main idea. They therefore need a great deal of development. In a paragraph, a major detail can be supported with a sentence or two. In an essay, you have an entire paragraph to explain a major point.

Above, you were shown an effective introduction to an essay on modern folk dancing. That introduction ended with this statement about the evolution of modern square dancing: "Three of the major changes that have taken place are in the type of music played, places dances are held, and the ability of the callers." To see if they deliver on that promise, read the body paragraphs that originally followed that introduction:

(1) Replacing the fiddle-playing, foot-stomping western beat of yesterday are the modern bands or the smooth-running turntables amplifying the latest hit tunes, only some of which are western. The beat has changed, as have the smooth maneuvers of those who follow it.

(2) No longer do the dancers do-si-do and promenade around in a newly swept but still-fragrant barn. Legion Halls, YMCAs, and churches offer rooms for this popular part of urban recreation. There are in some areas specially built square-dance halls with hardwood floors set in rubber for ease of motion of the dancers. At gala festivals and conventions one can see thousands of square-dancers in four-couple squares, dancing at fair grounds, in hotel ballrooms, and even outdoors under the stars.

(3) Callers have probably been the most influential in changing the barn dance to the modern square dance. Everyone and his brother took a turn at shouting out directions, a set pattern for each song, in the olden days. Sophisticated modern callers design their own choreography, picking out figures from hundreds on hand, setting them to music to challenge their able followers. A series of lessons, given by callers, prepares the dancers for this mentally and physically stimulating activity. Callers often make a career out of calling, touring America and other countries.

Which body paragraph above was least successful? A lot of readers find paragraph 1 lacking. We are told modern bands use sophisticated equipment. Does that mean Moog synthesizers? Electric cowbells? Readers should not have to guess. Also, we learn the beat has changed, but to what? Explanation of these key claims is lacking. This paragraph tells a lot but shows little.

By contrast, the second body paragraph, which has twice as many sentences, is better supported and much clearer. It even details the special floors created for the modern square dancers. This is not to equate length of paragraph with effectiveness of a paragraph. Some long paragraphs are rambling or vague. This one is not.

The third body paragraph, the longest of the three, sets up a comparison and contrast between callers then and callers now. Because it gives plenty of examples, its points are also easier to grasp than those of paragraph 1. It is not, however, "drenched in particulars." For example, it would be interesting to see examples of the kinds of new calls that have changed square dancing.

To summarize, the square-dancing essay has an effective introduction and conclusion, but its first body paragraph shows less support than the other paragraphs. Each paragraph flows from the main idea expressed at the end of the introduction and sticks to its point. Transitions ensure that the reader is never confused about which kind of dance is being explained. The body paragraphs are fine on unity and arrangement. A bit more support would, however, be useful to the reader.

Taking stock of these strengths and needs, the student rewrote her paper. Here is her complete final draft:

From Barn to Ballroom

How would you like to swing with four people of the opposite sex all at one time? Sounds anything but square, right? No, not when you're considering America's most popular folk dance, the modern square dance. You must, however, include the other three of the same sex that it takes to fill the square, four couples being the basic unit of the dance. Modern square dancing has fashioned major changes from old-time barn dancing. Three of the major changes are the type of music played, the places dances are held, and the sophistication of the callers.

Replacing yesteryear's fiddle-playing, foot-stomping western beat, entwined with the twanging Jew's harp flavor, are the modern bands or the smooth-running turntables amplifying the latest hit tune, only some of which are western. The beat has changed, as have the smooth maneuvers of those that follow it, from the high-kicking and jerking, resembling the Russian Bear Dance, to the weaving in and out, twirling and shuffling, feet hardly leaving the floor, the music greatly influencing the action.

No longer do the dancers do-si-do and promenade in a newly swept but still-fragrant barn. The straw-covered floor served well but the American Legion, YMCAs, and churches offer rooms for this popular part of urban recreation. There are, in some areas, specially built square-dance halls with hardwood floors set in rubber for ease of motion of the dancers. At gala festivals and conventions one can see thousands of square-dancers in four-couple squares, dancing at fairgrounds, in hotel ballrooms and even outdoors under the stars.

Callers have probably been the most influential in changing the barn dance to the modern square dance. In the olden days, everyone and his brother took a turn at shouting out directions, a set pattern for each song. Hog callers and auctioneers had the advantage. Who needed to carry a tune if he had the beat? Today, sophisticated modern callers design their own choreography, picking out figures from hundreds on hand, setting them to music to challenge their able followers. "Curl the wave," "Scoot back," "Swing star through," "Spin chain through," "Weave the ring," would confuse the oldsters used to "Birdie in the center and three hands around" and "Duck for the oyster." Today, instead of amateur callers, professionals who often make a career out of it, do most of the calling.

If you're interested in swinging, do-si-do-ing, and promenading, you'll find these and many more in the challenging folk art of the square dance. Both barn and modern square dancing capture the spirit along with the step, but modern square dancing, its spirit now tamed and its step smoothed, has moved far from the old barn.

Joan Weiler

In this final revision, note the particular details added—for example, some of the actual calls cited in paragraph 4. To summarize, this well-detailed student essay has an *introduction* which begins with a catchy question, states a central idea to be developed (how modern square dancing differs from barn dancing), and suggests three major changes that have occurred in this dance form.

The *body* of the essay covers in order in separate paragraphs the three major changes: music, place, and callers.

The *conclusion* picks up the idea of "swinging" from the introduction, summarizes, and repeats the claims of the introduction.

For comparison, here are some body paragraphs taken from another student essay:

(1) I can't remember the first bowl of chili I made. I can't say I remember the first bowl I ate either. But I can say I remember whose chili I ate first—Grandmother's. I've known her chili all my life. For years now, knowing this recipe has not allowed me to duplicate Grandma's chili exactly. Oh, I've been able to duplicate such properties as color, density, and almost, but not quite, the same flavor. One thing I did learn was how to make chili. Actually, I cooked a number of dishes, and the secret to cooking is the cook must taste what he or she is making. To control the taste of food the person preparing it must first know what the food tastes like raw or cooked without seasoning. I've never known anyone to exactly duplicate any home cook's or professional's dish.

(2) Now, let's make chili. The first thing you have to believe is that no matter what recipe you are using, others will like it. If you prepare something you like, there will always be someone who will like it too. Be your own best critic. Find a large cooking pot, the larger the better. Plan on preparing chili well in advance. Chili is much better after it has set twenty-four hours prior to serving. If this is not possible, steal as much time as you can; this allows for the seasoning to take effect.

(3) Beans are the basis for chili, so carefully prepare them. You may use several types, large red kidney beans, small red kidney beans, small or large pinto beans, or even a chili bean if you can find such. I usually use large red kidney beans. The beans yield a good texture as well as a rich broth. They also have the right amount of starchy taste. Dried beans are better, as they allow consistent taste. Canned beans may change in taste and vary in taste from brand to brand. This could cause various results. Canned beans also provide an inconsistent chili broth.

Without reading the entire essay, you can tell that these three body paragraphs are from an essay that explains how to make chili. The student writer went on for several paragraphs to explain that process and ended with his own recipe. Paying attention to unity, support, and arrangement, reread the body paragraphs above. Then do the following exercise.

EXERCISE   Body Paragraphs

1. Find one place where the author violates the unity of a paragraph by drifting from the specific subject of that paragraph. Cross out the sentences that don't belong.

2. The sequencing of steps is crucial when you explain a process. Which paragraph presents its steps in a confusing order? Circle one number.

   1   2   3

3. Which paragraph presents the most detailed development? Circle one number.

   1   2   3

Not just the body paragraphs, but all the paragraphs in an essay require a lot of attention to unity, support, and arrangement. After a section on essay titles, you will be shown a prewriting plan. This plan will help you unify, arrange, and support your own essays.

The Title of an Essay

After you have written the body of the paper, concluded it, and added an interesting lead, all that remains to be written is a suitable title. Titles may seem insignificant, but they can influence whether or not someone voluntarily reads a particular work. If you've ever picked up a magazine from a rack to find out "The Real Woman in Tom Selleck's Life" or "Fifteen Ways to Improve your Sex Life," you can attest that titles do sell stories.

Suggestions for Titles.   Avoid dead giveaways, such as "My Weekend" or "How College Has Affected My Life." These may work as suggested topics for writing, but as actual titles they are too literal and tell the reader too much. The reader needs a title, not a table of contents. The titles used in magazines will serve as better models than the headlines used in newspapers.

What makes a good title? Some attention-getter that fits without giving away too much about your topic. Keep it short. Titles are usually not full sentences. "No Flesh in the Pan" was how one magazine head-lined a review of a vegetarian restaurant. The play on words suggested the subject without spelling out too much. A news headline, such as "Vegetarian Restaurant Now Open Downtown," tells the essay reader too much too soon.

For a title you can often lift a key word or phrase from your own essay. For a paper on how college affected her family life, one student used "Sockless Wednesday." The point is that your title should be a lively point of entry, not an obvious giveaway. It should be obvious which of the following is a better title:

My Weekend in the Country   Fun in the Haystack

The title is the first thing a reader sees when evaluating your writing. Like any part of an essay, the title can be written at any stage of the writing process. As mentioned in chapter 2, some writers like to have a title in hand to give them a focus on what they are writing. Because they serve as temporary reminders to writers while they work, I call such titles "bookmarks." In the example above, "My Weekend in the Country" is a bookmark title. It's simply a heading that reminds the writer what he or she is writing about. As a working title, it is OK, but readers probably would not need or want such a giveaway title.

EXERCISE Effective Titles for Essays

Circle by letter only the one title you prefer in each pair listed.

1. **a.** Being a Disk Jockey
   b. Spinning the Wax

2. **a.** King vs. Baldwin
   b. The Comparison–Contrast of Two Subject-Related Essays

3. **a.** What Was Wrong with My High School
   b. My High School: A Factory of Failure

4. **a.** Koalas and Kangaroos
   b. Australian Animals

5. **a.** Let's Draft Women
   b. My Thoughts about the Draft

The following titles were all submitted by one writing class that was assigned the topic "Describe your composing process." You can see what the teacher had to face:

Sitting Down to Write
A Time to Write
My Way of Writing a Paper
My Writing Hang-ups
My Talent for Writing
Preparing a Writing Assignment
Setting the Mood
My Writing Procedures
Writing: Sweet Inspiration
Writing
How I Write a Paper
Back to the Drawing Board
My Excuses for Not Writing

Essay Troubles
The Noise in My House
Preparing to Write at Home
What I Do to Write
Getting Ready to Write
How I Avoid Writing
What I Do to Get Ready to
   Write
My Method of Writing
What I Do before Writing
Writing and Me
My Writing Rituals
Writing Fears

Circle two of your favorite titles from the list above. Briefly, tell why you chose them:

_____

_____

_____

Cross out two titles you think are the least successful. Briefly, tell why:

_____

_____

_____

_____

We have reviewed the parts of an essay:

Title
Introduction
Body
Conclusion

Isolating each of these parts is a way of cutting an essay down to size. The title is only a short phrase. Introductions and conclusions are single specialized paragraphs. The body of an essay features a series of linked paragraphs.

To write an essay, however, you have to know not only what makes up an essay but how to plan one.

How to Plan an Essay

Step 1: Find a Limited Subject

First, as with all the writing you do, find a subject; a limited subject. Writing about a general subject is a sure way to wind up with an essay that lacks specific detail. There's not enough room in a short paper to develop and support a too-general topic. If entire books have been written on the subject you have picked, that subject is too broad. What you are after instead is a limited subject, one that would be at most a single chapter in a book or an article in a magazine.

One good place to find subjects is in your own freewriting or journal writing. Look there for a topic that still intrigues you. Wherever you get your subject from, the more specific the better. You can, however, begin with a general subject or idea. Just be sure to cut it down.

How? Here is one way: Add modifiers or substitute more restricted words. For example:

general subject = _gardening_

plus a modifier

> vegetable = *vegetable* gardening
> *limited subject*

plus another modifier

> backyard = *backyard* vegetable gardening
> *a more limited subject*

Substitution: Replace "vegetable gardening" with a more restricted phrase:

> growing cucumbers = *growing cucumbers in your backyard*
> *an even more limited subject*

Here's another example:

television shows	general subject
+	
daytime	modifying word
=	
daytime television shows	limited subject
+	
soap operas	substitute word
=	
daytime soap operas	more limited subject
+	
All My Children	substitute word and specific subject

Here is another way to convert a general topic to a specific or limited subject:

General subject	My relatives
Who?	Uncle Bill
What about him?	His manners
When?	At dinner

Asking questions is a way of interviewing yourself to get to a subject you can do justice to in an essay. Asking only three questions moved the writer from a larger subject (relatives) to a limited subject (the behavior of one relative.) More questions can, of course, be asked. We still don't know whether Uncle Bill's table manners are splendid or disgusting. That can be shown later when the writer arrives at the controlling idea of the essay. For now, even though she started out with a rather general topic, the writer got down to a more limited, that is, a more specific topic. That sure beats trying to write about all of your relatives in one essay.

EXERCISE   Limiting a Subject

Using modifying and restricting words or questions, create a limited subject suitable for an essay for any *four* of the topics listed below.

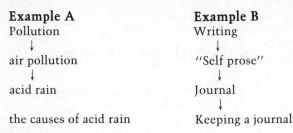

Example A
Pollution
↓
air pollution
↓
acid rain

the causes of acid rain

Example B
Writing
↓
"Self prose"
↓
Journal
↓
Keeping a journal

1. Vacation spots
2. Photographic equipment
3. Winter sports
4. Magazines
5. Fads
6. Games
7. Stereo equipment
8. Nursery rhymes
9. Columnists
10. Crime prevention

Step 2: Include a Point of View

Once you find a limited subject that interests you, ask the "what about" question. What about fluoride in drinking water? What about the drinking problem on college campuses? What about break dancing? Whether you are writing about hula hoops, handball, or hydroponics, you have to include a point of view or attitude toward a subject. For example:

Home decorating (General topic. Entire books have been written on this topic.)

Wallpapering (Better. One process to decorate walls. But who is wallpapering what?)

Wallpapering your living room (A more limited subject, but what about it?)

Wallpapering your own living room is not difficult. (A limited subject and a point of view that answers the "what about" question.)

Here are some more limited subjects with sample points of view:

Break dancing can be dangerous.
  limited subject   *point of view*

Julius Erving ("Dr. J") is the greatest professional basketball player.
  limited subject   *point of view*

Our student president should resign.
    limited subject   *point of view*

It is easy to keep a journal.
point of view   *limited subject*

It is difficult to keep a journal.
 point of view   *limited subject*

Notice that there can be contradictory points of view. A point of view would not be a point of view if it did not express an arguable or debatable point. A point of view cannot be added to a factual statement or a settled issue such as "John F. Kennedy was assassinated." This statement has a limited subject, John F. Kennedy, but adds no point of view. It is simply true, not debatable, that President Kennedy was assassinated. Explaining *why* he was assassinated or some of the major *effects* of his assassination would be an open topic, one that could take a point of view.

Compare these two statements:

Woody Allen is an actor.
Woody Allen is a comic genius.

The first statement presents an obvious fact. Only the second statement has a point of view to be explained or proven. Facts close off differing points of view. In the Middle Ages you could have maintained that tomatoes were poisonous or that the earth was flat. Unlike these dead propositions, the limited topic you pick should allow a point of view. You might argue that Julius Erving is the best professional basketball player. Someone else might argue that this distinction belongs to Kareem Abdul-Jabbar or Ervin "Magic" Johnson. You might want to show that break dancing is dangerous. Another writer might want to show that the number of physical ailments some break dancers suffer has been exaggerated. That is the nature of an open topic—it allows for various points of view, any of which can be defended.

Adding a point of view to a limited topic creates a thesis sentence. Just as a paragraph is often controlled by a topic sentence, an essay is controlled by a thesis sentence. What the topic sentence does for a single paragraph, the thesis sentence does for a whole essay:

Topic sentence—paragraph
Thesis sentence—essay

It is called a thesis sentence because it expresses a thesis, that is, a point of view on an open topic.

The two parts of the thesis sentence are (1) a *limited subject* and (2) a *point of view* about that subject. For example:

Smoking on airlines should be banned.
    limited subject   *point of view*

Smoking—a general subject
Smoking where?—the limited subject
What about smoking on airlines?—the point of view

That is all there is to a thesis sentence, a limited subject plus a point of view presented in one sentence. As a forecast of what you will prove or explain, the thesis sentence usually appears in an essay's first paragraph. The thesis sentence itself presents no proof for its point of view. Such will be supplied later in the body paragraphs.

Guidelines for Thesis Sentences

1. *Pick an open topic*—that is, one that can be debated or argued. Take this example: "We have telephones in our dormitory." This is a sentence, but it is not a thesis sentence because it states an established fact, not an opinion. It lacks a point of view.

The telephone service in our dormitory is inadequate.
  limited subject   +   *point of view*
        = *thesis statement*

Some other student might find the telephone service adequate. There-fore, the thesis sentence is arguable.

2. *Be sure the thesis statement is a grammatically complete sentence.* Sentence fragments, such as these, will not do:

Something about acid rain.
The drinking age in Wisconsin.
Whale watching in the Atlantic.

These thesis ideas need verbs that represent a point of view or a stand.

If you cannot express the limited subject in a full sentence, you have probably not yet fully explored a point of view. If all you can say is that you are going to write an essay *about* something, you are zeroing in on a topic, but you are not ready to write an essay. An essay about acid rain or whale-watching would very likely be just that, a bunch of words about a topic which lacks a definite stance. To cure the "some-thing about" problem, add a verb that expresses a point of view or takes a stand:

Acid rain is endangering a river in my hometown.
The drinking age in Wisconsin should not be raised to 21.
Whale watching in the Atlantic Ocean is an unforgettable experience.

3. *Make sure the verb expresses a point of view.* These would-be thesis sentences lack a real point of view:

I am going to write something about headaches.
My topic is wombats.

These sentences merely announce their subjects. You could begin with such general statements to help prime your prewriting. The reader will expect to see your topic tied to a stand or point of view. For example:

There are three major causes of migraine headaches.
      point of view   *limited subject*

The wombat is a vanishing animal that should be protected.
      limited subject   *point of view*

The ending of *The Grapes of Wrath* is inappropriate.
      limited subject   *point of view*

EXERCISE   Thesis Sentences

Draw a line through those thesis statements which do not express a point of view because they are not sentences or are statements of obvious fact. Circle the words that indicate the point of view in the remaining thesis statements.

1. Using too much salt.

2. Cars should be banned from our campus.

3. An ineffective teacher.

4. Texas is our largest state.

5. Ronald Reagan was our first divorced president.

6. Pope John Paul II has charisma.

7. Many video rock programs are sexist.

8. Shirley MacLaine is a great actress.

9. Winter is my favorite season.

10. Jabba the Hutt is a fictional character.

WRITING ASSIGNMENT   An Essay Built on a Thesis Sentence

Using any of the thesis statements that were not crossed out above, write an essay. You may change the thesis sentences to fit your own point of view—e.g., "Most video rock programs are not sexist."

Another way to help discover a thesis sentence is to apply those familiar questions: **who, what, where, when, why,** and **how.** For example, a student wanted to write about junk food. That gave her this for openers:

    What? Junk food
    Who?   Me

Those two quesions and answers were enough to lead her to the limited topic "My addiction to junk food." To arrive at a thesis sentence, she had to ask more *W* questions:

When?	Childhood on, but especially during teen years
Where?	Corner store and at school
Why?	Lots of reasons: spending money, insecurity, boredom, etc.
With what results?	Became overweight

Thesis sentence:

My addiction to junk food, which made me overweight, was my biggest problem before I became an adult.

It *is* hard to know what to write about. Asking the right questions and searching for definite answers can at least move you from rough idea to thesis sentence. The search for a limited, debatable subject and a point of view may take a large chunk of your prewriting time. Because the thesis sentence you discover will become the controlling idea for the entire essay, it is worth taking time with it. Again, It is easier to move bricks (words) than walls (sentences and paragraphs).

EXERCISE   Thesis Sentences

Take any four of the following limited subjects and add appropriate points of view to form thesis sentences. The points of view can be negative or positive. You may, if you wish, limit the subjects even more. For example:

Miss Piggy
limited subject

Miss Piggy is the most entertaining of the Muppets.
                    point of view

or

Miss Piggy is not very amusing.
                point of view

1. Clint Eastwood movies
2. Essay examinations
3. Flying in an airplane
4. Ice skating
5. Ironing clothes
6. Diet soft drinks
7. Newspaper advice columnists
8. Pigeons
9. The funniest comedian
10. This year's best musical group

WRITING ASSIGNMENT   An Essay Built on a Thesis Sentence

Take any thesis sentence that you formed in the preceding exercise. Use it as the controlling idea for an essay you write. State the thesis sentence in the introduction to the essay you compose. Be sure to follow all the stages of the prewriting and writing process that remain: listing, organizing, writing, editing, and rewriting.

After you (1) find a limited subject and (2) add a point of view to create a thesis sentence, there is one more step in planning an essay:

Step 3: Create a Chickenfoot or Other Outline

A thesis sentence helps you know what point of view you will be supporting in an essay. A chickenfoot is one way to outline the major support for that point of view. To illustrate, let's assume you are writing an essay about credit cards. Your thesis statement is "Using credit cards can create major problems." What do you mean by "create major problems"? That's what a chickenfoot will help reveal. It is quite simple to use: first, put the thesis sentence on the horizontal line. Then add the major reasons or explanations on diagonal lines:

Credit cards can create major problems / *because it is hard to remember what you spent* / *because they can be stolen.* / *because they encourage you to spend beyond your income.*

Here's another example:

Television soap operas can be harmful. — *They are escapist fantasies.*

They keep viewers from more important tasks.

They perpetuate sexism and racism.

EXERCISE: Chickenfeet

On separate paper, make up three chickenfeet using any three of the thesis statements below. Provide at least three supporting reasons for each thesis sentence chosen. You may add more supporting reasons if you wish; just add more diagonal lines.

1. Too much caffeine can be harmful to your health.
2. There are several ways to survive a cold winter.
3. Being at the beach on a hot day can be very uncomfortable.
4. Being at the beach on a hot day can be quite comfortable.

5. Smoking should be banned on all airlines.
6. Fraternities and sororities are important to campus life.
7. Fraternities and sororities are not important to campus life.
8. Cramming for exams is useless.
9. Cramming for exams is helpful.
10. State lotteries should be made illegal.

WRITING ASSIGNMENT   An Essay Built on a Chickenfoot

Using one of the chickenfeet you have just developed, write a five-paragraph essay. Draw and fill in the chickenfoot you used and turn it in with your final draft of the essay. Be sure to provide plenty of proof, illustration, and examples to support the paragraphs you have written. Specifying a particular audience and keeping that audience in mind should help.

Putting It All Together

Here is how one student followed the three steps of planning an essay. "Writing" was the general topic he started with.

Step 1: Limiting a Subject

He added modifiers and substitute words to arrive at a more limited subject:

Writing *(general subject)*
My writing *(limited subject)*
My writing rituals *(more limited subject)*
My prewriting rituals *(still more limited subject)*

Step 2: Including a Point of View

Next, he asked the "what about" question: What about my prewriting rituals? After thinking them over, he decided there were three kinds of activity he engaged in when he had to write an essay. So he had a thesis sentence:

My prewriting rituals require three kinds of activity.
limited subject   *point of view*

Step 3: Creating a Chickenfoot or Other Outline

My prewriting rituals require three kinds of activities. / *taking a walk* / *looking for solitude* / *cleaning my work area*

If he had used a formal outline, it would have looked like this:

Thesis Sentence: My prewriting rituals require three kinds of activity.

  I. Taking a walk
 II. Looking for solitude
III. Cleaning my work area

Each major heading would then be fleshed out with details, which would be labeled A, B, and so on. However, using a chickenfoot, he decided he could brainstorm details to fit each major section of the chickenfoot without any further divisions or outlining. The chicken-foot he used suggested a five-paragraph essay, which is what he developed. Without showing the entire writing–editing–rewriting process he went through, here is his final draft:

> I take the craft of writing seriously, perhaps too   *Introduction*
> seriously. He who writes well has the potential to influence
> the world, so the gift of writing must be taken seriously.
> Perhaps there is just a touch of self-importance on my part in
> taking this view, but I cannot help that. Every time I pick up
> a pen, I feel the ghosts of Shakespeare and Melville peering
> curiously over my shoulder as if to say: "OK, kid, let's see if   *Thesis*
> you have anything." **Since writing is almost a sacrament with**   *Sentence*

me, it requires a certain set of prewriting rituals that simply must be observed if I am to write effectively.

The first such ritual is my walk. I simply must take this walk. This walk may consist of a trip to the kitchen to see if the refrigerator and all its contents are still there, or it may include a trip to the living room to check on any new magazine arrivals. One thing is certain, not a damn syllable will be put on paper until I take my walk. Whether it is a walk from one room to another or to the park and back, my creative juices will not flow until I take that walk. Preliminary goofing off is what it actually is, but I tell myself that I am communicating with my literary angels or demons.

Chickenfoot 1

After I have completed my walk and I have received sufficient inspiration from the muses, *I then arrange for solitude.* I simply must be alone! No children, no wife, no chirping birds or tail-wagging puppies! I must have solitude. The life of a creative genius is a hard, lonely one at times. Imagine a creature like me trying to put together a piece of deathless prose that will last for the ages. Imagine a wife insisting that she be not ignored and abandoned while she cleans up after dinner. Imagine a daughter demanding that I enjoy *The Three Stooges.* To write effectively, I must have peace and quiet.

Chickenfoot 2

Once I acquire the necessary solitude, by waiting for these lovely ladies to fall asleep, I then go on to the next ritual. Things get serious now, folks. "Nitty-gritty" time is here. *I indulge in an orgy of neatness and cleanliness.* The setting must be perfect. The area must be spotless. All pencils must be sharpened, the wastepaper basket empty, the desk must be wiped clean of all traces of soot and grime. No clothes on the floor, everything must be in its proper place. If writing is a sacrament, then my desk, which I view as an altar, must be in a state of perfection. My writings I view as a gift offering to the literary gods. Pretentious balderdash! My cleanliness jag is just another "bulljive" evasion that helps me put off the actual act of putting words on paper.

Chickenfoot 3

Writing is a serious endeavor, and great are its rewards to those who take it seriously. The thought-gathering walk, the patient wait for quiet solitude, my orgy of neatness, all my prewriting rituals prepare me mentally for a productive session with my pen and paper.

Conclusion

Anthony Rangel

EXERCISE   Analyzing an Essay

All the questions below are based on the model five-paragraph student essay you have just read.

1. What kind of paragraph pattern is used in the introduction?

   a. problem solution   **c.** restriction of topic (TRI)
   b. question answer

2. What two reasons are given for his walks before writing?

   _____

   _____

3. The author uses a lot of specifics to illustrate his point. List three specific details used by the author in the fourth paragraph to explain his third ritual—cleaning his work area.

   _____

   _____

   _____

4. The conclusion

   a. summarizes   **b.** predicts   **c.** offers a solution

WRITING ASSIGNMENT An Essay on Rituals

Besides writing, there are many activities around which we develop rituals. In an essay, explain what you do to get ready for a particular activity. Choose any activity you wish. Here are a few ideas:

Jumping off a diving board   Grocery shopping
Jazzercise   Washing the dog
Praying   Preparing for a date
Preparing a dinner party   Studying for exams
Getting ready for a particular holiday

Essay writing needs careful prewriting. At a minimum, such writing deserves a thesis sentence and an organizational plan. To illustrate this point, read the student essay that follows:

Over six million Americans are hooked on the style of running known as jogging. Jogging is one of the most popular and fastest-growing sports in America.

It is easy to jog; if you can walk, you can jog. Jogging is fun. You can get a very good feeling and a physical high from jogging. Most people take to jogging because it helps to maintain good health.

A five-to ten-minute warm-up is all it will take. Muscles and cardiovascular system need the readiness for increased activity. This will enable one to jog further with ease.

Jogging is cheap; you can spend less than fifty dollars to purchase needed items.

Jogging is convenient; it can fit almost any schedule. You can step out of your front door onto the sidewalk, or go over to the park, or run on any bike path.

You can jog the first thing in the morning, or the last thing in the evening. Approximately fifteen to twenty minutes is all that is necessary.

Jogging can firm and tone the body. Your legs will get lean and your hips will tighten. Jogging can help improve a woman's chest and improve her complexion.

Jogging is good for the heart in that it will improve circulation. Learning how to monitor your heart at rest and after jogging is very important.

Jogging can help insomnia. Once you begin to run, you should sleep better and need less sleep. You will wake up feeling rested and refreshed. A long and a good jog can help relax one at the end of a hectic day.

Jogging can help you to lose weight and maintain your weight loss. Usually after running you find you are not hungry. Your appetite is reduced, and the only desire is for a lot of fresh orange juice and water.

Jogging is good for mental alertness and memory improvement. After running, you are more creative in thinking and better in everyday activities.

When exercising before running, toe touching, leg raising, sit-ups, and side bends are the most important types of movements.

After all the readiness for running is accomplished, you are ready to begin. I began jogging five years ago; so far I've liked every minute of it. I am feeling great by now and ready to run as long as my legs will hold up, maybe the rest of my life.

Although this essay touches on many particulars about jogging, the paragraphing is skimpy. A lot is said about jogging, but many books have been written on this subject. The student should have begun with a more limited subject: for example, the cardiovascular benefits of jogging or her own personal jogging regimen.

The writer did not begin with an outline or chickenfoot. This would have helped her structure the writing more consistently and set up the reader for the particular aspects of jogging she covered. As it is, whole sections of the essay could be moved around without affecting the loose organizational plan of the writing. Having a lot to say is not enough to get you ready for an essay. First limit your subject, discover your thesis sentence, and outline the territory you will be covering.

Here is a much more carefully organized essay. However, the paragraphs will be shown in scrambled order. The essay is so tightly arranged you should have no trouble finding which paragraph parts fit together.

(A) Finally, there are the noisy people on the train. In the morning the train ride downtown is peaceful. On the way home, it is something else again. Some passengers try to read, others try taking a nap, and the rest are screaming and laughing. At the end of the day when I'm exhausted and worn out, I need a nap, not raucous partying. I wonder what those revelers do for a living. If it means coming home with so much energy, I'd like one of their jobs.

(B) I'm an easygoing person with few problems or troubles. Not many things irritate me, but I do have pet peeves. There are three aggravating things I can't endure. They are people who chew gum noisily, those who talk loud at the movies, and those who are noisy on the train. Most annoyances I can block out. These remain.

(C) There will always be gum crackers, loud laughers, and noisy talkers, so I'll have to live with them. Just as there are limits to my patience, however, there should be a limit to their rudeness.

(D) Then we have those who talk during a movie at a theater. They've seen the movie, so they're telling those next to them what the movie is about. Well, since I'm either in front of or behind them, I can hear everything being said. I don't want to know what's going to happen even if their dimwitted friends do. There are also those who laugh loud and long. I enjoy comedies, but let's not get carried away. They laugh extremely loud to the point where my eardrum feels as if it's going to burst. To top it off, it isn't a short laugh, but a three- to four-minute laugh. So much for hearing the movie. Perhaps there should be a one- to two-minute laughing section and a three- to four-minute laughing section. Anyone who laughs after four minutes should be committed.

(E) My first pet peeve is gum cracking. I can't tolerate it when people chew gum noisily, especially in a quiet place like a library or a classroom. While sitting, they're either reading or writing with their gum cracking away. Those who sit around such a person usually have their fingers in their ears, but the gum chewer is oblivious to this. Gum cracking is a function of someone else's boredom. On a bus you can see people cracking away and hear them crack, crack, crack, chew, chew, crack. Maybe they do it because they're nervous. Someone should suggest nail biting to these offenders. At least that isn't so noisy.

EXERCISE   Scrambled Essay

Using the letters that precede the paragraphs above, indicate the correct arrangement of the essay paragraphs above.

Paragraph 1 _____   Introduction

Paragraph 2 _____ ⎤
Paragraph 3 _____ ⎬ Body Paragraphs
Paragraph 4 _____ ⎦

Paragraph 5 _____   Conclusion

Because there was a clearly stated thesis sentence and a tight arrangement, you probably were able to put the paragraphs in the original order in which they were written. The jogging paragraph showed you how not to organize an essay; the paragraph on pet peeves shows you a standard way to do so. Here is the original arrangement of that essay.

Introduction

I'm an easygoing person with few problems or troubles. Not many things irritate me, but I do have pet peeves. **There are three aggravating things I can't endure.** *They are people who chew gum noisily, those who talk loud at the movies, and those who are noisy on the train.* Most annoyances I can block out. These remain.

Thesis Sentence

Advance Organizers

Body Paragraph 1

My first pet peeve is gum cracking. I can't tolerate it when people chew gum noisily, especially in a quiet place like a library or a classroom. While sitting, they're either reading or writing with their gum cracking away. Those who sit around such a person usually have their fingers in their ears, but the gum chewer is oblivious to this. Gum cracking is a function of someone else's boredom. On a bus you can see people cracking away and hear them crack, crack, crack, chew, chew, crack. Maybe they do it because they're nervous. Someone should suggest nail biting to these offenders. At least that isn't so noisy.

Body Paragraph 2

Then we have those who talk during a movie at a theater. They've seen the movie, so they're telling those next to them what the movie is about. Well, since I'm either in front of or behind them, I can hear everything being said. I don't want to know what's going to happen even if their dimwitted friends do. There are also those who laugh loud and long. I enjoy comedies, but let's not get carried away. They laugh extremely loud to the point where my eardrum feels as if it's going to burst. To top it off, it isn't a short laugh, but a three- to four-minute laugh. So much for hearing the movie. Perhaps there should be a one- to two-minute laughing section and a three- to four-minute laughing section. Anyone who laughs after four minutes should be committed.

Body Paragraph 3

Finally, there are the noisy people on the train. In the morning the train ride downtown is peaceful. On the way home, it is something else again. Some passengers try to read, others try taking a nap, and the rest are screaming and laughing. At the end of the day when I'm exhausted and worn out, I need a nap, not raucous partying. I wonder what those revelers do for a living. If it means coming home with so much energy, I'd like one of their jobs.

Conclusion

There will always be gum crackers, loud laughers, and noisy talkers, so I'll have to live with them. Just as there are limits to my patience, however, there should be a limit to their rudeness.

Yolanda M. Ferreira

This essay is clear and easy to follow. The thesis sentence (shown in boldface type) is followed by an advance organizational plan, the three types of behavior that annoy the writer. Each body paragraph starts with a topic sentence that takes up the pet peeves in turn. A concluding paragraph summarizes the three types of annoying behavior.

This essay outlines where it is going and signals every turn. The advantage is that readers always know where they are and where they are headed. This easy-to-read essay may seem too obvious. For some purposes, it might be. There are more subtle ways to organize an essay, but such a clear presentation helps an audience. As you found, it was certainly easy to follow in the essay on square dancing earlier in this chapter. Like that essay, the one above uses advance organizers—that is, it tells you where it is going before it gets there. And it ends with a summary. Such a straightforward plan is extremely helpful to the reader. This format is useful for many essay situations, including essay exam questions. (The next chapter has a section on taking essay examinations).

An essay, then, is nothing more than a linked series of paragraphs that form an introduction, a body, and a conclusion. You have worked on these essay parts and on a plan to help fit them together. The next chapter offers direction and practice with more specialized essays.

EXERCISE   Analyzing an Essay

Read the following student essay and answer the questions that follow it.

Doing One Thing Well

Developing a certain shot has enabled certain professional basketball players to stay in the league a long time and become superstars. Julius Erving has mastered the slam dunk, Kareem Abdul-Jabbar has mastered the sky hook shot, and Elvin Hayes has developed the turnaround jumpshot. Each of these players has had a long career in professional basketball, and each is an established superstar.

During Julius Erving's twelve-year career in professional basketball he has mastered a crowd-pleasing shot known as the slam dunk. The slam dunk is the highest percentage shot that anyone can take. It's the safest shot to take because the player is so close to the basket, and he doesn't release the ball until it goes through the rim, so it's almost impossible to miss. Erving dunks so well because he is able to take off and hang in the air for a long time, and he can hold a basketball one-handed as easily as you and I hold a softball. Very tall people find it easy to dunk, but no one does it with the consistency of Erving.

Kareem Abdul-Jabbar has been able to remain in the league and become a superstar mainly because he has been able to develop the sky hook shot. At seven feet two inches tall, Jabbar is difficult to block. His percentage of successful sky hook shots is quite high. When Jabbar takes his sky hook shot, it's money in the bank, meaning that if he gets the sky hook off, it's going to be two points. If Jabbar hadn't developed his specialized sky hook, with his thin frame it is likely he wouldn't have stayed in the league as long as he has and become a superstar.

Another superstar who has been able to remain in the league over the years by developing and mastering a certain shot is Elvin Hayes. Elvin Hayes has mastered the turnaround jumpshot. He just gets the ball and backs the defender in around the basket, turns around, and backs the ball in softly off the glass. Hayes has consistently made the turnaround jumpshot throughout his twelve-year career in professional basketball. The turnaround jumpshot has enabled him to become the sixth leading scorer in National Basketball Association history.

Without these very special shots which Erving, Hayes, and Abudul-Jabbar have been able to master, they probably wouldn't have been so effective for such long periods of time in professional basketball. These three players have proven that the key to a successful career in basketball is finding something you do well and mastering it.

Gregory Landfair

1. Label the *thesis sentence* for the essay.
2. Circle the *advance organizer* used in the introduction.
3. Underline the *topic sentence* of the body paragraphs.
4. What kind of *conclusion* was used?

   a. prediction
   b. summary
   c. solution

7

Kinds of Essays

The strategies used to develop paragraphs also develop essays. But since it is composed of many paragraphs, an essay is likely to use more than one rhetorical strategy. For instance, a persuasive essay might use a comparison–contrast paragraph to illustrate one of its major points. Narrative essays will include descriptive details.

Persuasion and explanation are the most common essay modes. This is because, except for an autobiographical account, the essay's focus is not on the writer, but on the audience or on an object or idea.

Writer's Focus	Writer's Intention	Forms the Writing Takes
"I" writing (self)	self-expression	"self prose," such as journals, diaries, plus autobiography, credos, etc.
"You" writing (audience)	argumentation or persuasion	advertisements, sermons, editorials, etc.

"It" writing (object or idea)	explanation	news articles, directions, encyclopedia entries, reports, textbooks, etc.

In chapter 5 you worked with some strategies to develop paragraphs. Let's see how they work within essays.

Narration

Narration uses description to some extent. A narrative paragraph meant to stand by itself will not ordinarily have room for extended description. Here is one such narrative paragraph:

> It was the perfect type of day Jeff and I had hoped for the night before, one suitable for excellent fishing. I went to the car to awaken Jeff, *a skinny young lad of six who sported a curly natural hair style that seemed to weigh half as much as himself.* Even though he was unaccustomed to getting out of bed at four o'clock in the morning, he quickly collected himself. Soon he was baiting his hook and casting his fishing rod like a pro out for a serious day of fishing. Hardly ten minutes had passed when, reeling like mad, he pulled in his catch. Holding the line straight out as far as possible from his body, he showed me his trophy, *a shiny little blue gill about four inches long and weighing as many ounces.* It was a wonderful feeling to watch my son catch his first fish.

A narrative essay would allow a lot more extensive descriptive detail. Here, for example, is an excerpt from a narrative essay about growing up in a run-down neighborhood:

> My sister and I attended Coleman School on the south side of town. At the beginning of fourth grade we were chased home every day by Edwina and Bobby Jean. As we ran home, we passed a storefront where an old lady lived. *She had all sorts of candles and jars in the window. Her head was always tied up in a rag. With a long dress which came down to her shoes, she scared us as much as our pursuers. Her skin was black and ashy; her eyes were gray and sharp; they followed you like the eyes of a portrait which seems to follow you around a room.* She would sit in her doorway and shout as we passed, "Here come my two fat angels."
> The old woman saw that we were being chased almost every day, so she stopped us. Any time someone tried to do us harm and we had done nothing wrong, she explained, we should *take a glass, fill it with water, write the name of the person on brown paper, place the paper in the water, cover the glass with a saucer, and turn it upside down and let it sit.* My sister and I put this formula to work; two weeks later Edwina and Bobby Jean's house caught on fire, and they had to move. I felt as though I had just dropped an atomic

bomb. Half of me said it was an accident; the other half said it was the work of that old witch. To this day, I am not sure.

Jewett Collins

The italics highlight the many descriptive details used, such as the woman's clothing, her skin, her eyes. Also described is the ritual of putting the name in the glass of water. About a third of the selection is given to such description.

Here is another narrative essay:

Pink Mohair Sweaters, Box-Pleated Skirts, and Daydreams

Last August my family and I were caught in between selling our house and buying another. When the dust cleared, we were living with relatives and our possessions were stored in the basement of my husband's locksmith shop awaiting the closing on the new house.

Among the crates in the basement was *a brown cardboard box.* It was full of *old photo albums from my high school days.* I have forgotten most of the names of the people in the pictures, and we don't have a lot in common anymore. But there was something about those faces that documented our hopeful but self-conscious adolescence. *It was a time of pink mohair sweaters, box-pleated skirts, daydreams, and first loves that left you feeling crushed forever.*

Before we closed on the new house, it rained. The shop basement flooded, and the cardboard box was *soaked.* All that was left of the pictures were *shriveled pieces of paper. The faces and smiles were gone, as if wiped away with a towel and plenty of soap.*

The rain came and wiped out a part of me. It's hard to remember those times now. My mind is clogged with so many new experiences that it grows hard to summon up those of the past. When relatives asked about the water damage, I was too embarrassed to tell them I mourned the loss of that box of photos even more than the soaked bottom of *my new velvet couch.*

Marie A. Norris

While this essay uses description much more sparingly than the last selection, its descriptive details are essential to illustrate its main point. To prove this, try reading it without the italicized sections.

Narration is simply a story, but not simply a story of what happened to someone on an ordinary day. That is what you will find in a diary and you might find in a journal. Narration, and other forms suitable for essays, was explained in chapter 5. (See pages 119–121.)

A narrative usually centers on a moment in which special insight was gained or something extraordinary happened. You would not write a story about grocery shopping unless there were some special point to be made about that event. A narrator must not just tell what happened, but also underscore the significance of that happening. Here's an essay about an extraordinary day and event:

Firecrackers

Celebrating Independence Day is something I looked forward to much more as a child in Mexico than I do now as an adult in the United States. Going downtown to see the fireworks display was fun, but more exciting than that was getting together with the other neighborhood kids. For once we could be as noisy as we could and not be punished for it. I would have saved a couple of pennies from my weekly allowance and by this time had enough money to buy some firecrackers to celebrate with the others who had done the same thing.

How well I remember this neighbor of ours who was unusually quiet, particularly for a young adult, but who would be just as noisy and irresponsible as we were on this carefree holiday. On this particular day, this young man had bought quite a few of the biggest firecrackers, the kind which were sold by the dozen, and which would explode and sound almost like a bomb. The whole group hid in his basement, where he became daring. We watched, fascinated, as he lit his dozen firecrackers all at once. This fascination did not last long; in fact it very quickly turned to panic and screams as we saw his left hand being blown to pieces by the deafening explosion.

Blood splattered all over his face, his clothes, and his shoes, and some blood splattered on the clothing of all of us children watching in horror at this incredible happening. There were bits of flesh on the ground, and for some unexplainable reason a fingernail landed right on my nose. When I touched my nose to clean it, I could feel this piece of fingernail and feel its warmth and wetness from the blood. It made my stomach turn.

Some other adults by then took the victim away to a hospital. I can't remember much of what followed. I only remember how quickly I learned that firecrackers can do more harm than just making noise.

Maria Perez-Masanek

Notice that the details are held back until the end of the essay, where they have a very dramatic and shocking impact.

Here's another narrative about an unfortunate day and event:

I'll never forget the most unfortunate day of my life. It was two days after my twenty-third birthday, Tuesday, August 23, 1983.

For almost a week my father had been in the hospital due to a heart attack but was slowly recuperating. That Tuesday, I was told that my father was doing much better. I felt elated and couldn't wait until the time when I could see him.

That evening, when my mother and I visited him, we saw that he was indeed doing much better. He could move and didn't seem to be in much pain when he talked. My father did much of the talking while we were there. He started with his childhood and went through his adult life. On the way home, my mother was so happy knowing that my father was doing much better. But I couldn't help remembering that I had once heard that a person who is dying relives his entire life seconds before he passes away.

At about 9:30 P.M. it started to rain. Then, the phone rang. It was the hospital calling to let us know my father had gotten worse. I knew, even though they didn't say it, that my father had already died.

For a time after that, I was afraid of the rain. I felt that the rain signified death. Of course, I now realize that this was silly of me, yet I still shudder when the phone rings on a rainy day. It still reminds me of that dreadful evening.

Myrna Hinojosa

EXERCISE Narration

1. To move the reader through this tragic event, the student took care with arrangement of details. After establishing the exact time of the tragedy, she used place and time transitions. Those in the second paragraph have been *underlined*. Underline three more in the paragraphs that follow.
2. The essay shows little descriptive detail, perhaps because the writer did not want to distract you from the somber subject. Which one of these, however, should have been at least briefly described?

   a. the hospital building   **b.** the weather   **c.** her father

WRITING ASSIGNMENT A Narrative Essay

Write a narrative essay about any one of these topics, assuming that your audience is a child or adult whom you would like to entertain or instruct:

Something you lost
Something you found
A lesson you learned the hard way

Something that scared you
Something that surprised you

Here is another student narrative. Read it and then do the exercise that follows.

Waking up, yawning, and stretching sleepily in the early morning hours, the young woman dreaded stepping out of the warm, comfortable covers of her bed. It was another Monday morning. Monday mornings were always bad, the first and worst day of the week. Wearily wondering if going to a dull, dreary job of caring for old men and women was worth leaving her comfortable haven, she silently and mechanically hit the cold floor.

Still half asleep, she felt the brisk air sting her soft cheeks as she opened the door to the bleak harshness of the outside air. It was cold. Laboriously but steadily, the now energetic young woman worked at removing the thick layers of frigid snow which covered the body of her compact car like thick white icing on a pound cake. Working quickly, she thought, "Will the car start?" Keeping her almost frostbitten fingers crossed and saying a silent prayer, she turned on the ignition. Listening to the sluggish sounds of the motor trying to awaken, she felt her heartbeat increase. Angry from being disturbed, the motor roared viciously alive. Relieved, the young woman began her long, tedious journey through the drifting snow, icy streets, and stalled autos to care for the illnesses, needs, and never-ending demands of the aged. Her only thought was "Is it worth it?"

Entering the warm but very definite sounds and smells of a home for the aged, the young woman stood momentarily and breathlessly tried to collect her thoughts. Gathering around her, like bees to a honey comb, were several old men and women with wheelchairs, walkers, and canes. "You look cold," said one little wrinkle-faced man, looking up from an oversized wheelchair. "We were worried about you," said a man with concern written over his anxious face. "How did you ever get here?" "You must really care about us," said another quiet voice.

"Maybe," thought the young woman reflectively, as she began taking off the numerous layers of bulky clothing, "that is the answer."

EXERCISE   Narration

1. This essay centers on

   a. an extraordinary event   **b.** a moment of insight

2. The second paragraph receives the most descriptive detail. Explain

   why. _____

   _____

   _____

3. Underline a time transition used in the second paragraph.
4. This essay uses many place transitions. Underline two used in the third paragraph.

Description

Description is an aid to narration and other modes of writing. However, to meet some specialized need or as a writing exercise, you might want a stand-alone descriptive essay. Here is an essay-length description of an object:

The House

If you have ever traveled on a country road in the deep South, you know the kind of house. White frame but with the glitter long gone.* One story, a wide gallery across the front with two huge posts supporting the shade over it.* A tin roof, which seems to sway when it rains, with faded streaks of rust showing red in the ridges.*

*Intentional sentence fragment.

The whole thing sits on brick pillows, screened on both sides to make it a cool closure underneath. At each end of the gallery is a live oak, casting its shadows in the early summer season in the quiet of the day. And there sits a respectable middle-aged woman in a clean gray gingham dress with white stockings and black patent shoes, the salt-and-pepper hair rolled on her head, sitting in her rocker with her hands folded across her stomach to take a little ease now that the day's work is done and to listen to the songbirds. Orange orioles hop like a music box and sing in the crooks of the branches. Bright-eyed sparrows sitting on spotted eggs peer restlessly through the light and shadow.

It sits pretty well back from the road, half hidden in the greens, down by the creek, in the warmth of a full summer afternoon. Flowers are blossoming profusely, brilliant in the dazzling sun, roses smelling sweet. On each side of the walk, there are two round flower beds, made by laying two automobile tires around and filling them with dirt and sand. Frogs chirp, hopping through the grass. Turtles swim to the bank as the sun dies when the creek is hardly cool. The faded white decent house itself sits there in the early afternoon in the absolute quiet of that time of day and year.

Emma Raynor

Here is an essay which describes a place:

A Look at the Rainbow

As you jockey for position in the already filled-to-capacity parking lot, you spot the many brightly colored, scantily dressed bicyclists zipping quickly by, heading for the bike path. The blistering sun scorches your body as you head for what looks to be another beautiful day in the sun at Rainbow Beach.

The picnic grounds are dotted with scores of happy families out for a day of sunshine and soul. In the distance you hear the rhythmic, funky beat of the drummers as they hammer out soulful messages for all to hear. While you stroll towards the beach, the whisper of the light, almost nonexistent breeze seems to add a special flavor to the whole setting.

The walkway at Rainbow is crowded with other sun soakers who also feel the good "vibes" emanating from their surroundings. On either side of the path are loving couples huddled together closely, speaking words of kindness sprinkled with light laughter. Here and there are small groups of brightly dressed people sharing a large bottle of ice-cold wine. The pungent odor of marijuana lingers in the air, mixed with the aroma of char-broiled ribs. Who can tell the difference?

At the far end of the long, well-trodden walkway you see the Good Humor man ring out his familiar tune while doling out the many treats he has come stocked with. The parched patrons gladly come up with the coins needed to make a purchase. Next to him is one of the primary reasons for your visit to this picturesque spot—the drummers.

The drummers, most of whom would rival professionals, are an artistic sight and sound to behold. Their pulsating beat lends a wildly exciting contrast to the otherwise serene atmosphere. The steady, driving thump of their quick, well-practiced hands against the hard, taut skin of the congos and bongos creates rhythms and sounds wondrous to the ear. Yes, they are truly magnificent.

Later on in the afternoon, the night people start slowly drifting to the sand, bringing their own special kind of togetherness to the setting. These people, mostly teens, have come for the moonlight festivities. The many portable phonographs and cassette recorders they bring add their own sweet melodies to the chirping of the crickets and the steady hum of the bees and mosquitoes.

The star-speckled moonlit sky appears very peaceful and tranquil as the crowd starts to settle down into some slow-tempo, even-paced grooving. You "lay back" and "dig" the parade of young people that stroll by. What a sight! What a day!

EXERCISE   Descriptive Essays

1. Which essay combines description with narration?

    a. "The House"   **b.** "A Look at the Rainbow"

2. Give one descriptive detail used in "The House" for these senses:

    sight: _____

    hearing: _____

    smell: _____

3. Give one descriptive detail used in "A Look at the Rainbow" for each of the senses:

    touch: _____

    sight: _____

    smell: _____

    taste: _____

    hearing: _____

4. The arrangement used to structure details in "A Look at the Rainbow" was chronological and

    a. spatial   **b.** emphatic

5. Which essay centered all its details on one dominant impression?

    a. "The House"   **b.** "A Look at the Rainbow"

    What is that dominant impression?

    _____

    _____

From these two student essays it is obvious that a descriptive essay is more than a string of examples. The examples must be easy to follow. To make them easy to follow, a writer often structures them in categories. This calls for spatial, chronological, affirmative and negative, logical, or emphatic arrangement.

Explanation

Explanatory writing is the most common mode of essay writing. To explain means to make something clear. But there are many ways to clarify an object or an idea. Like an explanatory paragraph, an explanatory essay might make use of one or more of these strategies:

1. Giving examples
2. Comparing and contrasting
3. Defining
4. Classifying and dividing
5. Explaining a process
6. Showing reasons and results

For example, you might, in explaining a process, compare and contrast one process with another.

Examples and exercises on these six specialized essay strategies follow.

Giving Examples

Examples work because they show rather than tell what you mean. An essay gives you the opportunity to use plenty of examples or to explain one or two examples in great detail. Compare these two ways of providing examples as seen in the student essays that follow:

Chocoholic

As far back as I can remember, I've always liked chocolate. When I was a child I would go every day to my uncle's grocery store to buy a package of chocolate cupcakes and devour them with a big glass of milk, chocolate of course. I would buy ten or more Kit candies and hide them when someone was around so I wouldn't have to share. Whenever my mother or grandmother would make a chocolate cake, brownies, or fudge, I would lick the bowl and spoon. If chocolate was in a food, I would try it, whether it was ice cream, candy, or cookies.

With all my meals I had a glass of milk laced with chocolate syrup. I even went so far as to have my chocolate milk with barbecued ribs. I soon found that those two foods did not mix very well. I became so nauseated, headachy, and just plain sick that I decided against that combination. I gave up the ribs, not the chocolate.

Now older and wiser, I diet, but I still have that desire for chocolate. Usually I don't ask co-workers or friends to sample their food, but if they have a chocolate bar or anything chocolate, I find myself begging for a bite. When I was attending Weight Watchers, I was doing quite well until my husband baked some chocolate chip cookies. As a result, I broke my diet and didn't lose my weight goal for the week. Now when I am dieting, I set my goal down to losing a pound a week because I can't give up chocolate entirely.

There have been times when I have tried to leave chocolate alone, but I became very irritable and shaky. I felt as though something was missing from my life. After going through this experience, I finally realized that all my life I have been a chocolate "junkie."

Sandra Jackson

EXERCISE   Giving Examples

1. Underline the thesis sentence in the essay "Chocoholic."
2. The first paragraph lists several examples to demonstrate a fondness for chocolate. How many specific chocolate foods are enumerated?
   _____
3. What kind of conclusion was used?

   a. prediction   **b.** summary   **c.** drawing of a conclusion

4. The essay uses a chronological arrangement.

   true   false

Not surprisingly, when you are developing an essay that uses examples, you need quite a few of them. The bare bones of such an essay would be a series of examples. You could, as in the essay above, give a series of examples in each paragraph. Here is an essay that uses one extended example in each body paragraph:

My rural Mississippi surroundings were high adventure when I was a child. It was the challenge of a hike into the woods or the excitement of a long walk across the cornfield. It was adventure because only a few roads had cut through the pasture, and only a few houses had trampled the fields of knee-high grass. It was adventure because there was a forest of weeds that was taller than a small child and a pool, or at least a pond that seemed like an ocean to me.

Valley Creek was one of the most exciting places that we went. Just down the gravel road around the curve, where a shaky old bridge spanned a creek about six feet wide, and where willow trees cast their shade, days would go by without any traffic on the road, and we regarded the area as our private property. Nothing was more fun than our sneaking away from home. Our parents were afraid of Valley Creek because of the snakes crawling across the road and lurking in the creek. But for us it was enjoyable to swim in the creek, to fish for minnows, and to capture frogs.

Next on our list of adventure places was Big Oak, a woody area far away from home and out of sight of the road. There we had our picnics, built tree houses, and played our games. Just down the road from Big Oak was our secret blackberry patch. We would pick berries during the summer. In the fall we would gather hickory nuts from the trees that grew in this woody area. It, too, was forbidden territory because of the snakes. But no child in our neighborhood missed picking the berries or gathering nuts in the fall. However, no parents could be fooled when they heard the cracking of nuts or saw our berry-stained lips and hands.

And then it all came to an end. Over twenty years ago, my parents moved to the North, but the memories of my childhood days still linger. Living in Baltimore pleases the adult in me, but the child in me still remembers what adventures awaited me in Buena Vista, Mississippi.

Linda Williams

EXERCISE   Giving Examples

1. The conclusion of the essay above

   a. predicts
   b. summarizes the main idea
   c. points back to the introduction

2. Underline two transitional words or phrases in the essay which express time or movement (*then, down the road,* etc.).
3. In the first paragraph, three sentences begin with the words "it was." These sentences

   a. lack variety and should be revised
   b. show deliberate repetition or parallelism
   c. show unconscious repetition

WRITING ASSIGNMENT   Giving Examples

Write an essay that uses examples to explain some of the high adventure you found as a child and where you found it: in books, vacant lots, parks, etc. Structure your essay so it is not a loose string of examples. Choose as your audience someone whose idea of high adventure is or was Saturday morning cartoon shows.

Comparing and Contrasting

Showing similarities (comparison) or differences (contrast) between two objects or ideas is another convenient way of explaining. They are listed as one technique because they are intertwined. Any two objects that can be compared will also have some differences. Any two objects that are contrasted will also show some points of similarity.

Like examples, the points of comparison or contrast need an easy-to-follow arrangement. As in paragraphs, that means chunks or slices, but in essays the chunks and slices will be much larger.

Chunk Method of Comparison and Contrast

Paragraph	*Essay*
All about topic A in several sentences	All about topic A in one or more paragraphs
All about topic B in several sentences	All about topic B in one or more paragraphs

Slice Method of Comparison and Contrast

Paragraph	*Essay*
Topics A and B alternate within a sentence or every other sentence.	Topics A and B can alternate after several sentences.

Read the following essays, which use comparison and contrast. Then do the exercises that follow.

Writing: Day and Night

(1) When it comes to writing there are two sides of me. One side is the shared-prose day person. The other is the "self prose" night person. Even though they end up differently, they both start out the same way. First of all, the music comes on. This relaxes me. It allows my mind to drain out all worries. I just stare and wait until my mind is emptied of all its present concerns. Now, I'm able to concentrate just on my writing. I think about what I want to write and how I want it written. Next, I get a fine-tip marker and six sheets of loose-leaf paper. Finally, I'm ready to write.

(2) I find that I enjoy writing "self prose" at night. I'm able to let out my frustrations. My writing starts out neatly, but as I go on and feel more anxiety, the letters increase in size. When I run into a mental block, I doodle on the corners or margins of the paper until something comes to mind. No drafts have to be done. If I have a problem, I write about it. I try to solve my problems by writing and then reading what they really are. When I write about my problems, they don't seem as horrible as I thought they were. I'm not so mad at the world as I had speculated. Sometimes my problems weren't problems to begin with. My wild imagination made a mountain out of a molehill. In fact, after a week or so, I'll read my piece of writing so I can really see how I felt. By then, my problem has been solved. I then compare and contrast how I wrote the solution and how I really did solve it. I'm able to see how serious and how deep I can feel and how silly I was to think of some of the things I thought. Sometimes I write letters to friends to tell them how I feel and what I think of them, with no holding back. These letters are meant to be sacred, and they stay that way. No one sees them but me, not even the addressee. The best part of writing such "self prose" is the relief I feel in being able to lift a burden from my mind and soul.

(3) My shared prose is written during the day when I have some spare time at work. Here the only writing I do for myself is personal letter writing. Looking at the pictures on my desk, I decide to whom I'll write next. After finishing the work in my "IN" basket and running errands for my boss, when

I think of something to write, I'll pull out the letter and put down what is on my mind. Since I keep the letter on hand for about six hours, you can imagine how long my letters are. If there are too many cross-outs, I just keep starting over, but starting over and over is tedious. This is when the word processor comes into the picture. On it I can easily move, reword, delete, add, or change my text. The letter comes out on clean, crisp bond paper. I feel good sending out such a neat and presentable letter. It shows how much I care.

(4)   Although I prefer "self prose" as opposed to shared prose, I compose both whenever possible. By sharing my thoughts just with myself or with a friend, I am always learning and communicating.

Yolanda M. Ferreira

EXERCISE   Comparing and Contrasting

1. Paragraph 1 deals with

   a. similarities   **b.** differences

2. Which paragraphs demonstrate the chunk method of comparison and contrast? _____ and _____

3. Which paragraphs illustrate the slice method? _____ and _____

The following essay illustrates the slice method of comparison and contrast.

Developments in the Dark

(1)   There are always people at picnics and weddings who can take good photographs. Few of these novices, however, can develop their own pictures. Most must resort to leaving prized snapshots in the hands of a drug store clerk and must return periodically to see if the pictures are ready. There are many advantages to developing one's own photos, one of which is control over how the pictures will turn out even if the negatives were overexposed or underexposed. For those who merely bring the pictures to a neighborhood store, there is no long waiting in the darkroom while solutions come to temperature, only the long wait for the store to finish the developing. Overall, however, the advantages of developing one's own pictures far outweigh the disadvantages.

(2)   The biggest problem with installing a home darkroom is the cost. Initially, the cost of modifying a closet or bathroom for this purpose can be quite prohibitive, while there is no cost in getting to know where the nearest Fotomat is. Buying someone's old equipment is the least expensive way to start a home darkroom. After this initial investment, though, the cost per picture is much less than that of the service provided by a film processor, while the cost of developing at the drug store remains constant. Therefore, developing your own photos is, in the long run, cheaper than paying someone else to do the processing for you.

(3)   One advantage of letting a professional company develop your pictures is the convenience. When dropping off a roll of film, there is no waiting in the dark for the enlarger to turn off, while the phone is ringing. Placing the film in an envelope cannot possibly leave brown stains on your

fingers or corrode your fingernails. Dropping off the film is far more convenient for the person who is probably going to be a "klutz" in the darkroom.

(4) Developing your own pictures, however, provides you with a great deal more knowledge than sending your son to the film store does. Instead of your son learning what is on sale at the store that week, what he wants for Christmas, or the phone number of the cute clerk who sells binoculars, you will learn how to mix chemicals, and how to rescue the slides you took without a flash. By developing your own pictures, you can decide which ones to throw away before you print them, and make many copies of the ones you like. If a good picture turns out from Fotomat, your son will have to go back there again, and he still won't learn anything about pictures. Based on what you can learn, and the control you have over the results, developing your own pictures is far better than having them developed for you.

(5) While home development may be messy, time consuming, and initially somewhat expensive, the pictures you will get will be superior to those from the photo store's darkroom. By contrast, bringing your film to the drug store for developing will save you some time, it will cost you more, and may give you pictures back that you don't really want to keep. Overall, however, home developing has advantages which outweigh both its disadvantages and the advantages of bringing the film to a professional lab.

Aaron Bator

WRITING ASSIGNMENT Comparing and Contrasting

Compare and contrast your two selves:

day person and night person
public person and private person

or two roles you play:

student and worker   spender and saver
worker and loafer   teacher and student
parent and child   friend and enemy (etc.)

Assume as your audience someone who knows only one of your selves, such as a co-worker who doesn't know what you are like at home or a fellow student or teammate who doesn't know what you are like outside of school.

Defining

Many kinds of essays use formal definitions to clarify important terms. A definition essay does not get its name from the use of such dictionary definitions. It clarifies instead by providing an extensive treatment of a word or phrase. Words that have many meanings, words whose meanings are often confused, specialized words whose meaning may not be well known—these are all candidates for a definition essay.

Strict definition involves a classification plus a listing of specific differences that separate a word from other words of its class. An essay that defines is not limited to strict definition. It may use any of the special strategies. Often it defines by providing a series of well-chosen examples.

Charisma

(1) *Charisma* is not a new word in my vocabulary, but it is one that pleases me. When I first heard the word, it sounded good and fascinated me. I looked up its meaning so I could add the word to my vocabulary. According to my dictionary it means "a personal quality of leadership arousing special popular loyalty or enthusiasm."

(2) I searched around for those people who I feel possess this quality. Some people show leadership and can move individuals to follow them. However, those who possess charisma can move large numbers of people to follow and be happy while doing it.

(3) John Kennedy; Martin Luther King, Jr.; Bobby Kennedy; Mrs. Hargrave, the director of the playground where I played when I was a kid; Mrs. Mary Herrick, a teacher who touched all her students with her own special magic of teaching, all had charisma. Some movie stars and television personalities display this quality. I remember when J. Edgar Hoover died, many people wanted Efram Zimbalist, Jr., to become the director of the FBI since he so convincingly played the role of Inspector Erskine in the TV series *The FBI*. Hitler, who almost ruined the world, had charisma but used it for heinous purposes.

(4) The mere presence of a person who has charisma is recognized in a group. The charismatic person can directly or indirectly affect you. They aren't necessarily beautiful or handsome. They radiate a beauty from inside. The person with charisma is able to pull the best from you without its causing you pain. You want to achieve, and you work hard to produce results for them. I feel charisma is a gift given to a few lucky people. It is a responsibility of the charismatic individual to use his or her gift wisely or many lives can be hurt. I wish I had this quality, but I'm not one of the lucky ones. I feel we are seeking a new charismatic figure in our world today, but he or she has not recently emerged. My hope is that he or she appears soon.

Narcissa Roberts

Beauty

(1) What is it about a rose that we find so appealing? Why is a junk-yard full of rusty auto parts and oil-soaked mud almost painful to look at while the wildflowers and early spring grasses of a meadow are pleasing to the eye? Whatever the reason, we can classify it under a vague and nebulous term called beauty.

(2) What is beauty? It is hard to say, exactly. We know it can take many forms and be found anywhere, anytime. It can be as seemingly insignificant as a dew drop on a leaf or as grand as a range of mountains, and

it isn't limited to the natural world. It can be man-made and have no purpose other than to be looked at, or it can be found in something having strictly utilitarian purposes—an old-fashioned steam locomotive, for example. Beauty can be conveyed through any of the senses: we can hear it in music, see it in art, and even feel it as we caress the skin of someone we love. It can be a simple act of kindness or the cold, towering vaults of a gothic cathedral.

(3) One reason it's so hard to define is because of its subjective nature; just consider the maxim, "Beauty is in the eyes of the beholder." True, there are universal symbols of beauty that would appeal to most anyone—a glowing sunset is just one example—but sometimes one wonders exactly where the beauty in something might lie; how many times has someone been seen scratching his head while viewing a modern sculpture that seems to be liked by everyone but himself? There is a tribe in Africa where men are considered handsome if they are able to roll their eyes in a cross-eyed fashion. To us this would look ridiculous, but in the context of their culture and their interpretation of beauty, it is considered alluring.

(4) Because beauty is such a vague word, covering a huge spectrum, maybe a way to define it is to invent a standard or a list of qualifications something has to meet before we can call it "beautiful." But half a minute of trying to think of prerequisites will show how hopeless this is. Maybe a better way to define beauty is to examine its effect on us. When we encounter something that we think of as having beauty, we are struck by a sense of peace, joy, awe, and wonderment. Beauty can take us away from everyday human existence and if it's intense enough, into a higher realm where we are offered a sort of metaphysical peek into a dimension beyond us. Beauty is an essential component of life—a quality that generates positive feelings within us—and without it our existence would degenerate into one of disillusionment and hopelessness.

James Szmurlo

"Cooking"

(1) The slang word "cooking" had its beginning around the jazz scenes of our world. The term, as used by jazz musicians and jazz lovers, at first defined a superb way jazz groups played, but now it can also be used to describe other situations. To understand the true meaning of "cooking," one must first believe that every thought and being in life is valid, for cooking means to be in complete harmony with life.

(2) Imagine you've just walked into a jazz set, to find each member of the band molded to his instrument as though they're one, individually doing his thing, yet in perfect harmony with each other. That's "cooking"! The melody being played in perfect harmony, suddenly the horn leaves the group, climbing to the top, telling his story of joy or sadness, and then returning to the perfect harmony of the melody. Brother, that's "sho-nuff cooking."

(3) We may use the same scene to see how people experience "cooking" by being a conscious part of life. There's a table with jazz lovers around it, eyes closed, heads nodding, feet patting, and fingers rapping the table keeping the beat of the melody. Then, as the soloist ends his story, they applaud. They're in perfect harmony with what's going on; that's "cooking."

(4) The slang word "cooking" has nothing to do with food, but as in

cooking food, it takes the proper ingredients. The ingredients of the slang word "cooking" consist of affirming all of life. To be able to mix joy, sorrow, victory, or defeat into one pot and to get into harmony with whatever comes out: that's cooking.

EXERCISE   Defining

Answer the following questions about the preceding essays by circling the letter of your choice.

1. Which essay makes use of examples?

    a. "Charisma"   b. "Beauty"
    c. "Cooking"   d. All three essays

2. Which essay cites a dictionary definition?

    a. "Charisma"   b. "Beauty"
    c. "Cooking"   d. All three essays

3. One technique in definition is enumeration—that is, making a list. Which essay or essays use such a technique?

    a. "Charisma"   b. "Beauty"   c. "Cooking"

4. Which essay defines a specialized word whose meaning may not be well known?

    a. "Charisma"   b. "Beauty"   c. "Cooking"

WRITING ASSIGNMENT   Defining

Write an essay in which you define one or more slang terms you are familiar with: for example, "hacker" or "glitch" (computer slang), to be "clean" (as used in a black dialect), "tacky," "nerd," "sleaze," or some other term.

Classifying and Dividing

Like *comparison* and *contrast*, the terms *classification* and *division* are intertwined, but they can be separated. Classifying means creating logical groupings or categories for a plural subject. Dividing means separating a single entity into its logical parts. For example, a newspaper can be divided into sections, such as sports, amusements, and editorials. Newspapers can be classified by location, type, circulation, and so on. As you read the following essays, decide whether they are classification or division essays.

Take Two Aspirin

(1) "I have a headache" is a statement so often heard. "Take two aspirin," someone might say automatically. But what if that simple headache

cure does not help? Let's look not at the patent remedy but on the pain of a headache and its cause.

(2) A headache can be caused by any number of things, such as tension, stress, depression, trauma, or an allergy. We all know whenever the blood vessels in the head constrict we will have pain.

(3) There are three types of headaches: muscular, vascular, and migraine.

(4) Muscular headaches can cause pain for persons of all ages, both male and female. The pain may begin with a dull, tight, bandlike pressure. The pain in the head is usually constant and may last for a day or so. Treatment may be mild analgesics or moist heat to the head.

(5) Vascular headaches, which are most frequent in men, may be caused by alcohol, trauma to the neck, or allergy. In this type of headache the pain is sharp and piercing. The eye on the side of the pain is usually red and tends to tear. The pain may appear one to three times each day for four to six weeks, then stop suddenly. Treatment with oxygen may be helpful, if used carefully. Steroids are usually prescribed for a period of seven days at a time.

(6) Migraine headaches are most frequent in women, even though men are victims also. Heredity plays an active role in this type of headache. This pain can be caused by swelling of the brain, alcohol, odors, fatigue, stress, and foods containing tyramines, like cheese. The onset is a sudden intense pounding or throbbing pain. Usually lateral, meaning "to one side," in most cases it is located in the right of the temporal lobe, above and below the right eye. The pain may cause vomiting, loss of appetite, fatigue, chills, weakness, and sensitivity to light and sound. One might have tearing of the eye, on the affected side, and running of the nose. This pain may last two or three weeks or even a couple of months.

(7) As a nurse trained to counsel headache patients, I can make a crucial difference in their recovery. For the patient with a severe headache, there is no simple solution—like a couple of aspirin. Referral and teaching are the first and last steps in bringing headaches under control.

Betty J. Coleman

Stylists and Sluggers

(1) Boxing is one of my main passions. I have been a fanatical enthusiast of this brutal sport since childhood. Only the Second Coming of Christ could be more important than a good match between two highly skilled boxers. The heroes of my childhood were Sugar Ray Robinson, Carmen Basilio, Joey Giardello, and Gaspar "El Indio" Ortega.

(2) Because I have been a fan for so long, I feel competent enough to describe the categories and types of boxers that exist in this fascinating sport. In boxing, there are three basic kinds of pugilists. I will give you a description of each type. Each type has its supporters.

(3) The first type is the classic boxer, the purist, the stylish and artful technician. This type gives scrupulous attention to proper boxing forms and technique. To win fights, the classic boxer will rely on scientific boxing skill and ring cleverness. He is the thinking man's fighter. He wins by using his skills and wits. His aim is to win by outpointing and outscoring the opponent in order to win the decision of the judges. The clever boxer often lacks a hard punch, so he must employ other skills. He is out to confuse and baffle a

stronger but slower opponent. In Europe this type of boxer is highly admired; in macho Mexico he is despised. A good example of this kind of fighter was the great lightweight of the twenties and thirties, Benny Leonard. Many experts consider him to be one of the best stylists of all time. Willie Pep, a great fighter from the forties, fits in this category also. These two epitomize the clever boxer, the smoothie, the slick Fancy Dan.

(4) The mortal enemy of the stylist is his total opposite, the slugger. His battle cry is "I'll moider da bum." He will too if you let him. Sluggers have but one aim in life, and that is to search, find, and destroy whatever is in front of them. Strategy, science, technique, proper form are alien concepts and "wimpy" abstractions to this beef-mitted brute. He is out to maul, brawl, pound, smash, and bash your living skull in. He is the hero of the working class, the blue-collar boxing fan. Jack Dempsey, appropriately nicknamed the Manassa Mauler, is a prime example of this type. How would you like to earn your daily bread by going a few rounds with Rocky Graziano, Tony Zale, Jake La Motta, Joe Frazier, and the slugger to end all sluggers, Rocky Marciano? No way, chum. I'd rather tangle with a wounded water buffalo. Me face that kind of mean-spirited goon? Surely you jest. Sluggers are all spiritual descendants of Atilla the Hun.

(5) The most formidable of the three types is that rare, precious boxer called the boxer-puncher. They are rare as diamonds, but, like diamonds, are a wonder to behold. How unfair life is. The boxer-puncher has it all, style, grace, smoothness, and ring cleverness combined with a heavy, powerful punch. Rooting for them is like rooting for IBM or General Motors. Boxer-punchers act as if they are invincible, and, in reality, they almost are. They have few fans who love them but many grudging admirers. They couldn't give a damn whether you love them or not. All they ask is that you pay your money to watch them fight. If you love them, fine; if you hate them, fine. Either way, they don't give a damn. Oh, such splendid arrogance! Joe Louis, Sugar Ray Robinson, Billy Conn, Sugar Ray Leonard, and Muhammad Ali, the greatest boxer-puncher of them all, are examples of that new breed of boxer who combines the grace of the stylist with the cruel power of the slugger.

(6) If you value style and nimble cleverness, the pure boxer is your type. You are surely an aesthete. Do you have thuggish tendencies? Are you a low-class, beer-guzzling, proletarian "goon"? Do you want to see "da fancy bums get moidered"? The crude slugger is your type. As for myself, I prefer the boxer-puncher. Why? Because he always wins. That's why.

Anthony Rangel

The Pool Hall

(1) Everyone has a little spot where he can go to get away from the noise of home. He finds a place of security, a home away from home. Be it the library, the drugstore, or the diner, there is such a place for everyone. A place where I seem to belong is the local pool hall. I would like to introduce you to some of those who also hang out at Mr. Q's Recreation Hall.

(2) The people in the pool hall range from eighteen to eighty-five. A racially and ethnically mixed bunch, they come from the East Side, the North Side, and mainly from South Chicago. Most of the younger guys attend midwestern colleges, such as Notre Dame, the University of Michigan, or the

local junior colleges. There are the rich, the dropouts, the "potheads," and even the police.

(3)   The first person one sees upon entering the door is the owner. He checks the age of the young people who come into the pool hall. The law stipulates that no one under the age of eighteen be allowed in, and the owner has no plans of losing his little gold mine. Every night the pool hall is filled. The price to play pool for an hour is quite cheap, but the owner is not worried because business is very good.

(4)   The quietest group in the hall is the older generation, which hovers near the coffee machine. They find the pool hall a place of refuge. These men bring the daily newspapers to keep them busy. Their day at the pool hall usually consists of conversation and a short slumber.

(5)   By the jukebox sits the younger generation. In this group are the dropouts, who wear their leather, and since they are usually broke, they very seldom play a game of pool. These guys make the pool hall their hangout, since there is nowhere else to go and usually nothing to do. The rich guys usually come to the pool hall to buy some pot from the pusher. The pusher makes an easy buck at the pool hall, and that is what he is there for.

(6)   At the other end of the pool hall are the regulars. The younger set of this group cut their afternoon classes to get a couple of games of pool played. They usually have an interest in this sport, and they find some pleasure in playing pool, but the daily cost of their enjoyment is high.

(7)   To round out the pool hall group, there are the people who come here about twice a week. Some of these are the girls who come to the pool hall looking for some guy to buy them a dinner. Other girls come to see their boyfriends. The girls spend a lot of time in the rest room. The majority of these infrequent visitors, however, are undercover policemen. They can be seen a mile away by the way they play pool and by the bulge of their guns against their jackets when they bend over to shoot. The word travels fast around the pool hall, and these policemen are usually foiled in their search for a "bust."

(8) The pool hall is a city within a city, with each individual playing a role. All of the characters—the potheads, the hustlers, the pusher, the police, the dropouts, the rich guys, and the girls—make Mr. Q's an interesting place.

Donald Skonicki

Night and Day

(1)   The most successful times for me to write have been late at night or between classes. I seem to have done most of my best writing after 11 P.M. It seems that after eleven I don't have to put up with anyone. The children are asleep, and the adults in the house are responsible for themselves. The television fills the need I have for motion and sound that people provide. I also am very comfortable sitting on my bed in my pajamas. The best thing about writing in my room is that when I get tired, I lie down and start again at my leisure. To motivate myself, I have, at times, watched test patterns.

(2)   The time between classes I also find excellent for writing. I seem to absorb more in this short time. Again, I'm not responsible for anybody but myself. I can go off and sit in the student lounge and create. I tune in to the surrounding sights and sounds: People walking in the halls, the different sounds

their shoes make on the tile floors, somebody running, another laughing, and still another spouting some new street jargon. I find myself looking back and forth at them and my paper. Constantly observing, absorbing, and recording, I have again satisfied my need for motion and sound. There is nothing that escapes me, but yet I am able to create.

(3) I find this is not true of the classroom. Here it is much more difficult to create. The instructor is dealing with us on a one-to-one basis. It has to be somewhat quiet.

(4) In short, I think that I need some kind of human distraction to write well. It also can be provided in some sort of mechanical way, like a television or radio. You might need quiet in order to write. I need some reassuring noise.

Barbara Urbani

EXERCISE   Classifying and Dividing

1. Which essay primarily uses division? (Circle the letter of your answer.)

   a. "The Pool Hall"
   b. "Night and Day"
   c. "Stylists and Sluggers"

2. Explain why the author of "Stylists and Sluggers" tells you he has been a boxing fan for a long time.

   _____

   _____

3. Which essay or essays use a summary as an advance organizer before presenting its classifications? (Circle as many as apply.)

   a. "Take Two Aspirin"   **b.** "Stylists and Sluggers"
   c. "The Pool Hall"   **d.** "Night and Day"

WRITING ASSIGNMENT   Classifying

Write an essay in which you classify any of the following:

persons who frequent a campus hangout	mail-order catalogues	theaters
	magazines	children's TV programs
bookstores	personal computers	radio stations
department stores	sneakers	newspapers

If you want, assume you are writing for consumers your own age. You can therefore give your categories a practical slant—for example, what kind of sneakers last the longest.

WRITING ASSIGNMENT   Dividing

Write an essay that uses division to explain the parts of any one of these subjects:

a computer	a newspaper	a choir
a light bulb	an orchestra	a flower

Explaining a Process

What description is to a static subject, explaining a process is to a dynamic one. Process explanation describes not just elements but a meshed sequence of elements. A process does not stand still. Whether the purpose of the writer is to give information or directions, there must be a well-thought-out sequence the reader can easily follow. As you read the following essays, see whether every step of their plans fits in order and is easy to follow.

The Art of Filleting

(1)   Filleting a fish is the best way to prepare it for eating. With a little practice this process is simple to learn.

(2)   Filleting can be done with almost any kind of knife, but it is much easier with a proper one. I use a Rapala brand knife, which is thin, flexible, and about six inches long. If you use a stiff-bladed knife, you'll waste a lot of meat because it won't ride along the surface of the backbone. Whatever kind of knife you use, make sure it is sharpened.

(3)   By contrast, if you leave a fish whole, you have to scale it. Scaling a fish is time-consuming and tedious. Anyone who does it creates a lot of work that is unnecessary. Actually, leaving the skin intact doesn't do anything to enhance the flavor of fresh fish. With filleting you won't have to scale the fish and you won't have any bones to contend with while eating.

(4)   Here is my procedure: The first cut is made adjacent to the gill cover until you strike the backbone, making sure you don't cut through it. Position your knife at a slight angle. Then, using a sawing motion, ride the knife closely along the backbone of the fish. Continue cutting until you reach the tail. This side of the fish should lift right off. Lay it aside for the time being. Turn the fish over and repeat this procedure. The next step is to put the knife slightly under the rib bones and cut toward the stomach of the fish. Make sure all bones are removed by sliding your fingers across the length of the rib cage lining. Starting at the tail section, cut through the meat until you reach the skin. With your knife at a slight angle, use a sawing motion to slice through the entire length of the skin.

(5)   Filleting fish not only makes them easier to prepare but also increases freezer space. In the art of filleting, as with any skill, the more you practice, the more proficient you will become. If you follow my procedures for filleting fish, in a few weeks you will master this important skill.

Gene Kudzia

Cop Talk

(1) "Two seventeen, two-one-seven, a domestic disturbance at 4724 Langley, Jones on the three." The terminology is familiar to many although understandable in its strictest sense to a relative few. It is the jargon of the police. The terseness is a necessary characteristic of such communications, necessary because of the volume of calls and the fact that most callers are in tense situations and are actually calling for help.

(2) The police officer is linked to the central communications center by radio. A constant stream of information is broadcast in parrotlike monotones by a dispatcher who sounds like an auctioneer. The storm of information is made intelligible by the use of the military time system (1 A.M. is expressed as 0100 hours, and 1 P.M. is 1300 hours), an alphabetic code (A–Adam, B–Boy, C–Charlie, etc.), and the codification of commonly recurring situations that require police attention.

(3) Of the three devices mentioned, the one most responsible for the expeditious reporting of incidents and police action taken is the miscellaneous incident code. The following is an illustration of its use. An intoxicated man is annoying passers-by at the bus stop. A citizen calls the police, and the dispatcher assigns a unit in this manner: "Two seventeen, a disturbance with a drunk at 47th and King Drive." The unit acknowledges with "Ten-four." The officers arrive, arrest the man, and, on completing the assignment, inform the dispatcher of the action taken thusly: "Two seventeen is back with a three [disturbance drunk] K-King [taken to district station] R–Robert one time [one person arrested]." The code includes numerals from one to nineteen that represent situations (disturbances of different types; lost, sick, or injured persons; escorts; fires; etc.). It also has letters of the alphabet (A through R plus X) that represent the police action taken: peace restored, arrest made, taken to hospital or home, etc.). There was a system that utilized the number ten in addition to numbers from one to one hundred: 10–1, 10–2, etc. This code, however, is now obsolete and only three sets of the original hundred are still in use. These are: 10–1 (an officer needs help), 10–99 (a one-man car), and the ever popular 10–4 (a two-man car).

(4) Although the broadcast, receive, acknowledge cycle is in the main a monotonous affair, at times a resourceful dispatcher can add a little levity or color to his job. Then a down drunk becomes a "sidewalk inspector," a group of winos drinking on the street a "bottle gang," a traffic accident a "fender bender," and instead of calling for help for a domestic disturbance, it's "Save the marriage" or "Referee Jones versus Jones."

Alphonse Rochon

EXERCISE   Explaining a Process

1. Which essay provides an informational explanation of a process as opposed to directional explanation?

    a. "The Art of Filleting"   **b.** "Cop Talk"

2. Which essay lacks a conclusion?

    a. "The Art of Filleting"   **b.** "Cop Talk"

3. In "The Art of Filleting" which paragraph is in the wrong place?

   2   3   4

4. Which paragraph should it follow? ____
5. Which essay uses comparison and contrast?

   a. "The Art of Filleting"   **b.** "Cop Talk"   **c.** both essays

---

WRITING ASSIGNMENT   Explaining a Process

Write a process explanation in which you explain how to do any one of the following. You can take a serious or humorous point of view toward the subject chosen.

1. How to embarrass a parent
2. How to embarrass a teenager
3. How to handle a pushy salesperson
4. How to irritate a teacher
5. How to save money while traveling

Showing Reasons and Results

Providing reasons and results is the last of the strategies for explaining a subject in an essay. As reasons are causes and results are effects, this strategy is sometimes called cause and effect. Process explanation tells

Copyright, 1981, Universal Press Syndicate

how to do something; this strategy tells why something happened (causes) or the results of an action or condition (effects). Do not confuse this kind of essay with persuasion or argument. A writer can provide the reasons or causes of an event without taking a stand. Although reasons and results are useful in persuasion, when used by themselves, they can also explain.

Self-Development

(1)   There are many reasons for taking up a hobby, but the best reason is that it can make you creative. Such a hobby is photography. Photography allows me to be creative in my special way. It also shows me things I never knew were there.

(2)   A lot of people still think that cameras take pictures and spit back bits of the real world. On the contrary: photographers take pictures, and a photograph does not show the real world. To be sure, photographs seem more like the real thing than drawings or paintings. But photographs are like those art forms in that they isolate only a part of a scene in a frame and they are only two-dimensional. Unlike most paintings and many drawings, a photo is also often black and white, which certainly does not reflect the real world. Even when the pictures are in color, those colors are never exactly those of the real world. The choice of frame and the use of black-and-white or color film are up to the photographer, and that's where many aspects of creativity come in.

(3)   Photography is also creative because a camera lets me capture the things that interest me, especially things that show a struggle to exist. I have also photographed leaves that refuse to drop from trees in late fall and flowers that survive a spring frost. And I have photographed a puppy summoning the courage to step into a stream and a child who climbed a pole for the first time. Photography lets me concentrate on those aspects in life I like. I know that my pictures aren't all there is to life, but then I wouldn't want them to be. They are my world. They are what I want to create.

(4)   Photographs also create their own worlds because a person can't always anticipate how a photograph will come out. A scene looks different through each pane of a many-paned window. A photograph is like a pane of glass. It has its own special angle that makes it different from any other photograph. If eight or ten photographers took pictures of the same scene, no photographer would see the same scene or shoot from quite the same angle, nor would the light or shadow be quite the same.

(5)   Photographs also make their own worlds by showing me things I didn't know I saw when I took them. Last week, I took pictures of a small child playing. A lot of the pictures were taken in a hurry. When I developed and printed them, I noticed the strangest things. In two or three of the pictures, the child looks scared or even terrified. I don't know what he was thinking about while he was playing, but my camera was quicker at seeing than I was. Those pictures seem really independent of me, yet I took them; thus the camera is an extension of me. Another example is a picture of a leaf I took a few months ago. I was concentrating so much on the leaf itself that I didn't notice my mother's hand come into the background. She was picking flowers.

(6)   In all of these ways, then, photography is not only an enjoyable hobby, but a creative art. It requires choices and imagination, and it returns the investment with surprises of its own.

Paper Chase

(1)   I am afflicted with an addiction that has complete mastery over me. I cannot break it. I cannot shake it. This habit, this vice dominates me totally. Drugs and alcohol rule over some meek souls, but my addiction is not of that dark, desolate sort. I am neither a twitchy, nervous doper nor a boozy, befuddled wino. I have never traveled down those hard, mean streets, nor will I ever. There, thanks to fortune, go not I.

(2)   My addiction is the printed word. My vice, my obsession, is reading. I am a magazine freak. I read magazines, periodicals, journals with the single-minded fanaticism of a kamikaze pilot zeroing in on an aircraft carrier. A true wacko, if I don't get my daily fix of *Time* and *Newsweek*, I get the shakes and become emotionally unstable. Thank God for newsstands!

(3)   Does my wife need affection and attention? Do my children need a father's guiding love? Of course they do, and love and tenderness they get, but not until I have polished off *The New Republic*. My order of priorities may irritate my loved ones, but I cannot help myself. Like Popeye, I am what I am. I have long ago reconciled myself to my shortcomings, and I will make no effort whatsoever to change my ways. If my addiction leads to my perdition and damnation, then so be it. I do not care. I will boldly face the unforgiving fires of hell just so long as William F. Buckley is one of the demons of Lucifer and he makes available to me a copy of *The National Review*.

(4)   Happy is the man who knows his strengths and weaknesses, his virtues and his vices. I am such a man. I am at peace with myself. I know I will never conquer my addiction, and so I refuse to try. Why should I? My addiction is my strength. If readers are leaders, as the library commercial claims, then I am destined to be Caesar someday.

Anthony Rangel

Decay from Within

(1)   The decay of books is one of the most serious problems that libraries have to deal with. The pages in the book grow old and, for various reasons, deteriorate. Dust, salt particles, carbon dioxide, ozone, nitric oxide, oils, and various other pollutants are many factors that lead to this deterioration. Even dampness or dryness can damage paper.

(2)   One of the most destructive enemies of paper is acid. Acids deteriorate the pages of a book by attacking its fibers, which are made up of cellulose. What are these acids and where do they come from? Nitric, sulfurous, sulfuric, and hydrochloric acid are found in the sizing of the paper and in the atmosphere.

(3)   A book can be on shelves under what is believed to be ideal conditions but still be eaten away. Even in a controlled atmosphere books can deteriorate. One might expect a book to be safe if left unopened for years, but the gas from the acid can penetrate into the fibers of the page and totally erode the book from the outside.

(4)   Even the printing inks used today in books contribute to the problem. Most inks used today are from "iron gall formulas," in which

sulfuric acid is used to stabilize the ink. Ironically, in order to stabilize the inks, producers are increasing the chances that the books will deteriorate from the acids in the ink.

(5) There are some de-acidification techniques that can be used not only to remove the acids but to add a buffering agent to protect against future deterioration. They are expensive and time-consuming. Without such preservation techniques, books in our libraries will continue to be destroyed by chemical pollutants.

EXERCISE   Reasons and Results

1. Which essay or essays focus more on reasons (causes) than results (effects)? Circle the letter(s) of your answer.

   a. "Self-Development"   **b.** "Paper Chase"
   c. "Decay from Within"

2. Which essay or essays focus more on results (effects) than on reasons (causes)?

   a. "Self-Development"   **b.** "Paper Chase"
   c. "Decay from Within"

WRITING ASSIGNMENT   Reasons and Results

In an essay explain the reasons and/or results of some stressful activity, such as taking an examination, undergoing an interview, giving a speech, leaving home.

Argument or Persuasion

Explaining is not the main focus of argumentative or persuasive writing. Instead, it seeks to move an audience to accept a point of view or act in a certain way. Strictly speaking, getting someone to *do* something is persuasion. Getting someone to *agree* with you is argumentation. The terms are closely allied. It takes carefully supported arguments to get an audience to do something. The distinction lies in the writer's intention. If he or she is trying to get you to do something, that is persuasion. If he or she is trying to convince you of the soundness of a position, that is argument. As you read the student essays that follow, decide whether the writer is trying to persuade you to do something or trying to argue a point of view.

To My Sister-in-law

(1) When I was in my sophomore year in high school, it was required that I keep a journal for my English class. At that time I found it a tiring

chore. This year, I am again keeping a journal for my college English class. However, even though it is still time-consuming, it is not so tiring as it was when I was in high school. Perhaps the reason I don't mind it as much is that now it is not a required task.

(2)   I have found that writing my daily thoughts or activities has made me more capable of dealing with my co-workers and myself. The journal acts as my confessor and as an outlet for venting my frustrations. I have been able to pour out all my anxieties over my guilty thoughts and actions. And, if I'm extremely angry, I let off steam by writing about it. This is the main reason that I suggest that you keep a journal. I have seen you angry and take it out on the closest person to you. By keeping a diary, you can do as I do and put your anger in writing.

(3)   Another reason I feel that you should write a journal every day is that it will help you become more fluent in the English language. Since English is not your native tongue, a journal may be very effective for you in breaking you of the habit of first mentally composing something in Spanish. It did for me.

(4)   Whatever reason you choose for writing a journal, I believe that it will benefit you. You will probably notice an improvement in your grades and with your personal life. Keeping a journal worked for me. I am sure that it will work for you.

Myrna Hinojosa

EXERCISE   Argument or Persuasion

1. The essay "To My Sister-in-Law" is

    a. persuasive   **b.** argumentative

2. This essay was addressed to the writer's sister-in-law. List two specific reasons the writer uses to persuade her audience to start keeping a journal.

    _____

    _____

Ann and Abby

(1)   I support advice columnists, such as Ann Landers and Dear Abby. While they are sometimes put down as gossip columnists, they do not deserve that title. They are eager to help those who write to them for advice.

(2)   In order to judge these advice columnists, we must first have an understanding of the meaning of the word *advice.* According to the dictionary, it means an opinion given for the practical direction of conduct or information given by letter. This is all an advice columnist is trying to do.

(3)   People who write to Ann Landers or Dear Abby are people who are unable to solve their own problems. For example: Joan, a teenager, writes to Ann Landers about her fear of dating and asks how to overcome this fear. Ann

tells her that her fear is due to a lack of confidence in herself. Ann suggests to Joan that she go out on double dates at first until her self-confidence is built up. Ann's advice to Joan is a suggestion, not an order. The columnist is not trying to run someone's life but only to provide objective guidance.

(4)   Instead of writing to columnists, we should go to our relatives and friends for help, some would argue. But we might feel uncomfortable revealing some of our problems to close friends or relatives. Besides, I feel that someone who makes a living out of advising people is more qualified to help than a friend or relative.

(5)   Here's another example. Paul wants to marry Linda, who is pregnant by another man. He asks his friends and relatives if they approve, but their advice to Paul is to leave this woman because of her condition. Paul is puzzled, and he therefore writes to Dear Abby about his problem. Abby tells Paul that the basis of marriage is love and that if Paul and Linda love each other, their marriage will succeed. The friends and relatives in this case were operating on what they would have done in Paul's case. They are too subjective to give out any other advice because they are less experienced in advising.

(6)   Professional advisers, such as Ann Landers and Dear Abby, will be in print as long as there are people who are puzzled and need someone they can turn to outside of or in addition to their friends and relatives. By performing such a valuable service, the professional advice columnist does not deserve the title gossip columnist. The real gossip mongers are the amateur advice givers, those people around us to whom we often go for help.

Sharon Ann Owens

Ask an Amateur?

(1)   In the nation's newspapers there are columnists who write about almost every subject. There are sports columnists, fashion columnists, and, of course, advice columnists. The advice columnist is supposed to be the great solver of problems. All you have to do is write or type a letter telling your problem and sign it with a clever name like "worried widow," abused adolescent," or, if you can't think of a name for yourself, there's always "anonymous." Then you wait and read the column every day until your letter is printed and your life-saving reply is there in black and white. Of course, if your letter is so personal that you don't want it printed, you can ask for a confidential reply instead.

(2)   I don't see how anyone could waste his time and energy sending in a letter. A very small percentage of the replies can be taken seriously. Many times a very serious letter is written, and a person expects a sympathetic reply, but gets a sarcastic or a flippant dismissal. Even when serious advice is given, I wonder how much of it can be carried out. For example, take the case of teenagers who write to complain about some problem with their parents. Are we to believe that parents will simply agree to follow the advice decreed by an outsider just because it is in print?

(3)   Another example of time-wasting is the insignificant problems that get treated *ad nauseam*. For example, do we really need to read dozens of letters about the right way to squeeze toothpaste or to hang toilet paper?

(4)   Whether the problems are earthshaking or trivial, I also question the authority of the advice givers. Columnists such as Ann Landers are

ordinary persons with no specialized training in counseling or psychology to qualify them to hand out advice. I realize that people have problems, some trivial, some very serious, but there are many people infinitely more qualified to help with problems, like lawyers, psychologists, doctors, and clergy. There are many professionals bound by legal and moral codes who can offer serious help to people with problems.

(5) Take your choice: Write to an advice columnist who is out to sell newspapers and risk having your problem trivialized or clucked over by ten million readers, or go to a professional who specializes in solving problems. To me the choice is obvious.

EXERCISE   Argument and Persuasion

1. "Ann and Abby" is

   a. persuasive   **b.** argumentative

2. "Ask an Amateur?" is

   a. persuasive   **b.** argumentative

3. Which essay uses extended examples?

   a. "Ann and Abby"   **b.** "Ask an Amateur?"

4. Which essay has a conclusion that returns to a point made in the introduction?

   a. "Ann and Abby"   **b.** "Ask an Amateur?"

WRITING ASSIGNMENT   Argument and Persuasion

Choose one of the following exercises.

1. Write an argumentative essay in which you prove which essay on advice columnists did a better job of defending its position.
2. Write an argumentative essay that states how you feel about a particular newspaper advice columnist or advice columnists in general.
3. Write a letter of reply to the writer of "Ann and Abby" or "Ask an Amateur." Try to convince the essayist that your position on advice columnists makes more sense. You may, if you wish, address the anonymous student writer by a fictitious name.

Mixed Strategies

You have seen sample essays illustrating the strategies and modes writers use. They help suggest a shape but don't dictate the content of what you write. You can see there is quite a range of variation in the ways writers use a strategy. Some of the writing assignments have directed you to work with a particular strategy. When you write on your own, the strategy you need will be discovered later in the writing process. For example, a writer covering an election doesn't know at first whether he will contrast two candidates or explain why a candidate won.

Sometimes the writer's strategies are so mixed it is hard to know how to classify the essay. Such essays could be called mixed-strategy essays. An example follows.

Rainy Days and Yesterdays

(1) I love when it rains. I can sit and wander back into my "remember-when days" and remember my old friends.

(2) I can remember one rainy day last week. I sat on the chair by the window in the living room. Gazing through the window filled with raindrops, I could see my neighborhood the way it was fifteen years ago. From my front porch, directly across the street is my girlfriend Franny's house. I see her brothers, Joe, Martin, and crazy Philip. I also see her baby sister, Caroline, sitting on their front porch. Next door to me is Armida, the 350-pound woman who's married to Pete, who weighs about 150 pounds. To this day, I still can't understand how—well, that's their business! Down the street is Jerry De Laurentis' Grocery Store, better known as Jerry's. That store had the best candy selection in the neighborhood. When the Christmas season came around, Jerry would dress up as Santa Claus. He would sit outside in front of the store with his wife, Julia, next to him. She would pass out cookies and hot cocoa to the kids who waited in line to sit on Santa's lap and tell him what they wanted for Christmas. As my eyes looked farther down the street I came across Shield's Book Store. That's where Franny and I would go to buy Archie and Jughead comics. We would also put a quarter in the pop machine to get a cold bottle of Kay-O chocolate pop. (We drank it in the store so we wouldn't have to pay the nickel deposit on the bottle.)

(3) As the lightning cracks through the sky, I find myself back in the present and everything has changed. Franny and her family don't live across the street anymore; Armida and Peter moved, too. Julia De Laurentis is a widow now, and Shield's Book Store, well, it's still there but it's not the same. The entire neighborhood isn't the same, and you know—neither am I.

Anita Gutierrez

This essay describes a neighborhood. It uses flashback to tell a story, but it also provides many examples. It concludes with contrast. What kind of essay is this? It's either (1) an essay that explains by examples but also uses narrative or (2) a narrative essay that uses examples. Let's just call it a mixed-strategy essay.

WRITING ASSIGNMENT   Comparison and Contrast

Write an essay in which you contrast some person, place, or thing that has changed a great deal. See "Rainy Days and Yesterdays" above for an example of how this kind of subject can be treated.

EXERCISE   Identification of Essays

Except for mixed-strategy essays, it is fairly easy to tell what main strategy a writer is relying on. To prove that, read the following essays and answer the questions that follow them.

I

My weekdays should begin with breakfast. Breakfast means putting fuel in my tank to boost me into orbit for my daily activities. However, breakfast never materializes because my wife is asleep at 5 A.M. I need plenty of energy to run up and down the steps at work and to walk to and from the bus stop. Also, listening to people talk, which I have to do all day, requires a lot of energy.

My workday starts at 7 A.M., so I begin to fizzle out about eleven. Taking lunch then will give me the refueling I need to boost me into the next phase of the day. But the supervisor is so unorganized that he fails to set up regular lunch schedules. Therefore, I seldom have lunch at eleven. The time I do get lunch varies; my hunger doesn't vary. By eleven my stomach is sending me messages. A delayed lunch brings anger and more fatigue.

The time is winding down to 3 P.M., and the thought of the best steak dinner you could dream of and a restful evening at home invades my thoughts. But, to my disappointment, there isn't any steak, and the house is a wreck and as noisy as a zoo. Oh brother, another annoying day.

Robert McCullough

1. This essay is *primarily*

   a. descriptive   **b.** explanatory
   c. argumentative   **d.** narrative

2. The *overall* strategy used is

   a. comparison–contrast (chunks)
   b. comparison–contrast (slices)
   c. classification and division

II

There are three kinds of college instructors I have encountered whom I regard as "bad news." These three types I call the Standard Bearer, the Good Buddy, and the Bull Artist. In this paper I will briefly describe the three types in terms of their behavior in the classroom. If you have not yet encountered any one of these losers, count your blessings, cross your fingers, and hold your breath.

The Standard Bearer is an instructor who prides himself on upholding standards. Examples are the instructor of the Shakespeare class who announces proudly that even old Will himself would have trouble earning a C minus in the course or the professor who, challenged by a conflict between what he says and what God or anyone else says, announces that he will have the Constitution, Ten Commandments, whatever, amended to bring it into line with his thinking.

The Standard Bearer firmly believes that if you are taking his class you should drop all other activities (quit your job, divorce your spouse, put your children up for adoption). He believes the course is falling apart if anyone achieves an A or if more than 10% of the students pass the course. The standards (educational objectives) exist out in the great beyond somewhere, vague, mysterious, known only to the professor and, perhaps, the Almighty. His motto is: "Many are called, but few are chosen." Damn few!

Good Buddy is a glad hander, a hand-slapping, cheek-kissing phony. He want to con the students into accepting him as just another member of the group. He takes pride in being on a casual first-name basis with everybody in class. Everything is brother so and so, sister so and so. The class resembles a prayer meeting half the time and a union social the other half. Everything is cool, everybody (or should I say every brother and sister) all nice, warm, snug, cozy, and comfy. And that's the problem.

When I want a friend, I call on a friend. When I want a mechanic, I call on a mechanic, not a friend. What I want at college is a teacher, someone who, like the plumber and mechanic, knows a job, does it, and expects to be paid for it.

The Bull Artist is very stimulating, always entertaining. The jokes are current and come one after the other. The B.A. is a storehouse of interesting anecdotes about life in general or about his hobby, sex life, spouse, or pets. However, I have yet to meet one as funny as Richard Pryor or Jonathan Winters. When I want entertainment, I know where to go for it—and it isn't school.

If you currently have any of the teachers described above, you have my deepest sympathies. Before the semester's over, you are really going to need them.

1. This essay is *primarily*

   a. descriptive   b. explanatory
   c. argumentative   d. narrative

2. The *overall* strategy used is:

   a. comparison–contrast (chunks)
   b. comparison–contrast (slices)
   c. classification and division

WRITING ASSIGNMENT   Classification

Write an essay in which you give your own categories for any one of the following groups:

police officers	waiters
cab drivers	bus drivers
salespersons	coaches
sportscasters	clergy

III

In today's society, many people are turning toward smaller cars for reasons such as economy, conservation, and ease of parking. I, however, prefer the larger models of cars for three important reasons. The most obvious reasons are size and power, but I also have a feeling of security when I'm driving a large car.

As I mentioned earlier, size is very important to me. I like to have plenty of room so that I can be as comfortable as possible when I'm driving. I also feel that I can maneuver the car more efficiently if I have plenty of room. Thirdly, large cars can accommodate more passengers and cargo than smaller ones.

Small cars offer a small engine, which means that the power is very minimal. So in order to get the power that I want, I must again turn to the large car. I don't want to give you the impression that I'm a speedster; it's just that I like to pass other cars and trucks on the expressway, and a 402, eight-cylinder, four-barrel engine is very capable of doing so.

My last and most important demand of a car is safety. While most cars are only as safe as the person who's driving them, I feel more safe in an Electra than I do in a Volkswagen. I feel that a large car can better withstand an accident than a small car. The longer hood or trunk on a larger auto more or less acts as a cushion between the struck object and the driver and passengers.

Even though large cars consume lots of gas and cost more to buy and maintain, I will continue to drive them because of their roominess, power, and the extra safety they offer.

This essay is *primarily*:

a. descriptive   b. explanatory
c. argumentative   d. narrative

WRITING ASSIGNMENT   Persuasion or Argumentation

Write a persuasive or argumentative essay in which you make a case for any of the following:

small cars	winter vacations
a vegetarian diet	traveling by train
jogging	cross-country skiing
homemade bread	

You will probably find it useful to contrast your subject with another, for example, cross-country skiing with downhill skiing. Assume that your audience is someone who knows little about your topic. For example, explain a vegetarian diet to a meat-and-potatoes person, or convince someone content with packaged sliced bread that he or she should bake some homemade bread.

IV

The secretary answered telephones with three hands and wrote with the other. She asked if my name was Fred Flealy and I replied, "Yes." She was very cute and her legs were simply dazzling. We started to smile at each other when I heard, "Next," and I jumped to my feet and followed the red line, winking at the secretary as I passed her. The line weaved through the enormous hairs of the collie being used as the staging area for recruitment of would-be flea circus performers.

Ringmaster Franklin was a short, stubby flea with large antennae and short arms and legs. He told me to have a seat and asked about my qualifications. I fidgeted in my tiny chair and began, "Well, sir, I spent eight months on a police German shepherd struggling with the meanest of human criminals. For five months I was on an Alaskan husky pulling a sled through blizzards, and I even trained with a very fast racing greyhound. That greyhound was so fast that I was the only flea left; all the others couldn't hang on and were probably killed on the track. My feet are very quick, and I can jump higher than most fleas. All four of my arms are very strong, and I have excellent reflexes in case a paw interferes."

With two arms tapping on the desk and the other two crossed, he got up and walked to the front of the desk. "This isn't just any old mutt circus; this is Fleeling Brothers and Barkum and Bathem Circus," he roared. "Our beautiful lady stars come from the finest French poodles and Afghans. Most of our strong and brave male stars come from fierce Dobermans and some from vicious wolves," he added. He went back to his chair and sat, scratching his chin and studying me. In a more relaxed tone he said, "I think that you have some solid work experience. If you have references to support your claims, you can join our circus."

Reaching into my pocket, I displayed the very tips of three hairs, a German shepherd hair, an Alaskan husky hair, and a greyhound hair. He examined them. With a big smile he said, "Mr. Flealy, you just might become one of my finest performers."

Hilario Perez

This essay is *primarily:*

a. descriptive   b. explanatory
c. argumentative   d. narrative

WRITING ASSIGNMENT   Narration/Description

Write a narrative or descriptive essay on any one of the following topics:

A day in the life of a parking meter
The life and death of a snowflake
A fear you conquered
An accident waiting to happen
An experience that deeply affected you

Answering Essay Exam Questions

Answering an essay examination question is not much different from writing an essay, period. The strategies you have been studying will prove especially useful. Time limitations are the only significant difference. The writing process has to be planned within the time constraints set by your instructor. Here are some suggestions to help you do just that.

1. *Read the essay question carefully to be sure you understand what it asks.*

2. *Budget your time.* If, for example, you have forty-five minutes to compose your answer, you might allot five minutes to planning your answer, thirty minutes to writing it, and ten minutes to proofreading and correcting. You will not ordinarily have the time to rewrite an entire draft of an essay.

3. *Plan your answer before you start writing.* Students who start writing essay responses without a plan often wind up contradicting themselves. A chickenfoot or other outline is helpful, but you do not have time for an extremely complicated outline.

4. *Guide your response by the key words in the question.* One biology professor used to ask his students to simply tell all they knew about blood. A question that wide you could drive a truck through! Most teachers are more exact in their essay questions—for example, "Explain the function of white blood cells." Here are key words to watch for and the writing strategies they suggest.

Analyze	classification or division
Describe	description
Explain	any explanatory essay, such as process explanation, reasons and results, etc.
Account for	reasons and results
Evaluate	argumentation or persuasion
Compare or contrast	comparison and contrast
Explain	examples, description, narrative

5. *Use specifics (proof, illustration, examples) to back up your answer.* In other words, separate yourself from Dumb Harry. Harry knows there were several causes of the Civil War. He can't specify what they were. He knows that Gilbert and Sullivan wrote a lot of operettas; he can't tell you how many.

6. *Proofread.* Don't just check for error. Find out where you can amplify what you wrote with further examples or specifics.

Here's a model essay examination. It was written in a history class in response to the following directions:

Pick any two of the people listed below and discuss their contribution to the early days of the United States under its new Constitution. Draw a conclusion as to which person made a more significant contribution.

George Washington   Thomas Jefferson
John Adams   Alexander Hamilton

Both Alexander Hamilton and George Washington were important leaders in the earliest days of the new nation under the Constitution. Washington was influential in that he set the tone for the Presidency as well as formed a policy of neutrality that, in large measure, lasted until World War I. Hamilton was a diehard Federalist who first articulated the "loose construction" principle and who also set the direction for American expansion into industry and commerce. While Washington's influence proved to linger into the future, Hamilton had more of an influence on the nation at the time he was in power.

thesis re Washington

thesis re Hamilton

contrast

The lingering effects of Washington's Presidency were not an accident. Washington knew he must set an example of a strong and effective executive. He took interest in the appearance of the office since he knew that all Americans would be watching him closely. Washington kept a kind of royalty about the Presidency, but not in the British sense. He was dignified, yet wasn't a monarch and did not pretend to be one. Instead, he worked to keep the balance of powers as dictated by the Constitution. Washington kept the cabinet his affair, so that cabinet members would not become tools of the legislature. Similarly, he rarely concerned himself with directing the legislature. Washington felt that lawmaking should not be directed by the executive. He only used the veto power twice in his two terms as President.

Washington's domestic policy

Another aspect of Washington's ideals was that he wanted as little as possible to do with the politics of other nations. He stressed that involving the U.S. in European affairs would lead the country into being a puppet of whichever European nation was in power. Washington recognized the need for trade with other nations; he warned against political involvement with other nations. This sentiment is especially apparent in his Farewell Address. The policy that Washington adopted in order to preserve political independence was that of neutrality, which basically meant that other countries should respect the decision of the U.S. to remain apart from their affairs. Except for the War of 1812, this policy of neutrality was the prevalent idea in foreign affairs until World War I, when the U.S. joined the allies in Europe to help finish that war.

Washington's foreign policy

While Washington was in the Presidency and acting in moderation, Alexander Hamilton voiced his opinions without any hint of moderation. Hamilton was Washington's

contrast with Hamilton

Secretary of the Treasury. He was an ardent Federalist and was in favor of a strong central government. One of Hamilton's first major fights with Thomas Jefferson came over the issue of the National Bank and the subsequent loose versus strict interpretations of the Constitution. Hamilton succeeded in convincing Congress that a National Bank was "necessary and proper" to the financial system of the country. This was a major point of government because it established the use of the "necessary and proper" Constitutional clause.

Hamilton was also the primary shaper of the early U.S. economy. He boldly paid off all U.S. debts in full at face value and assumed part of the state debts. His overview was of a nation of manufacturers. He wanted to move the nation toward increasing its industry. In many ways he was successful in sowing the seeds for this growth.

Hamilton

It seems, then, that Hamilton's influence was more immediate than Washington's. He raised Constitutional questions which had a bearing on his peers' interpretation of the Constitution. He set up the financial system, paying off debts in full to strengthen the nation's credit. The nation followed much of the economic policy which Hamilton set. Washington was influential also, primarily by setting up the nature of the Presidency. He was, in terms of Presidential manner, the President to be emulated. Also, the foreign policy of neutrality which he established had a long-lasting influence on the nation.

summary:
comparison
and contrast

Daniel Hollander

PART III

Writing Systems

8

Language

Word Choice

Writing planned for an audience puts special demands on your word choice. Word choice is the focus for much editing and rewriting. That does not mean hunting for the most learned or most impressive word. No capable writer deliberately chooses words that are too difficult for an audience.

Neither does good word choice mean simply writing the way you speak. Why not? For one, when you write you don't have an audience in front of you offering instant feedback. You also have to do without gesture, tone of voice, and body language, all of which can help you make your point when you talk.

Language must be tailored to the needs and expectations of an audience. To sound impressive, students sometimes lean on evasive or high-sounding language. Here's an example of a student who, trying to impress an audience with terminology, confuses and loses the reader:

> To refer back to the aforementioned chapters shows a great cognizance in the previous works comprised to make our English class more comfortable.

The student forgot that language should be clear and specific. I think all he was trying to say was that he likes the fact that his textbook includes references to and builds on material already covered. You can see how unfortunate word choice can hinder communication.

Word choice is sometimes called diction. Diction in speaking means clarity; in writing, diction also calls for clarity.

Getting to Specifics

To illustrate, suppose you were in a shopping center and heard the following announcement: "Will the owner of a late-model blue Buick with Ohio license plates ST 5420 please come to the security office." While this statement starts out in general terms, it does not stay there. Otherwise, most of the car owners in earshot would be lined up at the security desk. Notice that as more detail is added, the description gets so specific it finally refers to only one car:

The owner	—Anyone who owns anything (motorcycle, van, bicycle, etc.)
Late model	—Not an exact year, but it excludes older objects.
Blue	—While it doesn't say what shade of blue, it excludes all other colors.
Buick	—Owners of Toyotas, Fords, etc., can stop listening.
With Ohio license plates	—Excludes 49 other states.
ST 5420	—At last, the one car that matches all of the above.

You will not always have to get that specific in writing, but you should remember that no one drives just "a car" (rather a Ford, a Mazda, etc.). That is, we live in a concrete world. Although we often don't have to be blueprint-specific ("I went to my Chemistry 205 class in room 2114 of Hellems Hall at 9:30 A.M."), we often must come up with something more specific than a general statement ("I went to class").

General terms do not provide the reader enough detail to form adequate word pictures. Compare the word pictures in the following sentences:

1. I went out last night.
2. I went out to eat last night.
3. I enjoyed a pepperoni pizza last night at Luigi's Restaurant.

Sentence 1 is so general the reader does not know what you did or where you went. Sentence 2 categorizes the activity but leaves too many suppositions. Did you go to a diner, snack bar, or restaurant? Sentence 3 ends a lot of mystery. It enables the reader to picture checkered tablecloths, wine bottles, comfortable booths, and cheese-laden pizza. The reader would not ordinarily expect to know the name of the waiter or the size of the bill. That would be getting too specific.

By contrast, not telling the audience too much but telling them too little is the problem of much student writing. Student writers sometimes express fear of "bothering a reader with a lot of details." Readers would rather be "bothered" with details than kept in the dark. We live in a world of details. Originality and truth lie in details, one author insists. No less than your spoken language, your written language should mirror those details.

EXERCISE   Specific Details

Take the following words, phrases, or sentences and make them more specific. That is, make them reveal more specific detail. For example:

> We worked on our schoolwork.
> Vera and I slaved over our term papers. (revision)

1. A nice party
2. A good time
3. The band performed.
4. The car made a noise.
5. The teacher was angry.
6. It was late.
7. Her shoes were not new.
8. Traffic was bad.
9. The bird moved in the cage.
10. The weather was miserable.

Clichés

Although they are sometimes quite specific, clichés can rob writing of specific detail. Clichés are once-colorful expressions that have been overused, like the following:

poor but honest   quick as a flash
birds of a feather   sly as a fox
dead as a doornail

You know they are overused when you can automatically finish them off after hearing just the beginning words of the phrase. For example:

a labor of _____
hard as a _____
last but not _____

Such worn-out expressions not only bore readers, they rob you of the chance to express images and ideas in your own way.

What's the cure for a cliché? Rewrite the expression so that it makes its point in a fresh way. For example, "high as a kite" becomes "high as a drunk on stilts"; "lonely as a hermit" becomes "lonely as a peanut in a boxcar."

EXERCISE Replacing Clichés

Rewrite any four of the following clichés so they make their point in a fresh way.

quick as a fox	sharp as a tack
one in a million	quick as a wink
white as snow	pure as the driven snow
tight as a drum	stubborn as a mule
busy as a bee	safe and sound

He couldn't punch his way out of a paper bag.

Redundancy

Another problem area in choosing words is unconscious repetition. Someone who calls the Sears Tower a "tall skyscraper" probably means a tall building. Ever see a short skyscraper? If you mention "the two twins," you probably don't mean two sets of twins, but simply one set. Another example of such unintentional repetition is the phrase "pizza pie." Since *pizza* already means "pie," that word is not needed. Redundancy means saying the same thing twice, like calling someone famous and well-known. Some repetition in writing is unavoidable and useful to the reader in bridging your ideas. In trying to give the reader a clear word picture, you might, however, sometimes unconsciously repeat yourself.

EXERCISE Redundancy

Cross out redundant words or phrases in the following sentences. For example:

Finally, they stopped the ~~argumentative~~ bickering.

1. My tour started at 8:00 A.M. on a Saturday morning.
2. The speakers were so large in size, they protruded out into the audience of people.

3. The annual yearly meeting was held in an abandoned store building.
4. This phrase has been used for many years past.
5. A ballad is a test of a singer's ability to sing.
6. Usually, as a rule, they sell novel new products.
7. My most favorite politician once more promised to reunite us together again.
8. The diner regularly served perch fish fillets once a week every Friday.
9. The reason we couldn't continue on was because the temperature was minus ten below zero.
10. I've never in my life met that well-known famous celebrity personally.

Wordiness

Wordiness in many ways is like redundancy. Redundancy, saying the same thing twice, is a specific kind of wordiness. A wordy expression is one that uses too many words to make its point. For example, look at how a student overstuffed this sentence:

> In performing the skills of a writing assignment, there are special and different types of rituals I must go through with before I can sit down to write what I plan to say.

To come up with 500 words for an essay, there is no need to pad your writing like that.

What was the student trying to say? Something like this:

> There are several rituals I must engage in before I can write.

The passive voice, as we have shown, is often the culprit that creates wordiness. Compare the following:

It has come to my attention *Tom Sawyer* was written by Mark Twain.	I just found out Mark Twain wrote *Tom Sawyer*.
Enclosed please find a copy.	I enclose a copy.

Wordiness also results from unconscious language habits. The examples you have just studied show how easy it is to cause (and to cure) wordiness. Take "bake up." I'd like to flatten the Pillsbury dough boy for that blob of wordiness. "Baking up" some cookies sounds folksy, but since nothing bakes down, *up* is mere filler. *Up* often unconsciously gets tacked on some verbs with illogical results. For example: How do you "wash up" a floor? What does it mean to "listen up"? Extra words, such as *up*, worm their way into our writing. However small, they mar clear meaning.

EXERCISE Wordiness

Rewrite the following sentences to eliminate wordiness.

1. The young teenager stepped off of the plane.
2. Let's all of us continue on.
3. The ending was not so bad as I had expected it to be.
4. The horse was old in years and gray in color.
5. At the present time I am going to bake up some brownies.
6. This is the most unbelievable thing that ever happened to me in my life so far.
7. At this point in time we have in the neighborhood of ten thousand dollars pledged.
8. In the not too distant future I will buy a computer.
9. Due to the fact that he got up late, he missed his early-morning class.
10. Until such time as he bought an extra-loud alarm clock, he overslept as a general rule by virtue of the fact that he was a heavy sleeper.

Denotation and Connotation

You may use accurate words, rid your sentences of wordiness, and still have word problems. One reason is that words mean on more than one level. That is, words do point out objects, but, at the same time, they can pick up multiple or very specialized meanings. Would you, for example, rather be in a crowd, a mob, or an assembly? These words all mean (denote) groups of people, but they suggest (connote) very different groups. A *mob* suggests an unruly crowd, while an *assembly* suggests an orderly group.

All words have some connotation. Take that assembly we mentioned. A teacher might say she "escorted" her students to such an assembly. A reluctant student might complain about being "herded" there.

escorted	**herded**
positive connotation	negative connotation
suggests a helpful, orderly movement of humans	suggests a forced roundup of animals

Over and above what they literally mean (denotation), words pick up special meanings they suggest (connotation). To illustrate, *peda-*

gogue is one term for a teacher, and a mother is a female parent, but don't try addressing your teacher as a pedagogue or your mother as your female parent. *Pedagogue* suggests an inflexible and dogmatic teacher. *Female parent* would be a cold, clinical way to address your mother.

EXERCISE Connotation

Circle the word or phrase that has the most positive connotation in each grouping. Underline the word or phrase that has the most negative or least positive connotation. For example:

    vintage automobile   old car   <u>a junk</u>

1.	used car	pre-owned car	jalopy
2.	mongrel	mutt	mixed breed
3.	shrieked	called	yelled
4.	smart	egghead	genius
5.	eat	ingest	dine
6.	worker	bureaucrat	payroller
7.	determined	headstrong	stubborn
8.	garbage collector	janitor	sanitation engineer
9.	crowd	mob	assembly
10.	odor	scent	stench

To know what words mean and what words suggest, writers have to become wordsmiths.

Language sometimes has to be customized for an audience. In some parts of the country, "My uncle passed" will provoke a puzzled reply: "Passed what?" In other parts, the listener will immediately know your relative has died ("passed away"). Another example: A mother who asked her son what he wanted for dinner was told, "Don't make me no never mind." She thought her dinner offer was turned down flat. Instead, her son was using a dialect expression to mean, "It makes no difference to me what you cook." To avoid such miscues, speakers and writers must constantly assess their language to match their audience.

Regional Expressions

Many words and expressions are common to one geographical area but not common to a whole country. These regional expressions work fine for those who share the code. As a midwesterner, I don't use the southern expression "you-all." But if I spend a few weeks in the South, I unconsciously start to pepper my speech with that expression. Regional expressions function clearly for those who know the code. For those who don't, there can be many miscues. For example, regular coffee in New York and some other parts of the East often means "coffee with cream and sugar." Where I come from, *regular coffee* means non-espresso. We all inherit and use localized terms like that. Whenever a clerk asks me if I want a *sack* for my groceries, I always expect burlap, not a paper bag. There are even regionalisms peculiar to one city. To a Chicagoan, downtown is "the Loop" and even the smallest vacant lots are "prairies."

Dialects

Many groups of people in this country use not just an occasional regional expression but a special vocabulary, pronunciation, and grammar. There are many dialects of English used by Polish-Americans, Chinese-Americans, Afro-Americans, and other groups. There are many such community dialects. For example, on the South Side of Chicago where I grew up, the word *mayor* was always a single-syllable word. Even the mayor called himself "duh mare." Chances are you are familiar with some community dialect. Such dialects are useful, and they often provide a rich source of new standard English words. Those who know a dialect can communicate in a special way with those who share it. The following student paper makes that point quite clearly.

The Two Languages of Fred

"Good morning. How are you?" When I'm at school this is the way I greet my associates, but when I get home it's "What's happening?" or "What's poppin'?" It's almost like learning two languages, one academic and one more relaxed or urban.

Here is a typical conversation I might have with someone from school:

FRED: Good morning, mind if I sit down?
MARK: No, go right ahead.
FRED: Mr. Armstead is really a good instructor. He gets his point across accurately and forcefully.
MARK: Yes, I agree with you 100 percent. I'm going to recommend him to all my friends.
FRED: His style is so fresh and alive.
MARK: And his lectures are really enlightening.

That's basically how a conversation at school would go. Now I'm going to use that same conversation at home.

ABBASI (Fred):   Hi, Blood, what's poppin'?
RICE (Mark):   Aw, you got it.
ABBASI: Mind if I cop a squat?
RICE: Go ahead, my name ain't on the furniture.
ABBASI: Brother Armstead is a smokin' teacher.

RICE: Yeah, I think he real down myself. I'm going to tell all my
partners to hook up with him.
ABBASI: Yeah, man, he believes in getting his word across.
RICE: I'm hip. His lectures don't make you want to catch forty
winks. They really put something on your head.

That's how a conversation at "the crib" would go. I like both my
languages and don't consider one any better than the other. I respect and like
the differences in them. So if you hear me at school and you hear me at home,
don't think I have a twin brother, just twin languages.

Fred A. Hendricks

The student might be exaggerating the differences here. His everyday language at school is probably less formal than the examples cited,
but he does illustrate and appreciate some differences between his community dialect and his more standardized language.

WRITING ASSIGNMENT   Your Language

Choose one of the following exercises.

1. Using a community dialect or lots of regional expressions, retell a
   story such as "Little Red Riding Hood" or "The Three Little Pigs."
2. If you are bilingual, illustrate in an essay the two languages you
   speak.
3. Explain how in the course of a day you adapt your spoken or written
   language to various audiences.

In a preface to your paper, explain the particular audience you are writing
for—for example, someone in another part of the country who is not
familiar with your regional expressions.

Another important point made in Fred's paper is that we shift how
we talk and write to suit an audience. Even if you do not speak a special
dialect, in the course of the day you are constantly changing the kinds
of language you use. Let's look at how you might switch language when
you simply answer the telephone.

CALLER: a friend who shares a dialect
with you   ANSWER: What's up, man?
CALLER: your mother   ANSWER: Hi, Mom.
CALLER: someone who asks for you but
whom you have never met   ANSWER: Hello. Yes, this is he.

The three ways of answering the phone listed above are, in order,
examples of slang, informal language, and formal language. Let's look
at those in reverse order.

Formal Language

Formal language is the language that we use in a formal situation. Examples include:

a business letter   a report or a term paper
minutes of a meeting   a speech at a formal occasion
newspaper editorials

    In the telephone response above, the speaker did not know his audience. Therefore, he used formal English. If you received such a phone call you would probably use formal English too. Formal English is the language we speak and write in a formal situation. This variety of language avoids contractions and other shortcuts of expression:

> NOT: I won't run for President. (informal)
> BUT: I will not run for the office of President of the United States.

Informal Language

When you are not using formal English, you are using some variety of informal English. The slang "What's up, man?" and the colloquial "Hi" both fit this extensive category. Informal English is everyday English, the kind you use when you are not aware that your language is being monitored. All of formal English and much of informal English is standard. That is, it represents a standardized way of communicating that can be used anywhere in the country. We have already dealt with regional language and community dialects. The dictionary labels these and slang as *nonstandard* English. That does not mean *substandard.* Substandard English would represent expressions that are not typical of English, period. For example, "The brick she falls off the roof."

Slang

Slang represents a body of figurative and colorful expressions often developed by a subgroup of the population. Prisoners, college students, jazz musicians, politicians, and other groups have developed a special slang.

    Some slang terms can make their way into formal English. *Mob* and *sham* are two such terms. However, slang terms often have many competitors. There are dozens of slang terms, for example, for being intoxicated (formal) or drunk (informal). Among the slang terms are:

wiped out   plowed
tanked   plastered
smashed   three sheets to the wind

Slang terms are faddish. Some of the expressions above have been around for decades. Others have "bitten the dust" (another slang expression). For example, sixty years ago, "ossified" was a catchy slang term for being intoxicated. Slang terms can die out more quickly than that. Surveying its own slang, one college found that "tuna," a 1980 term for an overweight person, was no longer in use four years later. Here is some college slang found in 1984 at one eastern college:

a "duck course"	an easy course
"air mail"	an empty mailbox
"comping in a cube"	studying in a library cubicle

An easy course may be known on your campus as a "gut course," as a "Mickey Mouse" course, or by some other slang expression. Slang words come and go.

In writing dialogue you can use slang as is. Outside of dialogue, put any slang you use in quotes to set it off from standard English. This helps a reader distinguish a word used in a slang sense from its traditional usage—for example, crib (a baby's bed) and "crib" (apartment).

WRITING ASSIGNMENT   Slang

Choose one of the following exercises. In either case, specify an audience. You might, for example, explain your campus slang to someone in another school or tell some young relative or friend about slang from your high school days.

1. In an essay explain some popular slang terms heard around your campus.
2. Write an essay about slang terms you know that are no longer popular: for example, some slang used in Hollywood gangster movies of the thirties and forties, or slang terms you remember from your high school days.

Edited American English

I have put the form of language called "Edited American English" last to highlight it. Edited American English is the language used in most newspapers, magazines, and books, as well as in television and radio newscasts. All dialects are useful. Because this widespread dialect represents the formal and informal English shared and used by the communication media, it is especially useful. Most college reading and writing will be in Edited American English.

Finding the Right Word

Another job of the wordsmith is coming up with the right word or phrase, not one of similar sound or meaning. Because you hear words more often than you see them in print, they can be easily confused. For example, one student wrote that she was feeling "out of source." She meant "out of sorts." That is like using pepper for paprika. In everyday speech her error was hard to detect. In print, she had to get the phrase right. Another student wrote about being caught "dead in his tracts." Don't be caught dead wrong in your tracks. Carefully distinguish similar-sounding words. The Glossary that follows should help you do just that—untangle many easily confused or misused words and phrases.

Glossary of Commonly Confused Words

a	Article used before consonants: a lemon a joystick a hit
an	Article used before vowel sounds except for long *u* sounds: an orangutan an umbrella an hour an onion BUT: a union a university
and	Linking word (conjunction). Do not confuse with the article *an:* bacon and eggs NOT: bacon an eggs
accept (ak sept)	To agree to or to receive (verb). Example: I accept your offer.
except (ik sept)	Excluding or with the exception of (preposition). Example: Except for Mondays, I like my week.
accidently	A common misspelling (see correct spelling below).
accidentaly	Another misspelling (see correct spelling below).
accidentally	The correct spelling of this adverb: I accidentally crushed my teddy bear in the trash compactor.
advice (ad vīs)	Recommendation (noun): Her advice was sound.
advise (ad vīź)	To give advice (verb): I advise you not to skip breakfast.
affect (a fekt)	To influence (verb): The weather affected his mood.
effect (i fekt)	The result of some action or cause (noun): The effects of unemployment are far-reaching. (Hint: Think of the phrase *cause and effect* to remember

the meaning of *effect.*) Also, to put into effect or to make happen (verb): The committee effected the new rules.

ain't	Nonstandard. Common in some dialects, but avoided in formal writing except when quoted in dialogue.
a lot	A large quantity: There is a lot of violence on prime-time television. Don't write as a single word: alot. Try this hint: A lot does not stand alone.
already all ready	Both spellings are correct, but the words have different meanings. *Already* (an adverb) applies to an act that is finished before some other action in the same sentence: By six we were already awake. *All ready* means "in complete readiness": By six, we were all ready to move.
alright all right	Nonstandard spelling of *all right.* The correct spelling of *all right:* That's all right with me. NOT: That's alright with me.
amount number	*Amount* refers to unspecified quantities or quantities that can only be measured or approximated: There is a surprising amount of sugar in most soft drinks. *Number* specifies something countable: A number of manufacturers now sell low-calorie soft drinks.
anyone any one	Singular pronoun referring to any person: Is anyone there? A more restrictive singular pronoun referring to any single person or thing: Any one of us could have handled the job.
are our	A verb—present tense plural of *to be:* They are weird. A pronoun: It's our turn. Do not confuse the words *are* and *our,* which sound somewhat alike.
as far as . . . is concerned	Do not leave out the concluding part of this expression. NOT: As far as people who leave off this ending, they should be beaten with sticks. BUT: As far as people who leave off this ending are concerned, they should be beaten with sticks.

awhile	An adverb that means "for a short time or period."
a while	*After a while* and *for a while* are prepositional phrases. Since prepositions take nouns as objects, do not use the adverb form after them. NOT: after *awhile* for *awhile* BUT: after *a while* for *a while*
beside	Near, next to: The creature sat beside me.
besides	In addition to, or over and above: Besides Godzilla, there were many movie monsters. Don't confuse these two words. "There was a grinning fool besides me" includes you as a fool. "There was a grinning fool beside me" means that the fool was next to you.

EXERCISE   Usage

Without consulting the glossary, do the following exercise. If the underlined words or phrases are used correctly, circle them. If they are used incorrectly, cross them out and write in the correction in the space above. Assume that a formal usage is called for. For example:

The death of the rock star deeply (affected) his fans.

Benjamin Franklin ~~lead~~ an interesting life.
 led

1. The gorilla wouldn't <u>accept</u> any more bananas.

2. The waiter <u>accidently</u> spilled chicken soup on my lap.

3. Horace Greeley's <u>advise</u> was, "Go West, young man."

4. Her resignation will have far-reaching <u>effects</u>.

5. Miss Piggy <u>ain't</u> beautiful, but she is <u>all right</u> with me.

6. <u>A lot</u> of blood has been wiped up <u>all ready</u>.

7. There were a <u>number</u> of planes <u>already</u> on the runway.

8. <u>Anyone</u> interested in a game of tiddly winks?

9. <u>As far as</u> tiddly winks, I haven't played for <u>awhile</u>.

10. It's <u>our</u> turn. <u>Are</u> you ready?

11. There was an empty chair <u>besides</u> me.

12. <u>Except</u> for dinner I don't eat <u>alot</u>.

13. Will <u>anyone</u> want to work for three dollars <u>an</u> hour?

---

brake	To stop (verb): I brake for wombats. A device used to stop (noun): Disc brakes will hold even when wet.
break	To reduce to pieces or to fracture (verb): It is bad luck to break a mirror. An interruption or rest (noun): I have a break between my spinal-injuries class and children's literature.
can't hardly can hardly	Since *hardly* is considered a negative word, *can't hardly* is a double negative. We can't hardly hear you. (nonstandard) We can hardly hear you. (standard)
capital	A noun or adjective with many meanings, including, Highly important or serious (adjective): A capital crime. The official seat of government (noun): Carson City is the capital of Nevada. Hint: A<u>ll</u> states have capita<u>ls</u>.
Capitol	The building where the United States Congress holds its sessions. The United States *Capitol* is always capitalized.
choose (chewz) chose (chōz)	To pick: Let's choose sides. Past tense of *pick:* The witch chose another broomstick.
clothes (klōthz)	Garments made of cloth: Put the clothes in the hamper.
cloths (klothz)	The plural of *cloth.*
complement	Something that completes or adds to: The red pillows complemented the black-and-white couch. Hint: A compLEment compleLEtes.
compliment	To praise (verb) or an expression of praise (noun): I want to compliment the chef. Hint: A compLIment is something you LIke.
complementary	Completing or forming a complement: Yellow and blue are complementary colors.
complimentary	Flattering or free: a complimentary remark or complimentary tickets.

conscience	Moral sense (noun): Jiminy Cricket was Pinocchio's conscience.
conscious	Awake or aware (adjective): The students were very conscious of the noise outside the room.
desert (déz ert)	A great sandy land mass (noun): The Sahara is a desert.
desert (di zúrt)	To abandon or to leave without permission (verb): The soldier planned to desert.
dessert (di zúrt)	A final course served after a meal, such as pie or pudding (noun): Dessert was strawberry shortcake. Hint: <u>S</u>trawberry <u>S</u>hortcake = de<u>SS</u>ert.
don't	A contraction that stands for *do not.*
doesn't	A contraction that stands for *does not.* Don't confuse these. In standard English do not use *don't* with third person (he, she, it). NOT: He don't get paid until Friday. BUT: He doesn't get paid until Friday.
etc.	An abbreviation for *et cetera,* a Latin phrase that means "and other things." Do not write *and etc.,* which would mean "and and other things." Drop the *and* to get rid of this redundancy. *Etc.* is *always* preceded by a comma.
ever since	Continuously: Ever since I can remember, the house has been haunted.
every since	*Every* means each. *Every since* is a typographical error for *ever since.*

EXERCISE Usage

Without consulting the glossary, do the following exercise. If the underlined words or phrases are used correctly, circle them. If they are used incorrectly, cross them out and write in the correction in the space above. Assume that formal usage is called for. For example:

The death of the rock star deeply (affected) his fans.

Benjamin Franklin lead an interesting life.

1. Security has been tightened at the <u>Capitol</u> in Washington, D.C., our nation's <u>capital</u>.

2. I do not <u>chose</u> to see any more swamp-monster movies.

3. I don't believe in killing animals for fur, so I wear a <u>cloth</u> coat.

4. In the prison were thieves, murderers, burglars, <u>and etc.</u>

5. Because we ushered, our concert tickets were <u>complementary</u>.

6. My history teacher is not very fashion-<u>conscience</u>.

7. While on a diet, Garfield gave up <u>desert</u>.

8. She <u>don't</u> like scorpions nibbling on her tiny toes.

9. <u>Every since</u> his nose turned red, his friends called him Rudolph.

---

fewer less	A smaller number. Often confused with *less*, especially in everyday speech and informal writing, as in signs for supermarket express lines for "10 items or less." Also, in commercials some soft drinks are touted as having "less calories" than a competing product. In formal writing, when referring to something countable, use *fewer*; otherwise, use *less*: Fewer students signed up for basket weaving this year. There was less swine flu last year.
forty fourty	The correct spelling of the number 40. An incorrect spelling of the number 40.
hardly	Almost, not at all, barely. Do not use *hardly* with another negative. NOT: We can't hardly wait for winter's end. BUT: We can hardly wait for winter's end.
have of	In some instances, these words sound somewhat alike. After *could, would,* or *should,* the word *have* will often appear, not *of:* NOT: I could of danced all night. BUT: I could have danced all night.
hear here	To listen (verb). Hint: Think of *ear*. In this place (adverb). Hint: Think of *here and there*. Example: Hear the wedding march? Here comes the bride.
I'm	Contraction of I *am:* "I'm just wild about Harry." Since I'am would mean "I am am," it is redundant. Use either *I'm* or I am.
knew	The past tense of the verb *to know:* He knew little about astrophysics.

new	Recent or not old. Pronounced the same way as the word *knew:* Poker is a new pastime for me; I never knew it was so much fun.
know	To have knowledge of: I know a little bit about a lot of things.
no	A negative response: No, I don't know the answer. Pronounced the same way as the word *know*.
now	At this time: The erotic bakery now delivers.
lead (lēd)	To direct (verb): I want to lead a band.
led (led)	The past tense of the verb *to lead:* She led the team with 25 points.
lead (led)	A noun or adjective meaning a metal: a lead mine. Spelled like the present-tense verb *to lead,* but pronounced like the past tense of that verb *(led)*.
loose (lo͞os)	Not tight (adjective). Hint: lOOse tOOth.
lose (lo͞oz)	To misplace something (verb): Don't lose your sense of humor.

EXERCISE   Usage

Without consulting the glossary, do the following exercise. If the underlined words or phrases are used correctly, circle them. If they are used incorrectly, cross them out and write in the correction in the space above. Assume that formal usage is called for. For example:

The death of the rock star deeply (affected) his fans.

Benjamin Franklin led an interesting life.

1. There are <u>fewer</u> detective stories on television this season.

2. For <u>fourty</u> days and nights it rained.

3. The monsters <u>couldn't hardly</u> wait to crawl in the slime.

4. I <u>should of</u> taken a typing course in high school.

5. <u>Here</u> comes trouble.

6. There is nothing <u>knew</u> to <u>know</u> for the examination.

7. The Mickey Mouse Club was <u>led</u> by a rodent.

8. Charlie Brown is a born <u>loser</u>.

9. *Any Which Way but <u>Loose</u>* is my favoite Clint Eastwood movie.

---

maybe	Perhaps (adverb).
may be	A verb phrase: It may be possible to keep from confusing these words. Maybe you will succeed.
of	A preposition that gives the origin or composition of a substance: a piece of cake.
off	Don't confuse the preposition *of* with the adverb *off*, which means "away from": The farmer chased the hunters off his land.
off of	The word *of* is not needed after *off*. Avoid this needless filler: NOT: She stepped off of the plane. BUT: She stepped off the plane.
passed	Past tense of the verb *to pass:* The ushers passed the collection plate.
past	Noun or adjective for time gone by: Scrooge was scared by the Ghost of Christmas Past.
personal	Private, or pertaining to a person (adjective): personal appearance.
personnel	The persons employed by one organization (noun): City Hall personnel are very busy on election day.
principle	Concept or idea (noun): the principle of justice.
principal	Major (adjective) or head of a school (noun): The principal reason for the change was the principal's incompetence. Also, money that earns interest: A monthly mortgage payment consists of principal and interest.
quiet (kwī et)	Not noisy (adjective) or freedom from noise (noun): Areas around hospitals are quiet zones. We must have quiet.
quite (kwīt)	Adverb that means *very* or an indefinite quantity: I've had quite a day.
reason is because	Since reasons are causes, the word *because* is not included in this expression, at least in formal writing. NOT: The main reason is because of pollution. BUT: The main reason is pollution.

right	Correct in judgment, or as opposed to the left side: in the right place at the wrong time; writing with your right hand.
write	To compose with words: Don't forget to write to Santa Claus.
should of	Use *should have* instead: I should have realized that sooner.
stationary	Not movable or standing still: A stop sign is a stationary object.
stationery	Writing material. Hint: LettERs are written on stationERy.
suppose	To guess or to assume.
supposed to	Ought or should. Always correctly spelled *supposed to*, NEVER *suppose to*: You're supposed to remember to add the *ed* ending to the word *supposed*.

EXERCISE Usage

Without consulting the glossary, do the following exercise. If the underlined words or phrases are used correctly, circle them. If they are used incorrectly, cross them out and write in the correction in the space above. Assume that formal usage is called for. For example:

The death of the rock star deeply (affected) his fans.

Benjamin Franklin ~~lead~~ *led* an interesting life.

1. You <u>maybe</u> wondering why the <u>principal</u> called this meeting.

2. Snoopy got so excited he fell <u>off of</u> his doghouse.

3. Walk <u>past</u> the <u>personnel</u> department to get to the exit.

4. You are <u>suppose to</u> be <u>quiet</u> in the library.

5. The <u>reason is because</u> other students are studying.

6. Brenda used perfumed <u>stationery</u> to <u>write</u> to Elbert.

then	Time past, as in the expression *now and then*. Don't confuse *then* with *than*.
than	A comparison word: College is harder than high school.

their	Possessive adjective for a plural pronoun. *Their* is often followed by a noun: their house. (Note *ei* spelling.) Hint: Think of an <u>heir</u> to <u>their</u> fortune.
there	At that place, as opposed to *here* (adverb). Hint: Use the phrase *here and there* to help you remember this usage.
they're	Contraction of *they are:* They're always sacking the poor quarterback.
theirs	Pronoun showing ownership: That aardvark is theirs.
there's	Contraction of *there is:* There's a tavern in the town.
to	Preposition showing direction toward something or someone: The owl and the pussycat went to sea.
two	The number 2. The two animals went to sea.
too	Very or also (adverb): The owl was too kind to the pussycat. Besides the owl, the pussycat was going to sea too.
used to	Familiar with. Don't leave off the ending. NOT: use to BUT: used to We've gotten used to chili for breakfast.
wait on	In some dialects this means "to wait for." In Edited American English, *wait on* means only "to serve": When will the waitress wait on us? Use *wait for* if you mean "to wait in the hope or expectation of" something: The acrobat waited for the trapeze.
weather	A noun: climate. Our weather is unpredictable. A verb: endure or exposed to the elements. We weathered the storm. The old barn was weathered.
whether	An adverb: He debated whether to join the Peace Corps or go back to school.
were	Verb in past tense and plural: The way we were.
where	Adverb of place: Where were we?
where is it at?	Redundant expression. *Where* already denotes an *at*. The word *at* is therefore not necessary: Where is it?
who's	Contraction of *who is:* Who's on first?
whose	Pronoun showing ownership: Whose boa constrictor are you holding?
woman	Singular noun.
women	Plural noun: The women voted her Woman of the Year.

your	Pronoun showing ownership: Your cat ate my canary. Avoid the overuse of *your:* Fry your liver until brown, cover it with your sauce, and put it in your oven. (incorrect)
you're	Contraction of *you are:* You're in trouble. Correct in informal writing. In formal writing, spell out this and all other contractions.

EXERCISE Usage

Without consulting the glossary, do the following exercise. If the underlined words or phrases are used correctly, circle them. If they are used incorrectly, cross them out and write in the correction in the space above. Assume that a formal usage is called for. For example:

The death of the rock star deeply (affected) his fans.

Benjamin Franklin lead an interesting life. *(led)*

1. If you do not have an appointment to see Santa, then you will just have to wait.

2. There pet rattlesnake usually sleeps on the floor.

3. Charlie Brown's sister is not too kind to him.

4. Our cat will never get use to the vacuum cleaner.

5. The weather is ideal in the Land of Oz.

6. "Where is it at?" asked the scarecrow.

7. "Whose sorry now," wailed the cabaret singer.

8. Your check is in the mail.

9. Woman outnumber men in our night school.

EXERCISE Glossary Summary

Correct the following nonbusiness letter. Assume that the punctuation is correct. Look for errors of usage, such as confusion of similar words (for example, a *sail* on winter coats instead of a *sale* on winter coats). Cross out the incorrect word or phrase and write in the correction right above it.

Dear Jill,

I should of written sooner. Thanks alot for the complementary tickets. Are you sure its alright to use them? Besides my girlfriend and me, many of my friends are already to go. I feel guilty excepting the tickets but there very hard to get, so I will take your advice and use them. I can't hardly refuse your offer. You are much to kind. You are quiet a friend.

See you there,

Jack

P.S. How do you like my new stationary?

EXERCISE Glossary Update

Use the space below to list any word confusion errors that are pointed out in your writing and that are not covered in the glossary. Also record any additions or clarifications to the glossary section that your teacher may give you.

_____

_____

_____

_____

_____

_____

_____

_____

_____

_____

_____

9

Parts of Speech

Parts of speech are traditional ways of classifying words by function or use. It used to be customary to require students to memorize elaborate definitions of parts of speech. Useful as it is to learn the parts of speech, that should be no end in itself. To a writer, learning how a word works in a sentence is more important than painstakingly precise definitions.

What's more, some words function as multiple parts of speech. Look at this example:

To surprise the gorilla, the zookeeper put on a gorilla suit.

A dictionary will tell you that the word *gorilla* names an animal and is therefore a noun. In the second part of the sentence above, however, the word *gorilla* describes and is therefore an adjective. Parts of speech represent general categories of words. To be accurate and useful, they need to be tested within actual sentences.

Learning the parts of speech is not so important as learning how to use them. It doesn't matter if you call adjectives describers or adverbs add-ons, so long as you don't use an adjective where a sentence requires an adverb. Parts of speech are meant to help you understand and form our basic communication units—sentences.

This chapter reviews eight parts of speech. Some writing texts dispense with teaching the parts of speech by themselves, and so might your instructor. In that case, you might want to look over this chapter on your own to see if it helps where it counts—in your writing.

Nouns

Nouns name. They point out:

who (persons, places)   or   what (things, concepts)

Nouns function as subjects or objects.

Diane stroked the tarantula.
subject   *object*

In the sentence above, since the *tarantula* is on the receiving end of the action, it is labeled an object.

The tarantula bit Diane.
subject   *object*

In this sentence, *Diane* is on the receiving end of the action and is therefore the object. The actor or agent that does something is the subject. In the first sentence, therefore, the subject is *Diane.* That sentence shows Diane doing something. In the second sentence it is the tarantula which did something. Therefore, in this sentence *tarantula* is the subject.

If a sentence tells you who or what the action happens to, that sentence includes an object. Subject and object tell how a noun is used in a particular sentence. Don't confuse noun, a *category word* that names persons, places, or things, with subject and object. Subject and object are *function words* that describe how a noun is used in a specific sentence.

Here is another way to distinguish nouns. Almost all nouns can take plural endings. Most nouns take *s* in the plural:

monster   monsters
cobweb   cobwebs
coffin   coffins
ghost   ghosts

Some nouns add *es* to form the plural:

box   boxes
church   churches
kiss   kisses
wish   wishes
lens   lenses
actress   actresses

Notice the endings above. Most nouns that end in *x, ch, s,* or *sh* form the plural as above.

Nouns that end with one *f* also usually add *es*, but the *f* is first changed to a *v*:

wolf   wolves
leaf   leaves
scarf   scarves
loaf   loaves

The following are exceptions:

dwarf   dwarfs
brief   briefs

Nouns that do not use *s* or *es* to form a plural are called irregular nouns. Some irregular nouns show no change from the singular to the plural:

deer   deer
cattle   cattle

Some nouns have no true plural. They are always in the singular. Here are a few examples:

blood
sunshine
rice
pork
punctuation
grief

By adding other words, quantity can be indicated for words that show no plural:

She had much grief. (NOT griefs)
I found many punctuation errors. (NEVER punctuations)

Some few irregular nouns use *en* to signal the plural:

ox   oxen
child   children

Some irregular nouns signal a plural by changes *within* the noun:

mouse   mice
freshman   freshmen
tooth   teeth
woman   women

Luckily, the vast majority of nouns are regular; that is, they form a plural with *s* or *es*. In fact, that is a useful way to classify a noun: a word that usually takes a plural in *s*.

word   +   *s*   =   *a noun*

lion   +   *s*   =   *a noun*

Warning: Don't confuse noun + *s* = a plural noun with noun + *'s* = a singular noun showing possession.

Christopher Robin was afraid of lions and tigers and bears.

NOT:

Christopher Robin was afraid of lion's and tiger's and bear's.

The *'s* is singular, not plural, and shows ownership:

the lion	=	one lion
the lion's den	=	the den of one lion
the lions	=	more than one lion
the lions' den	=	the den of more than one lion

(For more on the apostrophe, see the next chapter.)

Nouns are capitalized only at beginnings of sentences or if they name an individual or a particular place or thing:

Ripon College		a college
Key West	BUT	a city
Bay of Fundy		a place
Butch Cassidy		an outlaw

EXERCISE   Nouns

1. Underline the nouns in the following nonsense sentence: "The dorps galumped the grocks."

2. Which word is the subject? _____

3. Which word is the object? _____

4. Cross out the *one* incorrect plural listed below:

   foxes   benchs   halves   wolves

5. Correct the mistake: _____

6. Cross out *all* incorrect plurals listed below:

   freshmen's   punctuations   oxes   pear's   children   deer

7. In the space below, correct all the mistakes in item 6.

   _____

   _____

8. Circle the one correct noun:

   a. Washington Redskin's
   b. Washington Redskins
   c. Washington redskins
   d. washington redskins

9. Circle the one correct noun:

   a. a high school freshman
   b. a High School Freshman
   c. a high school Freshman
   d. a High School freshman

Pronouns

Pronouns, like substitute players in a game, replace nouns. They thus cut down on repetition and help link sentence units. Here is an example of that.

> Jack was sent to sell the cow. Jack traded the cow for a handful of beans. The beans were thrown out, but the beans grew overnight into an enormous beanstalk.

> Jack was sent to sell the cow. *He* traded *her* for a handful of beans, *which* were thrown out, but *they* grew overnight into an enormous beanstalk.

Neither passage is great prose, but the pronouns make the second version hang together better and certainly cut down on the annoying repetition.

Like nouns, pronouns can be singular or plural, but unlike nouns, they never take a plural that ends in *s*.

Singular		**Plural**
I	speaker	we
you	spoken to	you
he, she, it	spoken about	they

Notice that *you* is the same in the plural or the singular. Only from the context of the sentence can you tell whether the writer is addressing one or several persons.

Some pronouns look like plurals but function as singular pronouns. *Everyone* is one such singular pronoun. *Everybody* is another. *Everyone* means each and every *one*. *Everybody* means each and every *body*.

Pronouns that are always singular:

anybody	anything	anyone
somebody	something	someone
everybody	everything	everyone
nobody	nothing	no one

However plural such pronouns might sound, grammatically they are treated as singular:

Everyone in the class will receive his grades by mail.
singular   *singular*

It is traditional in English grammar to use the singular masculine pronoun even when it refers to a male or a female. To avoid the impression that everyone in the class is male, the sentence could be rewritten:

Everyone in the class will receive his or her grades by mail.

Many writers, however, would simply recast the sentence this way:

All students will receive their grades by mail.

The plural subject takes a plural pronoun. Since *their* does not indicate gender, this gets around the confusing gender reference.

When used as *pronouns*, the following words are always plural:

both   many
few   several

Many are cold, but few are frozen
Both her shots were blocked.

Unlike nouns, many pronouns change form when used as objects.

Ken left Barbie.   Barbie left Ken.
He left her.   She left him.

When used as objects or to show ownership or possession, pronouns change forms.

Subject Pronoun	Object Pronoun	Possessive Pronoun (Ownership)
Singular		
I	me	my, mine
you	you	your, yours
he	him	his
she	her	her, hers
it	it	its
Plural		
we	us	our, ours
you	you	your, yours
they	them	their, theirs

Personal pronoun errors are easy to spot: *Me* don't like you. *Them* are ready.

Who and *whom* create much of the pronoun difficulty. These pronouns, along with *that* and *which*, are used to refer or point back to persons and things. For example:

the mouse that roared
The doggy bags which restaurants give away seldom go to dogs.

Who or *whom* always refers to persons, never things.

INCORRECT: The students *which* have been preregistered avoided long lines.
CORRECT: The students *who* have been preregistered avoided long lines.

INCORRECT: Ours is a company *who* can be trusted.
CORRECT: Ours is a company *that* can be trusted.

The pronoun *that* is usually used to refer to animals and things:

the beast that ate Brooklyn

That can also be used for persons when the reference is collective or anonymous. Both of the following are correct:

The salesperson that we wanted was not in.
The salesperson whom we wanted was not in.

Unlike *which* and *that*, *who* changes forms much like the personal pronouns (*I, you*, etc.):

Subject Pronoun	Object Pronoun	Possessive Pronoun
he	him	his
who	whom	whose

Who/Whom Hint: If you can't decide between *who* and *whom*, substitute *he* and *him*. Where *him* makes sentence sense, *whom* is correct; if *he* makes sentence sense, *who* is correct. For example:

Who/Whom is there?
He is there. NOT: Him is there. Therefore, *who* is correct.
He is someone who/whom we trust.
Him we trust or We trust him.
Since *him* fits, *whom* is correct.

Following a preposition, *whom* is often correct:

For whom are you voting?

In informal speech, where the preposition does not come before the pronoun, *who* is generally used:

Who are you voting for?

The who/whom choice is difficult where there is a tug-of-war construction, that is, when one part of the sentence calls for *who* and another calls for *whom*. Try these:

The clown presented the balloons to whoever/whomever she wanted.
The clown presented the balloons to whoever/whomever smiled.

In the first sentence *him* would fit ("presented the balloons to him" and "she wanted him" would both make sense). Therefore, *whomever* belongs in the first sentence. In the second sentence there is a tug of war between the preposition and the verb. In this case, the verb wins out: *smiled* must have a subject *(he)* even though *to* needs an object *(him)*. Thus, "to whoever smiled" is correct.

Do not choose *whom* simply because it sounds formal. If you need a subject pronoun, pick *who*. If you need an object pronoun, pick *whom*.

Another common pronoun confusion is between *its* and *it's*. This one is easier to solve than *who* versus *whom*. *No* pronoun takes an apostrophe to show ownership or possession. You would not write, "He saddled his' horse," or "The dagger was her's." Do not use *it's* if you mean something belonging to "it":

The chick pecked its way out of the shell.

NOT:

The chick pecked it's way out of the shell.

It's always means "it is." If *it is* can be substituted in a sentence and make sense, use *it's;* otherwise, use *its*.

It's/Its a long way to the North Pole.
Since *it is* a long way to the North Pole, *it's* is correct.

Readers expect consistent pronoun usage. In other words, don't shift pronoun usage unexpectedly. For example:

INCORRECT: There comes a time in every man's life when he needs advice and you have no one to turn to.
CORRECT: There comes a time in every man's life when he needs advice and he has no one to turn to.

Another pronoun error is unnecessary use of pronouns:

My friend he is a clown. (*He* is unnecessary.)
The doctor she said to take two aspirin and lie down. (*She* is unnecessary.)

Self Pronouns

There are some special pronouns designed for repetition or emphasis. They all end with the suffix *self* or *selves:*

Singular		Plural
myself	speaker	ourselves
yourself	spoken to	yourselves
himself	spoken about	themselves

They are often called *reflexive pronouns* because they reflect back on the words they refer to:

Sam scared himself.
The prisoners freed themselves.

Reflexive pronouns can also be used to add emphasis:

The teachers themselves thought the test was too hard.
She herself rescued the pilot.

Do not use a self pronoun as an all-purpose pronoun:

It was an unfortunate day for myself at work.

And do not use reflexive pronouns as a cover-up when you are not sure what the correct pronoun form should be.

INCORRECT: They invited Kim and myself to the party.
CORRECT: They invited Kim and me to the party.

Note that when a pronoun is linked with a noun, the pronoun comes *after* the noun.

the King and I   NOT   I and the King
for Kim and me   NOT   for me and Kim

The pronoun *I*, which is always capitalized, is quite common. If too many sentences begin with *I*, rewrite the sentences. Some students mistakenly believe that the word *I* is forbidden in formal writing. That is not so. As a matter of fact, trying to avoid *I* entirely creates some very wordy and contorted prose.

In the opinion of this writer the sky is falling.

instead of:

I believe the sky is falling.

EXERCISE   Pronouns

In the sentences below cross out all pronouns that are incorrect and insert corrections in the space above each error. In some cases, you may also have to change other words in the sentences.

1. Everyone at a football game is screaming for their favorite team.

2. A fair-weather friend will expect you to have money to lend them whenever they ask.

3. I hate when people are jealous of me, especially when the person who is jealous tries to hurt you.

4. The doctor he is not seeing any more patients today.

5. Somebody is playing their stereo awfully loud.

6. Whomever is responsible should stop.

7. The purple mashed potatoes were a weird idea of her's.

8. She did not know who she could trust.

9. The team lost it's star quarterback.

10. The players which were traded were glad to go.

EXERCISE Pronouns

Some sentences below use pronouns correctly. In the same way as in the preceding exercise, correct those that have pronoun errors.

1. It's clear that our city still has its pollution problems.

2. Me and Phyllis are going to the flea market.

3. Everyone is entitled to their own opinion.

4. My roommate is someone whom I can trust.

5. Whoever is making that noise, stop it.

6. The booby prize is for whomever has the most wrong answers.

7. The orders were hers.

8. Pulling dandelions kept myself busy.

9. Many of the weeds are as pretty as flowers.

10. Several of the enemy were missing.

Verbs

Verbs express action, tell what happened, or describe a state of being:

> Bubbles *jogged.*
> Bubbles *passed* her exam.
> Bubbles *is* a bomber pilot.

Present and Past Tense

Verbs change to indicate when an action or condition took place or came to be. Such changes that add a time frame to a described action are called *tenses*. The present tense describes what happens regularly. The past tense describes an action begun in the past but is now over and done with.

Present   **Past**
I work every day.   I worked yesterday.

Verbs, of course, can also be applied to persons other than the speaker:

Singular

Present   **Past**
I work.   speaker   I worked.
You work.   spoken to   You worked.
He/she/it works.   spoken about   He/she/it worked.

When the verb applies to more than one person, it follows these forms in the present and past tense:

Plural

Present   **Past**
We work.   speaker   We worked.
You work.   spoken to   You worked.
They work.   spoken about   They worked.

Notice that there is a change only in the verb endings. In the past tense the ending *(ed)* is used whether the verb is applied to the speaker, the audience, or someone spoken about. The present tense is almost as regular: I work, you work, they work, we work. Only for *speaking about one person* is there any verb ending *(s)*: he works, she works, it works.

Because a noun plus *s* creates a plural, some students assume that a verb plus *s* creates a plural. That is a logical but mistaken assumption.

CORRECT: noun + *s* = plural noun
INCORRECT: verb + *s* = plural verb
CORRECT: verb + *s* = singular verb (with *he/she/it*)

The *s* ending on the verb is hard to notice when someone is talking. In writing, the *s* cannot be left off when (1) you are using the present tense and (2) an individual or thing is the subject of a sentence.

He jogs.   She jogs.
The bathroom sparkles.   Vera feels no pain.

Otherwise, use the present-tense verb form without any special ending.

I jog.   You jog.   We jog.   They jog.
The diamonds sparkle.   The students feel cheated.

To summarize, most verbs take no special endings in the present tense. An important exception is the verb that is linked to one individual or thing which is being spoken about. This verb always takes an *s* ending:

Ella Fitzgerald sings a lot of Gershwin tunes.

The present-tense verb form is easy to recognize. It is the form of the verb that can be used after the word *to:*

to + present-tense verb form = infinitive

to float   to read
to deliver   to vomit
to charge

If a verb makes sense with the word *to*, it is in the present tense. For example, *float* fits, but *floated* or *floating* does not. *Deliver* fits, but *delivered* or *delivering* does not. This present-tense form is often called the present stem of a verb. If you are not sure of the present stem of a verb, check a dictionary. It is the verb form dictionaries list first.

The most common use of the present tense is to *describe what someone or something does regularly:*

Mares eat oats.
The Cookie Monster devours cookies.

The present tense can also be used to *state general truths:*

April showers bring May flowers.
Being nice has a price.

The present tense can be used to *indicate a predictable future action:*

The department store closes this Saturday for inventory.
The sale starts on Monday.

The present tense can be used to *describe characters or events or what an author does in a work of art or literature:*
King Kong scampers up the Empire State Building.
Huckleberry Finn is always trying to run away.
Mark Twain lets Huckleberry Finn escape on a raft.

To stress that an action is happening at the time of writing or speaking, use *am/is/are* plus the *ing* form of the verb in the present tense.

I am freezing.
It is snowing.
We are leaving.

(See pages 267–268 for all the forms of this, the present progressive tense.)

The verb form dictionaries always list right after the present stem is the past tense. In the past tense, regardless of whom the verb applies to, most verbs take an *ed* ending:

> The Goodyear blimp floated by.
> The dog vomited on my socks.
> They laughed when I played the kazoo.

EXERCISE   Present and Past Tense

Fill in the blanks below with the appropriate form of the verb *to laugh*.

Present tense	**Past tense**
1. I laugh	I _____
2. you _____	you laughed
3. she _____	he laughed
4. we laugh	we _____
5. you _____	you laughed
6. they laugh	they _____

Fill in the blanks below with the appropriate form of the verb *to pretend*.

7. Every day, Snoopy _____ he is the Red Baron.

8. Last night, Snoopy _____ he was the Red Baron.

9. Right now, Snoopy ____ _____ he is the Red Baron.

10. He is not really who he usually _____ to be.

Future Tense

The present tense verb stem plus *will* or *shall* expresses an action that has not yet happened but that you expect will happen:

> Tomorrow we will work.
> I will work.
> I shall work.

The future tense also is used to indicate a promise or willingness to do something:

> I will invite you to dinner with the Macbeths.

For comparison, here are the three simple verb tenses in the *singular:*

Past Tense	Present Tense	Future Tense
(then)	*(now)*	*(later)*
I worked.	I work.	I will work.*
You worked.	You work.	You will work.
He worked	He works.	He will work.

And in the *plural:*

We worked.	We work.	We will work.
You worked.	You work.	You will work.
They worked	They work.	They will work.

To express an action more precisely than in the simple past, present, or future tense, there are some special tenses. These special tenses are called perfect tenses because they can *perfect* the time being described.

Present Perfect Tense

This tense describes some action that began in the past and has not been completed or was just recently completed.

> We have walked for two hours.
> The mail has arrived.

To form this tense, just add *has* or *have* to the last of the three verb forms as listed in the dictionary. This form (the past participle) will sometimes be the same as the simple past, as in

Present	Past	Past Participle
work	worked	worked

But some verbs show a past participle different from the past form. For example,

take	took	taken

> They took the train. (past tense)
> They have taken an early flight. (present perfect tense)

Singular	Plural
I have worked.	We have worked.
You have worked.	You have worked.
He *has* worked.	They have worked.

Note the only difference is the helping word. *Has* is used with a singular subject spoken about: He *has* arrived. She *has* arrived. It *has* arrived. BUT: We/You/They *have* arrived.

---

*Shall is sometimes used to stress determination: I *shall* return. But *shall* and *will* are commonly used interchangeably in the United States. Note that *shall* only appears with the pronoun *I* or *we.*

Past Perfect Tense

The past perfect tense describes an action completed before another event which is also in the past:

> When I *had* worked for three hours straight, I took a rest.
> *an earlier event*   *a later event*

> We had waited for an hour before our luggage arrived.
> *an earlier event*   *a later event*

This tense is fairly easy to form. Just use *had* plus the past participle of the verb *in all cases*:

> I/You/He/She/It   had worked. (singular)
> We/You/They   had worked. (plural)

Future Perfect Tense

The future perfect tense describes something that will be completed on or by a specific time in the future:

> By the time I get to Phoenix, she will have arrived.
> *specific time in future*   *expected action*

> By the end of summer, I will have earned a thousand dollars.

This tense is formed by using *will have* plus the past participle of the verb.

> I/You/He/She/It will have worked. (singular)
> We/You/They   will have worked. (plural)

If the speaker of the sentence is doing the action, you could also use *shall:*

> I shall have worked.

or

> We shall have worked.

BUT NOT:

> You shall have worked, He shall have worked, etc.

Summary of Tenses

I had worked.	past perfect	
I worked.	past	Then
I have worked.	present perfect	
I work.	present	Now
I will have worked.	future perfect	
I will work.	future	Later

EXERCISE   Perfect Tenses

Circle the correct verb form of those provided in parentheses.

1. He (had, has, have) just waxed the floor before the dog padded in with its muddy paws.

2. By June, Maria (will, shall) have saved enough to go to Peru.

3. Harold (have, has, had) just opened a topless shoeshine parlor.

4. The police (have, has, had) closed it down.

5. She (had, has, have) learned to read in Spanish and English by the time she was five.

6. They (have, had, has) worked on their motorcycles all day.

7. By the time I get out of school, all the beaches (will have, shall have) opened.

8. My cousin (has, have, had) opened all the mail.

9. The child (has, have, had) squashed every tomato in the house before he was whisked away from the mess.

10. The movie (had, have, has) just started when I dropped all the popcorn on my date's lap.

Progressive Tenses

These tenses deal with action in progress (present progressive tense), action that was in progress (past progressive tense), and action that will be in progress (future progressive tense).

Present Progressive Tense.   The present progressive tense emphasizes action happening right now more exactly than the simple present tense, which stresses action done regularly.

This tense is formed with the present stem of the verb plus *ing* and *am, is,* or *are:*

I am working.	We are working.
You are working.	You are working.
He is working.	They are working.

Think of action in *progress* to help you remember this and the next two *progressive* tenses.

Past Progressive Tense.   This tense shows action that *was* in progress at a certain time in the past:

> In 1978 I *was working* as a busboy.
> In winter of 1983, shoppers *were mobbing* the stores for Cabbage Patch dolls.

I was working.	We were working.
You were working.	You were working.
He was working.	They were working.

Future Progressive Tense.   Use the future progressive tense to describe an action that *will be* going on at or by a specified future time.

> In the year 2000, my youngest child *will be entering* college.

I will be working.	We will be working.
You will be working.	You will be working.
He will be working.	They will be working.

EXERCISE   Tenses of Regular Verbs

1. Add any verb in the past tense that fits the following frame: Yesterday,

   I _____.

2. Using the correct form of the verb *to walk*, add the correct endings below.

   a. Every day I _____ the dog.

   b. Every day he _____ the dog.

   c. Every day they _____ their dogs.

   d. Right now they _____ _____ their dogs.

Cross out the one verb form in each of the sentences below that is incorrect.

3. **a.** She has jogged for an hour.
   b. She jogs every day.
   c. When she has jogged for an hour, she took a rest.

4. **a.** They delivered our furniture yesterday.
   b. They was waiting all day for that delivery.
   c. He delivers furniture for a living.

5. **a.** By summer I will have finished all my courses.
   b. I have finished my coursework tomorrow.
   c. She is starting work on her degree.

6. He (has/had/have) passed the halfway point in the race.
7. They (have/had/has) played two innings of softball before the rain halted play.

Regular versus Irregular Verbs

Verbs that add an *ed* ending in the past tense (that is, most verbs) are called regular verbs. The verb that we have been using *(work/worked)* is one such verb. Verbs whose past tense is formed in any other way are called irregular.

Regular Verbs

Present	Past	Past Participle	Present Participle
talk	talked	talked	talking
create	created	created	creating
jump	jumped	jumped	jumping

Some Irregular Verbs

Present	Past	Past Participle	Present Participle
begin	began	begun	beginning
blow	blew	blown	blowing
break	broke	broken	breaking
choose	chose	chosen	choosing
do	did	done	doing
drink	drank	drunk	drinking
eat	ate	eaten	eating
fly	flew	flown	flying
freeze	froze	frozen	freezing
go	went	gone	going
lay (to place)	laid	laid	laying
lie (to recline)	lay	lain	lying
ring	rang	rung	ringing
run	ran	run	running
shake	shook	shaken	shaking
swim	swam	swum	swimming
take	took	taken	taking
write	wrote	written	writing

Some irregular verbs show no internal changes to form the past and the past participle. For example:

Present	Past	Past Participle	Present Participle
burst	burst	burst	bursting
cut	cut	cut	cutting
shut	shut	shut	shutting
spread	spread	spread	spreading

Although most verbs signal the past tense by an *ed* ending, don't try to regularize irregular verbs: "bursted," "spreaded," and "cutted," for example.

Unfortunately, there are many irregular verbs. Fortunately, you don't have to memorize their forms. The dictionary will supply you with the present, the past, and the past participle forms of irregular verbs. There is, however, one irregular verb that you must master because it is our most common verb. In some dialects the verb *to be* is regularized to *I be, you be, he be, we be, you be, they be.* In standard English, however, this verb is very irregular.

In the **present tense:**

I am   you are   he/she/it is (singular)
we are   you are   they are (plural)

In the **past tense:**

I was   you were   he/she/it was (singular)
we were   you were   they were (plural)

In the **future tense:**

I/you/he/she/it   will be (singular)
we/you/they   will be (plural)

Notice that the verb *to be* often changes depending on whether it describes

the person(s) talking   (I/we)
the person(s) being talked to (you)
the person(s) talked about   (he/she/it/they)

Here is how the past tense of *to be* changes depending on who is talking or talked about.

Singular	**Plural**
I was	we were
you were	you were
he/she/it was	they were

By comparison, regular verbs in the past tense, use *ed* for all persons, singular or plural:

I screamed	we screamed
you screamed	you screamed
he/she/it screamed	they screamed

There is another category of irregular verbs you should know something about: helping verbs. These verbs usually appear with another verb, which they help express. Some helping verbs are

will	must	should
can	would	do
may	could	does
shall	might	did

Two of these (*will* and *shall*) you have seen used in the future tense. Besides indicating tense, these helping verbs can be used with a main verb to indicate shades of meaning or mood:

Obligation
You should exercise more.
You must remember this.

Willingness
You may borrow my pompons.

Capability
She could bench-press her own weight.
He can touch his nose with his tongue.

A wish
I would have liked to have smashed that pie in his face.

EXERCISE   Irregular Verbs

Use the correct form of the irregular verbs called for below.

1. Last Christmas, we _____ to Atlanta.
   (fly)

2. It was so cold last night, the milk _____.
   (freeze)

3. How many miles have they _____?
   (run)

4. Yesterday, she _____ fifty lengths in the pool.
   (swim)

5. Our club has _____ an armadillo for its mascot.
   (choose)

6. After finishing the exhausting rehearsal, he _____ down to
    take a nap.   *(lie)*

7. She has _____ the phone off the hook.
            (took)

8. The dryer was broken, so we _____ our underwear on the
    lampshade to dry.   *(lay)*

9. Who has _____ the last of the pomegranate juice?
            (drink)

10. The crumbs were _____ out of his beard regularly.
                    (shake)

EXERCISE The Verb *to be*

Fill in the appropriate form of the verb *to be.*

1. The biology exam _____ easy, or so it seemed to me.

2. We _____ up very late studying for the exam.

3. Last semester's exam _____ more difficult.

4. We _____ expecting some trick questions, but there _____
    none.

EXERCISE Noun and Verb Endings

Read the following selection. Look for errors in word endings of nouns and
verbs. Assume the writer is writing in the past tense. Add the missing endings *(s, es, d, ed)* and cross out those endings that are not necessary.

>   The attire of the many guest gave me feelings of insecurity. I
>
> felted out of place. Over in one corner was a woman adorn with a
>
> formal evening gown. Her shoes looked like they were fresh from the
>
> box. Next to her was a typical teenager dress only in desert boots, neatly
>
> press jeans, and a trendy T-shirt. It seem as though everyone at the party
>
> was dress right out of one of the fashion catalogue.

Subject–Verb Agreement

Verbs change endings because of tense, because of number, and because
of person. That means verbs change depending on the time of the action

described, whether the action is stated about one person or many, and whether the action fits the speaker (I, we), the audience (you), or a third party (he, she, it, they).

With singular subjects, use singular verbs; with plural subjects, use plural verbs:

> The snake crawls.   The snakes crawl.
> *singular   singular*   *plural   plural*

Hint: Think of this as balancing an equation. The noun *and* the verb will hardly ever end in *s* in the same sentence. *S* plus a noun makes a plural. It does not follow that *s* plus a verb makes a plural.

Subjects and verbs must agree in number. That is, a singular subject cannot be linked with a plural verb or vice versa. With a singular verb and a singular subject that should be no problem, so long as you avoid the false plural—*s* plus a verb. Remember, a verb ending in *s* will *always* be singular.

Coordinating conjunctions make subject–verb agreement trickier. Whether to use a plural or singular verb with two or more nouns joined by coordinating conjunctions depends on which conjunction is used.

Subjects Joined by *And*.   Ordinarily, subjects joined by *and* take a plural verb:

> Spinach and okra are not his favorite vegetables.
> Poker and pinochle are her favorite card games.

There are a few exceptions to this rule. Some words joined by *and*, especially those that are often linked together, can be considered as a single entity:

> Ham and eggs is a fortifying breakfast.
> Corned beef and cabbage was served again.

Another exception to a plural verb after subjects joined by *and* occurs when the word *each* or *every* comes *before* words joined by *and*:

> Every local church and synagogue is helping to run the food pantry.
> Each dorm and fraternity house is contributing food.

But note that when *each* comes *after* a compound subject, it does *not* call for a singular verb:

> The owl and the pussycat each want to go to sea.

Subjects Joined by *Or* or *Nor*.   Since *or* and *nor* separate, they ordinarily create singular subjects and therefore need singular verbs:

> Today's soup is either cream of refrigerator or cream of Friday.
> Neither cream of coyote nor cream of parrot is recommended.

When *or* or *nor* separates two subjects, one of which is plural and one singular, make the verb agree with the noun or pronoun *closest to the verb:*

Either the police or *he* is lying.
Either he or *the police* are lying.

Words between Subject and Verb. When deciding whether the verb should be singular or plural, ignore any modifying words that come between the subject and the verb.

One of the submarines *was* missing. (not *were*)
One of the actors *is* sick. (not *are*)

Also ignore interrupting phrases:

Cumin, in addition to cayenne, belongs in the chili pot.
subject   verb

Ken, together with Barbie, is moving to Malibu.
subject   verb

After the Word *There*. In sentences that begin with the word *there*, the subject comes *after* the verb.

There are exceptions to all rules.
      verb   subject

There is no joy in Mudville.
      verb   subject

After Titles as Subjects. All titles take singular verbs—even those with plural nouns.

The Attack of the Killer Tomatoes is a film so bad that it is worth seeing.
The Grapes of Wrath is an important novel.

After Some Nouns. Some nouns might cause you to make subject–verb agreement slipups. Some nouns, for example, end in *s* but are considered singular:

mathematics   civics
physics   measles

Therefore, use singular verbs to agree with these nouns:

Civics is one required high school subject.

Some nouns are always considered plural:

scissors   trousers

Therefore, they take plural verbs:

The scissors were rusty.

Nouns that express an amount of time, measure, money, or weight are considered singular even when they end in *s*:

Two hours was too long to wait.
Four miles is the most I can jog.
Five dollars seems a lot for one movie ticket.
Two hundred pounds is one-tenth of a ton.

Nouns that name a group usually take a singular noun, unless the writer or speaker is stressing the individual members of the group. Here are some common examples of such *collective nouns:*

crowd	class	family
team	committee	jury
orchestra		

The jury has reached its verdict. *(stresses whole group taking one action)*

The jury are badly divided on the verdict. *(stresses individual members of a group)*

Do/Does, Don't/Doesn't. These word pairs are often confused. *Does* is singular, as is *doesn't.* Use *does* or *doesn't* when speaking about *one person* or *thing:*

CORRECT: Dracula does sleep during the day.
CORRECT: Dracula doesn't sleep at night.
INCORRECT: Dracula don't sleep at night.

Otherwise use *do/don't:*

We do work hard, but we don't complain.
I don't like loudmouths.

EXERCISE Subject–Verb Agreement

Circle the verbs that agree with their subjects.

1. A line of students at the copy machines is/are common.

2. *Of Mice and Men* is/are worth reading.

3. There was/were a few flies in the ointment.

4. Thirty-two degrees Fahrenheit is/are zero degrees Celsius.

5. Five settings on a microwave oven seem/seems plenty.

6. These cars come/comes with five gears.

7. There was/were bats in the belfry.

8. One of the sopranos appear/appears nervous.

9. The team is/are on the field.

10. Your chrome don't/doesn't shine.

EXERCISE   Subject–Verb Agreement

Circle the correct verb of those provided in parentheses.

1. My mother, in addition to my grandparents, (was, were) applauding loudly when I accepted my diploma.

2. Either the beach or the mountains (is, are) fine with me.

3. Each car and truck (was, were) made ready for a safety inspection.

4. Every card and letter (has, have) to be answered.

5. Neither the Congress nor the President (want, wants) to deal with that issue.

6. Over three-fourths of the earth's surface (is, are) covered with water.

7. Physics (seems, seem) difficult to me.

8. The soccer team (has, have) won the state championship.

9. Many of those clothing stores (play, plays) loud music.

10. One of the elevators (break, breaks) down a lot.

Verbals

Some verb forms can function as adjectives or nouns. Compare the verb *rotate* as used in the following sentences.

Cheryl <u>rotates</u> her car's tires once a year.
subject   verb

<u>To rotate tires on a car</u> <u>is</u> time consuming.
   subject   verb

Rotating tires on a car is time consuming.
          verb

Rotating her car's tires, Cheryl felt a sense of accomplishment.
   adjective phrase   *subject verb*

Rotated tires last longer.
adjective subject verb

A verb or verb phrase used as a noun or adjective is called a verbal. Verbals are verb-like words or phrases that are not used as verbs. There are three kinds of verbals: infinitives, participles, and gerunds.

Infinitives

Infinitives are formed with the word *to* plus a verb.

to wander   to scratch
to dig   to annoy

Infinitives often function as nouns in a sentence, either as subjects or objects.

The referees tried to stop the brawl.
   subject   verb   *object*

To write an essay takes time.
      subject   *verb object*

Notice that the whole infinitive phrase functions as a subject or object. Infinitives can also function as adjectives:

They ordered pizza to go.

or as adverbs:

The lawn mower was difficult to start.

SALLY FORTH by Greg Howard, © 1983 Field Enterprises, Inc. Courtesy of News America Syndicate.

Warning:

1. Infinitive phrases never take verb endings:

>   to stop   NOT   to stopped

2. Since an infinitive phrase is never used as a verb, an infinitive phrase cannot, by itself, be a sentence.

> To spin your wheels (fragment)
> To get ready for a very important interview (fragment)
> <u>To find a summer job</u> is not easy. (sentence)
>   *subject*   *verb*

Participles

Verbals used as adjectives are called participles. Like true verbs, they can take a present or past tense. Compare:

1. Steve <u>ironed</u> even his blue jeans.
        verb

2. Do we still need an <u>ironing</u> board?
                     adj.

3. The <u>ironed</u> towels were a surprise.
         adj.

Only the first sentence uses the word *iron* as a true verb. Sentence 2 uses a present participle *(ironing)*. Sentence 3 uses a past participle *(ironed)*.

Past or present participles are used to describe. Do not try to make them the main verb in a sentence:

> The cars spinning out of the turn (fragment)
> The cotton candy spun by a machine (fragment)

A verb ending in *ing* will always have another helping verb when it functions as the main verb of a sentence.

> The cars <u>were</u> spinning out of the turn. (sentence)
> The cotton candy <u>was</u> spun by a machine. (sentence)

Participial phrases can also be attached to independent clauses:

> <u>Flashing a smile,</u> the salesman invited us in.
> *present participle*   *(modifies* salesman)

> <u>Stuck to the tar baby,</u> the fox cried for help.
>   *past participle*   *(modifies* fox)

Gerunds

Besides infinitives and participles, there is a third kind of verbal. This is a gerund, a kind of verb–noun that functions only as a subject or an object. It is formed by the present tense of a verb plus *ing*:

Ironing is a chore.
subject

Susan hated vacuuming.
object

Notice that a gerund looks like a present participle, but is used as a noun. Since a gerund functions as a noun, it cannot be the main verb in a sentence.

Washing all the dishes from last night's party (fragment)

But an entire gerund phrase can be the subject or object of a sentence:

Washing all the dishes from last night's party took hours. *(gerund phrase as subject of sentence)*
He feared waking up the hibernating bear. *(gerund phrase as object of sentence)*

EXERCISE Verbals

The following word groups contain verbals. Label them with this code: **I** for infinitive phrases, **G** for gerunds or gerund phrases, or **P** for participles or participial phrases.

_____1. Brushing the reporters aside, she refused to answer any questions.

_____2. To camp in the desert

_____3. Putting an astronaut on the moon

_____4. A smoking gun

_____5. Smoking is not permitted in the theater

_____6. I want to work with computers

_____7. Shaded by the sun, we didn't mind the heat

_____8. The carved jade ring that my aunt gave me

_____9. Everyone hates cleaning the oven

_____10. The semitrailer blocking traffic on the Long Island Expressway

Now circle the numbers only of those word groups above that are fragments.

Dangling and Misplaced Modifiers

Misusing verbals sometimes creates confusing modifiers. A student once asked where she should put her dangling modifiers. The answer is nowhere. Here is a dangling modifier:

> Crawling on the window, I saw a scorpion.

Unless the speaker is Spiderman, the sentence should show that it is the scorpion which is crawling, not the person who saw it. Here are two ways that the sentence could be corrected:

> I saw a scorpion crawling on the window.
> Crawling on the window, a scorpion got my attention.

Dangling modifiers often occur when you begin a sentence with a participial phrase but fail to follow it immediately with the subject it modifies.

> Before sitting down in a cozy chair, the radio is turned off.
>   *dangling modifier*

Following the modifier immediately with the proper subject will solve the problem:

> Before sitting down in a cozy chair, I turn the radio off.
>   *modifier no longer dangles*

A classic example of a misplaced modifier is this very old joke:

> MOE: I just met a man with a wooden leg named Fred.
> JOE: What's the name of his other leg?

While corny, it does illustrate how putting a modifier in the wrong place can cause ambiguity or confusion.

Here's another example of a misplaced modifier—one that I inadvertently wrote in an earlier draft of this text:

> On a TV program a famous cook once dropped a fish dish she was cooking on the floor.

See anything wrong with that sentence? I didn't—until a colleague asked why the cook was cooking fish on the floor. I should have written:

> On a TV program a famous cook once dropped on the floor a fish dish she was cooking.

Here's a more gruesome example of a misplaced modifier:

> He saw a wasp crawling out of the corner of his eye.

Keep verbal phrases from crawling all over your meaning like that. Simply rewrite the sentence so the modifier no longer confuses.

> Out of the corner of his eye, he saw a wasp crawling.

The exercise that follows will check whether you now know what to do with dangling or misplaced modifiers.

EXERCISE   Misplaced and Dangling Modifiers

Rewrite each sentence below to fix any misplaced or dangling modifiers. If the sentence has no such errors, mark it OK.

1. While fixing dinner for my nieces, they asked me why they always got milk with their meal.

2. Talking on the phone, my dinner got cold.

3. Analyzing the test, it has some clear information.

4. Pen in hand, words cease to come.

5. Answering two questions at once, he got confused.

6. I let the cat out with my bathrobe on.

7. I saw a jellyfish walking on the beach.

8. The orphan was flown to Washington for an eye operation aboard *Air Force One*.

9. The desk clerk called for a bellhop with a smile.

10. Tickets are available for the football game in the lobby.

Adjectives

Adjectives describe. They modify—that is, add detail to—nouns or pronouns. Some adjectives are easy to spot:

<u>broken</u> record   <u>rusty</u> metal
<u>tired</u> feet   <u>wooden</u> door

Words that function as nouns can also serve as adjectives if they occur in adjective position (before nouns):

a <u>dog</u> collar   the <u>typewriter</u> ribbon   my <u>car</u> keys

Any word that occurs after *a* or *the* and before a noun will function as an adjective:

A _____ noun
     adjective

The _____ noun
      adjective

Any word that fits these test frames can function as an adjective. In the phrase "a dog collar" the noun is *collar*, but the word *dog*, ordinarily a noun, here tells what kind of collar.

When comparing one or more objects, adjectives change form.

Strong	**Stronger**	**Strongest**
a quality	a quality compared with one other thing	a quality that stands out among three or more things

Here's a memory aid:

Add a *two*-letter ending (ER) to an adjective when you are comparing *TWO* things.

Add a three-letter ending (EST) when comparing *THREE* or more objects:

weak	weakER	weakEST

Some adjectives form their comparisons in a different way:

beautiful	more beautiful	most beautiful

Adjectives of more than one syllable often form their comparisons as above, while one-syllable adjectives often use the *er/est* forms to make comparisons:

lean	leaner	leanest

Exception: Adjectives that end in *y*, even if longer than one syllable, usually take the endings associated with one-syllable adjectives:

pretty	prettier	prettiest
angry	angrier	angriest

Some adjectives form comparisons in a completely different way.

good	better	best
bad	worse	worst
little	less	least

Because *more* and *most* often occur with words of more than one syllable, some writers get trapped into calling something "more better" when they simply mean "better." That's like calling something "more beautifuler." Crossing comparison wires causes such adjective overload.

Adjective overload results from using two or more adjectives where one will do. Examples:

A huge tremendous mountain   today's modern world

Except for such adjective overload and some tricky comparison forms, adjectives are not very problematic. A confusion of the adjective with the next part of speech, the adverb, is a bigger problem.

Adverbs

Like adjectives, adverbs modify, but they don't modify nouns. <u>Adverbs</u> <u>add</u> detail to verbs, adjectives, or other adverbs.

> The slow hedgehog crawled.
> adj.

> The hedgehog crawled slowly.
> adv.

In the first sentence *slow* describes the hedgehog; in the second sentence *slowly* tells *how* it crawled, that is, it describes an action, not an actor. By answering questions such as When?, Where?, How?, and Why?, adverbs modify verbs, adjectives, and other adverbs.

An adverb can also modify an entire clause:

> Finally, my room was clean.
> Ordinarily, I don't read the sports pages.

Many adverbs end in *ly* (*slowly, really, noisily, truly,* etc.), but not all words ending in *ly* are adverbs (*oily, curly,* etc.). And some adverbs do not end in *ly:*

very   rather   too

Besides verbs, adverbs can also modify adjectives:

<u>very</u> tired   <u>rather</u> hot   <u>too</u> noisy

Or they can describe other adverbs:

<u>very</u> slowly   <u>rather</u> carelessly   <u>too</u> rapidly

> The very old turtle crawled rather slowly.
> adv. adj.   adv.   adv.

Very tells how old the turtle was.
Slowly describes how the turtle moved.
Rather describes how slowly the turtle moved.

Because adjectives and adverbs both describe, speakers and writers occasionally confuse them.

> INCORRECT: Donald Duck does not speak very clear.
> adv.   adj.

> CORRECT: Donald Duck does not speak very clearly.
> adv.   adv.

In this example, the last word in the sentence describes a verb—how the cartoon character speaks. That's an adverb function. Adjectives only modify nouns. Therefore, the *adverb (clearly)* fits above. In conversational English the distinction between adjective and adverb sometimes gets mangled:

> That is a real nice iguana.

Again, the test is what the describing word modifies. In the statement above, the speaker is not saying your iguana is real; the speaker is saying that it is nice and intensifying that adjective. Therefore, an adverb is called for:

> That is a <u>really</u> nice iguana.

Adjectives describe nouns. Adverbs describe verbs:

> The swift vultures ate swiftly.
>   *adj.*   *adv.*

Adverbs also intensify or qualify adjectives or other adverbs:

> The film was <u>quite</u> gross. The campus sponsor of the film
>   *adv.*   *adj.*

> apologized <u>very</u> sheepishly.
>   *adv.*   *adv.*

Adverbs and Adjectives after Verbs

Modifying words that come after verbs will ordinarily be adverbs:

> He cracked his knuckles constantly.
> The gloves fit perfectly.

NOT:

> The gloves fit perfect.

BUT: After *linking verbs*, the modifier will ordinarily be an adjective:

> The essay was perfect.

That is because a linking verb *links* a subject to a word that renames or describes it.

> Terry seemed anxious.
> *subject linking   adj.*
>   *verb*

> Orange is a warm color.
> *subject linking   noun*
>   *verb*

Linking verbs include *to be* (all forms, such as *is, was, were,* etc.) plus the following:

feel	look
appear	taste
become	seem
sound	

After a linking word, if the modifying word describes the subject, use an adjective.

> The defendant looked angry.
> subject linking verb adj.

If the modifying word describes the verb instead of the subject, use an adverb:

> The defendant looked angrily at the judge.
> subject linking verb adv.

When the words following the linking verb rename the subject, a noun will be used instead of an adjective or adverb:

> The defendant was a gang member.
> subject linking noun
> verb

Conjunctions

Conjunctions can connect words, phrases, or sentences. There are two major kinds, coordinating or subordinating.

Coordinating Conjunctions

Coordinating conjunctions keep the sentence elements they link in the same rank or level of importance. (**Hint:** Think of a <u>co</u>-worker, your equal, to remember <u>co</u>ordinating conjunctions.) Seven conjunctions coordinate:

and	but	or
		nor
yet	so	for

Learn them. Chapter 3 showed how these conjunctions join sentences. Coordinating conjunctions can also link words or phrases.

and *And* links by adding detail. It keeps the reader headed not just on the same level but also in the direction already begun.

> nuts and bolts (words)
> blowing a whistle and signaling a penalty (phrases)
> The game was over, and our team lost. (sentences)

but These turnaround conjunctions prepare the reader for an abrupt
yet shift.

> poor but honest (words)
> saying no but meaning yes (phrases)
> Most people like chocolate, but I don't. (sentences)
> It was Juan's day off, yet he couldn't relax.

or These conjunctions separate.
nor

> coffee, tea, or milk (words)
> on the piano or under my bed (phrases)
> Make me captain, or I'll take my bat and go home. (sentences)

With a negative (like *neither* or *never*), *nor* substitutes for *or*.

> neither rain nor storm (words)
> never around to work nor to help (phrases)
> She was never absent, nor was she late. (sentences)

for This conjunction means "because" or "since," but, unlike those words, it does not make a clause subordinate.

> He was kept on the job, for he was too valuable an employee to lose.

so *So* sums up or concludes.

> The road was washed out, so they turned back.
> I'll be busy tomorrow, so don't call me.

There are only seven coordinating conjunctions to learn. Memorize them because they are common and useful ways to link words, phrases, or sentences. One student came up with this memory aid, which might help:

F	A	N	B	O	Y	S
For	And	Nor	But	Or	Yet	So

Another way to remember these important connectors: Think of *and* and *but* as opposites; *or, for,* and *nor* all rhyme. That leaves *yet* and *so* to be remembered by themselves. However you learn them, notice that they are all single-syllable words. Therefore, words like *therefore* and *however* are NOT coordinating conjunctions.

Warning: The common one-syllable sequence words *then* and *next* are NOT coordinating conjunctions.

Subordinating Conjunctions

There are many **subordinating** conjunctions (see the list on the inside back cover). They include time words:

while   after
when   until
before   whenever

and conditional words:

if	unless
although	as
because	though
since	even though

These conjunctions do not maintain the equal rank of what they join. They <u>subordinate</u>. They make one sentence element dependent on another. (**Hint:** Think of someone who is your <u>subordinate</u> at work, as opposed to a co-worker.)

I was ready for the exam, <u>but</u> I failed it.
coordinating
conjunction

<u>Although</u> I was ready for the exam, I failed it.
subordinating
conjunction

In the first sentence the coordinating conjunction balances the two clauses: *I was ready* and *I failed the test.* In the second sentence, the subordinating conjunction *(although)* makes its clause dependent on the clause with the main idea *(I failed the test).*

Prepositions

Prepositions get their name from the fact that they are *positioned* before nouns or pronouns. There are dozens of prepositions. Here are some common ones:

about	beneath	into	through
above	beside	like	till
across	between	of	to
after	by	off	under
against	down	on	until
among	during	outside	up
at	except	over	upon
before	for	since	with
below	in		

Some prepositions are made up of more than one word, for example:

because of	in front of
except for	instead of
in back of	in spite of

Prepositions are pointing words that identify or show time, place, and other relationships of nouns and pronouns to other words in a sentence.

Prepositions form phrases with the nouns or pronouns to which they are linked:

around the corner   toward him
across the tracks   among friends
during winter   for centuries

Prepositional phrases can function as adjectives:

The gates of the kingdom were shut.
       (describes which gates)

or as adverbs:

Dorothy hurried toward the Emerald City.
       (describes where she hurried)

Nouns or pronouns that follow prepositions are treated as objects. Which of the following phrases is correct?

Just between you and I   or   Just between you and me

Since *between* is a preposition, it takes an object, not a subject. Therefore, the phrase should be "just between you and me."

Hint: Try mentally reversing the pronouns if you can't tell which one to use. If you would not write "just between I and you," don't write "just between you and I."

Warning: *Than* is not a preposition; it is a subordinating conjunction. Therefore, it is NOT followed by an object:

She is taller than me. (incorrect)

Instead, it is followed by a *subject:*

She is taller than I.

Note: There is an implied verb after *I:*

He is taller than I [am].

If a preposition is followed by a pronoun and a noun, it is usual to put the pronoun *last:*

They gave the award to Henry and me.

NOT:

They gave the award to me and Henry.

Interjections

Interjections are interrupting statements or expressions that indicate strong feeling or emotion. They can be:

Single words   Oh!
Phrases   Not again!
Sentences   Stop or I'll shoot!

Even when the interjection is not a complete sentence, it can appear by itself.

Wow!
Ouch!
Help!

Within a sentence, interjections are set off with a comma, unless the writer wants to emphasize strong feeling:

Stop, he shouted.
Stop! he shouted.

EXERCISE Adjectives, Adverbs, Prepositions, Conjunctions, and Interjections

1. She exercises _____.
   Fill this test frame with a single word. Then tell what part of speech it is:

   a. adjective   **b.** adverb   **c.** preposition

2. The coffee tastes _____.
   Fill this test frame with a single word. Then tell what part of speech it is:

   a. adjective   **b.** adverb

3. Masking tape is _____ than cellophane tape.

   a. stronger   **b.** more strong   **c.** strongest

4. All words ending in *ly* are adverbs.

   true   false

5. Old Max moved very sleepily.
   This sentence contains how many adverbs?

   1   2   3   4

6. The lorpy clads marsed the glebe rilkens.

   Circle the adjectives in the nonsense sentence above.

7. Which of these is NOT a coordinating conjunction?

   and   yet   so   then

8. Which of these is NOT a subordinating conjunction?

   for   although   since   if

9. The judges have to decide between

   a. him and me   **b.** him and I   **c.** he and I   **d.** me and him

10. Whole sentences are never interjections.

    true   false

11. Alice fell <u>down the rabbit hole</u>.
    The underlined prepositional phrase functions as

    a. an adjective   **b.** an adverb   **c.** an object

12. Nobody knows the sport better than

    a. she   **b.** her

13. The fire spread

    a. quick   **b.** quickly

14. The room looks

    a. neat   **b.** more neater   **c.** neatly

15. Moses was found <u>among the bulrushes</u>.
    The prepositional phrase above is used as

    a. an adjective   **b.** an adverb

16. A suit of armor was very uncomfortable.

    Underline the prepositional phrase above.
17. It functions as

    a. an adjective   **b.** an adverb   **c.** a noun

18. What part of speech is *very?* _____

19. What part of speech is *uncomfortable?* _____

Punctuation, Capitalization, and Spelling

Inconsistencies in punctuation, capitalization, and spelling may seem minor, but they can cause readers to miscue what you wrote. Here is a passage whose content should be quite clear, but the punctuation and the capitalization have been removed:

all creatures great and small an autobiography by james herriot was published by st martins press in 1972 it is hard to say exactly how this 442 page book is arranged obviously there is flashback relating herriots first veterinary practice during the 1930s however there is more to herriots strange arrangement for some chapters are somewhat related while others show no chronological relationship

Clearly, punctuation and capitalization (not to mention correct spelling) make writing easier to follow.

Punctuation

Some students expect punctuation to cue every pause and inflection the reader will make, but punctuation is not an exact science. It represents printing conventions that evolved centuries after the English language was first formed. Not every pause will be signaled by punctuation. Nor is there a separate function for each symbol. And in many cases, you can choose from several equally correct punctuation symbols. In some cases you have a choice of whether to punctuate at all.

To help straighten out the confusion of punctuation, let's look first at the major ways those symbols are used. Knowing the punctuation symbols won't help much unless you also know their function.

The Function of Punctuation

To Link

-	hyphen	ex-offender mother-in-law post-season game
—	dash	Love and attention—that's what he wanted.
:	colon	There are many college expenses: tuition, books, room and board, etc.

To Omit

'	apostrophe	can't I'd wouldn't
.	period	R.N. Ph.D.
. . .	ellipsis	"Give me liberty or . . . death."

To Separate

Between sentences:

.	period	There is a walrus on the couch. (after a statement)
?	question mark	Is that a walrus on the couch? (after a question)
!	exclamation point	There's a walrus on the couch! (to indicate surprise or strong emotion)

Between closely related sentences:

;	semicolon	There was a walrus on the couch; he had it all to himself.

Between words or phrases in a series and between very short sentences:

,	comma	oats, peas, beans two turtle doves, three French hens, four calling birds Get ready, get set, go.

Between numbers and between words that are alternatives or opposites:

/	virgule or slash	1/3/85	dates
		How about skating and/or skiing?	
		a love/hate relationship	

To Enclose

, ,	paired commas	For nonessential or interrupting details: Expressway driving, especially in bad weather, is something I avoid.
" "	double quotation marks	For direct quotations: "War is hell."
		For titles of works found within longer publications: articles, essays, short poems, etc.: "Twinkle, Twinkle, Little Star."
		For colloquial or slang terms used within more formal writing: We "pigged out."
' '	single quotation marks	For quoted material within a direct quotation: The teacher told the class, "Remember the rule: '*i* before *e*, except after *c*.'"
[ ]	brackets	For adding or correcting information within a direct quotation: "It [war] is hell."
( )	parentheses	For setting off nonessential information: The Dr. Who books (published by Target Books) are very popular at campus bookstores.
— —	dashes	Also for setting off parenthetical information. I didn't mind the hard work—that's why I took the job—I did mind the boredom.
_____	underlining	For setting off titles of books, newspapers, magazines, plays, films, paintings, etc.: <u>Damien</u>, <u>The New York Times</u>, <u>Newsweek</u>
		For words referred to as words: <u>Irregardless</u> is not standard English.
		For foreign words: We'll see you <u>mañana</u>.

Link + Omit + Separate + Enclose = LOSE

You are less likely to LOSE your way in choosing punctuation if you check it against the function you need to fulfill. Punctuation can be confusing sometimes, but it is not guesswork.

Punctuation would be a lot easier if there were separate symbols for each function. While some symbols, such as exclamation marks, do serve only a single function, many symbols, like the comma, are used in several ways.

Comma (,)

The comma is the most common punctuation symbol. *Single* commas are used

1. to separate items in a series:*

    Sleepy, Sneezy, and Doc

2. between sentences joined by coordinating conjunctions:

    Many are cold, but few are frozen.

3. between geographical and time units, such as city and state, date and year, etc.:

    Baltimore, Maryland   September 1, 1939

4. after a long introductory phrase or dependent clause:

    After nineteen innings and five hours, the game ended.

5. after transitional words or phrases at the beginning of sentences:

    Nevertheless, I quit smoking.

6. in direct address:

    Bertha, peel me a grape.

7. before short direct quotations:

    Sally said, "Wash your hands; you touched the dog."

8. to separate adjectives:

    tart, succulent rhubarb
    a loud, arrogant boor

But the comma is often omitted, especially when the adjective before the noun commonly precedes that noun:

    a local business group
    the old spinning wheel
    a new laundry detergent

*The comma before the linking word is optional, but inserting it is a common publication practice.

Hint: If the word *and* could be inserted between the adjectives and make sense, then the comma is usually used:

> a dirty, cluttered room (Since you could write *a dirty and cluttered room*, the comma fits.)
> small craft warnings (Since you would not write *small and craft warnings*, the comma does not belong.)

9. after the greeting in informal letters and after the closing in all letters:

> Dear Roberto,
> Sincerely yours,

10. to prevent misreading:

> After we moved the furniture collapsed.
> After we moved, the furniture collapsed.

Paired commas are used to enclose extra information or an identifying phrase that is not essential to a sentence:

> Muhammad Ali, the former heavyweight champion, spoke at our school.
> He is, in my opinion, a spellbinding speaker.

When NOT to Use Commas

1. *For essential phrases or clauses.* If the modifying clause or phrase is essential to the sentence, do not set it off with commas:

> CORRECT: All students who drive on campus must get a permit.

Adding commas would mean that all students, even those who don't drive, need a permit:

> INCORRECT: All students, who drive on campus, must get a permit.

Hint: A clause introduced by *that* is seldom set off by commas:

> The mess that you made in the living room must be cleaned up.
> The dishwasher that you just bought is now on sale.

2. *To separate a subject from a verb.* Don't separate a subject from its verb unless an interrupting phrase comes between:

> INCORRECT: My uncle Charlie, has a horse farm.
> CORRECT: Charlie, my favorite uncle, has a horse farm.

3. *Between two words or phrases joined by a coordinating conjunction:*

> INCORRECT: The dwarfs picked up their axes, and went to work.
> INCORRECT: Play-off hopes ended today for the Tigers, and the Pirates.
> CORRECT: The dwarfs picked up their axes and went to work.

4. *After the last item in a series:*

INCORRECT: Allosaurus, stegosaurus, and brontosaurus, were all dinosaurs.
CORRECT: Allosaurus, stegosaurus, and brontosaurus were all dinosaurs.

EXERCISE   Commas

In the following paragraph look only for comma errors. You can insert commas, delete commas, and/or replace commas with other punctuation marks. Make all corrections directly above the mistakes.

"Do you mind if I smoke?" This used to be a rhetorical question, today it is a required one. Those who have suffered in silence in elevators, or theaters now demand their right to breathe clean air. Taking their complaints to administrators and legislators, they are, in some cases, getting action. Nevertheless, this is not happening instantly, In Nebraska, for example, smoking is prohibited in elevators, theaters, and public buses. Violators are supposed to pay fines. The laws however are not always enforced. While one can sit in no-smoking sections on an airplane, train, or bus some college classrooms remain holdouts where no-smoking signs, posted for years, are routinely ignored.

Period (.)

Periods are used to

1. end statement sentences:

    The werewolf was hungry.

2. form some abbreviations:

    M.D.   R.N.   Apt.

(Many abbreviations, especially of names of organizations, do not require periods: UN, PTA, TWA, etc.)

Note: If a sentence ends with an abbreviation that takes a period, do not add an additional period. For example:

> Don't play with burning candles, matches, etc. (correct)

You can use three periods in a sentence when you need to show something has been purposely left out of a direct quotation:

> "Birds . . . flock together."

If the omission comes at the *end* of a statement sentence or if you leave out one or more sentences, add the usual sentence-ending period as well as the three periods:

> "Birds of a feather flock . . . ."

Remember, the triple period (called an ellipsis) is used only *within a direct quotation.*

Correct Use of Periods

1 period.	OK at end of statement sentence
2 periods in a row . .	Never correct
3 periods in a row . . .	OK only to show omission in direct quotations
4 periods in a row. . . .	OK only to show omission at *end* of direct quotation

Semicolon (;)

Semicolons are used to

1. end closely related sentences:

> He got up late; he skipped breakfast.

2. separate items that contain commas:

> On stage were these celebrities: Alan Pakula, the director; Meryl Streep, the actress; William Styron, the novelist.

Do not confuse semicolons (;) with colons(:).

Colon (:)

Colons are used

1. after greetings in formal or business letters:

> Dear Sir:

2. to signal that a list follows:

> To fix errors, the typist kept these supplies on hand: erasers, tape, and correcting fluid.

3. to introduce a long quotation or one introduced by a separate sentence:

> On her desk were these words from Francis Bacon: "Some books are to be tasted, others to be swallowed, and some few to be chewed and digested."

4. in some time subdivisions and between parts of biblical citations:

> The 8:15 train   Mark 3:5

Apostrophe (')

The apostrophe is used to

1. show that something is left out:

> We're   I'd

2. show possession or ownership:

> Bill's Barber Shop   The Lord's Prayer

3. form the plurals of letters and numbers that are not written out:

> 8's and 9's   ABC's

To show ownership or possession for singular nouns, just add 's:

> Alice's Restaurant   Bill's Tap   the disk jockey's patter

If the singular noun ends in s and is *one* syllable, add 's:

> Gus's job   Charles's team

If a singular noun ends in s and is *more than one* syllable, add only an apostrophe:

> Jesus' parables   Ulysses' journeys

For plural nouns that end in s, just add an apostrophe *after* the s:

> the actors' dressing rooms   the umpires' strike
> The Supremes' performance

For plural nouns that do *not* end in s, add 's:

> children   children's

Don't confuse the possessive with the simple plural of nouns:

CORRECT: lions and tigers and bears
INCORRECT: lion's and tiger's and bear's

Warning: the apostrophe is never used with verbs:

INCORRECT: He create's trouble.
She warm's up first.

CORRECT: the cat's pajamas
the puppet's nose

And never use the apostrophe with personal pronouns:

INCORRECT: The bird hurt it's wing.
CORRECT: The bird hurt its wing.

INCORRECT: The package was her's.
INCORRECT: The package was hers.

Dash (—) and Hyphen (-)

Another pair of easily confused punctuation symbols are dashes and hyphens.

The dash — is longer than the hyphen.

This is a way to remember that the dash deals with larger elements than the hyphen.
The dash signals a strong break in thought or change in tone:

The exam was easy—so I thought at the time.

Note that there are no spaces before or after a dash. On a typewriter a dash is formed by two strokes of the hyphen key --. In handwriting a dash is simply longer than a hyphen. The dash can also be used in pairs to indicate a parenthetical thought:

When the cashier said, "You all come back now" the teacher—a stranger to southern dialect—thought he had forgotten to pay his bill.

A dash can also signal interrupted speech in dialogue:

"Would you mind if I—"
Cutting him off, she replied, "Yes."

A hyphen links

1. some words:

father-in-law

2. some prefixes and suffixes:

ex-addict   post-Thanksgiving sale   governor-elect

3. all prefixes before a capitalized noun or adjective:

    anti-Soviet position   pro-Israel demonstration

4. compound adjectives that come **before** the nouns they modify:

    A blood-splattered gymnasium was depicted in the movie *Carrie*.

5. compound names:

    Neiman-Marcus   Ann-Margret

6. syllables at the end of one line and the beginning of another:

                                                               chil-
dren.
                                    BUT: Never hyphenate a one-syllable wo-
rd.

Hyphens are also sometimes needed to help eliminate word confusion or awkwardness:

    co-worker   re-enlist

Underlining (_____)

Words underlined in a manuscript are set in type by printers as italics.

    The Joy of Cooking = *The Joy of Cooking*

Use underlining to signal titles of books, magazines, newspapers, plays, films, and works of art:

    Newsweek   The New York Times   The Sound of Music
    Moby Dick

Underlining is also used to set off words and phrases that are foreign and not yet Anglicized:

    amore   Zeitgeist

and to set off words referred to as words:

    Our most common conjunction is and.
    People who lisp like Barbara Wawa have trouble with the letter s.

Quotation Marks (" ")

Double quotation marks are used

1. to enclose titles of published works that are not published by themselves (poems, articles, short stories, chapters of books, etc.):

    "Casey at the Bat"   "The Lottery"

2. to enclose someone's exact words:

> "What's your sign?" the singles-bar regular asked. *(direct quotation)*

If the statement is put into your own words, the quotation is no longer direct:

> He asked what her sign was. *(indirect quotation)*

Single quotation marks are used only for quotations or titles that require quotations found within direct quotations:

> "Please sing 'Amazing Grace,' my favorite hymn," the preacher asked the choir.

Single and double quotation marks always appear *in pairs.*

Quotation Marks with Other Punctuation

When used with quotation marks, some punctuation goes inside the quotation marks, and some punctuation goes outside.

Always inside: commas (,) and periods (.)

> My favorite Robert Frost poems are "Fire and Ice," "Birches," and "The Road Not Taken."
> While in prison, Martin Luther King, Jr., wrote "Letter from Birmingham Jail."

Always outside: colons (:) and semicolons (;)

> The student protested, "That don't sound right to me"; the teacher replied, "That doesn't sound right to me."
> There is much to keep you busy in "The Big Apple": theaters, museums, restaurants.

Sometimes inside, sometimes outside: question marks (?) and exclamation points (!)

Within a sentence, if only the quoted material is a question or exclamation, put the question mark or exclamation point *inside* the quotation marks:

> She asked, "Do you know the way to Pismo Beach?"
> "Help!" we screamed.

If the entire sentence is a question or an exclamation, put the question mark or exclamation point *outside* the quotation marks:

> In what play do you find the line "Was this the face that launched a thousand ships"?
> "Don't let your sons grow up to be cowboys"!

EXERCISE Underlining and Quotation Marks

Supply the missing underlining and quotation marks in the following passage.

Hint: There is only one missing set of quotation marks.

Last spring I went to New York City. I bought The New York Times and a guidebook entitled Fun in Fun City to see what was going on. I was lucky to find an old Marx Brothers movie, Duck Soup. Also, I caught a matinee performance of Lorraine Hansberry's play, A Raisin in the Sun. I topped that off with a visit to the Museum of Modern Art to see my favorite painting, Pablo Picasso's Guernica. Europe can wait; there's a lot to do in The Big Apple.

EXERCISE Punctuation Review

In the following paragraph, replace incorrect punctuation and delete any punctuation that is not needed. Besides comma and period errors, there are some errors in the use of apostrophes and one missing hyphen.

The sound of guns filled the autumn air in Arkansas, because it was the beginning of the deer season. It was a very, cold morning in November, with the suns rays peeking through the tall, pine trees along with a silence found in a funeral parlor. Breaking the silence of the early morning was the crackling of the fire that was built by the faithful, Indian guide, and the howling of hound dogs. A new experience for me this was my first hunt after one of natures most sought after game, the mule deer.

EXERCISE Punctuation Review

By adding, deleting, or replacing, correct all incorrect punctuation in the paragraph below. Make all corrections directly above each error.

While reading The Los Angeles Times I came across an article, called the Snail: Sea Scavenger. It showed snail teeth, that can't be seen with the naked eye. Taken with an electron microscope these photographs were in my opinion fascinating pictures. I had a few, tropical fish so I read some books on snail classification, and became quite interested in their background. Now I am I think the local authority on snails, and similar sea life.

Capitalization

Capitalization also helps a reader decode a writer's message. As with punctuation, conventional usage as seen in the print media dictates what is regularly capitalized.

Here are some categories of words, the first letters of which are regularly capitalized:

Beginnings of Sentences

The doorbell rang.
Is anyone around?
Answer the door.

Note: Do NOT capitalize after a semicolon:

The doorbell rang; the guests arrived.

Geographical Units

countries	India
cities and states	Reno, Nevada
streets	Skyline Drive
rivers, lakes, etc.	Truckee River
sections of a country	the South, the Midwest

but NOT a general direction: turn south

Adjectives derived from countries: French perfume   Japanese car

Most Calendar Units

months	July
days	Monday
holidays	Thanksgiving

but NOT seasons: summer   autumn

Brand Names

Canon cameras   Prince spaghetti

Religions, Races, and Languages

Buddhism   Caucasian   Spanish

Specific Places, Institutions, and Organizations

Independence Hall   Yellowstone National Park
Rockefeller Plaza   the United Nations   Western Union
Amtrak   Columbia University

but NOT a general reference to any of the above
NOT: She works for a large Corporation
BUT: She works for a large corporation.
OR: She works for Standard Oil.

Names of Persons and Titles That Occur before a Name

Isidore Mudge   Dr. Alvarez
Professor Tower   Uncle Joe

BUT:

My uncle was a doctor.

Titles of Works of Art: The First Word and All Important Words

Murder at the Vicarage   *Of Mice and Men*

Historical Events

World War II   the Reformation

Beginnings and Closings of Letters

Dear Prudence,   Sincerely yours,

NOT:

Sincerely Yours,

The Pronoun *I* and the Interjection *O*

I know a little bit about a lot of things, but I don't know enough about
you.
Hear, O Lord, our prayer.

Oh is not capitalized except at the beginning of a sentence: She told me she loved me, but oh how she lied.

Avoid BLOCK capitals and do not capitalize words just because they are important to you.

INCORRECT: Come to a PARTY at my House.
He is a Pastor at my Church.
She does Cancer Research.

CORRECT: Come to a party at my house.
He is a pastor at my church.
She does cancer research.

EXERCISE   Capitalization

There are several capitalization errors in the following passage. To correct them, follow the format of the first two corrections which have been done for you. If a letter should be in lowercase, draw a line through it and put the correction *below* the mistake. If a letter should be in uppercase, draw a line through the mistake and put the correction *above* the line.

A Member of the elks and a Professor of American History, my

Brother lives in the east. He teaches at a small college in Elm Isle,

Maine. He is also a member of the Maine senate, the knights of

Columbus, and the Kiwanis. When he is not involved with these

organizations, he can be found on Main street every friday Morning of

every summer saluting the Flag in anticipation of labor day.

EXERCISE   Punctuation and Capitalization

Supply the missing quotation marks and underlining in the following selection. Also correct any errors of capitalization.

A children's book that adults often borrow is The Lion, The Witch

and the Wardrobe. This science fiction book is centered in a kingdom

called narnia, which lies North of Archenland off the Eastern Ocean.

Most exciting is the Chapter called "The Triumph of the Witch, but the

suspense does not end until the Witch is routed and Spring returns to

the frozen land. The author, Professor C. S. Lewis, was an Anglican

Priest who felt that children would never be harmed by far-out fantasy.

This view is confirmed by thousands of child and adult readers who

have enjoyed not just this book but the whole Narnia series.

EXERCISE   Punctuation and Capitalization

At the beginning of this chapter (see page 291), you were shown a passage with all punctuation and capitalization omitted.

Adding all necessary punctuation and capitalization, rewrite that passage below:

_____

_____

_____

_____

_____

_____

_____

_____

_____

_____

Spelling

Don't confuse spelling errors with transcription errors. In writing a draft of an essay, you might leave out or transpose letters. Writing *teh* for *the* is miswriting (or mistyping), not misspelling. Blocked by the slowness of handwriting or typing, your brain leaps ahead, and you may write *Goconut Grove* for *Coconut Grove.* Careful proofreading *just for spelling* will catch such transcription mistakes. Don't confuse words you know how to spell but miswrite with words that make up your real spelling problems.

To improve your spelling, you have to find out what words you often misspell. Your own writing can give you that data. Finding a word you misspelled is just a beginning. Finding out why you misspelled it marks the start of the cure. Three main causes for spelling mistakes are:

1. mispronouncing a word.
2. misunderstanding a word or phrase or confusing it with another.
3. not knowing the correct spelling of a word.

Mispronouncing won't always create a spelling error, but a syllable added orally might affect how you write a word. To illustrate: *realtor* and *athlete* are often mispronounced. Each word has two syllables—only two. *Ath-lete*, not "ath-e-lete." Accurate pronunciation gives you a better chance of spelling a word correctly.

Word confusions occur when you hear a word that you are not used to seeing in print. One student wrote that, in the Job Corps, she was "a sign to a counselor." She meant "assigned to a counselor." Another student wrote about having everything "down packed." He meant "down pat." "Down packed" was the way he made mental sense out of an expression he was not used to seeing in print. We have all had the surprise of discovering that a word or phrase stored the way we heard it does not match the word or phrase in print.

And there are words that have two different spellings which change depending on the meaning. Would rhubarb pie be a *desert* or a *dessert?* Is writing paper *stationery* or *stationary?* When you trip over such words, the dictionary is the safety net.

Another help is to come up with some word association that will help you untangle the confusion. Think of strawberry shortcake as a typical dessert. The two *s*'s in *strawberry shortcake* and the two *s*'s in *dessert* should keep you from confusing shortcake with sandy plains. So if you can't remember how a word is correctly spelled, use a memory aid. For example, is it *friend* or *freind?* Use a word association, such as A true fri<u>end</u>ship should never <u>end</u>. You can make up your own memory aids. <u>O</u>ne student came up with this elaborate way for remembering how to spell the word *arithmetic:* <u>A</u> <u>r</u>at <u>in</u> the <u>h</u>ouse <u>m</u>ight <u>e</u>at <u>t</u>he <u>i</u>ce <u>c</u>ream. As revolting as that sounds, this trick did help her conquer one of her spelling demons.

For words you often simply misspell, you can rely on some rules.

1. Doubled Consonants

When adding a vowel ending, double the final consonant of a one-syllable word or of a final-stressed syllable if (a) it ends in a single consonant *and* (b) it is preceded by a single vowel. (In the following examples, *V* = vowel and *C* = consonant.)

> pin + ing = pinning   flat + er = flatter
> VC   VCC   VC   VCC
>
> trip + ed = tripped   refer + ed = referred
> VC   VCC   VC   VCC

BUT:

> drift = drifting
>   VCC

Drift ends in *double* consonant, so rule does NOT apply.

> rain + ed = rained
>   VCC

Final consonant preceded by *two* vowels, so rule does NOT apply.

2. Words Ending in *e*

Adding *ing*.   Words ending in *e* will drop that vowel before adding *ing:*

shine	shining
write	writing
refine	refining
observe	observing

Do NOT combine the two rules above:

shine	shinning
write	writting

A helpful double check is a phonics rule: A double consonant makes a vowel that comes before it short, not long. *Writting* would have a short *i* sound and be pronounced *ritting.*

Writing has a long *i* sound and is pronounced *rīting.* Since that is the sound you want, *writing* is the spelling you want.

Adding Other Vowel Suffixes: *able, ible, ous.*   Just as with the *ing* ending, drop the final *e* before adding these vowel endings:

> force + ible = forcible
> presume + able = presumable
> virtue + ous = virtuous

BUT there are many exceptions, especially words that end in *ge* and *ce:*

> notice + able = noticeable
> courage + ous = courageous
> service + able = serviceable

3. *Y* Endings

If a word ends in *y*, change the *y* to *i* before adding *es* or *ed*:

apply	applies	company	companies
sky	skies	study	studied

BUT the *y* does not change to *i* before adding *ing* or when adding a *consonant* ending:

study	studying
monkey	monkeys

4. *IE* or *EI?*

Use *ie*, not *ei*, for some long *e* sounds, except after *c*:

believe retrieve   conceive receive

Use *ei* when the sound is long *a*:

neighbor   weigh   freight

The old saying, "*I* before *E*, except after *C* or as sounded as *A* in *neighbor* or *weigh*," still helps. But there are some exceptions:

either   their   height   foreign   leisure

Such rules help. You may know others. Rules, unfortunately, will have exceptions. The dictionary remains the ultimate fail-safe when you are unsure how to spell a word. If you are a poor speller, the reader doesn't have to know it so long as, dictionary in hand, you proofread your final drafts thoroughly for spelling errors.

EXERCISE Spelling

Cross out the *one* misspelled word in each line.

1. receipt   neighbor   thier   believe
2. defining   writing   buying   forceible
3. supplies   applies   applying   payed
4. skiped   tripped   applying   transferred
5. wrapped   warped   warpped   rapped
6. tripped   conserving   rainned   shined

Circle the <u>correctly</u> spelled word of each pair in parentheses.

7. The floor was just (moped, mopped).

8. The champagne cork (poped, popped) off easily.

9. He was (contending, contendding) for first place.

10. The Tasmanian devil (weighhed, weighed, wieghed) a lot.

EXERCISE   Spelling

Keep a list below of misspellings marked in your writing this term. List the *correct* spellings only, but underline the parts of each word you misspelled.

_____   _____

_____   _____

_____   _____

_____   _____

_____   _____

_____   _____

_____   _____

_____   _____

_____   _____

_____   _____

_____   _____

_____   _____

_____   _____

11

Manuscript Format

There are some standard manuscript regulations that cover how a piece of writing is presented to an audience. Many of these you know. They cover everything from size of paper to color of ink. If your instructor has supplied you with manuscript instructions, follow them. Since writing teachers deal with hundreds of papers, they often standardize their instructions. Following them will ease the teacher's job of evaluating your writing. There is usually some method behind even the most stringent manuscript specifications. The specifications will vary. Some teachers get alarmed if a composition is written in green ink; others are grateful you didn't use pencil or crayon. However observant your audience is, observe standard formatting. How your writing is presented should enhance, not take away from, what you are saying.

When you do not have more specific instructions for your composition, follow these suggestions:

1. *Use standard size paper: 8½ by 11 inches.* That is the conventional size. A jumble of sizes is hard to deal with, and smaller pieces of paper would force you to squeeze your writing in, giving it a cramped look.

2. *On a cover sheet, center the title but do not underline it or put quotation marks around it. Capitalize the first letter of the first word*

in the title and of all other important words. Cover sheets are traditional in business reports. Underlining or quotation marks would signify that your title was already published somewhere.

3. *Put your name, date, instuctor's name, course title, and section on the cover sheet in the lower right-hand corner.* With dozens of papers to correct from several classes, a teacher who has this information is less likely to misfile your writing.

4. *Type your paper or write it in blue or black ink. Do not use pencil or some lurid color of ink.* Formal writing is typed or printed to ensure legibility. Some teachers will insist on typed final copies of student writing; others will also accept handwritten essays, provided they are neatly done. Orange or purple ink doesn't look very dignified.

5. *Write or type on only one side of the paper.* Otherwise, writing from one side might show through on the other, making it hard to read.

6. *If you type, double-space.* It is easier to read and gives the teacher more room to make comments and corrections. For this reason, some instructors expect double spacing even in handwritten essays.

7. *Provide ample left, right, top, and bottom margins.* It is conventional to leave an inch or an inch and a half of space for margins. Framed by white space, a paper is easier to read.

8. *If there are a few corrections on the final draft, don't hesitate to make them. Make them clear: erase or "white out" any errors completely. If there are many errors to be corrected, redo a whole page.* Students sometimes leave in errors they detect at the last minute because they do not want to blemish the typed page. Although neatness and accuracy are both important, a paper with a few last-minute corrections is preferable to one perfectly typed but with uncorrected errors.

9. *Number the pages in the upper right-hand corner. It is not necessary to number the first page.* If the pages get out of order, the reader can figure out what goes where.

10. *Paper-clip or staple the pages, and make sure they are in correct order.* This obviously helps to keep the pages in order.

Additional Format Advice

1. *Abbreviations:* In general, be sparing in the use of abbreviations and avoid the more informal ones, such as &, +, or =. Spell these out: *and, plus, equals.* You can, however, use standard abbreviations, such as *i.e.* (that is), *e.g.* (for example), and A.M. or P.M.

2. *Numbers:* Spell out all numbers that can be expressed in one or two words: forty-five, two hundred, sixteen. If it takes three or more words to express a number, then show the number as figures: 3,389;

214; 12,500. Exception: Use figures for all dates (including the year) and for addresses:

> September 1, 1939   100 East Bellevue

Also use figures for hours of the day if expressed in digital numbers or if used before A.M. or P.M.:

> 9:10 A.M.   9 P.M.   BUT   nine o'clock

3. *Punctuation:* Punctuation rules are reviewed in the previous chapter. In a manuscript, except for quotation marks, never begin a new line with punctuation.

If your instructor has given you any additional or different manuscript instructions, list them below:

_____

_____

_____

_____

_____

_____

_____

_____

_____

_____

_____

The sample student theme that follows illustrates standard manuscript format for an essay.

Midsummer Tropical Night

George Gonzalez

January 15, 1985

Ms. Thomson

English 101 D

It was summer vacation, and my friend Diego and I were hitchhiking from Cali, Colombia, on our way to the Caribbean coast of that country. The idea of free traveling and adventure to the coast had attracted us. I carried my bright yellow backpack, my water canteen, my sleeping bag, and enough money to spend four to five days in a flophouse somewhere on the coast. I was also carrying a small hardshell suitcase filled with clothes, which, when I stood it on end, served nicely as a seat. For those long waits by the sides of the highways, I had my stool. This precious idea of the suitcase was knowledge passed on from my grandfather to my father and then to me.

We hitchhiked to Medellín in three days. About forty-five miles before Medellín, a police trooper stopped us to see if we were any menace to society. After a few minutes, he let us go, but not until we heard a lecture on safety rules on the highway. After two days in Medellín, we headed straight for the train yards, which happened to be our best choice for free traveling. That night we tiptoed through the yard and found a train aimed in the right direction. Spotting an empty box car, we climbed in and hid in the shadows at the far end of the car. It was a long night. For me, anyway, there was no sleep. A couple of years earlier I dozed off in the open gondola of a train that lumbered into a long tunnel in the Andes. I suddenly awoke, and the noise, heat, and fumes of the steam engine and the blackness of the tunnel convinced me that I had died in my sleep and gone straight to hell. That day I vowed never to fall asleep while riding a freight train. Next morning, after great crashes and jolts, we moved out. By late afternoon the train stopped at another yard and was broken up. Keeping our hopes high, I asked the first person I saw, a yard worker near a ditch, where we were. "Cartagena," he said. We were already on the Caribbean!

That afternoon we took another train, but kept heading north. This time our car was an open double-tiered one, designed to carry automobiles. We climbed to the top level, sat down, and enjoyed the beautiful plains of the north. Far away to the east and west we could see the high Andes with their snowy peaks. It was beautiful scenery. At sundown the air was cooler. A deepening red violet flooded our beautiful sky. Small towns drifted by. The people picking cotton waved at us, and I felt the vibration of the Andes coming to rest.

Something hit me on my arm, and I jolted alert. Then another plink hit my chest. There were gold spots whizzing through the air, sticking to the beams of the car, tangling in my hair. We were passing through a valley of freshly cut hayfields, and we were bombarded with flecks of yellow light. All around the train and fields, tiny sparkles of hay wove in the air. The afternoon went by, and darkness started to surround us while thousands of lightning bugs appeared in the dark, filling the fields like the stars in the sky. First one, then the second, and the third, and after a while we were surprised by the thousands flickering in the night in a dance of passion of the midsummer tropical night. This made me remember when I was just a little boy how I had captured them in jars, brought them to my room, and then fallen asleep watching them flickering like Christmas lights. Their glowing light always seemed strange, but I satisfied myself with my mother's answer, "That is one of God's marvelous creations." Coming to reality, I found myself in the middle of a massive orgy; the car was festooned with the blinking lovers, joined together with fantastic sparkles. I was so delighted with the extraordinary spectacle I whooped and hollered and laughed with my friend.

The train hurried on. There were schedules to meet and cargo to deliver, and soon the firefly party was far behind us. It wasn't long before the northern sky began to brighten. We were in different terrain. The air was humid. The palms began to appear— a sure sign that we were close to our destination. While the north was completely different from what we expected, the magic of that firefly night stayed with us all the way up the coast and long after we were back home.

Correction Abbreviations and Symbols

Below are some common correction abbreviations and symbols. They are useful to know because your instructor may use many of them. You may also wish to use them as shorthand when editing your own writing.

Abbreviations

agr	agreement error in subject and verb or in pronoun reference
awk	awkward word phrase or clause
cap	capitalize
cs	comma splice
coh	error in coherence
frag	fragment
ital	italics (underlining) error
lc	lower case (noncapital) letters needed
ref	reference error, usually vague or confusing pronoun
rep	repetition
ro	run-on or fused sentence
shift	shift in tense or person
sp	spelling error
sva	subject–verb–agreement error
uc	upper case (capital letters) needed
v.g.	very good
ww	wrong word

Symbols

∧	insert omitted material at this point
ℰ	delete
∿	transpose: \man old\ means the manuscript should read: *old man*
no ¶	no new paragraph here
¶	new paragraph needed
⌒	close up gaps
#	insert space

Listing or Brainstorming Sheets

Use the sample sheets below for your writing assignments. Brainstorm—that is, simply flood out what comes to mind about your subject. Do not, at this stage, be concerned with complete sentences. Jot down single words or short phrases. Do not censor what you list. You will not be using all of your jottings. You can get rid of repetition and what doesn't fit later. Think of what you write as a shopping list of ideas about your subject. Later you can renumber and group the items you decide to use in your writing. If your list does not turn up enough specifics, brainstorm it again.

Listing (Brainstorming) Sheet No. 1

1. _____

2. _____

3. _____

4. _____

5. _____

6. _____

7. _____

8. _____

9. _____

10. _____

11. _____

12. _____

13. _____

14. _____

15. _____

16. _____

17. _____

18. _____

19. _____

20. _____

You needn't fill every line, but if you can't list several specifics, you need to revise your subject or find out more about it. If you run out of sheets, make up your own.

Listing (Brainstorming) Sheet No. 2

1._____

2._____

3._____

4._____

5._____

6._____

7._____

8._____

9._____

10._____

11._____

12._____

13._____

14._____

15._____

16._____

17._____

18._____

19._____

20._____

21._____

22._____

23._____

Listing (Brainstorming) Sheet No. 3

1._____

2._____

3._____

4._____

5._____

6._____

7._____

8._____

9._____

10._____

11._____

12._____

13._____

14._____

15._____

16._____

17._____

18._____

19._____

20._____

21._____

22._____

23._____

Listing (Brainstorming) Sheet No. 4

1._____

2._____

3._____

4._____

5._____

6._____

7._____

8._____

9._____

10._____

11._____

12._____

13._____

14._____

15._____

16._____

17._____

18._____

19._____

20._____

21._____

22._____

23._____

Listing (Brainstorming) Sheet No. 5

1._____

2._____

3._____

4._____

5._____

6._____

7._____

8._____

9._____

10._____

11._____

12._____

13._____

14._____

15._____

16._____

17._____

18._____

19._____

20._____

21._____

22._____

23._____

Listing (Brainstorming) Sheet No. 6

1. _____

2. _____

3. _____

4. _____

5. _____

6. _____

7. _____

8. _____

9. _____

10. _____

11. _____

12. _____

13. _____

14. _____

15. _____

16. _____

17. _____

18. _____

19. _____

20. _____

21. _____

22. _____

23. _____

Listing (Brainstorming) Sheet No. 7

1._____

2._____

3._____

4._____

5._____

6._____

7._____

8._____

9._____

10._____

11._____

12._____

13._____

14._____

15._____

16._____

17._____

18._____

19._____

20._____

21._____

22._____

23._____

Listing (Brainstorming) Sheet No. 8

1._____

2._____

3._____

4._____

5._____

6._____

7._____

8._____

9._____

10._____

11._____

12._____

13._____

14._____

15._____

16._____

17._____

18._____

19._____

20._____

21._____

22._____

23._____

Afterword: Becoming a Better Writer

So you want to be a better writer. If you put enough time and effort into the entire writing process, including prewriting and rewriting, you should be creating acceptable final essays. Here are some suggestions to help make those written products better match your intentions and your abilities.

Conferences

Read your writing teacher's comments carefully. They are important clues to assessing your writing, but they are often not enough to go on. A teacher will have dozens of essays to correct at one time. His or her comments will not be as specific as you (or the teacher) would like. This is where a conference comes in. Some instructors schedule regular conferences with students to help them improve their writing. In class or out of class, whether these are regularly scheduled or you yourself set them up, conferences provide important feedback.

Conferences work best when you participate actively. Come to the teacher prepared with specific questions, not a general "What's wrong with my paper?" Such general questions often provoke general

327

responses. Instead, you want focus. Ask specific questions about individual papers that you bring with you. Remember, your goal is not to argue a past grade but to get directions for future writing assignments.

Specific questions will help your teacher show you just where and how to improve your writing. And don't just focus on error. Find out your writing strengths so you can build on them. Take notes during the writing conference or as soon as it is over, so you won't have to rely on your memory when you next sit down to write.

Keep Your Writing

Many students dispose of their writing because it is not always as good as they would like. Keeping your writing (even drafts leading up to a final copy) will show you how you compose. Art students leave school with a portfolio of their work; music students leave with a repertoire. Writing students often don't realize they have created a writing portfolio, that they do produce a body of writing, not just for English classes but for many other classes. Keep a file folder of *all* your college writing, not just your best work. Go over it regularly to see your writing strengths and weaknesses. Your file can also be a handy reference source that will show you the errors that recur and how to avoid them.

Freewriting

Chapter 1 showed how to do the unedited, nonstop writing called freewriting. These five- or ten-minute sessions will help you over the terror of the blank page. Calling on yourself as critic too soon can create writer's block. In freewriting, if you can't think of what to write, you simply write your name or "I can't think of what to write." A few minutes of this and you should get unstuck, and some thought will insist on being put down on paper. Freewriting is an exercise. It won't create the final copy of a coherent essay, but it will show that writing is something you can generate easily and without terror. Since it can show how you feel about many subjects, it might also help you locate subjects for writing assignments. Some students even use freewriting as a way of brainstorming a subject without making a list. Used in these ways, freewriting becomes a part of prewriting.

Journal Writing

Journal writing is daily writing you keep just for yourself. This "self prose" is like a diary, but you are not confined to what happened to you that day: you can write about anything you wish. Since there is no audience but yourself, there is no need to correct or revise it. Writing every day, you will discover you can write about a wide variety of things. One student who had written only what she had been assigned discovered that in journal writing she could write about anything. That is no small discovery. It is hard to squeeze in time every day for writing, but it only takes fifteen or twenty minutes at a time. You'll find you're in good company: famous artists and writers like Leonardo da Vinci and Henry David Thoreau kept journals. You should too, even if no one reads them but you. One of my students was able to bring to class entries for the day and year of her birth from a set of journals her uncle had kept for forty years.

Reading

Reading is another important prewriting tool. Reading attentively will improve your spelling, punctuation, and vocabulary. Writers constantly make choices. To see how an author chose to communicate to one audience will help you see a fuller range of your own writing choices. This does not mean modeling your prose on Herman Melville or Maya Angelou. It does mean finding reading passages you especially like, whether on the sports pages or in some classic novel, and analyzing them to find out what the writers did to get and keep your attention.

Analyzing Your Errors

Look over your writing to get a feel for where your errors come from. Are you misspelling words or mistranscribing them? To find out where your errors are coming from is to get at your own error patterns—mistakes you regularly make. Focus on mistakes that recur. You have to find out why you left off an *ed* ending or why you wrote a fragment. The number of errors is not so important as why the errors occur. Don't let the number of errors wear you down. One word misspelled six times stems from one error. A student who forgets to capitalize the word *I* will make zillions of errors, but they stem from one easily correctable mistake.

Finding Your Voice

An important breakthrough in writing occurs when what you write sounds like who you are. Whether you are bubbly, sarcastic, or witty, your writing should reflect your personality. Kurt Vonnegut, a famous U.S. novelist, swears that every time he forgets to write like who he is—a midwesterner—his writing falls flat. Don't try to sound like somebody else. You are somebody; let your readers know who that person talking to them really is.

Don't Duck Writing Opportunities

Taking notes at a meeting, writing a friend instead of calling—there are many chances we have to write even when writing is not an assignment. No less than music or dance, writing is a performing art. A lot of practice by yourself and with your writing teacher as coach will move you through process to product, from those who write because they must to those who write because they have something to share with an audience.

Index

"DON'T YOU DARE MENTION LUCK TO ME, BEN CORBETT!"
MORGAN GLARED AT THE MAYOR OF ROCKY BLUFF.

"This is the worst day of my life. I should have seen the writing on the wall when my flight was canceled. Then there was the foul-up with my car reservation, my luggage was stolen, and I was thrown in this jail because some jerk ripped off my driver's license. Now I'm locked in this cell in the middle of a ferocious storm, the rain is pouring in, the ceiling's about to collapse, and you've lost the key. You really think you'll open the lock? Forget it! I'll drown in here if I'm not crushed to death first."

As if she had a direct line with fate, a large piece of plaster fell on Morgan's shoulder just as Ben sprang the lock. He rushed in, and as he touched her shoulder, she screamed, "No! No!"

Ben thought she was telling him not to touch her, but by the time he realized she meant that the door was closing behind him, it was too late. . . .

CANDLELIGHT ECSTASY ROMANCES®

TAKE-CHARGE LADY

Alison Tyler

A CANDLELIGHT ECSTASY ROMANCE®

Published by
Dell Publishing Co., Inc.
1 Dag Hammarskjold Plaza
New York, New York 10017

Dell ® TM 681510, Dell Publishing Co., Inc.

Candlelight Ecstasy Romance®, 1,203,540, is a registered trademark
of Dell Publishing Co., Inc., New York, New York.

ISBN: 0-440-18478-9

Printed in the United States of America

July 1986

10 9 8 7 6 5 4 3 2 1

WFH

To Our Readers:

We have been delighted with your enthusiastic response to Candlelight Ecstasy Romances®, and we thank you for the interest you have shown in this exciting series.

In the upcoming months we will continue to present the distinctive sensuous love stories you have come to expect only from Ecstasy. We look forward to bringing you many more books from your favorite authors and also the very finest work from new authors of contemporary romantic fiction.

As always, we are striving to present the unique, absorbing love stories that you enjoy most—books that are more than ordinary romance. Your suggestions and comments are always welcome. Please write to us at the address below.

Sincerely,

The Editors
Candlelight Romances
1 Dag Hammarskjold Plaza
New York, New York 10017

CHAPTER ONE

Her day began disastrously and went from bad to worse. The Continental Airlines strike, which was supposed to have been settled by midnight, was still in full swing. The union decided at the last minute to hold out for classier uniforms for the flight attendants. So, while the stewards and stewardesses hunkered down to some serious bickering over jackets and skirts, Morgan Gerard was forced to jockey around the L.A. airport at the last minute trying to come up with another flight to New York.

She was on standby all morning, finally nabbing a flight on Trans Oceanic at noon. The plane sat on the runway for another hour before getting clearance to take off.

Twenty minutes in the air the flight attendants were racing up and down the aisles with lunch platters, now nearly two hours late. Just as a pretty blond stewardess was setting down Morgan's lunch on her fold-out tray, the seat-belt sign flashed on and the pilot's baritone voice came over the loudspeaker announcing some rough weather over the Rockies. At the same moment the plane hit an air pocket. Only those passengers fortunate enough still to be waiting for their hot, open-faced turkey sandwiches and cranberry sauce were saved; all the others got at least half their lunch in their laps. The brown gravy, which had looked less than appetizing on the white plastic plate, looked particularly revolting on Morgan's white linen skirt.

There was a mad rush for the four bathrooms in the tourist-class section, and outraged passengers picked off turkey, cranberry sauce, and peas from their clothing as they waited their turn to wash off the damage as best as they could. By the time Morgan managed to get into one of the tiny bathrooms, the gravy had congealed on her skirt and she noticed that her soft gray-blue blouse had a glob of cranberry decorating her breast pocket. She looked for all the world as if she'd been stabbed. A fitting image, she thought ruefully, since she'd been feeling just that way for the past three days.

She hadn't wanted this New York assignment in the first place. Four days ago she'd been getting her wardrobe ready for the French West Indies. Fremont Studios was doing a movie which had two weeks of location shooting in such sunswept tropical isles as Martinique, Guadeloupe, and St. Martin. Morgan's job was to go down a few weeks ahead, check out the locations, line up some locals to act as extras, and acclimate the townsfolk to the onslaught of a movie crew.

Most of the time her job was a cinch. Everybody, it seemed, wanted to be in the movies. And the town fathers usually got a kick out of seeing their little villages on the silver screen, not to mention that the influx of movie people with lots of ready cash did not hurt a town's economy.

Morgan had been looking forward to a few weeks of emerald waters, tropical sun, and the intoxicating beat of calypso music. Especially as her last assignment had been six weeks in a godforsaken little town one hundred miles from civilization, if one could call Juneau, Alaska, civilization. Morgan couldn't.

The morning of the day she was to take off for Martinique, Harris Palmer called her into his elegant office suite at Fremont Studios—replete with an ebony desk that looked like a dark, glistening pool, Moroccan leather walls, and two stunning Picassos "to lighten up the place," as he was fond of saying. All Morgan had to do was take one look at his effervescent smile to know that she might as well tear up her plane ticket. Palmer, a man whose bow tie was lost under his double chin, was not one of those jolly fat men. He was a tough-as-nails VIP who hadn't made it to the top by glad-handing people. And he never smiled unless he was about to stab you in the back.

He didn't take long to wield the knife.

"Rocky Bluff, New York?" She gave him such a wide-eyed stare that one of her contact lenses dislodged and fell into the lush black carpet. The conversation went on hold while she took to her knees to search for it. Palmer walked over and helped her to her feet.

"Don't worry about it, honey. I'll spring for a

9

new one for you." His smile broadened, a bad sign. "Hey," he went on in his smooth Hollywood croon, "I know you were looking forward to Martinique, but Fred West asked for you specifically. He's the biggest producer our studio has in its fist. You don't turn a man like West down."

"But Rocky Bluff, New York?" Morgan grimaced. "That's a far cry from tropical splendor."

"It's a great little town. Right on the tip of the Long Island Sound. Real pretty coastline, great beaches . . . Okay"—he shrugged—"Guadeloupe it's not. But it's a hell of a lot better than Alaska."

Not a great deal better, from her perspective. "Why me? There are a dozen other scouts he could use."

"He feels you're the only one with enough smarts to iron out the rough spots."

Morgan gave him a wary look.

"The thing is," Palmer continued, "West's director for his new film, Lloyd Bergson, spent several summers as a kid in Rocky Bluff. He's got his heart set on doing a good half of the film there."

Morgan narrowed her blue eyes, tucking a strand of chestnut-brown hair behind her ear. With only one contact lens Harris Palmer's smile had blurred, but Morgan didn't need twenty-twenty vision to know that the prolonged upward curve of his generally grim lips meant that there was a tricky catch to this assignment.

"You better give it to me straight." She sighed.

Palmer leaned his bulky frame against the desk. He took a lingering look at Morgan's long, slim legs, her neat, slender body, her attractive if slightly too angular face, and marvelous blue eyes the color of turquoise. In any place but Hollywood, where the competition ran rampant, Morgan Gerard would have attracted attention. Palmer liked her. She had a tough kind of prettiness and a no-nonsense style that was assertive without being unattractively aggressive.

"There might be a few problems," he said slowly. "One in particular." Morgan was amazed at how slowly Palmer could drag out a sentence when he wanted to. "Ben Corbett."

"Who's Ben Corbett?" Morgan asked rapidly, hoping to speed Palmer up a bit.

"He's the mayor of Rocky Bluff. And when Lloyd Bergson called to tell him the good news about using his town in the filming of *Windswept,* Corbett told him to forget it. Seems the mayor of Rocky Bluff has a less-than-positive opinion of us folk in Hollywood."

"So let Bergson get another town in the area. Don't tell me Rocky Bluff is all that unique."

Palmer shrugged. "Come on, Morgan. You know Bergson. He's a nut. When he gets his mind set on something, that's it. He's driving Fred West crazy, if you want the true scoop. Only, keep it under your hat. Bergson's ego gets bruised easily, and we need him to do this picture. He's got the best reputation in town and horror is big in the box office now. This film could get Fremont Studios out of a . . . little slump."

He came over to Morgan and put his fulsome arm around her. She heard the soft crunch of her contact lens under his left foot. Palmer pretended not to notice. He guided her toward the door. "West wanted you to leave for Rocky Bluff tomorrow, but I insisted you take a couple of days to . . . get ready."

Morgan directed a cool gaze at Harris Palmer. "It will take that long for you to get me a new pair of contact lenses. Goldfarb's down on Linda Street has the prescription."

"Sure. Sure. Don't worry about a thing."

"Yeah, I know. Just go have myself a great time, right?" Morgan was searching for her sense of humor, but was having no luck finding it.

Palmer gave her a vigorous nod. "Right. Someone with your experience and powers of persuasion should have no trouble with a small-town mayor. After that it'll be a piece of cake."

If her flight was any indication of the rest of the assignment, she was in trouble, Morgan thought as she toweled off the remainder of the lunch from her clothing. It was hopeless. She'd have to change into a clean outfit in the ladies' room at Kennedy Airport when she landed in New York. The plane lurched again, throwing Morgan against the commode. The pilot's voice came back over the loudspeaker, sounding disturbingly intimate in the close quarters of the bathroom.

"Sorry, folks, but we're going to have to set down in Reno until this storm clears. I estimate a delay of no more than forty-five minutes."

The forty-five minutes dragged into two and a half hours. At this rate Morgan would arrive in

New York close to six P.M., just in time to join the traffic jams heading out of the city.

The pilot made up for some lost time, landing at Kennedy at five twenty-five, the very heart of the rush hour. Morgan was sure her luggage would be lost, and nearly hugged the bald-headed man beside her as she spotted her matched set of gray canvas bags slowly revolving toward her on the baggage conveyor. She hurried into the ladies' room, pulling out a wrinkled but nonetheless clean gray linen dress, and slipped it on. She began to comb her hair only to find that several strands were sticky with gravy. She ended up brushing it into a tidy chignon that hid most of the stiff mess.

As she waited at the car rental counter for the short, stocky manager to straighten out the confusion about the car she insisted had been ordered for her from L.A. the day before, Morgan forgot about her good fortune with her luggage and silently began cursing her lousy luck again. The man behind her was more expressive about his irritation.

"I'd like to get out of here today. How about stepping out of the line, lady?"

"So you can grab the car that's supposed to be mine? Not on your life," she retorted, standing firm.

The manager, anxious to avoid a scene, moved the red tape along, then finally hurried over with a sheaf of papers.

Morgan signed all of the forms and turned to the man behind her to give him one last sneer. He was gone. So was her luggage.

She found the alleged thief at a competitor's rental line. It turned out that he hadn't stolen her bags after all. Not that it was any real consolation. She was still missing her luggage. And the man was extremely rude to her, telling the policeman she'd grabbed to have the thief arrested that he wouldn't be surprised if this was some kind of a con job. He swore he didn't recall seeing any gray luggage while he was in line behind her.

Morgan spent a half hour filling out more forms, knowing damn well she was never going to see her baggage again. As she got on the clogged Long Island Expressway, she wondered what kind of dress shops they had in Rocky Bluff. The thought alone proved too depressing to mull over.

It was almost nine P.M. when she pulled off onto the Rocky Bluff exit. Morgan didn't see any bluff to speak of as she drove into town, but she had to admit the village did have a certain picturesque charm with its neat rows of clapboard houses sitting in the shade of old elms and maples that were in full bloom on this balmy May night.

Morgan had learned from Lloyd Bergson that the sleepy town of Rocky Bluff was a bit more lively in the summer. Vacationers didn't arrive in droves, he had told her, but there was a steady group that returned to their seaside cottages each July to swim, sail, and relax. It was a toss-up which was the most exciting summer activity in Rocky Bluff—the regular Wednesday-night bingo game or the Saturday-night contredanse at the town hall.

Morgan stopped a young man walking his large

14

mutt and asked directions to the Bluffside Inn, where there was supposed to be a room awaiting her. Not that she had great hopes at this point that anything would go according to plan.

It turned out she was right.

Bluffside Inn was seven miles out of town. Befitting its name, it was supposedly on a bluff overlooking the Sound. Morgan was exhausted. The seaside road was empty. She stepped down on the gas, eager to crawl into a nice soft bed and forget this day had ever happened. When she heard the siren behind her, she realized she'd been going maybe ten miles over the speed limit.

The officer, a tall, gaunt fellow with sallow complexion and watery eyes, must have had a bad day himself. He wasn't moved by Morgan's explanations or apologies.

"Can I see your license and registration, miss?"

That was when she remembered that she'd tucked her white pocketbook into her suitcase when she'd changed clothes in the ladies' room at Kennedy, pulling out a gray one to match her new outfit. She had her wallet, but her driver's license was in a separate billfold with her credit cards, and they were now in the possession of the creep who stole her luggage. Morgan tried valiantly to explain about the switch in the bathroom, the hassle at the rental counter, and her stolen bags, but the officer maintained a blank stare. In addition to Morgan's being without her license, it turned out that the manager at the car rental had fouled up the forms, giving her the papers for a Cougar. She was driving a Mustang.

"I'm afraid you'll have to come down to the station with me until we clear this up." He opened her door. "You can ride in the cruiser."

Morgan made a few more vain attempts at gaining his sympathy, then gave up, resignedly walking ahead of him to his car. He opened the rear door. Morgan felt like a criminal as she got in. She had to move his half-eaten dinner of fried chicken over to make room to sit down.

The station house turned out to be a large room with one makeshift cell at the back of the Rocky Bluff General Store. Officer Jack Dunne was reminded by the burly man closing out the register that Police Chief Moe Hawkins had left that afternoon for two weeks of fishing in Connecticut.

"I guess I better call Mayor Corbett and ask him what he wants me to do," Officer Dunne informed her.

Morgan gasped audibly.

Officer Dunne smiled for the first time. "Don't worry. He'll probably let you off with a fine."

"What do you mean, probably?"

His smile disappeared. "He's strong on law and order. He has been known to let a lawbreaker sit in the cage for a night or two"—he motioned to the tiny cell in the corner of the room—"to kind of think things through." He looked at her more closely. "You haven't been drinking, have you?"

"Of course not," she said, affronted. The truth was, she'd love nothing more at that moment than to drown her sorrows in a tall gin-and-tonic, possibly two.

"Corbett really comes down hard on drunk drivers."

"Listen officer," Morgan said with an earnest smile, "don't you think you could give me a break just this one time? It's late. I'm sure the mayor must be settling in for the evening. You wouldn't want to bother him with such a small misdemeanor."

But the officer was already dialing the phone.

She should have known something like this would happen after the disastrous events of the day. Now, to add to all of her other calamities, she was going to have her first meeting with Mayor Ben Corbett in the local jail.

Mayor Corbett arrived at the general store fifteen minutes later. He stayed up front for a good ten minutes having a real friendly chat with the same man who'd reminded Officer Dunne that the chief had gone fishing. His deep baritone voice wafted into the back. Morgan decided he sounded pleasant enough. Surely once she explained . . .

She was in for quite a few surprises. For one thing, Mayor Corbett was much younger and far more attractive than the image she'd conjured up in her mind. It threw her off. She'd expected some fatherly figure with graying hair, ruddy cheeks, and nice country manners. Ben Corbett looked to be in his mid-thirties, was at least six feet tall with an athletic build, light-brown hair, and deep-brown eyes. He had a very distinctive aquiline nose and very thick eyebrows. His were the kind of craggy good looks Morgan associated with a dude ranch in Montana instead of a sleepy little town on Long Island. More than once she found herself staring. It was his sensual eyes and half smile that were disturbingly insinuating.

As for his pleasant country manners, they were decidedly absent as soon as Morgan explained who she was and what had happened. After patting his officer on the back for a job well done, he sent him merrily off to catch more criminals and finish his chicken dinner. Then he sat down behind the ancient wooden desk and gave Morgan a long, hard stare.

It took a while for Morgan to figure out why Mayor Corbett was so enraged. After all, she hadn't committed the crime of the century. It turned out not to be her lack of a driver's license and mistaken registration forms that really got his goat, but her audacity at showing up after he'd told "those clowns" in Hollywood in no uncertain terms that he wasn't about to have his fine old town turned into a three-ring circus.

"Hold on a second," she said heatedly. "The way I heard it from Bergson, you weren't exactly taken with the idea, but he believed you would keep an open mind about it. There are a lot of advantages—"

"Save it," he said sharply. "You've got more pressing problems, the way I see it."

Morgan gave him a wary look. "I explained about the license and the mix-up with the car rental papers. If you don't believe me, you can check with the rental office. And the airport authorities will confirm the theft—"

He cut her off again. "Be that as it may, Miss

18

Gerard, speeding, driving without a license, and possessing erroneous registration papers are all against the law. And we take the law seriously in this town."

"So I've heard," she muttered sarcastically.

He ignored the remark. "It's punishable by a fine of up to five hundred dollars and/or a jail sentence of up to thirty days."

Thirty days was exactly the amount of time she had to convince Corbett to allow Bergson to film in Rocky Bluff; she had little hope of doing that from a jail cell.

Morgan found herself disliking Ben Corbett more and more. She decided he was pompous, vain, rigid, and about as warm as one of those snow caps she'd gotten to know so well out in Alaska. Still, she had no intention of spending the next thirty days in a jail cell in the back of the Rocky Bluff General Store. She decided to appeal to his sense of fair play, if he had any.

"Please, Mayor Corbett, can't we behave like two rational people? I'm only out here to do my job."

"So am I," he said coolly.

Morgan worked hard at holding her temper, since Ben Corbett was holding all the aces. "I'll be happy to pay the fine," she said with as much equanimity as she could muster.

His brown eyes narrowed. "I guess you people are used to getting off the hook by greasing palms with a little cash."

Morgan glared at him, fingers pressed to her temple. "I am not 'you people.' And for your information, Mr. Corbett, I don't get into the kind of situations where the need to—to 'grease palms' even comes up."

"From where I'm sitting, you're in one of those situations now," he pointed out blithely.

Morgan came to the fast conclusion that Mayor Ben Corbett not only lacked any sense of fair play, he was greatly enjoying himself at her expense. She was astute enough to realize it would be a bad move on her part to call him on it. She needed another angle, something that would put him on the defensive.

"I'm well aware of my current dilemma. Just as you're aware that a speeding ticket usually means a twenty- to fifty-dollar fine. The fact that you're asking me to fork up five hundred could be seen as extortion." She allowed a pregnant pause. "I doubt you'd like me to press the issue with my attorney."

He smiled sardonically. "The five-hundred-dollar fine has nothing to do with your speeding ticket. You'll have to pay separately on that. The five hundred is for driving without a license or registration."

Morgan groaned. "Didn't you listen to one word I said? My license is in a purse that was stolen at the airport, along with every last item of clothing I brought with me on this trip, including a gravy-stained linen skirt and a cranberry-smeared blouse, thanks to one hell of a plane trip. I don't even have a toothbrush to call my own, never mind a driver's license." She gathered herself up, refusing to fall apart at the seams.

Ben Corbett's expression softened for the first time. "I'm sure I can dig up a toothbrush for you."

Sensing that she was finally getting somewhere, Morgan decided it was worth falling apart at the seams a little after all. "I'd very much prefer to go out and get my own." She forced a little catch in her voice and gave Ben Corbett her best damsel-in-distress smile.

"I'm afraid that won't be possible, Miss Gerard. At least not tonight."

"You don't mean you're honestly going to—to lock me up here for the night?"

"You might as well learn the lesson now as later. Then you can report back to your Hollywood crew that this town takes a harsh view of lawbreakers. We don't look the other way. In fact, we keep a close eye on everything that goes on in this town. And when someone breaks the law, they have to face the consequences. It's as simple as that. To-morrow, I'll bring you over to the county judge and he can decide on a ruling."

Morgan's temper erupted. Her turquoise eyes seething at him, she exclaimed, "You—you can't do this to me! I know what you're up to, Mister Corbett. And let me tell you something, you're not going to get away with it!"

Ben Corbett tipped back his wooden seat and retrieved the cell key from the top desk drawer. "And just what am I supposedly up to, Miss Gerard?" he asked as he meandered over to the cell, opened it, and held the barred door for her.

Fuming, Morgan stormed over to him. "You're trying to humiliate me. Spending the night in jail has nothing to do with my supposed crimes, and you know it. You're just planning to have yourself a good laugh at having one-upped 'one of those Hollywood people.' But let me tell you something, Mayor Corbett: You hold an elected position in this town, and after I get finished telling the folks of Rocky Bluff about all the fame and fortune to be garnered with a big movie filming here, they're not going to be pleased with your veto."

Ben Corbett grinned. He had to admit Morgan Gerard was on target. He could just as well have let her go, simply ordering her to appear in court in the morning. Not that he had any intention of letting her know that. He did want her to go back to L.A. and tell Bergson it wouldn't be worth the hassle to film his movie in Rocky Bluff. Ben was sure there were a large number of townsfolk who felt the same way he did about it, but he was also aware that Morgan Gerard could stir up trouble, causing the town to splinter off into opposing groups. She was a very determined young woman. He wondered if she'd be as feisty after a long night in jail.

He opened the cell door wider. "There's an extra blanket on the shelf over the cot."

"Wait one minute. I don't remember being read my rights. And—and I'm supposed to be allowed to call my lawyer," she said indignantly.

"Your rights?" He grinned. "Right."

Morgan had no idea if he gave her the correct spiel, but it sounded official enough. She shrugged.

"And the call to my lawyer?"

He twisted the phone around to face her.

"That's a ten-cent call you're allowed," he commented in that same sardonic fashion.

"I'll call collect," she retorted.

Morgan's index finger remained poised on the dial. She really didn't have a lawyer out West, and she certainly didn't know any on the East Coast. She finally decided to call Harris Palmer, since he'd gotten her into this mess in the first place.

She was relieved to find Palmer still at his office, but her relief was short-lived.

"I'll give Joe Irwin a call, Morgan, but I doubt there's much he's going to be able to do about the situation tonight. I'll have him get someone in New York to come out first thing tomorrow."

"You mean you're going to let me sit in jail all night?" she shrieked.

Ben Corbett, sitting off to the side, mumbled something about there being a perfectly good cot in the cell so she could stretch out comfortably. Morgan glared at him, then focused her glare back on the receiver.

"Morgan, relax. It won't be so bad. Something to tell the little kiddies about one day."

Morgan knew he must be smiling again.

"You're just full of comforting thoughts," she said icily. "I'd better see that lawyer here tomorrow morning, or as soon as I get out of this place I'm hopping the next plane to L.A."

Ben Corbett smiled at her words. But at that point Morgan couldn't care less if he got his way. Let them all go fly a kite. She slammed the phone back in the cradle.

"I guess I'll be taking you up on your accommo-

23

dations for the night," she said with a cool shake of her head. A few strands of damp hair loosened and fell against her cheek, reminding her of the shampoo she'd planned on having tonight. She gave a resigned sigh and walked toward the cell.

"Your belt."

"What?" Morgan looked over at Corbett in confusion.

"I'll have to ask you to remove your belt."

"You've got to be kidding." But she could see from his expression that he was serious. Morgan had thought she'd managed to get her temper under control, but this was the last straw. She fumbled furiously with the clasp on the belt and literally threw it at him. "Anything else? Oh, you'll probably want my jewelry," she said tersely, lifting her gold chain over her head, tugging off her college ring, twisting off her bracelet, and slamming them down on the desk. "And I suppose if I were desperate enough to hang myself I could use my panty hose." She turned her back to him, ready to pull them off too.

Ben Corbett cleared his throat. "That, uh, won't be necessary."

When Morgan turned around he was smiling broadly. He opened the cell door wider still. "I'll go see about a toothbrush for you out front. I won't be long."

Morgan had no choice but to step inside the cell. "Don't hurry back on my account." She was in a five-by-eight cinder-block room, improbably painted with a thick coat of pastel pink enamel. It was lit by a caged bare bulb at the center of the

24

ceiling. There was a metal cot attached to the far wall, with a plastic-covered foam slab mattress on it. The cell provided absolutely no privacy, as the entire front wall was constructed of the same metal bars as the door itself.

"Hey, this is no bed of roses for me either," Ben said. "We're short-staffed this week. I'll have to sack out on the couch in here to keep an eye on you."

"You mean, with all the rest of the indignities I'm being made to suffer, I'm going to have to spend the whole night with you?" she asked in choked anger.

Ben Corbett grinned. "Only in a manner of speaking, Miss Gerard. Unless that was some kind of a bribe." He gave Morgan a provocative wink, watching her silently fume as he locked the cell door.

CHAPTER TWO

"Soft, medium, or hard?"

Morgan, who'd sat down wearily on the cot, looked up sharply at the sound of Ben Corbett's deep voice. She gave him a stinging glance. "What?" Then she saw the assortment of toothbrushes in his hand.

"We're well stocked here," he said with an amused expression. "You even have a choice of colors."

"How fortunate can I get?"

He walked over to the cell, displaying the brushes. "So?"

"I don't really give a damn."

He pulled one out, extending it toward her. "I prefer the hard bristle, myself."

"You would."

He laughed. "If you promise to behave, I'll let you out to brush and clean up."

"Clean up? Now, that's a laugh." She stood and walked over to the bars. When Ben opened the door, Morgan stepped out.

"Aren't you going to handcuff me?" she asked sarcastically.

"It's hard to shower and brush your teeth with handcuffs on. But if you're thinking of trying any funny stuff, forget it. There's only a narrow vent window in the bathroom, and I doubt even someone as"—he gave her an infuriatingly thorough survey—"as slender as you could squeeze out. Besides, I'll be waiting just outside the door."

No doubt trying to stare through the peephole, Morgan thought. However, she was so happy to hear him mention a shower she decided not to push her luck by sharing the thought with him.

Ben led her out of the office and then through a tidy storeroom to what turned out to be a surprisingly clean bathroom replete with shower stall. As she stepped inside the open door, Morgan glanced up at the narrow window. He was right about her not slipping through. Not that she had any intention of trying it. She could just see the mayor's gleeful smile when he personally tracked her down, which she had no doubt he would. He was just the type to do the job himself. Anyway, she was confident Harris Palmer would keep his word and see to it that his L.A. lawyer got some legal help out to the boondocks in the morning to straighten out the mess. At worst she'd end up with a sizable fine—which she'd be pleased to charge to her expense account.

Ben remained outside the door. "I took the liberty of picking out a shampoo for you. It's in the shower. And a new towel and some toothpaste."

Morgan nodded. "I'll reimburse you," she said coolly.

"Your toothbrush."

He was still holding all three types.

Morgan gave them a closer look and took one from him. "I prefer the soft bristle myself."

Ben gave her another of his assessing glances. Then he smiled broadly. "You would."

"Very amusing," Morgan snapped, stepping further into the room and slamming the door in Ben Corbett's face. She turned the bolt and, noting the keyhole, made certain to drape the towel over the doorknob, blocking any possibility of a view.

As she showered, Morgan felt her spirits reviving. A night in a jail cell, she reflected as she washed her hair, wasn't so awful. Okay, so it wasn't exactly the Ritz—or even the Bluffside Inn—but it was clean and she had to admit the cot had a decent foam pad and there was a fresh sheet on the shelf. If she could get the mayor to do a vanishing act, she might actually get some much-needed sleep. Somehow, she doubted Corbett would oblige. She didn't buy, for one minute, the line he'd given her about having to keep an eye on her. Just where would she go, locked up in a jail cell? No, he was just trying to intimidate her, make her first hours in Rocky Bluff so miserable she'd give up and go home.

But Morgan Gerard didn't intimidate so easily. Maybe she'd had a minute or two there when she'd considered giving in, but now that the last remains of that turkey lunch had been washed away, Morgan felt ready to tackle the world again. And more than ready to tackle the irritatingly smug Mayor Ben Corbett.

As she stood in front of the mirror and took a

look at her wet, tangled hair, she remembered that Corbett had taken her purse from her. She looked around the bathroom to see if he'd thought to supply a brush or comb. No such luck. She smoothed her thick brown hair as best she could and slipped her clothes back on.

She was surprised to find the hallway empty when she opened the bathroom door. For a moment she actually considered taking off, then immediately decided Ben Corbett was probably setting a trap for her. Oh, she could just see it! Two minutes after her flight through the general store into the street, Corbett and Officer Dunne would pick her up. She didn't even have a car outside to make her getaway. Besides, she reminded herself, she'd already figured out she stood to gain nothing by skipping off, whereas Corbett had everything to gain.

Morgan strolled leisurely back into the jail. As she opened the door, a succulent, aromatic scent assaulted her nostrils. For the first time she remembered that she hadn't eaten all day. The last food she'd seen was that open-faced turkey sandwich on her lap. Her stomach made a low, grumbling noise.

Ben Corbett was sitting behind the desk. Spread out in front of him were a large bowl of beef stew, a hefty chunk of French bread, and a can of root beer. Morgan didn't realize she was staring until Ben grinned.

"Hungry?"

Morgan shut her mouth. "What do prisoners get? Bread and water?"

He chuckled, breaking off a piece of the bread. "I don't always play it strictly by the books," he said in a teasing voice. "I'll throw in some stew and we can substitute root beer for water, if you don't mind sharing."

Morgan considered her pride. Then she considered the uncomfortably hollow feeling in her stomach. "Okay. I'll share." She looked over to the cell. "Your place or mine?"

Ben laughed. "You know something, Miss Gerard? You're not so bad after all." His laughter turned into a disquietingly sensual smile as he pulled a chair over to the desk for her. He stared at Morgan, her chestnut hair falling in a profusion of thick waves around her shoulders. When she'd had it pulled back in that slick, sophisticated chignon, he'd assumed her hair was straight. Now he could see that it was almost curly—and strikingly attractive. His smile lingered.

Morgan stared him down, her hand going to her tangled hair. She told herself that his good looks and seductive manner were having absolutely no effect on her. However, her voice sounded oddly husky when she spoke. "You took my purse. Can I have it? I need my brush."

He shook his head, his eyebrows arched. "No, you don't. Your hair looks good like that."

"You like women looking like they've just stepped out of a windstorm?"

"No, like they've just stepped out of a shower, though. Scrubbed clean, all fresh and smelling faintly of Ivory soap." He grinned. "You look . . . real down-home now."

"Down home? Terrific."

"Have a seat. The food's getting cold and I'm starving. We had a no-hitter that ran into overtime tonight. I didn't get in until close to nine. Softball," he added, as she stared blankly at him. "I was just about to eat when Jack phoned to tell me he'd nabbed himself a wrongdoer."

Morgan sat down. "Innocent until proven guilty. Or do you write your own laws out here?"

"I'm willing to reserve judgment." He dished out some stew on a plate and slid it across the desk to her.

"That isn't the way I see it." She reached for a fork and took a large bite of stew. "Mmmm. That's delicious." She took several more eager bites. She really was starving.

Ben watched her with amusement for a couple of minutes. She looked as though she were digging in for her last meal.

"How do you see it?" he asked as Morgan buttered a piece of bread.

"Huh?"

"You said you didn't think that was the way—"

"Oh." She nodded, her mood lifting with each bite. She smiled at Ben, waving her empty fork at him. "You made your mind up the minute you set eyes on me. No, before that. The minute you first heard about Bergson wanting to film out here. You have a head full of preconceived notions about what it will be like, what—"

"Are you always on the job?" He gave her a sly look. "I was only reserving judgment about you, not the film industry."

31

"I'm part of that industry. And did you ever consider that if you can reserve judgment about me, you ought to do it about broader issues?"

He smiled. "In my line I have to take strong stands on certain issues." His expression turned serious as he leaned forward. "Like upholding the peace, making sure people's rights are respected, keeping the town free of crime, drugs . . . you name it. It isn't always easy. And I'm not always successful. Three months ago the Rocky Bluff Bank was held up. It's two buildings down from here. Al Franklin, the guard at the bank, was shot when he raced outside after the crooks. He's nearly seventy, and those bastards knew there was no way in hell Al would be able to stop them. But they hit him anyway."

Morgan looked across the desk. "Is he . . ."

"Dead?" Ben smiled. "No. Al's a tough old geezer. And mighty lucky. The bullet hit his thigh. He was up and hobbling about the next day. Went back to work a couple of weeks later."

"Did the police find the holdup men?"

"Two of the four men were picked up a week later in New Jersey, but they'd ditched the money and they weren't about to steal and tell. The heist was good for over thirty thousand dollars. Banks keep a lot of cash on hand for the late spring and summer trade. The thieves will sit tight, do their time, and go dig up their share in about ten years. Unless their other two buddies get greedy."

Ben shrugged. "The only reason I'm telling you this bit of news is that just that one episode turned this town topsy-turvy. Suddenly our sleepy little oasis felt like a hotbed of crime. People panicked. This is the kind of town where no one bothers much about locking their doors. Half the time they don't even remember to take their car keys out of the ignition when they're in town to pick something up at one of the shops. After the holdup everyone took to bolting their doors, locking their cars, putting all their worldly possessions in safe deposit boxes."

Morgan gave him an exasperated look. "What does a bank holdup have to do with a few honest, hardworking people coming here for a month or so to film a movie? Believe me, the cast and crew are going to be too busy from dawn to dusk to think about robbing banks."

"Look, Miss Gerard, half the people out here are potato farmers. The rest run the few shops in town or work in the post office, the electric company, or down at the harbor. I'd say two thirds of the population lived in Rocky Bluff all their lives, and most of the others migrated out here from the city to find peace and quiet. They were looking for a wholesome place to either raise their families or retire in an atmosphere of tranquility. We're over two hours from New York City, and I'd hazard a guess that less than a handful take a ride into the Big Apple more than once a year. Even the summer folk are a low-key group who spend most of their time on their boats or gathering seashells on the beach."

He paused, shifting back in his chair. "I'll admit there are some people who might get carried away by the idea of seeing glamorous stars parad-

33

ing down the streets. But on the other hand, they're not going to take any too kindly to the drugs, the wild parties, the carrying on that goes on after dusk. And don't tell me those things don't happen, or that all the items you read in the paper about movie people are just bad press."

Morgan sighed. "Okay, I'll admit there's a modicum of truth to those stories on some sets. But Lloyd Bergson runs a tight ship. You'd have his guarantee that his people won't act up."

"And if he's not a man who keeps his word?"

Morgan shrugged. "You could always throw any rabble rousers in jail for the night."

Ben smiled. "I'm afraid our quarters aren't big enough to handle a crowd."

Morgan pushed aside her empty plate and met Ben Corbett's provocative smile. It was clear that while he didn't take very well to her profession, he had less negative feelings about her personally. And from the way those warm brown eyes of his assessed her, she had a fair idea just where his thoughts were running.

Morgan had the distinct impression that if she really turned on the charm and asked him to release her on her own recognizance, he might condescend to let her take a local room for the night instead of having to rough it in a jail cell. But she also knew it would mean one big point scored for his side. She couldn't afford to let him do her any favors, especially as she was damn sure he wasn't the type to let her forget that he had.

Without a word Morgan stood up, walked across the room, and stepped inside the cell, slamming the door shut after her. Ben gathered the plates up and set them on a tray. He lifted Morgan's barely touched glass of soda.

"Should I save it for you in case you get thirsty later?"

"I wouldn't want to trouble you," Morgan said snidely, pulling down the extra blanket from the shelf and painstakingly smoothing out the wrinkles as she laid it over the cot.

Ben picked up the tray. "I'll just run these back home. Otherwise Laura would have a fit. She likes to clean up before she goes to bed."

Morgan looked a little surprised. She hadn't pictured Ben Corbett with a wife. What was he doing flirting with her, when his tidy wife was sitting in the kitchen waiting for her husband to return with his dirty dishes? "Doesn't your wife mind your sleeping here tonight?"

"You mean alone with another woman? A real pretty one, at that?" His eyes sparkled with amusement.

"That's the first positive quality I've noticed in you, Mayor Corbett. You have good taste," she said airily.

Ben laughed. "Hey, what about that toothbrush and that first-class dinner I fed you instead of bread and water? I happen to have a large number of good qualities. I'm honest, generous, dependable. . . ."

"You must have been an A-one boy scout."

"As a matter of fact, I was." He grinned, starting for the door and then coming to an abrupt stop. "Oh, Laura is my housekeeper, not my wife." He

35

looked over his shoulder and gave Morgan one of those provocative smiles of his. "I've managed to stay clear of the marriage trap up to now. I like the role of being the most eligible bachelor in town. There are a number of benefits that go along with the part."

"And I'm sure," Morgan said with a cutting glance, "that you take full advantage of them."

"I prefer taking advantage of all situations, Miss Gerard, rather than being in a position where I end up being taken advantage of. The latter is not a position I find myself in very often."

Morgan was about to ditto that, but she realized it wouldn't sound very convincing standing on the wrong side of jail bars. From the sly smile Ben Corbett bestowed on her, she had a feeling he'd just read her mind. She turned and attacked another wrinkle in her blanket.

"Aren't you going to lock me in?" she muttered as Ben started for the door.

"How careless of me." Ben shook his head, pursing his lips together. He looked down at the tray in his hands. "You know what, Miss Gerard? I'm going to put you on scout's honor. I'm going to trust you to stay put until I get back."

"I was never a girl scout," Morgan said pointedly.

Ben smiled. "I'll trust you anyway. You've got an honest face."

She almost replied, honest enough to let her go, but caught herself in time.

"I only live around the corner," Ben said, balancing the tray on one palm as he opened the door. "I'll be back in a flash."

"I won't wait up for you," she said dryly.

After he'd walked out, Morgan stood and walked over to the barred door. She decided to get her brush from her purse, which Ben had stashed in the top drawer of the desk. She pushed the door. It didn't budge.

The bastard. The cell door was fitted with a self-locking device and he'd known it all along.

Morgan pretended to be asleep when Ben returned fifteen minutes later. She had the cover pulled up to her eyes, but managed to catch a quick glimpse of him spreading a sleeping bag on the old sofa. Her only compensation for this miserable experience was that Ben Corbett was bound to have as lousy a night's sleep as she was going to get.

Despite it's being mid-May, the night air was chilly. And it had started raining, the raindrops making annoying pinging sounds on the metal roof. Morgan heard a sound of water dripping somewhere in the cell, and was grateful that it wasn't leaking over her bed. She was cramped and uncomfortable, but didn't want to move around and give Ben Corbett the satisfaction of knowing she was still awake.

A flash of lightning streaked past her window. The next moment came a crackling sound of thunder, followed by a new torrential burst of rain. Another leak broke out, this one only inches from

Morgan's cot. She actually felt a tiny splatter as the water hit the concrete floor.

"Damn," Ben grumbled.

The next minute Morgan heard him shoving the couch a few feet across the floor. She grinned in the dark and rolled over onto her side.

"You will let me know if you start to drown in there." Ben's voice broke through the stillness between claps of thunder. "We get some wicked spring storms in these parts, and I see the roof in this place needs a bit of plugging up."

There was no point pretending to be asleep; only the dead wouldn't be awakened by this cacophony. Morgan turned onto her back. "How long do they last?"

"Usually a few hours, but a couple of years back we had one of those nor'easters that lasted three days. Rocky Bluff and all the towns around here were declared disaster areas. We lost close to thirty beach cottages, and people were canoeing down Main Street."

"Well, at least I'd be able to get around without any problems. Unless you require canoeing licenses," she added.

Ben laughed softly. "You'd be all right unless you rowed faster than the speed limit."

Morgan laughed too. A splash of water on her cheek stopped her laughter abruptly. "I think I just might drown in here." Several more drops of water landed on her face. "Hey, did you hear me? It's really raining in here. Even a prisoner is entitled to a dry night's sleep," she said hotly, the leaks springing with more fury.

38

"All right. Come on out of there."

"Very funny, Mr. Corbett. The door's locked, and you know it."

"I didn't . . . Oh, it must have clicked into automatic by accident."

"Some accident. Will you unlock this door and get me out of here before this cot starts floating across the cell?"

"Hold on," Ben muttered. "The zipper on my sleeping bag jammed."

She heard him mumble some curses under his breath as he rolled off the couch onto the floor with a thud, finally squeezing himself out of the top of the bag.

The room was pitch-black. Just when Ben could have used a flash of lightning to see his way to the desk, that aspect of the storm had stopped. He stumbled into the wastepaper basket, then slammed his shin against the file cabinet. He let out a rapid spate of curses.

"Why don't you put on a light?"

"In case you haven't noticed, the whole town is in the midst of a blackout. The electricity always goes in these storms." He rubbed his wounded leg and hobbled over to the desk.

"Will you hurry up? It's raining as hard in here as it is outside."

She heard him rummaging around the desk.

"Where the hell did I put the key?" he muttered.

"How am I supposed to know? You had it last." In a lower voice she said harshly, "And you were

39

going to put me on scout's honor. If you'd meant it, I wouldn't be sitting here having a cold shower."

"I didn't realize about the lock. I told you that."

"Look, let's forget it. Just find the key, will you, please?"

"I'm looking. It isn't easy in the—ouch!"

"What happened?"

"I just jammed my finger into something sharp." He felt around carefully to see what it was. "One of Moe's extra fishhooks. Damn, that hurts."

"While you're bemoaning a pricked finger, I'm sitting here with the ceiling starting to crumble around me. Will you hurry up? Look in the drawers. Or maybe it fell on the floor."

"Are you always so damn selfish and impatient?"

"Only when I'm about to have a roof cave in on me."

"Maybe I left it in the storeroom when you went for your shower. Don't go away."

"You're a laugh a minute."

Morgan heard Ben carefully make his way across the room. It took several seconds for him to find the doorknob. While he went off in search of the key, Morgan moved about the cell trying to find a dry spot to wait. It was impossible. Wherever she stood, water splattered on some part of her head or body. She wrapped the already damp blanket around her shoulders, but it afforded little warmth and no comfort. What was taking Ben so long?

Finally, getting nervous, she shouted out his name.

He didn't answer, but she heard his footsteps coming back toward the jail.

"I feel really embarrassed, Miss Gerard. I just can't find the key anywhere."

"If this is some sort of perverse prank you're pulling . . ."

A blinding light aimed at her face made her shut her eyes.

"Calm down. I picked up a flashlight and a few tools from the store, just in case." He walked over to the desk and began hunting for the key. "I can't imagine where the blasted thing went."

"Did you check your trouser pockets?"

He gave her a condescending grimace, but a few minutes later stuck his hands in his pockets again. He came over to the cell. "Maybe I can jimmy open the lock."

"I hope that was one of the skills you learned in your boy-scout days," Morgan said, looking on dolefully as Ben attacked the bolt mechanism.

After five minutes she said, "There must be a locksmith in town. Couldn't you call—"

"The phone lines are down."

"Well, then, go get him. This is an emergency. I've got pieces of plaster in my hair. What if this roof caves in?"

"It's made it through at least fifty storms," Ben remarked, regarding the lock thoughtfully. He slipped a small awl through the hole and began jiggling it. "Anyway, George Klein lives over in the Point Roy area. You'd have to cross Willow Road, and that's always the first one to flood over

41

in one of these storms. Just sit tight. I think we're beginning to have some luck."

"Don't mention luck to me tonight. This will have to go down on record as the worst day of my life. I should have seen the writing on the wall when Continental didn't end that strike. Then there was my lunch landing in my lap, the foul-up with my car reservation, my luggage getting stolen, then being thrown in jail because some idiot gave me the wrong registration papers and some bastard ripped off my driver's license. And now I'm locked in a jail cell in the middle of a ferocious storm, the rain is pouring in, the ceiling's about to collapse, and you really think you're going to get the lock opened. Forget it. I'll probably drown if I don't end up being crushed to death."

As if Morgan had a direct line with fate, a large piece of plaster came smashing down on her shoulder. She screeched in pain just as Ben managed to spring the lock. He rushed in to see if she was all right.

As he touched her shoulder, she screamed, "No! No!"

Ben thought she was telling him not to touch her shoulder because of the pain. It was too late by the time he realized that what she was trying to tell him was that the cell door was shutting. Running true to form it snapped closed with a clank.

CHAPTER THREE

Morgan was too busy coping with the shock of the cell door locking Ben Corbett in with her to think about her injured shoulder—until Ben touched it gingerly.

"Ouch." She jerked her arm back.

"Does it hurt badly?"

Morgan glared at him. "Leave me alone. This is all your fault."

"You better let me see it," he said authoritatively.

"I have no intention of letting you see anything. Besides, it's pitch-black in here," she retorted.

Ben pulled out the flashlight from his back pocket and turned it on. "See? All is not lost."

"No, just one minor thing—the key that would get us out of this chamber of horrors."

Ben flashed the light on her shoulder. There was a small red stain spreading on the gray linen material. He leaned over.

"I told you to leave me alone."

Ben ignored her, gripping her arm. His hold wasn't hard enough to hurt, just firm enough to inform Morgan he was not going to pay any attention to her. He reached for the zipper on her dress.

Morgan shrieked.

"Will you stop acting like a child? You're bleeding all over your dress. Now let me see the damage."

Morgan's shoulder throbbed. She looked over at the bloodstain and groaned. "All right. Switch off the flashlight."

Ben grinned, but did what she asked. He listened to her struggle with the zipper. Then he heard the soft rustle of material. He also heard, or more correctly stopped hearing, the splash of water on the roof. "Hey, I think the storm's letting up."

"It must be my lucky day," Morgan replied, her voice laden with irony. "Okay, put on the light."

Morgan turned her wounded shoulder in his direction. Ben aimed the beam. For a moment he forgot about the injury as he saw Morgan standing in a provocatively alluring pose, her wild mane of hair flowing around her face, her dress pulled down on one side to reveal the sensual curve of her neck. He forced his attention to the wound.

"It doesn't look too bad," he said. "But we should bandage it to stop the bleeding." He rested the lit flashlight on the floor and began unbuttoning his shirt.

"What the hell are you doing?" Morgan's voice registered alarm.

Ben slipped off the shirt. Underneath he was wearing an army-green tank-style T-shirt. It hugged his broad chest and accentuated what

44

Morgan could not avoid noticing was a perfectly magnificent build. When he started to take off the T-shirt, Morgan's hand shot out to his wrist.

Ben cocked his head, meeting her concerned gaze. "It's nice and soft. And very absorbent. Besides, the first-aid kit is out there." He nodded in the direction of the file cabinet.

Morgan dropped her hand, looking away. Ben tore off a long piece of the cloth and carefully, gently, wrapped it around her shoulder. He pulled the dress down a little lower. Morgan stiffened.

"Just making sure the plaster didn't get you anywhere else."

Morgan suddenly felt very vulnerable and very uneasy, locked in with a very good-looking, half-naked man administering to her. She quickly pulled the dress up over her shoulder and moved back. "I'm fine. It didn't get me anywhere else."

Ben took a step closer to her. Without warning he put his arms around her.

"What the hell are you—" Before she finished her sentence, Ben casually zipped up her dress and then immediately dropped his hands. He gave her an innocent smile as she stood glaring at him. She knew damn well he had intentionally wanted to provoke her into thinking he had been about to make a pass.

"How do you feel now?" he asked, tossing what remained of his T-shirt over to the corner and slipping his plaid shirt back on.

Morgan assiduously avoided watching him dress. She was less successful at getting her rapid pulse under control. But she covered her momen-

45

tary physical betrayal with a sharp tongue. "Except for the fact that I'm now staining your T-shirt instead of my dress with blood, I feel cold, wet, miserable, and I think I'm about to get one of my migraines."

Ben gave her a sympathetic smile. "At least the ceiling won't collapse now that the rain's stopped." He took her hand and led her over to the cot. "Come on, sit down. I have a special treatment for headaches."

Morgan stopped abruptly, refusing to sit. "Oh, no. I'm not interested in your special treatments. How about concentrating on getting us out of here? Can't you reach your tools and—and do whatever it was you did before to spring the lock?"

Ben swung the light over to the small pile of tools outside the cell. From this angle he doubted he'd be able to do much. The truth of the matter was, he had no idea what he'd done before to release the door. But he walked over and reached out for the awl. He spent ten minutes fiddling with the lock, but his position was awkward and he couldn't get the instrument in at the right angle. He finally gave up.

Morgan was sitting on the cot, resting her head in her hands. Ben came over and sat down. He took her hands away, placing his own against her temples. Morgan stiffened.

"Relax. My mother used to do this to me when I had a headache," he said, gently but firmly massaging her temples. "It's perfectly respectable. Anyway," he continued, feeling Morgan start to relax, "I'm the mayor of this town. It's going to look bad enough for me that I went and lost the key, then got myself locked in here with you, much less for me to be fool enough to make a pass at my prisoner. I do have my reputation to uphold —along with law and order," he said in a teasing tone. "As it is, the townsfolk are going to have quite a chuckle at my expense." He stopped massaging her temples and looked into her remarkable turquoise-blue eyes. "You know, it is kind of funny when you think about it."

Morgan's wary expression softened, and a half-smile curved her lips. However, she wasn't about to concede the point. Until Ben began to laugh.

"It isn't that funny," Morgan argued, but she found Ben's laughter infectious. "Stop." A laugh erupted, but she tried to pull herself together. Her effort made Ben laugh harder.

She couldn't hold back the laughter then, even though she told herself that nothing about this crazy, maddening day was a laughing matter.

The two of them sank back against the wall, leaning into each other as they laughed and fought for breath at the same time. Morgan wiped at the tears rolling down her cheeks as she tried to stop giggling. She gripped her side, motioning with her other hand for Ben to stop laughing so that she could.

He put his arm around her, taking a deep breath. "Okay, okay." But as soon as he looked at Morgan he broke into laughter again.

Morgan gripped his arm. "This—is—ridiculous."

Ben continued laughing, his arm still around

her. Morgan found herself being pulled closer to him as he tried to stop again.

Her hair brushed against his cheek. Ben, as though noticing it for the first time, realized they were almost embracing. He looked over at his arm around her waist, then down at Morgan's hand still resting on his arm. His laughter began to fade. So did Morgan's.

Her eyes moved to the flashlight. "You're going to—to burn out the batteries," she said raspily. She took her hand from his arm and placed it primly on her lap.

Ben's gaze shifted from the light to Morgan's eyes. He felt her stiffen as she sat straighter, all laughter effectively halted. "I remembered to stick some extra batteries in my pocket," he said in a low voice.

Morgan found the touch of Ben's arm around her unnerving, and yet she made no move to dislodge it. Neither did Ben.

She knew she was experiencing a purely sexual response to Ben Corbett. He was provocatively attractive and sensual, even though as far as his personality went she still considered him an uptight man with a small-town mentality. Her assessment, however, did little to dislodge the tingling sensation deep in her stomach.

This kind of thing had happened to her before—feeling physically drawn to someone she didn't particularly like. After all, living in Hollywood, working around dozens of beautiful men, Morgan would have had to be deaf, dumb, and blind not to fall prey to the charm of a few of the heartthrobs around. But after a couple of painful but well-learned lessons, Morgan stopped letting her emotions alone guide her choice of partners. She had grown far more selective by the ripe old age of twenty-seven.

So what was she doing sitting on a damp cot in a jail cell contemplating what it would be like to be kissed by the mayor of Rocky Bluff? Not only contemplating—hoping to find out. And from the quick glance she allowed herself to take at Ben, she was pretty sure his hopes were running in the same direction.

There was a potent silence as both seemed to be trying to make up their mind about the next step. Morgan shifted slightly toward Ben. She always did have a problem with curiosity. Once she got something in her head, she couldn't let it go. Everything else about this day had been insane, so why stop now?

Ben felt the subtle change in Morgan's position, and he could sense some of the tension leaving her body. Their eyes met. When his hold tightened around her waist, Morgan tilted her head up ever so slightly.

And then suddenly Ben's expression turned wary. Thoughts began flashing through his mind. Was this some kind of game she was playing? One minute she was ranting and raving, the next she was angling for a kiss. Did she think she could con him into going along with the dumb movie business? Oh, no, he thought. He wasn't some naive pushover she could wind around her finger. No deal. He wasn't biting.

He dropped his hand abruptly, leaving Morgan feeling decidedly frustrated and more than a little embarrassed by Ben's obvious rejection.

He got up and retrieved the flashlight. Neither of them said anything. Out of the corner of his eye Ben saw Morgan shiver and pull the blanket up around her shoulders. He aimed the light into the room, resting it on the sleeping bag that was still lying in the middle of the floor. He swung the light around, looking for something long enough to use to reach the bag. Where was that well-placed broom just waiting for a moment like this to be useful?

He made some hapless attempts with the tools he had on the floor outside the cell, then joined Morgan on the cot. "Sorry. I thought I could at least get you something dry to put around you."

Morgan glanced over at the sleeping bag. "It would have been nice." Then she bit down on her lower lip thoughtfully. "Wait. I have an idea." She got up and walked over to the bars. "Come here and help me."

Ben started over.

"Your arm's longer. Reach through," she said, "and see if you can grab those pliers."

Ben pushed his long arm between the bars and, straining mightily, just managed to get hold of the plastic-jacketed handles. "I don't get it. What are you—"

"You'll see," she cut him off, turning toward the cot and pulling the extra sheet down from the shelf.

Two minutes later Morgan had tightly coiled

50

the sheet and handed one end to Ben to fasten securely to the pliers.

"Now what?" he said, giving the sheet a good yank to test his knot.

"Now," Morgan said brightly, "we're going fishing."

Ben grinned. "Hey, it just might work." He started to aim the heavy tool toward the sleeping bag, but Morgan grabbed his arm.

"Uh-uh. My idea, my victory," she announced airily.

Ben turned the pliers over to her. "Be my guest."

She stuck her arm as far out of the cell as it would go, took careful aim, and tossed the pliers over toward the bag. It turned out to be a more difficult task in actuality than theory. As the number of tries mounted, the strain got to her and she broke into a harangue. "If you hadn't decided to be such a damn jerk about this whole thing, we wouldn't be sitting behind bars fishing for a sleeping bag. You could have behaved reasonably instead of trying to teach me a ridiculous lesson. It serves you right. I hope every man, woman, and child in this town has a good laugh over this. I hope it makes the headlines in all the local papers." The bag refused to budge. "In fact, if I have any say in the matter, I'll see to it that the story makes headlines. Damn." She sat back on her heels in frustration, relaxing her grip on the sheet for a moment. "Stop sitting there looking so smug. Here, you try it."

Ben smiled. "I do happen to be a pretty good

fisherman." With a cocky grin he stuck his arm through the bars, threw out the sheet, and swung the pliers back and forth a few times as if he were fly fishing—only upside down, aiming the bulky weight for the center of the bag. It took him a couple of tosses, but he actually lodged the tool dead center, and with a surprising touch of good fortune, the handle of the pliers—as planned— lodged inside the sleeping bag as he reeled in the sheet. He gave Morgan a self-satisfied grin as he tugged the sleeping bag through the bars and handed it to her.

"All right, Mr. Corbett. You're very clever— sometimes," she said with a begrudging nod, clasping the sleeping bag.

"Climb in."

"What about you?"

"We'd make a very tight fit in there," he said, amusement clear in his voice.

"I didn't mean that. We could open it out."

"It is pretty damp and chilly in here." He pressed his hand to his chest. "Especially without my T-shirt," he added with a teasing smile.

"Here," Morgan said, "let's see how clever you are unjamming the zipper."

Ben sat down on the cot and aimed the flashlight on the spot where the zipper had wedged tightly into the seam. In his earlier efforts to open it he'd only succeeded in jamming it more. Now the task seemed hopeless.

He looked up at Morgan. "Forget it. I'll be gallant and freeze in silence." A soft smile curved his lips. "I guess you're right about me deserving this."

Morgan stared at Ben Corbett in surprise. The last thing she'd ever expected was an apology. "I am?"

"That's not saying I condone your speeding through our town the way you did. But as for the license and the registration . . ." He shrugged. "I wanted to give you a hard time so you'd go back and tell Bergson he'd picked himself the wrong town."

She walked over and sat down beside him. "I already figured that out. Believe me, Rocky Bluff wasn't my choice for location shooting. I'm sure there are a dozen other towns around here that wouldn't feel the way you do. If Bergson wasn't so damn stubborn, I wouldn't have been sent out on this dismal escapade. In fact, if I'd had any luck at all, I'd be sipping piña coladas under tropical palms right now. I was supposed to be doing the setup work for a film shooting in the French West Indies."

"What happened?"

"My boss decided I was tough enough and smart enough to deal with an uncooperative small-town Long Island mayor and get him to see his way clear to approve the shoot."

Ben grinned. "How did you plan to go about it?"

"You think I'd be fool enough to give away trade secrets? Oh, no, Mayor Corbett. I may not have asked for this assignment, but I am not going back to L.A. with a demerit on my score card. I still plan to get your permission to let Bergson do his film." She tilted her chin up in determination.

Ben found the tilt very becoming. Actually, he found a number of qualities about Morgan Gerard very becoming. Not that he had any intention of letting her use those qualities to get him to change his mind. On the other hand, since she fully intended to stick around awhile and try to convince him to do just that, he had to admit the idea of spending more time with the lovely Miss Gerard held a definite appeal.

Ben stared at her, then slowly lowered his face to hers, about to kiss her. Morgan's head held its tilt. This time Ben didn't change his mind midmotion. And Morgan realized just how disappointed she'd been before when he had. He put his arms around her, his lips finding hers. The sleeping bag slipped to the floor. The flashlight followed, the clank dislodging the batteries and sending the room into darkness again.

All of their senses were focused on touch. As their kiss deepened, Ben ran his hands through Morgan's silky hair, then skimmed her shoulders, careful not to press too heavily on the one that was bandaged.

But Morgan was not feeling any pain now. Ben's embrace and warm, demanding lips were intoxicating. She felt suddenly light-headed, almost dizzy. She couldn't remember the last time she had actually swooned like this in a man's arms. A strong, sensual, intensely attractive man's arms, she mused as his lips left hers to run a string of kisses down her neck.

Ben breathed in the scent of her perfume—a hint of lavender mingled with spice. Unusual. But then, Morgan Gerard impressed him as an unusual woman. And she was a fantastic kisser.

He sought her lips again, this time finding them slightly parted. As he held her closer he could feel her thighs press against his. Her arms moved around his neck, her grip tightening as his tongue slipped past her lips into the inviting warmth of her mouth.

For those few magic moments Morgan lost all sense of where she was and what had gone on before Ben's lips captured hers. His kisses were so intense and yet at the same time so tender that she was left feeling almost giddy with delight. In a day filled from the start with lousy luck, she wasn't about to balk at this kind of a finish. Responding with a desire that she'd only barely realized an hour ago, she kissed Ben back with ardor.

When he finally released her, Morgan sat breathless. She was thankful for the darkness, needing a few minutes to pull herself together. In the heat of the moment the passion had made sense, but now she was at a complete loss to figure out just what the sense of it was. Ben Corbett was practically a stranger. A stubborn and uncooperative stranger at that. And she was sure she could come up with a long list of reasons why she wouldn't like him even if they weren't on opposing sides. It was just that she couldn't quite think straight at the moment.

It didn't help matters that Ben took her hand between his. There was an amused tone in his voice when he said, "I guess this is a first for both of us."

Morgan pulled her hand away. She made a feeble attempt at smoothing down her hair. "I thought you weren't going to make a—a pass. Your reputation and all." She wished her tone weren't so breathy.

"That was more than a pass," he said. "And it felt pretty mutual. What about your reputation?"

Morgan had to laugh. "I figure I'm already a marked woman, locked in jail and all, so I threw caution to the winds—for a minute anyway." Her tone took on a note of severity. "Don't let it go to your head, Mayor."

He touched her cheek. "I'm afraid it already has." He pulled her to him again, but this time she struggled out of his grasp.

"I don't know why I let you kiss me. . . ."

"Or why you kissed me back?"

Morgan glared at his shadowy image. "Or why I kissed you back. This has been the strangest, worst day of my life."

"Was I that bad?"

Morgan grimaced. "You know damn well what I'm talking about, just as you know that you have a —a certain amount of sex appeal."

"I do?"

"So do a lot of men I meet. It's not the cover that counts, as the saying goes, it's what's inside."

"What's so bad about my insides?"

"You're very small-minded. All you can think about is your precious law and order. You're so worked up about that one small bank robbery that now any event that's a little new and different happening here has you in a veritable panic."

"I'm not in a panic. And it wasn't a small robbery. Besides, I only used that as an example of how easily this town can be disrupted. And now that everyone's settling back into their normal routine you want to turn this place into a three-ring circus for a few months."

"Two at the most," she argued. "And the cast and crew can find quarters outside of the area. I'll make sure that every single person knows you run a clean, quiet, proper little town. There won't be any problems, I promise. You might even discover it could be good for the town. Bring in some life, add a few sparks."

"We've managed pretty well without the sparks, thanks."

"And it will help the economy. Restaurants, shops, gas stations . . . Hey, some of the townspeople will even make some money working as extras." She cocked her head. "If you give your okay, I'll try to wangle you a small talking role."

Ben laughed. "You make it all sound so tempting."

"Really, Ben. I'm serious. It could be a lot of fun. I could stay around to keep tabs on everyone, make sure they all behave themselves. Will you at least think about it?"

"And what will you do while I'm thinking?"

Morgan grinned. "Well, if I ever get out of jail, I'm supposed to cover the area, do some videotaping, study the locales that fit Bergson's needs, line up the extras, make arrangements for where people can stay . . . I play an all-around Gal Friday. But I draw the line at fetching coffee."

"Sounds like a lot of work."

"It's fun and it pays well. And I get to see the world without joining the WACs."

There was a moment of silence.

"Okay," Ben said softly.

"Okay? You mean—"

"I mean I'll think about it. You can look around while I weigh all the pros you can come up with against all the cons I can count."

Morgan leaned over and kissed Ben demurely on the lips. "I take back that line about you being small-minded."

Ben returned the kiss, his not nearly as demure. "I might not change my mind, you know."

"I like to think positively." She laughed softly. "Even on the worst of days." Shivering a little, she leaned closer to him.

Ben reached down for the sleeping bag. Not bothering with the zipper, he took his Swiss army knife from his pocket and cut down through the binding. Getting to the bottom, his hand touched something hard. His fingers reached around the object.

In the darkness he smiled broadly. It was the key to the cell. During his contortions earlier in the evening to get out of the jammed bag, the key must have fallen out of his pocket. It was the one place he'd never thought to look.

Morgan had heard him rip through the zipper. She took hold of one corner of the sleeping bag, then leaned back against the wall and draped the material over her and curled her legs up on the cot. She moved slightly to the right to make more space for Ben. "Do you have enough room?" she asked softly, her voice hinting of her awkward discomfort but still carrying an enticing ring of warmth.

Ben continued to palm the key as he felt the pressure of Morgan's hip against him. It really would be a lousy thing to do. . . . Then again, morning was only a few hours away. Morgan pressed closer. He slipped the key into his pocket.

Morgan welcomed the comforting warmth of the makeshift blanket as well as the enticing warmth of Ben's arms. Closing her eyes, she rested her head on his shoulder and fell asleep.

CHAPTER FOUR

Morgan awoke to the sound of metal rubbing against metal. She opened her eyes, sleepily gazing toward the direction of the sound. She sat up abruptly, staring in shock.

"I don't believe it."

Ben, who'd just unlocked the cell door and was painstakingly trying to swing it open as silently as possible, stopped in his tracks at the sound of Morgan's voice.

He looked over his shoulder, casting her a sheepish smile. "I—uh—found the key."

Morgan leapt off the cot. "You had it the whole time? How could you—"

"Whoa." He held up his hand. "I found it in the bottom of the sleeping bag. It must have—"

"Just when did you find it?" she asked accusingly. And then, not giving him a chance to answer, she barreled on. "You let me sleep in this damp, cold cell all night long when the whole time you could have let me out!"

"I was in there too."

"Small comfort," she retorted icily, starting across the cell to the open door.

Ben blocked her way. "Settle down a minute, Morgan. Where do you think you're going? The court doesn't open until ten." He glanced at his watch. "And it's barely six in the morning."

Morgan was so incensed, she couldn't find words. Doing an abrupt about-face she stormed over to the cot and sat down resolutely.

"Fine," she said haughtily. "I'll wait for my lawyer." Her turquoise eyes narrowed. "I have quite a few things to tell him about my night in jail."

Ben was still standing at the open door. He smiled broadly at her. "I was going to suggest, before you jumped to conclusions, that we head back to my place and have some breakfast. You could even stretch out for a while in a dry, clean bed before I take you to see Judge Kallen. Of course, you'd still be in custody and I'd have to keep a close eye on you. . . ." He rubbed the back of his hand across his lips, regarding her contemplatively. "But you're very easy on the eyes."

Morgan folded her arms across her chest. "I'd rather have bread and water and this cot, if it's all the same to you."

Ben grinned. "Suit yourself." He made no move.

Morgan stared out of the dirty cell window, but she could feel his eyes on her. Not looking at him, she muttered, "Don't let me keep you. Now that you've conveniently found the key, you can lock me back in and go stretch out on your nice dry bed. I imagine you didn't sleep particularly well either."

Ben walked over to her. "You're right."

She found his nearness more unsettling than she

61

cared to admit. While she hadn't gotten much sleep during the night, she had found it cozy indeed, snuggling up against Ben Corbett's broad chest and feeling his arm resting lightly but protectively around her waist as he dozed off and on. In those twilight hours, holding on to each other hadn't seemed any stranger or more foolish than those few passionate kisses. Now, as the bright sun began streaming through the dismal little cell, Morgan felt very much the fool.

"Given what I'd been through yesterday," she said in a low voice, "I think that I had some excuse for behaving so—so uncharacteristically. I read somewhere that captives occasionally respond in —in physical ways to their . . . jailers. I was depressed, angry, scared, and exhausted. You intentionally put me in a very vulnerable situation and then proceeded to take advantage of me." She glanced up at Ben for a brief second, then stared back out the window. "What do you have to say for yourself, Mayor Corbett?" she asked in a formal tone, drawing her shoulders back and tilting her chin up in the way that Ben found so beguiling.

"I guess it's a poor excuse," he said softly, his hand lightly cupping her chin, "but I found you irresistible. You have a certain way about you, a certain look that kind of got me right here." He thumped his heart. "Believe me," he added, "my behavior last night wasn't any more characteristic for me than yours was for you."

Morgan pushed his hand away. "I thought you were the town's most eligible bachelor."

"Yeah, but you haven't seen the eligible bachelorettes," he teased.

Morgan grimaced. "I haven't seen much of anyone or anything since I landed in this town," she reminded him.

"Come on. Let's go have some breakfast. How are you at cooking omelets?"

"Lousy. I don't like to cook."

"Who cooks for you when you're home?"

"I'm not home all that much. I probably average ten months out of twelve on the road."

Ben took her hand. "Well, then, it will do you good to have a nice home-cooked breakfast. Today's Laura's day off, but I'm not too bad around a kitchen."

"All right," she said begrudgingly, the thought of even five more minutes in that cell making her shiver. "But I'm still mad as hell about you holding out on that key." She stood up, then came to a sudden halt. "In fact, I'm mad as hell about the whole thing. You admitted yourself that you tossed me in jail purely out of spite."

"Well, that's one interpretation of my motives. I saw it as a way to make my point clear about this being a law-abiding community. I only wanted to be sure you didn't miss the point." He glanced down at her with his dark, compelling brown eyes. "Anyway, I did apologize for being a little rough on you. And I was telling you the truth about finding the key in the sleeping bag. By that time the rain had stopped and . . . and I guess the idea of snuggling together on that cot didn't seem like a bad one. It was worth not getting much sleep." He

63

took her hand and their eyes met. "I'll make a deal with you, okay? You stay off the road until you get another license and straighten out the registration, and I'll give the judge a call and explain the extenuating circumstances. You'll have to pay the speeding ticket, but I think he'll waive the other charges."

"How am I supposed to get around and check out the town if I can't drive? It could take several days to get another license." Her eyes narrowed. "Or is this your way of effectively keeping me from doing my job?"

Ben shook his head. "My, my, you have a suspicious mind."

"I wonder why."

"I'm willing to offer my services as all-around guide if you stop thinking the worst of me. You do seem to get into strange situations on your own, Miss Gerard. I wouldn't want any more bad luck to befall you while you're a visitor in my town."

"What else could happen to me?" She smiled ruefully. "I feel pretty sure I covered all bases yesterday."

Ben led Morgan out of the cell. "Maybe our town is bewitched," he said lightly. "Did you ever think that's why Bergson is so determined to film his horror movie here? He did write me all about how he used to spend summers here as a kid and how he was convinced this town was the only place that would effectively capture the special mood he needed."

"He's particularly interested in a huge white

elephant of a house out near the bluff. Which, he informed me, is now town property."

Ben nodded. "The old Caspel estate. It's quite a relic. Woodrow Caspel died five years ago and left the estate to the town. He wanted to see the place turned into a folk-art museum, but the town inspector says the building would need a lot of work to get it into shape, which means a lot of money. The issue comes up for debate every year and inevitably gets vetoed. Most voters think the money could be put to more practical uses. And then there are some people around here who believe the old place is haunted and they don't want to rile up the ghosts. I guess that's why Bergson's so hot on filming there," he added with a wink. "He's probably hoping to get some of the ghosts as extras."

Morgan glanced at him, her turquoise eyes sparkling. "I wouldn't be surprised. Bergson's the king of horror. Maybe he's so successful because he knows something we don't."

Ben gave Morgan an amused smile. "What about you? Do you believe in ghosts?"

"After yesterday I'd believe anything's possible." Her cheeks colored slightly as she realized Ben could interpret that statement in various ways.

He moved closer. Those big brown eyes of his were studying her face, enjoying, no doubt, the blush that was a sure sign of her vulnerability, a sign that rarely occurred. He was about to say something when the door opened. Officer Dunne, the cop who'd picked Morgan up for speeding last night, stood at the entry. His eyes moved from the open cell to Ben and Morgan.

"I, uh, just thought I'd stop by to see how things went in that storm last night and if you wanted me to escort the, uh, prisoner to the courthouse later, Mayor Corbett."

"That's all right, Jack. I'm going to escort our prisoner over to my place for breakfast." He looked at Morgan. "I think Miss Gerard's night in jail has taught her a lesson. She's agreed to watch her speed and pay the fine. And I've agreed to give her another chance. But the next time you catch her racing through town—after she gets her new license and the right registration—we're going to toss the book at her. We'll lock her up and throw the key away."

It took Jack a minute to realize Mayor Corbett was kidding. Oh, the mayor had a good sense of humor and did a fair share of ribbing, but Corbett rarely kidded about prisoners who broke the law. Then again, Jack Dunne couldn't remember a prisoner in the Rocky Bluff jail who looked anything like Morgan Gerard. Even after a rough night in a leaky cell, the woman was a real showstopper. He couldn't blame Corbett for going light on her.

Morgan maintained a wry expression during Ben's little speech. Then she looked across at Officer Dunne. "Perhaps you'd do me a favor and see if you could put the wheels in motion for me to get another license? You do remember that my first one was stolen. And," she said, pulling out the top drawer of the desk and reclaiming her purse, her jewelry, and her belt, "if you could call about my car and get the registration straightened out I'd be very grateful." She slipped on her belt, catching Dunne's swift glance over at Ben and Ben's subtle nod.

"Thanks," she said casually, slipping on her watch and heading toward the door. She looked over her shoulder at Ben, who was sharing a smile with the police officer. "I'm ready if you are."

"Two omelets coming up."

She stopped in the bathroom to wash up and give her hair a thorough brushing. Her dress looked much the worse for wear, but she'd cope with that problem later, she decided. Ben was waiting for her in the general store. He was holding up a pair of jeans.

"I think these will fit you. And," he said, plucking a red T-shirt from the bin, "this seems appropriate." The shirt had the words, ROCKY BLUFF emblazoned in white lettering across the front.

Not exactly the outfit Morgan would have selected, her tastes running more toward understated sophistication, but it was a lot better than the wrinkled, bloodstained dress she was wearing.

"You can shower and change back at my place if you like."

She nodded, walking over and taking the clothes from Ben. She checked the price tags, then opened her purse to take out some money.

"I put it on my account," Ben said. Then, seeing her eyes narrow, he added with a smile, "We can settle up later."

She handed him a twenty-dollar bill. "Let's settle now. I like to keep my accounts balanced. And I don't like owing people, it puts them at an advantage."

He took the money and laughed. "This leaves me owing you seven cents. But I'm willing to give you the advantage."

Morgan grinned. "I don't believe that for one minute."

"Smart woman."

They had started out the door when Morgan remembered the lawyer who was supposed to show up this morning to bail her out of jail and straighten out the charges. Thanks to Ben she wouldn't need him now. Of course, thanks to Ben she'd gotten into this mess in the first place. However, Morgan wasn't the type to hold a grudge. And today was a new day.

She called Harris Palmer's exchange and left word for him that she'd handled the problem herself. It didn't hurt her image with her boss for him to believe she'd maneuvered her way out of a jam without needing to be rescued. One small step toward her goal had been accomplished. She'd managed to get Ben Corbett to keep an open mind. But she was a "smart woman" and she knew that the real prize—getting Ben's okay for the filming—remained dubious. Still, she was making considerably more progress than she'd dreamed possible ten hours ago when he'd first locked her in that cell.

It was a little past seven in the morning as they stepped outside. Morgan was surprised to see blue skies and feel a warm, salty ocean breeze after such a cold, stormy night. The small main street, consisting of little more than the general-store-cum-jailhouse, a drugstore, a couple of boutiques, coffee shop, and convenience market, was nearly empty. Only the coffee shop was open, with a few men in work clothes sitting at the counter.

Ben led Morgan around the corner to a residential tree-lined street. Small cottages intermingled with old but well-cared-for Victorian houses. Morgan could see, as she looked off to her right, that they were much closer to the water than she'd realized last night. Most of the north side of Rocky Bluff hugged the Long Island Sound. And this far down on the Island, the distance from the Sound to the ocean was less than three miles, so that the south side of the town looked out to sea. It was, she conceded, a town with a special feeling.

Morgan hadn't really thought about the kind of place Ben Corbett would hang his hat in, but she was surprised when he led her to the front door of an absolutely beautiful gingerbread Victorian house set on a knoll at the end of the street. There was a light, whimsical charm about the place that didn't mesh with her image of the man who resided there. Ben noted her surprise and her hesitation when he swung the door open.

"Don't worry," he teased, "it isn't haunted."

"Does this place come with the position?" She passed Ben and stepped inside a wide foyer covered in an attractive Oriental rug. The walls were painted a soft buttery yellow that gave the old oak woodwork a lovely golden hue. A wide staircase led upstairs and the side of the foyer was set off by a wooden alcove with a delightful inglenook fireplace. A cozy spot to remove boots and parkas on a cold winter day.

"This house has been in my family for three generations."

"Then you grew up here?"

"Part of the time. My folks were divorced when I was seven. My father moved back here with my grandfather and my mother stayed in New York City. I got to play country mouse, city mouse until I was eighteen and went to Chicago to college. Then I bummed around the country for a few years trying to find out what I wanted to be when I grew up."

He shrugged. "I never actually figured that out. But my grandfather died fourteen years ago at the ripe old age of eighty-nine, and my father decided to move out to Arizona. He was toying with the notion of selling the old place. I came back for my grandfather's funeral and never left. I don't know why, but of all the places I'd been, this felt like home. More than that. It always felt somehow removed from the grit and grime of the 'civilized' world. Quiet, serene, low-key."

"A haven from the storm?"

Ben grinned. "We do have our storms on occasion. I can't control the weather, so I have to put all of my energies into keeping manmade chaos from battering down the boards."

He took her elbow and led her down a long hall past the stairs to a real, honest-to-goodness country kitchen, complete with an old woodstove, wicker hanging baskets, and antique copper

70

molds. As in the hallway, there was oak wainscoting halfway up the walls, the rest decorated in softly faded flower wallpaper.

Morgan's eyes shone. "It's a great room. God, wait until Bergson sees this house. He's going to flip. I read the script and this place would be a perfect setting for—"

"Stop racing to conclusions. I haven't gotten close to making a decision yet. And even if I do give my okay, the last place I want to see that film crew is anywhere around my home. If you so much as mention it to Bergson I'll scotch the deal on the spot."

Morgan raised her hand in girl-scout pledge. "Okay. Okay. I'll keep the hounds from your door."

Ben handed her the bag with the dungarees and T-shirt. "There's a guest room upstairs, first door to your right. It's got a private bath, so you can shower and change."

She tucked the package under her arm and nodded.

"Do you want to rest for a while?" Ben asked.

"No," Morgan said, heading for the door. "I'll come back down and help you. I can at least beat the eggs."

She was walking out the door when Ben called to her. "Thanks about this morning."

She looked at him with a puzzled expression.

"For not telling Dunne about me locking myself in the cell with you. It would have spread through town like wildfire. You've saved my reputation."

Morgan smiled impudently. "I guess that gives

71

me a bit of an advantage, Mayor Corbett. I could blackmail you, you know."

"You could. But I don't see you as the blackmail type."

"I guess we'll have to wait and see," she replied blithely as she sauntered out of the room.

Twenty minutes later, clean and refreshed, she walked back into the kitchen. Ben was peeling an onion at the sink. Morgan noticed that he'd also changed his clothes. Like her he was wearing jeans and a T-shirt. He turned around, giving her an admiring survey. "Hey, you look great." He set the onion down and walked closer to her. She saw that his hair was slightly damp and she picked up the pleasant scent of soap and after-shave lotion. Morgan suddenly had the urge to run her palm over his newly shaved face. She felt the heat rise in her body, and she was shaken as much by the notion that he was reading her thoughts as she was by the feeling.

She walked a little too fast over to a large picture window facing west. "What a beautiful view," she muttered, gazing out to the Long Island Sound across a salt marsh overgrown with wild flowers and willows. She looked at Ben over her shoulder, more composed again. "I'm beginning to see why Bergson was so taken with Rocky Bluff. It feels a little like the Scottish lowlands or the Devon moors. Almost eerie, yet very romantic." She stopped speaking because Ben was smiling in that intoxicating way of his. This was crazy, she chided herself, feeling a flurry of excitement streak down her spine.

72

Ben picked up a shiny red apple from a ceramic bowl on the counter. "Here, catch."

Morgan watched the apple fly at her. She raised her hand, more to protect her face than to catch the fruit, which she didn't do. It landed on the floor at her feet.

Ben laughed, crossing the room and bending down to pick it up. When he stood again, he was very close. He took a small bite of the apple, then pressed the fruit to Morgan's lips. Instinctively she took a tiny bite next to his.

Her eyes were very large as she made an attempt to stare around him. His own gaze was very alert, vibrant, taking in the striking planes of Morgan's face. For a brief second he let his eyes run down her body, then raised them again.

Morgan took a long, slow breath as Ben stretched out his arm, grazing her hip, and set the apple on the counter. "Shall I start the eggs?" he asked in a low voice. It was hard to guess from his tone that he was talking about cooking.

Morgan shifted her position a foot or so away from him. "Good idea." She found his continued gaze unnerving. "I'll get the eggs." She crossed the room and walked over to the refrigerator, taking a little extra time finding the eggs so she could collect her wits. The potent electrical charges between her and Ben were coming a little too fast and too intensely for her own comfort. She briefly thought about trying to use that attraction calculatingly, but just as quickly pushed the idea aside. Morgan didn't work that way.

She smiled to herself. Contrary to Ben Corbett's

fantasy, Morgan was about as un-Hollywood as people came. She assiduously avoided the fast crowds, the wild parties, the drugs, the round-robin change of partners. But she did have certain assets that made her a success in that crazy, make-believe world. She was stubbornly determined to succeed, she had a tough hide, and she kept her feet firmly planted on the ground. Until yesterday few things ruffled her. She prided herself on never panicking when problems arose, and she always managed to get things done with as little hassle as possible.

Morgan liked the fact that she was independent, made her own choices, and paid for everything she wanted herself. She was resourceful, competent, cool.

As she whipped the eggs, Morgan reminded herself of all those admirable qualities—qualities that seemed to have taken a nose dive during these past twenty-four hours. Well, she thought, today was a chance to start fresh.

Her confidence would have been greater had she not been standing in a cozy country kitchen preparing breakfast with a man who had ha-rangued, humiliated, and seduced her. Begrudg-ingly she admitted to herself that she had had some part to play in that seduction. And even now she was unable to say she wished those few inti-mate moments had never happened. The prob-lem was quite the opposite: she kept wishing it would happen again. A foolhardy wish, she chas-tised herself. For one thing she made it a point of keeping her business dealings separate from personal involvements. She also didn't like brief encounters. They left a very empty feeling in the pit of her stomach. She preferred casual but relatively long-term relationships, the kind that were easy, uncomplicated, undemanding. *Give me a call when you're back in town and we'll take in a movie, catch up on gossip.* It suited Morgan perfectly.

"How are you coming with the eggs?" Ben asked, looking up from the onions and peppers he was chopping.

Morgan looked up blankly. She had been so deep in thought, she wasn't even aware she'd nearly beaten the eggs to death. Her hand stopped in mid-motion. "I guess they're ready."

Ben observed her with a smile. "I'll take care of the rest."

Morgan set the eggbeater in the sink and then leaned against the counter, watching Ben expertly prepare the omelets. Her eyes kept drifting to the firm brownness of his arms where the band of his T-shirt ended, then up to his face. In profile he reminded her of a young Gary Cooper—the lines of his face rough-hewn yet conveying a touch of tenderness. She relived that first tender kiss they'd shared. He really did have a gentle, warm side.

Hold on, she warned herself. *Slow down, kid.* He was still the opposition. And even though he'd agreed to consider the filming, Morgan knew he was still very leery. It was up to her to prove to him that Bergson and his crew wouldn't upset his tranquil domain too much. There were bound to be a few minor mishaps, but once Ben gave his okay, he wasn't likely to throw them out after they started shooting. And Morgan would play watchdog, making sure the mayhem was contained.

She looked back out the window. Rocky Bluff wasn't Martinique. But then again, she decided, Harris Palmer was right. There were worse places to spend a few months. She glanced back at Ben. He was quietly watching her, and a long silence ensued.

"What do you want to do after breakfast?" Ben asked finally.

"Well," she said slowly, "I need to pick up some clothes and get settled at the inn. But"—she tilted her chin—"let's go hunting for ghosts first."

"Aren't you testing your luck a little too soon? What if the ghosts at the Caspel estate aren't friendly?"

"When I tell them that they could be in the movies, they'll fall right into line." Her chin tilted a fraction higher. "Then, Mayor Corbett, you'd better watch out for those ghosts if you turn me down."

Ben walked over to her, his hand cupping her chin. "You're making life very hazardous for me, Morgan Gerard."

"I usually get what I want. Even if it means enlisting the aid of ghosts."

"I usually get what I want too. I guess we come from the same school."

Morgan met Ben's insinuating gaze. "Now, wouldn't it work out nicely if we both wanted the same thing?"

CHAPTER FIVE

As soon as Ben pulled past the wrought-iron gate of the old Caspel estate, Morgan understood fully why Lloyd Bergson had been so adamant about filming *Windswept* in Rocky Bluff.

"It's absolutely perfect," she murmured. "The quintessential backdrop for a Bergson supernatural horror-romance motion picture." She cast a glance at Ben, but he merely shrugged.

Undaunted, Morgan went on. "Can't you see Lauren Chandler, the beautiful young bride, arriving here with her handsome husband, Douglas? They look into the distance for their first hazy glimpse of this large, eerie mansion overlooking the sea. But to them it's beautiful . . . a sanctuary. They're so much in love."

"Not my idea of an idyllic love-nest," Ben quipped.

Morgan grinned. "It turned out not to be Lauren and Douglas's either. Poor Lauren."

Ben gave her a bemused look.

"You did read the script?" she asked accusingly.

"I never did go in for ghost stories."

"But it's such a powerful idea. Lauren is deeply

77

in love with her husband, yet she is pulled by some, at first, inexplicable force within the mansion. Douglas is frantic as Lauren drifts farther and farther away."

"Sounds more like your typical marriage-gone-awry tale."

Morgan grimaced. "How amusing. It turns out that Lauren has become possessed by the spirit of Charlotte Cobb, who, as a young bride, seventy-five years earlier, came to the same house with her austere older husband."

She shot a glance at Ben as he pulled the car over.

"Why are we stopping here? Aren't we going to the house?" She saw the disconcerted look on Ben's face.

"In a minute. Tell me the rest of the story."

Morgan smiled. So he was getting interested after all. She silently congratulated herself and continued the tale.

"After living in the house for a short time, Charlotte met and then fell passionately in love with Eliot Franklin, the young, handsome grounds keeper on the estate. She begged her husband for a divorce, but he refused. Instead he killed her. He threw her over the balustrade of her bedroom in a fit of jealousy. Then he set out to destroy her lover, who ended up committing suicide in one of the rooms in the mansion."

Ben turned to her now, more attentive. "I think I've heard this story before."

Morgan grimaced. "Not with the passion and intensity Bergson puts into it. Picture Lauren, in reality, passionately in love with Douglas. But Charlotte's demented spirit is compelled to seek revenge on her own husband for her murder and Eliot's suicide. Possessed by that force, Lauren is being driven to murder her own husband."

"How does it end?"

Morgan smiled. "I thought you'd never ask. Ultimately it's the power of Douglas's love for Lauren that helps him succeed in combating Charlotte's spirit and saving both himself and Lauren from destruction. Finally they leave the mansion. Charlotte's spirit remains, but having been confronted by the great passion the Chandlers felt for each other, Charlotte finally stops seeking revenge and in so doing, allows the spirit of her dead lover Eliot to be freed. They are reunited at the mansion for all eternity."

"A happy ending. Well, that part's all right," Ben conceded.

"I can't tell you how exciting the script is. You have to read it for yourself. It's the idea of the dual love story, one so real, the other so ethereal, that gives the tale a twist. There's so much intensity in both relationships. Unlike some of Bergson's other scripts, this one plays down the gore." She paused, smiling. "Of course there are still plenty of chills while good and evil do battle."

She saw Ben's scowl and laughed. "Okay, that part's not my cup of tea either. But the love story more than makes up for the horror angle."

She turned away from Ben. "Let's go up to the house. I'm dying to get a close look."

Ben hesitated, then started slowly down the

long dirt path. As Morgan looked out the car window, she could vividly picture Douglas and Lauren driving up the path the day of their arrival. The camera would catch the car moving down the long, crushed-stone path, large leafy elms forming a natural arch and casting a shadowy half-light over the scene. There would be a foreboding sense of evil and excitement. Yes, she could picture it perfectly—feel it.

"You look like you're in a trance," Ben remarked, touching her shoulder. "Don't tell me you're already communing with the spirits."

Morgan laughed, shaking herself free of the fantasy that had gripped her. It wasn't like her to drift off like that—into the midst of a horror story, no less. When she looked down at her arm she saw goose bumps. "If there are spirits anywhere, they must be here," she said lightly, refusing to admit a vague uneasiness as they neared the mansion itself.

She glanced over at Ben. "I wish you'd read the script. Then you'd see why Bergson—"

"The film itself has no real bearing on the issue," he said, cutting her off as he pulled up in front of the Caspel mansion. He was about to go on to give Morgan another of his little speeches when he heard her sharp intake of breath.

"What's wrong?"

Morgan didn't answer. Actually she hadn't heard Ben's question. Her eyes were wide with a strange blend of excitement and awe as she stared at the house.

He touched her arm, but she seemed oblivious to the sensation.

"Morgan?"

She heard him then and looked over, a soft smile turning the corners of her lips. "It's even more perfect than I thought." She looked up at the mansion and stared hypnotically at the rambling place built of wood and fieldstone. There was no real classification for its design; it was a hodgepodge of architectural styles. The front porch was sagging badly, most of the windows had been boarded up, and the few that weren't covered had been victims of vandalism. The lawn was overgrown with weeds, and patches of grass even sprang up through the floorboards of the porch. The place hadn't been painted in years; time and the elements had worked their mischief. Yet there was something magical, certainly Gothic, about the place: turrets on each corner, peaked gable roofs, leaded glass windows, a widow's walk that gave the watcher a clear view of the sea beneath the bluff.

"Do you want to walk around?" Ben asked as he stopped in front of the house.

Morgan nodded, her hand already on the door handle.

Ben was a little disconcerted by Morgan's reaction to the old Caspel place. She might be enchanted, but he had always hated the mansion. What he saw was a developing fire hazard, an unsavory hangout for teenagers, a monstrosity that would cost more money to restore than it could ever be worth. However, the Caspel mansion had been one of the first grand homes built in Rocky Bluff, giving the building a certain distinction. The local historical society had blocked the bill each year to tear down the building itself and use the land as a town recreational area. Although old man Caspel had wanted to see his home turned into a museum, he'd gone bankrupt several years before his death, leaving the town with the responsibility of footing the bill for the restoration.

Ben was just as happy Caspel's finances had dwindled. The idea of a museum didn't thrill him. He had been the one to first propose that the Caspel mansion be razed and the estate turned into a park. He envisioned a public beach, picnic grounds, playing fields—a place that would benefit the overwhelming majority. He had many of the farmers and retired folk behind his idea.

But the business people in the community believed that a folk-art museum would draw more tourists to the town. The Historical Society liked the idea of the museum because it would preserve the building. And there was a small but powerful monied group that considered the museum a nice prestigious touch to the quaint town of Rocky Bluff.

This year Ben was planning an all-out campaign to get a majority vote for his proposal, which was one of the main reasons he was so opposed to Bergson filming here. To use the Caspel estate certain improvements would have to be made and the studio backing the film had the kind of money necessary to do the job. Not that they planned to restore the entire building, but it would be a good start. Supporters of the museum would have a real advantage in pushing for the additional money to save the house that was the centerpiece of a famous Hollywood movie. And Ben Corbett wanted to hold on to his advantage.

Morgan was already out of the car and walking up the path to the front porch when Ben called out for her to wait.

"Why don't we just walk around the outside? The house is badly run down. Vandals have done quite a number on it. Not to mention the ghosts."

"Ghosts?"

Ben grinned. "Anything's possible, right?"

"I think you're the one that's nervous about meeting up with a ghost."

"Well, we might run into Charlotte Caspel if the winds pick up."

"Charlotte?" Morgan stared wide-eyed.

Ben leaned against the newel-post as they stood together on the creaky porch. "She's the resident spirit," he said in a light, teasing tone. "Just like in Bergson's script. In fact, rumor has it that on blustery evenings her cry can be heard over the howl of the wind."

"You're just trying to spook me," she said, a note of accusation in her voice. "There really is no such rumor."

"Ask anyone in town. It's been a local legend for years."

"Tell it to me," she demanded.

"Well, the story goes that Captain Wescott Caspel built this place at the turn of the century for his French bride, Charlotte. Then, six months after they began living here, the lovely bride took up with the gardener of the estate. Caspel had the man fired and thrown into jail on some trumped-up charges." He gave her an amused glance. "Sound familiar?" When she didn't answer, he went on. "A few nights later sweet Charlotte was found—"

"Dead on the bluff beneath her bedroom window," Morgan finished his sentence, her eyes shining with excitement.

Ben gave her a bemused look. "Just like in the script."

"What happened to Caspel?" she asked.

Ben shrugged. "I guess there were a lot of people who did believe he gave his wife a hefty push out of her window. But Captain Caspel was a very wealthy, upstanding citizen and word of Charlotte's infidelity had spread through the community. In the eyes of the chaste citizens of Rocky Bluff, Charlotte Caspel had committed an unpardonable sin. The authorities ruled her death a suicide. Supposedly Charlotte was so ashamed and grieved by the scandal that she took her own life. Caspel remarried soon afterward and had a son. . . ."

Morgan was no longer listening. She shook her head vigorously. "No. He murdered her, all right. What happened to the gardener?"

"Eliot? He was found dead some time after that, I think."

Morgan's voice was raspy. "Eliot killed himself in the mansion—just like in the *Windswept* script. Charlotte came back to haunt Caspel. She wanted to seek her revenge. Then, in the end, her lover rejoined her, and the two of them are . . . still together in this house."

Ben laughed. "I guess the folks of Rocky Bluff are less romantically inclined than Bergson. They just believe old Charlotte comes around whenever the winds howl to scare the poor Captain out of his mind. And I guess no one's been able to convince the spirit of the blushing bride that Wescott's been dead and gone for over fifty years now. She's still hanging around waiting for him to show up."

Morgan looked up at Ben. "Let's go inside and see if we can find sweet Charlotte and tell her about the Captain's demise."

Ben took his time searching for the key on his ring. The truth was, for all of his teasing, he had always found the Caspel estate rather spooky. Once, as a kid, he'd accepted a dare to sneak into the house in the dark when Caspel was away on business. He was frightened to death, sure he'd meet up with the ghostly Charlotte, but he refused to admit he was scared. So he had gritted his teeth and gone in. When he heard low moans wafting through the air, he'd nearly jumped out of his skin and raced out, but as soon as he saw his friends waiting for him just beyond the gate, he'd acted very cool. Then he'd proceeded to have horrible nightmares for weeks—until he found out that Mark Kiley, the boy who'd egged him on the most, had been the one doing the moaning. He'd sneaked up to the house after Ben and used a cheerleader's megaphone to create effectively Charlotte's eerie cries.

Except for one tour with the building inspector a few years back, Ben had not set foot into the building since. And he wasn't particularly eager to do so now. Not that he was really spooked, but even on that inspection tour he'd felt as though he were walking through a mausoleum more than a home. For all its vast rooms the place gave him a claustrophobic feeling.

Morgan stood by, impatiently waiting for him to come up with the key. He was puzzled by her fascination with the estate. Her reaction was so different from his. Maybe she was just more of a romantic. He considered telling her he couldn't find the key, but he could see from the set expression of her face that Morgan would figure out a way to get into the place with or without his assistance. And given her track record for bad luck, he decided it would be wise for him to stick close by. Anyway, the idea of sticking close to Morgan had a definite appeal.

Maybe he didn't believe in spirits, but there was certainly something about Morgan Gerard that had bewitched Ben Corbett. He wasn't sure whether it was her startling and unusual turquoise eyes, her lithe, slender body, the tilt of her proud chin, her warm, full lips, or her feisty spirit. Probably a combination of all of them. He was bewitched, all right. And he'd have to watch his step. While he liked the idea of Morgan staying around for a few weeks, he really doubted he would change his mind about the film, even though he had told her he would think about it.

"Try a few of them," Morgan suggested. "You

really are lousy with keys. Maybe we should just knock and see if Charlotte will open the door for us."

"Ah, the lady is glib. Wait until you hear the old bride's wail coursing through the place. Then we'll see if you still whistle the same tune."

He held up the key and handed it to Morgan. "Go on, brave lady. Open the door."

Just as Morgan inserted the key in the lock, a strong breeze whistled through the trees.

"Charlotte is sighing." She grinned, but she did feel an odd chill. Between Bergson's story, Ben's true-life tale, and her own curious fascination with the old place, Morgan found herself slightly unnerved as she swung the door open. True to all horror stories the doorknob rattled and the hinges creaked loudly. She glanced over her shoulder at Ben. He looked a bit unnerved himself. But she knew there wasn't a chance in the world either one of them would admit it to the other.

Morgan stepped inside the vast hallway. It was a dark, gloomy space, all sunlight effectively blocked out by the boarded windows. It took a few moments for her eyes to adjust. Then, leading the way, she walked through an elaborately arched entry that led into the formal living room.

Her first thought when she looked about the sparsely furnished and badly damaged room was that it looked more like a movie set than a home. It had a cold, hollow feeling and somehow seemed not quite real.

Puddles of water, most likely from last night's storm, had formed on the dark wooden floors, but

Morgan discovered them only after stepping into one. She lost her balance and grabbed on to Ben. Caught off guard he, too, lost his footing and the two of them landed on the floor, flat on their butts in another puddle.

"See?" Ben grimaced. "I told you we ought to stick to the outside. Charlotte obviously doesn't want any visitors." He stood up, then helped Morgan to her feet.

"It's only water. We'll dry off. Charlotte will have to do more than that to scare me away." She realized as she spoke that Ben was still holding on to her. His grip was firm and his eyes lingered on her face.

"What was it you said about the power of passion subduing the spirit's thirst for revenge?" He leaned down and kissed her, but Morgan's response was guarded, tentative. She took a step back, sloshing into another puddle.

Ben pulled her into his arms again. "I don't think we were very convincing. Let's try that again." Slowly, deliberately, he teasingly ran his tongue over her lips. His touch was light but insistent. Morgan leaned into him, her resistance wilting. She lifted her arms, putting them around his neck, and both of them forgot their jangled nerves.

Ben could feel Morgan's body trembling against him. She met his searching tongue with her own, and their kiss deepened. Ben pulled her closer, then ran his hands down the back of her thin T-shirt and over her tight jeans. She felt wonderful, he thought dazedly.

Then suddenly he felt her stiffen. When he released her, Morgan looked up at him, wide-eyed and slightly pale. "Did you hear anything?" she asked in a low voice.

"Only the sound of our hearts beating wildly." He stroked her cheek.

"Right." She laughed a little shakily.

"What did you hear?"

"Just the wind, I guess. And our hearts beating wildly."

He took her hand. "Come on, Morgan. Let's get out of here. I know lots of nicer places to get better acquainted." He gave her a sly smile.

"Slow down, Mayor. In case memory fails you, we hardly know each other. And to put it mildly, we got off to a lousy start. Let's take it slow, okay? We have a few weeks to . . . get to know one another. And then, if you give your okay to Bergson, a couple of months."

He took her hand, bringing it to his lips. "You make it sound tempting. Of course, you could stay around for a while even if I tell Bergson to go find himself another haunted house. After all, Charlotte might not like a lot of wild, noisy goings-on here."

"If you nix the deal, Ben, I'll be on the road checking out other haunted houses. Speaking of which, let's continue checking this one out. Too bad my camera was stolen. I'll have to pick up a new one tomorrow and come back. I'm supposed to send Bergson pic—" She stopped abruptly, her eyes darting up to Ben.

He made an effort to smile, but it came off a

trifle grim. This time he, too, had heard something. "It's probably a creaking board."

Morgan cocked her head to the side, listening. "Yeah, but who creaked it?"

She crossed the room and walked back into the entry, Ben following her. She looked around. "It sounded as if it came from upstairs."

"Do you want to have a look?"

She hesitated.

He could see her curiosity warring with her nerves. "If you're afraid . . ."

Morgan gave him a defiant look. "Are you?"

He started toward the stairs. Morgan remained where she was. "It could be a rat—or something," she added, rubbing her hands over her arms.

"It's very possible." Ben had his hand on the banister. "How do you think your Hollywood starlets are going to feel about filming in a building overrun by rats—or something?"

Morgan gave him a rueful smile. "We'll get an exterminator in here if there's a problem."

"How about an exorcist?" he teased.

Morgan walked over to the stairs. "Let's find out which it's going to be," she said more bravely than she felt.

Ben felt his palms grow clammy as they climbed the stairs. This was ridiculous. He certainly didn't believe in ghosts, and he wasn't particularly bothered by a scurrying rat. So why was that feeling of claustrophobia returning? The house had a somber aura that was very compelling despite all of his rationalizations. Still, he'd be damned if he was going to give Morgan a hint of his uneasiness. He walked briskly up the stairs, Morgan having to move quickly to keep up with him. He stopped at the first door to his right.

"Shall we start here?" His hand gripped the knob.

Morgan nodded.

Ben turned the knob firmly. The door didn't budge. "That's odd." He pushed harder, and it gave way. "Just warped, I guess," he said, swinging the door open.

A narrow shaft of light filtered in through the boards covering the large picture window. It was an enormous bedroom, and an old brass bed was still sitting in the center of the room. Morgan felt a chill run down her spine as she stepped inside. This was Charlotte's room. She knew it instinctively, could even imagine a soft, delicate scent of perfume in the air. She stepped inside. Ben stayed at the door, watching her as she walked over to the window. Through the narrow opening she could just make out the ragged bluff and the water beyond. When she turned back she stumbled over something. She bent down and picked up a small velvet-covered box. Opening it she found a few pieces of costume jewelry and a tiny heart-shaped locket. Inside was a picture of Charlotte. Morgan stared at it, transfixed.

Ben came to her side, curious to see what she had found. He looked over Morgan's shoulder, studying the miniature sepia photo. "There's a vague resemblance," he said slowly, glancing from the photo to Morgan. "Around the eyes mostly. I wonder what color her eyes were."

Morgan closed the locket. "This is ridiculous. I'm getting carried away by ghost stories."

Ben smiled, brushing her hair from her cheek. "We're also both exhausted. Let's go. I'll drive you over to the inn and we'll come back another time."

Morgan nodded. She felt a sudden urge for sunlight and fresh air.

They both heard the door close at the same time.

"How the hell . . . ?" Ben reached for the knob, tugging. Nothing happened.

"Pull harder. It was jammed before."

Ben leaned slightly, getting more leverage by placing the ball of his foot against the molding at the side of the door. Still nothing happened.

He straightened up. "The lock must have released. It won't budge."

"We certainly seem to be making a habit of getting locked into places together," Morgan said dryly, making a great effort not to get carried away by fantasy. "I don't suppose you have a key."

Ben doubted the key to the front door would work, but he tried it anyway. It didn't.

"Now what?" A hint of panic creeped into Morgan's voice. This really was too much.

"Take it easy," Ben said softly. "We've been in tighter spots." He smiled at Morgan, taking her hand. She was shivering. He pressed his lips to her palm.

"My luck really has gone bad." Morgan managed a thin smile.

"I don't know." Ben placed his hands on her

shoulders. She flinched and he immediately remembered the cut she'd suffered when the plaster
struck her last night. Poor Morgan. She really had
been having quite a time of it. When he tenderly
took her in his arms, Morgan didn't resist. Especially when she heard another creaking sound outside the door.

"Maybe some vagrant broke into the place."
Morgan's voice was a whisper. She pressed closer
to Ben, her lips brushing his ear.

He gently stroked her back, then dropped his
hands. "The place is pretty well sealed up. I still
think it's probably rats or field mice scrambling
about."

"Or Charlotte," Morgan added, watching Ben
move to the window to try removing the boards.

"Look around for something—"

They froze in place. Morgan's brow broke out in
a cold sweat at a rumbling sound and then another
followed by a low moan.

"It's only the wind," Ben said, his own voice
lower. "It's always windier by the sea. Or gulls. It's
very likely a combination of the two—our imagi-
nations are playing tricks on us."

"You thought of Charlotte too."

He walked over and took her in his arms.
"There's no such thing as ghosts, Morgan. Maybe
you were right before. Some vagrant could have
broken in. I'll get a couple of men out here later to
search the place."

The low whine returned. Morgan gripped Ben
tighter. "Hold me, Ben. Just hold me for a moment."

He tilted up her chin, planting a warm, moist kiss on her lips. "That's for courage."

She smiled. Ben did inspire courage—and other feelings as well. So much of what had happened to her these past twenty-four hours seemed crazy. At this point she was beyond trying to figure it out. Anyway, she was too scared right now to bother. All she knew was that if she had to be locked in a bedroom of a haunted house, she was awfully glad she was there with Ben Corbett. When they got out of this new fix, she'd concentrate on sorting out her quickly escalating attraction to the mayor of Rocky Bluff.

They set about looking for something to use to pry the boards from the windows. Ben came up with a rusty nail file, but it broke off almost immediately. Then they tried the low heel of Morgan's shoe. When that snapped off, she gave him the other one, more to even out the two than because of any hope the second shoe would work any better. In the end it was Ben's brute strength that dislodged the nails. His fingers were cut and scraped and his T-shirt was damp with perspiration. Morgan dug out a few tissues from her purse and wiped his brow.

"I'm impressed." She felt better with the bright sunlight streaming into the room. Instead of looking dark and ominous now, Charlotte Caspel's old bedroom simply looked old, worn, and unused.

He kissed the tip of her nose. "You inspire me." He turned to the window, struggling with the rusty latch. Managing it, he swung the window open.

There was a small balustrade, at the edge of a narrow parapet. It looked considerably thinner than it was when Morgan looked down to see the craggy stone bluff below. One false step . . .

"Maybe we should try the door again," she said anxiously, her high spirits sinking fast. The thought of climbing out on that ledge made her feel positively ill. She looked out of the window and cast her eyes down. For a moment she could actually envision poor Charlotte's slender body splayed out on that bluff. She shivered, wrenching herself free of the image.

Ben touched Morgan's cheek. "You wait here. I'll climb out and get to the corner of the building. I haven't slid down a drainpipe in a while"—he grinned—"but it shouldn't be too tough. Then I'll find something to break down the door and—"

"No, I'll come with you. I don't particularly want to be locked in here alone. I can slide down a drainpipe as well as the next guy."

They argued for a couple of minutes, but she was adamant. Five steps along the parapet Morgan changed her mind.

"Come on. You're doing fine. You've made it this far," Ben coaxed, carefully reaching toward her hand and placing his own over hers as she gripped the shingles.

"I—I can't. I'm dizzy."

The wind kicked up. Morgan gasped as she watched the window to Charlotte's room slam shut. She knew she'd never be able to get it open. There was no choice now but to go forward.

Ben cheered her on with each step, his hand

over hers, his smile warm and reassuring. Morgan clung to the wall, taking slow, tiny steps to the right. It felt like an eternity before they reached the corner.

There was a drainpipe all right. The only problem was the bottom half had broken off a good nine feet from the ground.

"You hold on," Ben ordered. "I'll slide down and try to find the missing piece and fit it back in."

He squeezed Morgan's good shoulder. "Are you going to be okay?"

She nodded. "I should have listened to you when you said there were better places to get acquainted."

He laughed softly. "Don't go away."

"Very funny." Then she said, "Be careful. It's a long drop. And we do seem to be testing the fates."

Ben gripped the pipe. "I'm leaving, Charlotte," he shouted in the wind. "And I'm taking Morgan with me. So go back and spook the rats and mice for a while." He grinned at Morgan. "There, that should appease her."

Either Charlotte didn't hear him or she wasn't so easily appeased. Just as Ben put his full weight on the pipe and started sliding down, the bracket holding it to the building began to give way. Morgan screamed, clutching the wall for dear life. Ben was a good fourteen feet off the ground when the pipe detached fully. Morgan stared, terrified and helpless as Ben went flying, at first in slow motion, and then accelerating frightfully until he landed spread-eagle in a rhododendron bush. That bush

96

had very likely saved him from breaking several bones, but he was badly scraped and bruised. Which was a minor catastrophe compared to the more pressing problem of Morgan Gerard, who was now shivering on that narrow ledge two stories up.

"Ben?" She couldn't bring herself to look down. She was too scared she'd find him smashed on the hard ground like poor Charlotte; too scared she'd lose her footing and land there beside him. "Ben . . . are you . . . okay?"

"Yeah," he shouted up to her, brushing himself off. "Nothing to it. Listen, Morgan. I want you to edge your way back to that balustrade. I'll come upstairs and break down the door and pry the window open again. Morgan? Do you hear me?"

"I hear you, but my feet don't want to move."

"You can do it. You've already done it once."

"I know," she said, trembling, "but there are some things in life you don't really want to do more than once. This is definitely one of those things."

She tried. She actually took one or two steps before she froze in fear. There was just no way she could get herself all the way back to that balustrade alone. Ben rushed upstairs, broke down the door, and in true heroic fashion climbed out the window and got to Morgan, leading her safely back into Charlotte's bedroom.

They were both very grateful that Morgan didn't faint until he got her inside.

CHAPTER SIX

When Morgan came to, she wasn't particularly surprised to find herself in Ben's arms; she'd been finding herself there so often since first setting eyes on him. She looked up at his concerned face and smiled.

"We did it. We defied Charlotte."

Ben leaned over and kissed her warmly on the lips.

Morgan sighed deeply, snuggling closer to him. "You saved my life. That makes me indebted to you. It gives you the advantage."

He helped her off Charlotte's bed. "I never take advantage of a damsel in distress." He slipped his arm around her waist. "Are you ready to leave?" He cocked his head. "Or do you want to continue hunting for ghosts, vagrants, and rodents?"

Morgan gazed around the room, her eyes falling on the tiny locket resting on the desk. She walked over and lifted it up. Flicking open the catch she stared down at Charlotte. There was something here in this house . . . a presence.

Ben came over and put his arm around her. Their eyes met.

He felt it too. She knew he did. It was in his eyes. Even if it were only that the house carried potent memories, both of them had been touched by the aura.

He took her chin in his hands and looked into her eyes. She smiled softly. He gathered her in his arms, and for just a moment they clung to each other silently. When he let her go, he seemed to have shaken off the strange mood. His expression was amused.

Morgan closed the locket and set it down. She decided she was getting too carried away. "I think I've seen enough for one day," she conceded. Then, regaining her sense of humor about the whole experience, she added, "Bergson is going to get a charge out of this little escapade of ours. He might even use it in the script somehow." She looked down at her arm. "Look, I still have goose bumps. There really is no other place to film *Windswept.*"

"Morgan . . ."

"I know what you're going to say, that there's no such thing as ghosts. But I *can* feel Charlotte's spirit here. There's a certain mood, emotions, a power. I know I sound a little wacky, but I can close my eyes and see Charlotte as she was, lying on this bed, running through the house and sneaking off to meet her lover. Bergson's got to do the film here. Don't you see that, Ben?" She looked up at him, her voice insistent, her eyes wide and filled with excitement.

Seeing Morgan's intense expression, he suddenly felt angry—angry at this house, at Charlotte

Caspel, at having let the horror stories about this place taunt him as a child.

"What I see is that this building is a death trap," he said harshly. "We almost—"

"We're just having a run of bad luck," Morgan said lightly, shrugging off the fear that had gripped her earlier. "If there were a film crew around here now, they would have gotten us out of the room without our having to play Spiderman."

Ben didn't answer. He took her by the hand and escorted her in fast order from Charlotte's room, down the stairs, and out of the mansion. It was only when they were outside that Morgan realized how scraped up Ben was from his fall.

"You're hurt." She examined his face more closely. Then his arms. She lifted his T-shirt. There were a good dozen reddened streaks crisscrossing his chest. "Oh, Ben, why didn't you say something?" She gingerly traced a gash on his arm where the blood was just drying.

He gave her a seductive glance. "You could use your T-shirt to bandage me up."

Morgan smiled wryly. "Come on. We'll stop at a drugstore and then we can go back to your place and I'll look after those cuts. It's the least I can do." Her tone was light, but then her eyes met his. "I don't think I could have made it across that ledge without you, Ben. I—I might have ended up like Charlotte Caspel. . . ."

He swept a strand of chestnut hair from her cheek. "I couldn't let that happen. You may be creating havoc in my life, Morgan Gerard, but you are the most beguiling woman I've come across in quite a while. I really do want to get to know you better."

They drove back into town, Morgan rushing into the drugstore for antiseptic ointment even though Ben had protested that he was fine and it wasn't necessary. He stayed in the car while she went inside the store, not particularly keen on meeting any of his constituents and having to explain why he looked the way he did. How the hell could he explain any of the wild events that had happened to him since Morgan Gerard walked into his life?

He was glad this was his housekeeper's day off. All he needed was for Laura to see him strolling into the house with Morgan looking like he just stepped out of a boxing ring. He could just imagine the kind of stories that would spread through the town. So far he'd been lucky enough to keep his bizarre assortment of mishaps from getting around. But he knew it was foolhardy, under the circumstances, to trust too much to good luck.

He went upstairs and took a shower, flinching as the hot water hit his cuts. He really did look as if he'd been on the wrong end of a boxing glove. When he'd finished he wrapped a towel jauntily around his hips.

Morgan, looking very efficient and maternal, was waiting in the bedroom, bandages and antiseptic cream set out on a small table by the window. Her maternal instincts immediately went to war with more primitive emotions when she saw Ben standing in the room with nothing but a towel

—and not a very big towel at that—wrapped around his waist.

He came closer and she busied herself opening up the tube of cream. Not looking at him she ordered him to sit down in the chair beside the window.

She looked around to find him sitting on the bed instead. She walked over slowly, cream, gauze, and tape in hand.

Her fingers were cool and gentle on his skin. Ben leaned back against the bed as she administered to him.

Taking care of Ben's wounds was not the simple task it should have been. Touching his broad muscular chest, running her fingers along his powerful arms, smoothing cream on his craggy jaw, and brushing his thick brown hair from his forehead to bandage a gash above his eyebrow made her nerve endings tingle and her hands tremble, and her thoughts drifted to fantasies of what it would feel like to lie naked on this bed with him. What was the matter with her?

"You—you don't look too bad." She knew her voice sounded breathy.

"Thanks. You look pretty good yourself." His hands rose to her face. "Especially when those amazing eyes of yours are sparkling with excitement."

"That's ridiculous." She fidgeted with the cap, trying to screw it onto the end of the tube of ointment.

"And when your cheeks are glowing with a gentle blush."

"It's—warm in here." The tube slipped from her hand. "Greasy stuff."

"I have a towel." He took her hands and placed them on the towel still draped around his waist. He slid her palms down so she could feel the firm, angular line of his hipbone.

Morgan gave him a helpless look. "Ben . . . things are happening too fast. We hardly know each other."

He pulled her down beside him on the bed. The ointment and bandages fell to the floor. "Just look at all the ordeals we've been through together," he said softly. "We survived the worst and came out okay. We're bound to be able to handle something far more pleasurable."

"Ben . . ."

His lips captured the rest of her words. He knew she probably had a long list of reasons why they shouldn't become intimate; he certainly could come up with a pretty long list of his own. But, somehow, nothing on those lists mattered right now. He could not recall ever wanting a woman more desperately than he wanted Morgan. He'd been through hell and back with her, and now he felt a burning need to get a taste of heaven.

Morgan's hand closed over his and she drew the back of it down her cheek. She lifted her eyes to his. "It could be very risky," she whispered softly, "considering our track record together."

He drew her to him. "I think our luck is beginning to change."

Her eyes were wide, and she could feel her whole body trembling. "Maybe you're right." She laughed softly. "Oh, Ben, this whole thing is crazy, but maybe you're right. I—I think I know how Charlotte must have felt when she first saw her lover's bare chest, his beautiful, powerful body, his hypnotic brown eyes. . . ."

Ben tickled her ear with his warm breath. "How do you know his eyes were brown?"

Morgan ran her hands slowly down his chest, over the few bandaged gashes, and then to the towel around his waist. It took the slightest tug to free it. "I just know they were brown. Just as I know Charlotte's eyes were blue, like mine."

She saw the flash of a frown cross Ben's face. She knew he thought she was merely letting her imagination get carried away, but she didn't mind. There really was no explanation for her certainty, but for some reason that didn't bother her.

She kissed Ben fully on the lips. "And I know that Charlotte felt the same desperate yearning for Eliot as—as I feel for you right now. She didn't understand those feelings any more than I do. But she couldn't help herself. Neither could Eliot." Morgan's turquoise eyes darkened. "They had to know it was foolhardy, that it would—"

"Morgan." He grabbed her tightly, smothering her lips with a fierce, hungry kiss, wrenching her from the fantasy so that all she could think of was how much she wanted him.

Her eyes were sultry with passion as Ben stripped off her jeans and panties and lifted her T-shirt over her head. He tossed them along with her lacy bra onto the floor and then encircled her in his arms.

It had to be fantasy, Morgan thought, for it to feel this extraordinary to lie in a man's arms. Never before, not in dreams or real life, had Morgan ever experienced such an emotionally charged intensity. Ben's caresses took her breath away, and his nibbling kisses that trailed over her body made her head reel. Every spot he touched seemed to come alive, making her skin feel as if it were burning with fire.

Her hand stroked down to his hard, firm stomach, her touch tentative at first, then more daring as he urged her on. She felt her inhibitions melt away at the same moment. She was consumed by desire, arching into him as he glided his hand down over her buttocks, slipping intimately between her legs.

She drew one leg over his hips, her heart slamming against the walls of her chest as his caresses aroused her to a fever pitch. Her lips opened over Ben's mouth and her tongue sought his as she stretched her long, supple body against him.

Ben's hands came up to each side of her face. He knew his eyes were filled with desire, and the raw intensity of his lust almost frightened him. He wanted to ravage her, possess her, never let her go.

She saw that he was trembling. So was she. Their eyes met and they both knew without saying a word that neither of them had ever felt this way before.

Her hand slipped down over his hard, muscled stomach. Ben throbbed at her touch. Her fingers closed around him and he buried his face in her hair, murmuring her name, groaning.

And then he caught her waist and turned her onto her back. He felt hungry, greedy. He wanted to feel, to touch, to run his lips over every part of her. He felt like a man starving, with blinding need to know each intimate curve and crevice, every inch of her.

Morgan responded with the same fierce hunger. They made love with a savage tenderness. As he thrust inside her, Ben's eyes burned into hers. Then he dropped his head, his hand arching her back so that he could taste her taut nipple. His tongue circled it, then his teeth lightly bruised the tip, creating an exquisite pain deep inside Morgan's body. Her other breast ached and she guided him to it.

Her hands moved over his back and down his buttocks, then as he thrust more deeply, more quickly, she clung to him tenaciously, her heart thundering. With each fierce thrust she breathlessly murmured his name.

"Ben. Ben. Ben." And then, when she was too breathless to speak, low moans of pleasure escaped her parted lips. She flung her head back, eyes closed, as she was engulfed in sensations until she was soaring, shuddering, every fiber of her body trembling. And Ben was with her, plunging so deep she felt as if they had become fused. The sensations were wild, fantastic, unbelievable. It was the ultimate surrender.

His hand moved over the lowest point of her abdomen and Morgan held it there with her own.

She looked over at him. He wore an intoxicating smile as he met her gaze. "I think there must be more than meets the eye here." His brown eyes shone. "Maybe we've both been possessed by spirits. I certainly never felt this way making love before. It was out of this world."

They laughed softly, but then Morgan's expression sobered. "It started in the Caspel estate. I could feel it, something inside of me was awakened for the first time. It isn't crazy. I really felt—I don't know, so strange. As if the wild passions that had been felt by Charlotte Caspel had been transported."

Ben's expression was slightly grim. "I'd much prefer to think it was purely my manly charms that took your breath away. I thought it started last night when we were locked in that jail cell together and we snuggled on that narrow cot. I know that's when my wild passion began to spring to life."

Morgan touched his cheek. "I guess that was the start. Except I was in no shape to recognize it. But everything was somehow heightened, clarified, when we stepped inside the Caspel house. No, as soon as I first set eyes on it, I knew that something extraordinary was going to happen."

"More than we bargained for. I'll admit, now that it's all over, I was pretty tense up there on that ledge. In fact, the Caspel estate has given me the creeps ever since I was a kid." He told Morgan about the dare when he was eleven. She put her arms around him, giving him a sympathetic kiss.

107

He leaned against the pillows, Morgan resting her head on his shoulder.

"Morgan?"

She picked up the tension in his voice. "Yes?"

"There are a lot of reasons I don't want Bergson filming here."

Morgan stiffened. "So you've told me. But don't you see, he wrote *Windswept* to be filmed in this setting. No other place would be right." She sat up and turned to him. "Nothing terrible is going to happen to your precious town in two short months."

"I particularly don't want him using the Caspel estate. For one thing, I just have bad feelings about it. Okay"—he grinned boyishly—"so I can be superstitious too. Didn't our escapade today leave a bad taste in your mouth?"

"Oh, I'll admit I was scared and spooked. But look what happened because of it." Her eyes sparkled. "The place had some very potent vibes."

"Stop, Morgan. You're just letting your fanciful imagination run away with your common sense. Things just clicked for the two of us. It was special." He placed his hand on her high cheekbone. "Very special." He paused. "Why don't we spend the next few days scouting around some other towns in the area? Then you can tell Bergson you've come up with a spot that would be just as good. And you'd be close enough for us to continue to get better acquainted," he said with a teasing smile.

"I think," Morgan said, studying Ben closely, "that we know each other well enough for you to

108

level with me. It isn't only the raucous Hollywood crew that you're worried about."

Ben sighed. "It's a big part of it. I just don't think this town is equipped to handle the onslaught." He saw Morgan's eyes narrow. "Okay," he admitted, "I am spearheading a campaign to get a majority vote to raze the Caspel estate. If your people come out here and fix it up, plus pay the town the hefty fee involved in getting permission to film there, I won't have a chance in hell of getting that vote. Right now the town is split pretty much down the middle. I think this community needs a public recreation area far more than it needs an obscure museum. But it will be hard to get people to agree to tear the Caspel place down once money gets thrown into it."

He was talking so fast he didn't hear Morgan's sharp intake of breath when he told her he wanted to raze the mansion. But when he stopped and looked at her, he saw that she was pale.

"Morgan, what's wrong?"

"Tear it down?" Her voice sounded hollow.

"The place is a white elephant. You could see that for yourself. Even if we did turn it into a lavish museum, what is that really going to do for this town? We don't need museums. We need—"

"You hate it, don't you?" She pulled the sheet around her.

"What are you talking about?"

"It frightens you. It does. I saw it in your eyes several times. You tried to hide it, but it was there."

"Morgan, that's absolute nonsense. You're getting swept up in—in Bergson's crazy fantasy. All this hogwash about Charlotte coming back to haunt old Caspel and then reuniting with her lover, two spirits living happily—well, I guess I can't say living. What does one call it?" he asked facetiously.

Morgan glared at him. "It has nothing to do with Bergson's script. I—I just know that you want to destroy something—"

"Something that should have been knocked down years ago," he said angrily. "I was voted into office because the people of this town believed I had the ability to get things accomplished, to help this town thrive. The Caspel place can be put to a hell of a lot better uses than keeping that mausoleum going. And if you weren't so caught up in the nonsense—"

Morgan stormed out of the bed, grabbing up her clothes and dashing toward the bathroom. "The only nonsense I got caught up in," she said tersely, "was—was this," she blurted, slamming the door to the bathroom so hard, a glass fell off the shelf of the medicine cabinet and shattered on the tile floor.

"Damn," she muttered, then leaned heavily against the closed door, taking deep breaths to calm down. At least it wasn't the mirror that broke, she thought ruefully. All she needed was seven more years of bad luck. She looked around the room for something with which to sweep up the shards of glass, settling for a discarded piece of cardboard in the trash. She gashed her foot in the process, but then that was par for the course. Tears

110

blinded her as she sat on the edge of the tub blotting the heel of her foot with a wad of tissue. She dressed quickly and hobbled over to the medicine chest, but all of the bandages and ointment were in Ben's room.

She opened the door. Ben was just buttoning his shirt. He saw her hobble across the room and pick up the gauze.

"I'm fine," she said sullenly. "It's just a little cut."

He walked over to her and pushed her onto the bed. She started to protest, but he grabbed her foot, ignoring her mutterings.

"That's quite a wound."

She tried to pull her foot away. "I'll take care of it myself."

He had a solid grip on her ankle. "I was a much more cooperative patient than you are, Miss Gerard." He looked up at her, a soft smile on his lips. "Can't you stay out of trouble for even a minute?"

Morgan sighed. "It doesn't look that way, does it?"

She flinched as he gently examined the cut. Giving up the battle she let him clean and bandage it.

"I don't think there's any glass in it, but we could have Dr. Spenser check it out."

Morgan shook her head. "It isn't necessary. But you might warn your housekeeper that I probably didn't get every piece of broken glass off the floor."

"I will."

She stood up gingerly, testing out the heel of her right foot. Not too bad. She reached for her shoes, laughing as she remembered that she'd lost both heels when Ben used them to try to pry off the boards from Charlotte Caspel's window. She held them up. "These are in worse shape than I am. I've got to pick up some things in town. I'll walk over and—and call a taxi to take me back to the inn."

"Call a taxi?" He smiled wryly. "I don't know if you'll be too successful. Al Harper does use his old Ford on occasion, but he went fishing with the police chief yesterday."

"I'll hitch a ride, then."

Ben looked down at his watch. "I'll give you a couple of hours to shop around and then I'll pick you up in front of Louella's and drive you out to the inn."

"I wouldn't want to put you to any trouble," she said archly.

Ben grinned. "Trouble? Trouble seems to be my middle name since we met." He moved closer to her. "I wonder," he said in a seductive voice, "what's going to happen next?"

Morgan's lips broke into a smile. "You're not the only one to wonder." She paused. "What's Louella's?"

"It's one of the two dress shops in town. You can't miss it," he said dryly.

"Let's make it an hour. Something tells me, given the number of choices I'm going to have, it won't take me very long."

"An hour it is."

There was a strained silence. Morgan saw that Ben hadn't finished with the buttons of his shirt. Her eyes lingered on his chest, a flash of the passion they had just shared hitting her full force. Her mouth went dry and she could feel herself tremble. She turned away abruptly, but Ben caught her in his arms.

She pressed her hands against his chest. "Don't, Ben. I've never acted so—so instinctively before. I need to sort it out." Her eyes reflected a blend of warmth, excitement, and a touch of panic. "Let's both give it some time. Okay?"

He hesitated, his hands gently running down her back before he released her. "Okay."

She smiled, then started toward the door. Once there she paused and turned slowly. "As far as what we talked about before, the film company using the Caspel estate, they wouldn't be putting a great deal of money into fixing it up. If you read the script you'll see that the place has to look pretty much like it does now. For the—atmosphere. So, as far as that's concerned, it shouldn't affect your campaign." She ran her tongue over her dry lips.

Ben studied her for a moment and then smiled faintly. "I suppose I always have been a little afraid of that place. Even before that crazy dare I took. I don't know . . . it always had bad vibes. I guess I'm more superstitious than I like to think. But," he said firmly, "those feelings are not guiding my campaign to raze the mansion. We really need that park, and the Caspel grounds provide the ideal setting."

Morgan watched him steadily, not saying anything.

His smile broadened. "I'll read the script."

"Oh, Ben, thanks. I know—"

"Whoa. I'm still not promising anything. Don't go running out to call Bergson. I still have to make sure . . . I think I may need to have my head examined." He let out a breath like a sigh. "If I do give my go-ahead, you better warn that film crew of Bergson's that they'd better toe the line or they'll—"

Morgan laughed. "I know. You'll squash them all into that cell and lose the key again."

"You've got it."

Morgan paused. "You know, for a while there I thought you'd really made up your mind to turn me down and were just leading me down the primrose path." She tilted her head, giving him a calculating look.

Ben came up to her. "For a short while you were right. Now . . . well, things are different."

She reached out and pressed her hand lightly to his chest. Then she finished buttoning his shirt. "Yes. Things are different now," she said softly. Then, with a bright smile, she said, "See you in an hour."

Morgan left the house and walked the block to town in the glittering sunlight. Her heel felt only slightly tender, not enough to affect her lilting step. She felt remarkably high-spirited, full of excitement and enthusiasm. Refusing to analyze her feelings, she proceeded to have herself a delightful shopping spree. Although the selection of clothes was limited, as she'd suspected, Morgan was surprised to find the selection in both Madison's and Louella's to be quite cosmopolitan. She

114

bought more than she needed, chatting amiably with the shopkeepers as she picked out her garments. When she mentioned that she was in Rocky Bluff to do some groundwork for the possible filming of a Hollywood movie, both the shopkeepers and the other customers in the stores got very excited, especially when they learned that Joe Shaeffer and the French beauty Françoise Perrin were starring in the film.

Morgan was sure that within hours the whole town would be buzzing with excitement about *Windswept.* She also knew that Ben would have a hard time turning her down now. Not that she was worried. She'd known as soon as he said he'd read the script that he'd already made up his mind to let Bergson do the film. He just needed a few days to make it seem like he wasn't making the decision too rashly.

Glancing out of Louella's storefront window she saw Ben pull up. She checked herself quickly in the mirror. Dressed in a soft peach cotton sundress with low sandals in a matching color, she looked much more like the Morgan Gerard she knew before this whole astounding adventure started.

CHAPTER SEVEN

Morgan and Ben were having dinner together at the Bluffside Inn. It was the third night in a row since the afternoon he'd brought her out there. Although the small seaside inn was a casual, country-style place, both of them had dressed up for dinner each evening.

Morgan thought Ben looked especially debonaire tonight in his light-beige suit, and the soft-blue shirt heightened his naturally tanned complexion. He'd removed the patch over his eyebrow and only a slight red line marked the spot. He was very handsome, she thought again. But it was more than his appearance that drew her to him. There was an intensity about Ben, hidden most of the time—by choice, she believed—she had seen it several times, but never as sharply as when they'd made love.

Ben had been a fierce, demanding, and yet tender lover. He'd responded to every nuance of change in her mood, following her rhythm, leading her smoothly into his. He had brought her to the most startling climax. She had never experienced the excitement, the uninhibited passion she'd felt with Ben that one heated afternoon.

Since then they had both pulled back. It was as if they were almost afraid to tempt the fates. At least that's what Morgan decided. She still felt that there was some special, powerful force drawing her to Ben, and while she told herself it was crazy to think that the Caspel estate and Charlotte and Eliot had anything to do with it, she could not shake the notion.

Ben had spent the past few days showing her the rest of the town, but he had assiduously avoided the Caspel place, telling her that Dunne and one of the other policemen had found signs of someone having broken into the place when they went to check it out. Morgan didn't believe him, but she hadn't wanted to push the issue. Besides, there were other locations she was supposed to cover.

It had been a lovely three days. Her bad luck seemed to have run its course and there were not even any minor disasters marring the time she and Ben had spent together. As he showed her around, Morgan began to understand Ben's strong feelings for Rocky Bluff. Beyond its being very quaint and picturesque, there was an air of warmth, friendliness, and tranquility that permeated the area.

Even Morgan, so used to the easygoing style of California, found the mood in Rocky Bluff especially soothing. Being here she realized for the first time in ages how much of a treadmill she'd been on these past five years. She'd traveled to many places, studying them, evaluating them, analyzing

117

them, and yet, as odd as it seemed, she'd never really seen them. Not the way she was seeing Rocky Bluff. But then, maybe it was her guide who made the difference.

"You look fantastic tonight. Even better than this fresh garden salad."

Morgan set down her butter knife and grinned. "I gather that's quite a compliment."

"Have you ever seen a fresher, prettier-looking salad? Just look at this tomato." He speared a cherry tomato with his fork. "Perfect color, fresh and ripe, exquisite shape. And the lettuce—cool, crisp, yet just the right hint of softness."

"And the vinaigrette dressing?" Morgan eyed him with amusement.

"Ah, the dressing." He paused, taking a bite of lettuce. "Mmm. Tangy, maybe a touch tart—but irresistible. However," he murmured softly, leaning closer to her, "not nearly as irresistible as you."

His voice was playful, but his eyes spoke of passion. Morgan was startled to realize how aroused she suddenly felt. She had not worn a bra with her nearly backless lavender sundress and the sensation of her hardened nipples pressing against the silky material was exciting and unnerving at the same time. It was also quite visible, as Ben's smiling gaze attested.

Morgan's cheeks reddened.

"I'm glad I still get to you."

Morgan tilted her head. "What does that mean?"

"Oh, just that you've acted very cool and professional these past few days."

"I thought we'd decided—"

"I can't get you out of my mind, Morgan. There's a song that goes like that—great lyrics. And very appropriate. You can't imagine how many cold showers I've taken since . . . since we made love the other afternoon. I'm even ready to concede there are forces beyond my control operating here. You've bewitched me, Morgan. I'm haunted by visions."

"Don't do this to me, Ben. It isn't fair." She emitted a small laugh. "How can I concentrate on this perfect salad?"

"I'm willing to skip the salad. Let's go take a long drive. I have a small cabin I rent each summer. It's just a few miles up the road, right on the Sound. Nothing fancy, but it's a beautiful spot. A kind of hideaway. You need a place like that sometimes in this kind of job." He took the fork out of her hand. "I took it as of today, actually. Do you want to come clear away the cobwebs with me?"

Morgan gave him a skeptical glance. "Is it haunted?"

"Absolutely not." He laughed.

Morgan hesitated. What had become of her resolve to take things slow?

"I have to be out of town tomorrow. There's a regional mayors' meeting in Nassau County. I'll be back late." It was his turn to hesitate. "I thought you might like to stay at the cabin while you're in town. It's a lot more private than the inn."

Morgan gave him a knowing look. As mayor of Rocky Bluff Ben had to be discreet. He couldn't very well pay Morgan a visit to the inn and leave

119

the next morning, the whole town would soon know about it. Just as they all now knew what she was doing here. Ben had told her, not too happily, that he'd been besieged by inquiries about the filming. There were more people in favor of the idea than against, and those in favor all wanted to get into the act. As for his decision, Ben had not said anything definite, and Morgan was trying very hard to be patient. It wasn't easy. Bergson had called at least half a dozen times so far. He was anxious to get started and wasn't particularly long on patience himself.

Morgan felt Ben watching her.

"You can make up your mind after you see the place tonight." His voice held a note of tender command. Morgan looked across at him. His eyes drew her like a magnet, and she felt slightly dizzy.

Very slowly she pushed the dish away. "We'll have to make up some excuse for running off like this without even eating our dinner."

"Leave it to me," he said with a soft smile. "I've had a lot of practice being diplomatic." He pushed his chair away from the table and stood up.

Morgan watched him walk over to Alice Holt, the owner and, in the off season, waitress at the inn. Alice, a small, tidy woman who exuded exceptional energy, nodded several times, glancing over at Morgan with an understanding smile.

A moment later Ben was helping Morgan out of her seat. He leaned close. "I told Alice you weren't feeling well. You think it's probably your allergy to zinnias acting up."

"The inn is surrounded by zinnias."

120

Ben grinned. "I know."

Morgan laughed, dismissing her reluctance. The truth was, she wanted to spend the night with Ben. She had a burning desire to see if it would be the same, if he would once more carry her off into uncharted worlds. And she wanted to wake up in the morning and see him lying beside her. That potent force she'd been fighting for days came rushing back with such power, she gripped Ben's arm for support.

A half hour later Ben pulled his small Triumph up in front of a gray shingled cottage. Pretty brass lanterns on either side of the door were lit invitingly.

Morgan gave him a knowing look. "You were pretty damn sure of yourself, Mayor Corbett."

He smiled sheepishly. "I was just being optimistic." He leaned over and nibbled her ear. "Do you mind?"

Morgan laughed. "Optimism has gotten us both through some rough spots."

Ben leaned farther, opening the car door for Morgan. He gathered her overnight bag from the tiny backseat after she got out.

The sun had slipped down over the horizon, and only a small band of vivid red hovered on the edge. It was just enough light for Morgan to see that Ben had been right about the cabin being both beautifully situated, perched right on a low bluff with easy access to a sandy beach, and very private. There wasn't another house in sight.

A slight evening chill was in the air, but Morgan, having grown used to the spring weather in Rocky

121

Bluff, had thought to wear a sweater. She'd also changed out of her sundress into more casual clothes, a print skirt and a blue blouse as close to the color of her eyes as anything she owned. She knew Ben was taken with the startling turquoise of her eyes, and it had been no accident that she'd chosen this particular blouse tonight. Even the sweater, a white cotton knit cardigan, was rimmed in the same blue.

"The door's open," Ben said, gathering up a few logs from the woodpile. Morgan came over and retrieved her overnight case so that he wouldn't have to do a balancing act.

She opened the front door and stepped inside. There were a couple of dimly lit lamps on in the large main room. Blended with the soft evening light filtering in through the windows, the space took on a beguiling, romantic glow. Most of the furniture was made of wicker, with bright, cheerful cushions adding warmth and sparkle.

"It isn't very rustic," she said, setting down her bag near the couch. "In fact, it's much more lavish than you led me to believe."

He dropped the wood by the hearth and walked over to her. "I know from our night in the jail cell how much you hate to rough it," he teased. "Anyway, it's not so lavish. Although there is hot and cold running water, an indoor shower, and a cozy bedroom . . . right this way." He took her hand and led her across the old pine floor scattered with colorful rag rugs.

The bedroom was as cozy as Ben claimed, with its big brass double bed, an antique rocker, and a lovely handmade quilt hanging quaintly over a carved wooden stand. On top of the one good-sized oak dresser sat a beautiful blue-and-white china bowl and pitcher filled with fresh wild-flowers.

Ben chuckled softly as Morgan walked over and breathed in the scent of the bouquet. "Optimism." He grinned.

Morgan plucked out a flower and cast him a devilish smile. "Zinnias? You know how they make me suffer."

"Come here," he said seductively. "Let me see if I can make you feel better."

When he slammed the bedroom door closed with his foot, Morgan felt as though they had just shut out the rest of the world. She walked into his open arms.

Ben drew her tenderly against him, his embrace filled with longing and promise. Morgan could feel every one of her nerve endings taut with anticipation and an almost uncontrollable excitement. And this time her feelings were completely removed from fantasies of Charlotte and Eliot. This time there was nothing eerie or strange about her desire. All her thoughts were for Ben alone. As their lips met, she knew that she had been waiting hungrily for this moment for the past three days. She knew that Ben Corbett was very rare, very special.

He gently massaged her neck, then slid the sweater off her shoulders. She leaned against him, feeling the heat of his arousal as he molded her to his body, his mouth covering hers for a deeper, more penetrating kiss.

Morgan's skin felt on fire. He didn't bother with the buttons of her blouse, instead tugging it up over her head. She shook her hair free and Ben smoothed it slowly to one side, kissing the sensitive skin behind her left ear. Then he slipped her skirt over her hips and gathered her up in his arms.

They fell together on the bed, Morgan grappling with his clothes, finding it unbearable not to feel his heated nakedness against her.

Finally, when they were lying naked in each other's arms, Ben spread a warm spray of kisses along her shoulder, his tongue leaving tiny tingling sensations that tickled and aroused her even more. As he caressed her body, trailing kisses and taking tender nibbling bites, Morgan felt as though she were floating, drifting, in a world that belonged only to the two of them. As Ben's lips and hands consumed her, she wrapped her arms and legs around him, urging him on, wanting more . . . more. . . .

Lost in his own passion, Ben felt an all-consuming need for Morgan. He was driven to experience every facet her exquisite body had to offer. He captured a sweet, taut nipple between his lips, letting his tongue rub across it, suckling it as Morgan cried out with pleasure. His hands moved down over her flat abdomen and her body arched to meet his exploring fingers. His mouth left her breast and drifted slowly down over her rib cage, trailing enticingly along the velvety plane of her

124

stomach. He could feel her muscles quivering as her legs parted and her breath came in rapid gasps.

He lifted her slightly, his caresses evoking an abandon in Morgan that matched his own. His searching mouth grew greedy, demanding, his hands smoothing, touching, fondling. Her sweetness was intoxicating.

Reeling with sheer, aching desire, he moved on top of her, entering her with an almost merciless thrust. A low groan escaped her lips, but very quickly she grew breathless, her senses rioting. She drew his lips to hers, their kiss wild and fevered. She tasted blood, but had no idea if it was his or hers, nor did she care.

Together they shared in the sensation of release to the fullest. Then, collapsing beside her, Ben let out one long, supremely contented sigh. He held her tight against him, his lips nuzzling her neck. In the aftermath Morgan still trembled, waves of passion continuing to undulate through her body.

They stayed like that for a long while. Ben pulled the cover up around them, taking great pleasure in feeling her lean, lovely body relaxing against him. It was very peaceful and quiet. For the first time in his life he was sharply aware of what he had missed. No, it was more than that, he realized. It was what he had always been waiting for. Were there fates, spirits, at work, guiding Morgan to him? Certainly he felt the magic, the enchantment, a myriad of feelings he'd never known before.

He ran his fingers along the softly rounded

curve of her hip. "Let's stay like this forever," he murmured against her ear.

"Impossible." She sighed. Then, feeling Ben stiffen, she tilted her head toward him and grinned. "I'm starving. If you remember, we skipped dinner. I don't suppose in your optimism you thought to pick up some food?"

He kissed the tip of her nose. "Don't move."

Morgan stretched. "I wouldn't think of it."

As she luxuriated under the soft, satiny comforter, she listened to Ben in the other room, rattling dishes and slamming cabinets. She propped herself up with several pillows as he walked into the bedroom, carefully setting the tray he was balancing in the palm of one hand on the bedside table.

Morgan laughed. "This is the first time in my life I've ever been served by a naked waiter."

"How do you like it?" he asked with a teasing smirk.

Morgan tilted her chin. "Turn around. I want to see if the back is as good as the front."

He did a mock pirouette, setting Morgan off into a spate of giggles. "Yes"—she nodded enthusiastically—"I like it." She pulled him down so that he fell on top of her. "I love it."

He pressed his lips to hers, cutting off her laughter. Then, in a voice filled with passion, he whispered, "I love you."

She stared at him, her turquoise eyes large and glowing.

He caressed her cheek. "I love you, Morgan," he said again.

"This is crazy, you know," she said softly.

"Is that your way of telling me you love me too?" he asked slowly.

"Ben . . ."

He pressed a finger to her lips. "What's wrong with being a little crazy, Morgan?"

"Probably a lot of things." She sighed. "But right this minute I can't think of any."

He kissed her, a hard, quick kiss—a seal.

They dined on croissants stuffed with fresh sliced chicken and a mustardy mayonnaise sauce, drank a bottle of cool, crisp white wine, made love again, and fell into a wonderful, languorous sleep.

The next day was anything but languorous. It started out well enough when Morgan awoke in Ben's arms to see his eyes smiling down on her. She moved against him for a hungry morning kiss that easily drifted into sleepy, tender caresses and then into a more familiar kind of lovemaking that made them feel very close.

The fight didn't begin until after breakfast. Well, not exactly a fight so much as a heated difference of opinion. It began with an order that made Morgan bristle.

"Listen," he said casually, dressing a bit hurriedly for the meeting he had to attend, "I'll drop you off back at the inn to pack. I'll also have Jack bring your rented car and your license there. So you're on your own today. There's only one thing." He stopped knotting his tie in mid-motion to glance at her. "I don't want you going back to the Caspel estate."

Morgan narrowed her eyes. "Why not?"

"I mean it, Morgan. Check out your other locations, do anything else you want to do, but you're to stay clear of the estate. Don't forget I haven't completely made up my mind yet about the film."

"Don't you think it's about time you did?"

"I wrote to Bergson. I told him that if he could find another estate, he could use Rocky Bluff for the other location shootings."

"He'll never agree to that. You know it's the Caspel estate that he wants to use the most." She walked over to him. "What is it, Ben? This campaign of yours to raze the place, or your fear that there's more there than meets the eye?"

He grabbed her, more violently than he meant. He immediately released her. "Will you stop it, Morgan? No more talk of ghosts, spirits, or crazy supernatural ideas."

"Last night you thought being a little crazy was fine," she said hotly.

"Dammit, don't twist my words." He looked down at his watch. "I'm late. Get dressed and I'll take you over to the inn."

"No, thanks," she said archly. "I'll walk."

"It's seven miles. Be reasonable."

"I don't want to be reasonable. I want to be crazy."

Ben sighed. "We'll talk when I get back tonight, but it will be late."

She started for the bathroom door. Before Ben left, he shouted, "I mean what I said, Morgan. Stay away from the Caspel estate while I'm gone."

* * *

Her anger and frustration made her not think about that seven-mile trek. She started out practically storming down the road. At least for the first four miles or so. A cramp in her side slowed her down then, and the strap of her sandal began rubbing painfully against her heel. She began to listen for the sound of cars so she could hitch a ride the rest of the way. Her luck, not a single car passed.

By the time the inn was in sight, she was tired and hot and she had several blisters forming from the new sandals she'd broken in so mercilessly. The only bright spot was that she saw her car waiting in the small parking lot. She walked into the inn, eager to have a shower and then take a nice long drive to cool off some more.

"Oh, Miss Gerard." Alice Holt stopped her as she started up the stairs. "Officer Dunne stopped by with your car."

"Yes, I know. I saw it in the lot. Did he happen to leave my driver's license with you?"

Alice slipped her hand in her pocket, pulling out the paper. "Here it is."

Morgan took it, thanking her. Again she started up the stairs.

"How did things work out in town?"

Morgan gave Alice a blank look.

"Do you think it was the zinnias?"

"Oh, zinnias. I, uh, don't think it was, Mrs. Holt. No, I'm pretty sure I'm not allergic to zinnias after all."

"Then will you be staying at the inn?"

Morgan hesitated. Flashes of last night's passion

mingled with the heat of this morning's tension. She took in a deep breath. "Yes," she said slowly, "I'll try it here for a while."

"Well, that's nice," Alice said cheerily. "I'd hate to think the Bluffside Inn was the cause of your distress."

Morgan slipped off her sandals and held them in her hand as she walked up the stairs. "No, Mrs. Holt. My feeling poorly . . . has nothing to do with the inn."

When Morgan was at the top of the stairs, Mrs. Holt called out, "Oh, Miss Gerard, I almost forgot. Mr. Bergson called again. He said—let me see . . . oh, yes, he'd see you at Charlotte's at ten tonight."

Morgan stopped in her tracks. "At Charlotte's?"

"Why, yes, that's what he said. I asked him if there was a last name, but he said you'd know who he was talking about."

Morgan felt a shiver crawl right down her back. "I know who he means." She stared down at Mrs. Holt. "Are you sure he said ten tonight?"

"I'm quite sure," Mrs. Holt said, a trace of annoyance in her voice. She certainly knew how to take a message after all these years running an inn.

Morgan picked up Mrs. Holt's irritation. "I'm sorry. It's just—I didn't think he would be flying out here so soon."

Mrs. Holt accepted the apology graciously and scurried off to the kitchen, where she was baking her special rhubarb pie. Morgan hurried to her room and went directly to her telephone. Her fingers trembled. She had to reach Lloyd Bergson before he left Hollywood. His precipitous arrival could blow the whole deal, not to mention the fact that Ben would have her head if she went off to the Caspel estate tonight. It wasn't that a part of her didn't want to defy him, and there was another part that continued to feel this strangely compelling desire to return, but it was trespassing. At this point neither she nor Bergson had any right to go communing with spirits.

Why, she wondered as she dialed Bergson's L.A. exchange, had he picked the dark of night to have her meet him out there? Why, indeed? Lloyd Bergson was the king of horror. It suited his personality perfectly to go stalking around those large silent rooms in the night. What really shook Morgan was that the notion of wandering those rooms with him did not frighten her in the least. Even as she listened to Bergson's phone ring, she knew that part of her didn't want him to answer. Then she'd have a perfect excuse for going out to the Caspel estate to try to head Bergson off.

The phone rang a dozen times before Morgan gently replaced the receiver in the cradle. Her hand rested on the phone, and a small smile curved her lips. She glanced out the window. The wind was beginning to whip up. By tonight there might be quite a storm. Tonight Charlotte might be racing through the halls to Eliot's outstretched arms. Morgan shivered. But her smile remained.

CHAPTER EIGHT

Morgan switched off the engine and let her car coast the last twenty feet. Two other cars were parked a few feet farther up, under a cluster of birch trees about ten yards from the wrought-iron gate. Morgan was puzzled. She hadn't expected Bergson to show up with anyone else. Trepidation rose in her throat. What did Bergson think he was going to do, throw a party?

Somewhere off in the distance a church bell tolled ten faint gongs. Morgan stepped out of the car. She was wearing a soft, sheer white dress with a black satiny poncho thrown over it. The expected storm had materialized. The wind whipped across the path and Morgan's hood flew off, her hair getting soaked before she could pull it back on. She hurried to the gate, wishing in earnest now that she'd been able to reach Bergson. It really was crazy to be stalking around this place in the pitch dark—not to mention a blinding storm.

There was a scratching noise. Morgan stopped in her tracks, looking around. She could barely make out the wrought-iron fence, and the Caspel estate itself was completely obliterated in the thick fog and rain. She told herself it was only the leaves of the trees and forced herself to go on.

The gate was padlocked. Morgan stared at it in frustration, then sighed. There had to be a way in. Bergson would have waited for her in his car otherwise. She started off to her left, hugging the half-wall for protection and cursing the darkness as she stumbled over a tree stump and nearly fell into the mucky leaves. She told herself she ought to forget Bergson, just turn around and return to the inn. But she continued walking, searching for a plausible alternate entry to the grounds.

She found it along the back wall of the estate, a crumbling section of concrete, the result of more than a hundred years of briny seawater smashing against the cliffs and slapping up at the wall. It wasn't an easy climb by any means, but it was possible. Morgan was sure Bergson had gotten in this way.

Stepping gingerly, the blackness and rain confounding each of her movements, she managed to get halfway up the wall. Her right foot was wedged into a narrow groove, and with her straining fingers gripping the concrete as best she could, she freed her left foot and attempted to find a second notch. She began feeling around frantically as her fingers started losing hold. A moment later she was sliding down to where she'd begun.

This was pure insanity, she told herself, starting the frustrating climb over again. But something was driving her on now. She had to get into the mansion, and if she'd let herself think about it, she'd admit it had nothing to do with Lloyd Bergson, *Windswept,* or her job. The same strange feeling that had taken hold of her that first visit was gripping her again.

This time she managed to scale the crumbling barrier with little difficulty. Once on the top she found her way down the other side made easier, as it was covered with hardy ivy vines for her to grab on to.

The Caspel estate came into hazy view, the rear of the building appearing to be as ornately designed as the front. The winds were slightly less violent inside the walled grounds, but the rain seemed to be coming down harder. Morgan felt a rush of excitement as she raced across the wet grass. She was oblivious to the soaking that her black canvas shoes were getting.

Racing toward the house, her black cloak and ruffled white skirt flapping almost rhythmically, she made an eerie, almost ghostlike vision in the stormy night. By the time she made it to the back door she felt anything but ghostlike. She was bone-cold and shivering, her whole body trembling with anticipation. And yet her feeling of decisiveness had gone. She hesitated, a wave of fear passing over her.

She thought she heard the not-so-distant snapping of twigs. She pressed against the back door, her muscles tightening. Was it Eliot hurrying in the stormy night to his love? *Stop it,* she chided. Ben was right. She was letting her imagination get the best of her.

The door gave way so suddenly, Morgan went

flying into the house. Unable to brace herself she stumbled to the floor.

It was hard and cold. And wet. Wet from Bergson's footsteps, no doubt. And whoever else he'd dragged along. Ben would be livid if he found out that Bergson had actually broken into the place. She flashed her penlight beam on the door, then down to the cement floor where she saw the broken lock.

Shining the light around, she realized she was in a small back hallway. It was damp and smelled sharply of mildewed plaster and old wallpaper. Morgan's eyes fixed on the slightly ajar door leading into what she supposed was the kitchen.

"Mr. Bergson?" She paused. "Lloyd?" The flat sound of her voice startled her. There was no answer. He was probably wandering around the front of the house.

Her poncho dripped more water onto the floor. Morgan lifted it over her head, hanging it on a wall hook. She shook her hair, then smoothed out her white dress. How strange, she thought suddenly, to have chosen this particular dress. She'd bought it the other day at Louella's on impulse, a strong impulse to buy something different from her usual style. The garment reminded her of an old-fashioned garden dress with its flouncy skirt and the soft ruffles along the modest V neck.

A small gasp caught in her throat. What was coming over her? Now she knew why she'd chosen that particular style. The dress she was wearing was a lot like the dress in that faded sepia photo of Charlotte. Morgan shut her eyes, seeing an image of Charlotte running through the halls . . . Charlotte in the same white garden dress.

Morgan's body froze as the image changed. She could see Charlotte in her bedroom, near the window, wearing that dress, that same white dress. Charlotte was looking out, smiling winsomely. There was a shadowy figure in the distance, waving. It was Eliot.

"Oh, my God," Morgan muttered, a rush of terror overpowering her. She closed her eyes tighter. Charlotte. She was tumbling through space, outstretched like an eagle as a low scream tore through the air.

Only it was Morgan's scream. It came as she watched Charlotte land against the bluff, her white dress billowing in the wind, her thin, lithe body motionless.

Morgan clutched her hand over her mouth. She was shaking uncontrollably, beads of sweat breaking out across her forehead. She stumbled toward the door, hurrying out of that tight, airless space and into the large kitchen.

She heard another sound, then, a new one. A thud, once, and then again. Morgan fought to catch her breath. Over and over she told herself these visions and sounds were only her mind playing tricks. She must have read those same scenes in the script. An overactive imagination. Yes, that was it.

Forget Charlotte, she ordered herself sharply. *Go find Bergson and his friends. And get them out of here.* She hurried from the kitchen and up the narrow passage to the front hall, her penlight showing the way.

She felt a little better. This area was familiar. She had entered into this hall with Ben that day.

She experienced a sharp pang of loneliness. Ben. She wished he were here with her now. But of course he wouldn't be. He hated this place. There was something here that truly frightened him. But what? Certainly he was not the fanciful type, not the type to let his imagination run away with itself.

Maybe the Caspel estate truly was haunted. Such turbulent emotions had existed here. Love, blinding passion, searing jealousy—and violence. If Ben didn't get his way and the place was made into a museum, Morgan wondered if these strange, eerie sensations would disappear from the house. She doubted they would. And for the first time she could sympathize a little with Ben's desire to tear it down. It might be for the best. Yet the thought still saddened her. Charlotte and Eliot would be gone forever.

Morgan was startled from her reverie by the return of that thudding sound. It seemed to be coming from somewhere beneath the floor.

The cellar.

God, she thought, how many horror movies were there where the innocent ingenue goes lurking about the silent house, creaking open the basement door, slowly, hesitantly, going down—

Skip the cellar, she decided firmly. *Leave it to the rats, or whatever else is down there.* She called Lloyd's name again from the bottom of the stairs.

There was still no answer. She felt edgy as she

roamed through the rooms on the first floor, going into the living room first. It was empty. A motor sounded in the stillness, making Morgan jump. But then the sound faded, and she realized it was only a car heading down the main road. Hurrying through the other rooms, Morgan found only cold, empty spaces. Maybe Bergson hadn't. gotten in after all. Maybe he and his pals were still searching the grounds. No, they'd be insane to wander outside in this storm. And the back door had been opened. Morgan had the disturbing thought that he was purposely trying to frighten her. She wouldn't put that past him. Lloyd had a warped sense of humor. He could be testing her reactions, using her as a chill-factor barometer. At this moment she'd likely register off the top.

It was her irritation at the possibility that she was the victim of a Bergson prank that urged her on. She started up the stairs, the renewed silence more unnerving, but her annoyance mounting. Damn Bergson. She hadn't wanted this miserable assignment in the first place.

But then, if she'd gone off to the sunny French West Indies, she would never have met Ben Corbett. She would never have known the unbelievable heights of passion she'd discovered with him. She would never have experienced such feverish, all-consuming desire. She might never have felt what it was like to fall in love.

She felt her cheeks flush. It was crazy to think she was in love with a man she had known for less than a week. How could she give the feelings she was having much credence? It took time to fall in love.

So when did it happen? she wondered. Did it take a month, a year, a lifetime? Morgan had known several men for long periods of time, even toyed with the notion that she might be falling in love with one or two. But never—never before—had she experienced the mind-shattering intensity of feelings that Ben Corbett evoked.

She did love him. She'd been afraid to admit it to him the night before. Loving meant having expectations. It meant making a commitment. What kind of a commitment could she make? In a few months she'd be gone, off on her next assignment, and then the next. There were so many places to go, so many new, exciting experiences.

But had she ever known the excitement she'd known these past few days with Ben? Would there ever be other experiences that would begin to measure up with these?

She paused at the top of the stairs, throwing off those thoughts, focusing on finding Lloyd Bergson. She took a few cautious steps.

She was standing directly outside of Charlotte's room. Her hand was poised on the doorknob, her heart pounding.

"Lloyd," she muttered, "if this is your idea of a joke, I'm going to murder you."

She swallowed hard. Best not to talk of murder, even figuratively. Then, chiding herself for such foolish superstitiousness, she boldly opened the door to Charlotte's room.

As her eyes tried to adjust to the darkness in the

antique bedchamber, she detected the soft scent of lilies. Though faint, it was cloying to Morgan's senses. Lilies. People covered coffins with pure white lilies, didn't they?

She could feel the color drain from her face. She wanted to turn and run from the room, but that same compelling force held her. She scanned the room with her penlight, which illuminated a desk in the room. She walked over to it and shone the light over its top. The light picked up the locket lying where she'd left it. Again she lifted it up, flicking open one half of the heart.

A low, haunting sound wafted into the room. Morgan, her eyes transfixed on Charlotte's image, began to tremble.

Though the photo had faded badly, Morgan could make out the almost haunted smile on Charlotte Caspel's face, her eyes—they must be turquoise eyes—looking at Morgan.

With a shudder Morgan wrenched her gaze away, clutching the locket in her fist. It snapped shut. She moved to the window, no longer boarded thanks to Ben's efforts the other day. She shivered, recalling her terrifying escapade on that ledge. Then she remembered Ben's daring rescue. She looked out into the stormy night.

She set her tiny penlight on the desk. Strange sounds drifted through the house, but Morgan ignored them. She stared down at the turbulent sea, not really seeing it in the inky blackness, but hearing its fierce, thunderous sounds.

She closed her eyes, listening to the roar of the waves crashing against the bluff. Her body began to relax a little, the tension easing off—only to come back with stunning force in one moment.

"Charlotte." It was a low, hushed murmur.

Morgan's hand rose to her mouth in stark terror. A figure, barely visible in the gloom, was framed in the doorway. She fought off the dizziness, afraid to faint.

The figure took a step forward. Morgan uttered a breathless moan. "No," she whispered. He continued walking toward her.

A hand gripped her shoulder. Morgan screamed.

Suddenly she was being shaken. "Morgan, Morgan. Get ahold of yourself."

The scream died in her throat. "Lloyd? Damn it, Lloyd, are you trying to scare me to death?"

"Of course it's me. Who the hell were you expecting? Old man Caspel? Or Eliot?" He gave her one of his charmingly quizzical lifts of his eyebrow.

"But—but you called me Charlotte."

He laughed. "You fit the image so perfectly I couldn't resist." He gave her a lingering glance. "Just look at you. Even the dress is right. And the look on your face as you stared out to sea. If I hadn't already signed Lisa Owens to play Charlotte in this picture, I'd hand you a contract instantly. You'd make a magnificent Charlotte. Absolutely dazzling."

"No, thanks," she said emphatically. She was breathing normally again. "Is this your sick idea of fun? I don't appreciate playing hide-and-seek in a dark, spooky mansion in the dead of night. And has the thought crossed your mind that we happen to be trespassing? Just how many people did you bring? I saw two cars—"

"Will you slow down?" His smile broadened. "I wasn't playing hide-and-seek with you. I got here about twenty minutes ago and I've been checking the place out. I didn't hear you pull up."

"I turned the engine off so . . ." So what? The ghosts wouldn't hear her coming? "Ben says a prowler may have broken in."

"And by Ben I take it you mean the honorable Mayor Ben Corbett?"

Morgan felt her cheeks redden, glad for the dim light. "Yes. Well, I was edgy that whoever had gotten in might still be lurking around. And I was nervous."

Lloyd Bergson gave her a sly look. "You think it too."

"Think what?" she asked defensively.

"That the house is haunted." He didn't wait for her to protest. "It's a fantastic place, isn't it? Do you know how long I've wanted to shoot this story? I wrote the script more than ten years ago, but I had to pay my dues, directing the work of big-name writers before I could get the go-ahead for my own. At my price, of course," he added with a low chuckle.

"We have to get out of here, Lloyd. Ben Corbett has given strict orders that this estate is off limits. He told me he wrote you."

Lloyd shrugged. "The guy just isn't making any sense. What's his gripe with using the Caspel estate?"

She told him about Ben's plan to raze the building and set up a public park.

"So let him do it in three months," Lloyd argued. *"Windswept* has to be done here, if for no other reason than the fabulous publicity angle it provides. Imagine, the story of Charlotte Caspel filmed on location, right on the very grounds where it all happened. Just think of it, Morgan," he said excitedly.

"Just think about this: If we don't get the hell out of here right now, I guarantee you Ben will see to it that your publicity plans go up in little puffs of smoke."

"Okay, okay. Relax, sweetheart."

He turned on his flashlight as Morgan picked up her penlight. They were walking to the door when they heard the bloodcurdling scream.

Morgan froze, panic gripping her like a huge vise. Even Lloyd gasped.

"Charlotte," Morgan whimpered, gripping Lloyd's wrist.

"Charlotte, my ass. It's Françoise."

"Françoise?" She looked up blankly.

"Françoise Perrin. She and Joe Shaeffer followed me out here to see the place." He threw open the door. "Hurry up. She must be hurt."

Morgan, dragged down the hall, muttered, "Maybe she saw Charlotte."

"Very funny. If she broke her leg or something, it will set the picture back months."

Right now that possibility didn't bother Morgan in the least.

Lloyd rushed to the stairs, Morgan still in tow.

"Where are we going?"

"I left the two of them upstairs on the third floor," he explained. "There's a small chamber there where Charlotte used to meet Eliot after old man Caspel was asleep. Eliot would climb up the vines and get in through the window. That's supposedly where Caspel found them together." His words were coming in little gasps. Despite his lean, wiry build, Lloyd Bergson was not in the greatest shape. Too many long hours working to take care of his body. He was out of breath by the time he got to the top.

Morgan was breathless herself, but it had nothing to do with her physical condition. She was nearing the room where Charlotte and Eliot had become lovers. Her pulse rate quickened. When they got to the closed door, Lloyd flung it open and rushed inside. But Morgan held back, her features blanched. She felt a need to brace herself before stepping into that room.

"Damn," Lloyd exclaimed. "They're not here. I told them to stay put. God, this is all I needed."

By that time Morgan had worked up her courage to enter. Lloyd swung around to her, gripping her shoulders. "Okay, listen. You stay right here. I'll go look around. Maybe there is a prowler." He went to the door. "You'd better lock yourself in to be on the safe side." He sighed. "Chances are, Françoise just got spooked. Hey, it happened to you, right?"

In a barely audible voice Morgan murmured, "Right."

Lloyd nodded.

144

"Maybe—maybe I ought to come with you," Morgan called to him in a tight voice.

"No. You better stay in case they come back here. This is no place to play hide-and-seek. You said it yourself. I'll check back in, say, ten minutes."

It made sense, so she did what he said. But as soon as he closed the door Morgan wished she hadn't agreed to stay and wait. She walked over to the door, her hand on the lock. She drew it away, remembering her past luck with locked doors. No, she thought, it was better to have a quick and easy exit . . . just in case.

She realized then that she was still holding Charlotte's locket. She eased her grip, then looked around the room with the aid of her penlight.

It was a plain room, with nothing special or particularly pretty about it. Spare and simple, it was unembellished in any way. There was a double bed set at an angle in a corner of the room. A narrow oak bedside table stood to one side. There was nothing on the other side. Beneath the leaded window was a built-in seat, the cushion worn so badly it was impossible to make out the pattern of the material. Probably because of its height, this window hadn't been boarded up. A straight-backed chair in front of a small Empire-style desk was the only other furniture in the hideaway.

Morgan again picked up the scent of lilies. Françoise's scent, she told herself immediately. But it wasn't only the scent that permeated the space. There was something else. She stared around the room, a cold chill washing over her.

145

This had been a haven where passion and love had blossomed. And Morgan felt absolutely certain that this was the very room where the heartbroken lover had taken his own life.

Morgan shivered. She sat down primly on the chair. Then, feeling restless, she got up and moved to the window seat. She shut her mind to the eerie sounds. Focusing her penlight on the locket, she opened it and once again gazed down at Charlotte, feeling that strange kinship once more.

As Morgan went to shut the delicate case again, Charlotte's photograph fluttered out. From her having opened the old locket so many times recently, the picture must have slipped from the tiny prongs that held it in place. Morgan bent to retrieve it and then moved to refit the photo in its setting, but she stopped abruptly. Her astonished eyes stared at the open locket and her lips parted. She made a small sound, a little gasp of indrawn breath.

There was another photo hidden beneath Charlotte's. Having been protected by the first picture, this one was slightly less faded.

It was the picture of a man, a youthful, strikingly good-looking man. But it was the distinctive aquiline nose and the thick brows that drew Morgan's eye. She stared open mouthed at the photo of a man who looked for all the world like a young Ben Corbett.

The similarity between the two went beyond any particular feature of the face. Even the expression was the same.

Morgan's fingers trembled as she lifted the

photo out of the locket. She turned it over. In faded script she read, *Eliot, May 1907.* A new chill plunged down Morgan's spine. Did Ben know? Or was it his instinct alone which lead him to dread this place?

She rushed to the door. The hell with Bergson's orders. She had to get out of here. She had to—

The door was locked. "No! No," she cried. "It's impossible." She turned the bolt, but it wouldn't budge.

Tears began running down her cheeks. She started banging on the door, shouting for Lloyd. She beat the wooden barrier until her fists bruised. She was gasping for air, suddenly overcome with claustrophobia.

Racing to the window, she flung it open. A fierce gust of wind hit her in the face. She screamed for help into the darkness. Then, growing hoarse, she sank onto the window seat.

Then she found herself assailed by the eerie night sounds. She imagined Lloyd, Françoise, and Joe Shaeffer hideously swallowed up by goblins. She felt all alone in the house, locked in the room where Charlotte and Eliot had known such wild, abandoned passion. . . .

Morgan shut her eyes. She could see herself lying on that bed. She could see the open window, hear the footsteps scaling up the ivied wall. Eliot was there at the window, smiling across at Charlotte, leaping into the room, hurrying to her. And then the image changed to Ben, and he was staring down at her.

Morgan forced her eyes open. Her skin felt cold

and clammy and her head was spinning. She was afraid she was going to faint again.

In a growing swoon she heard footsteps. Lloyd. Lloyd was coming back. She pulled herself together and rushed to the door.

The handle rattled loudly.

"It's locked," she shouted. "I can't open it."

She stepped back as the knob turned and the door slowly opened.

He was standing there in the doorway. She ran the beam of her penlight over his face. His eyes were hard and cold, his face set and grim. Nothing like the warm look in the tiny photograph.

"Eliot," Morgan gasped beseechingly.

CHAPTER NINE

In the faint illumination from his flashlight Ben's face was as hard as granite and as eerie. Morgan watched him walk toward her. She felt strange, disoriented. She couldn't wrench her eyes from his.

He nearly lunged at her. "Have you gone absolutely insane, Morgan?"

"What do you mean?"

"Your mind has obviously snapped. First, you break in here—"

"I didn't—"

"Second," he cut her off ruthlessly, "you brought Bergson and his two star players out—"

"Françoise?" Morgan gripped his arm. "We heard her scream."

Ben shrugged off her arm. "She wrenched her ankle. Serves her right for sticking her dainty feet where they don't belong." He glared at her. "I haven't finished my count."

"Ben, please listen," Morgan entreated.

"Ah, that was to be point number three." Ben's flashing brown eyes narrowed momentarily. "But I see you've remembered my name again."

She stared at him blankly.

"When I walked in here, you called me Eliot." He didn't add that hearing her call him that name had made his body grow suddenly cold. And, inexplicably, in that instant the name had felt . . . right.

Morgan opened her mouth to explain, but Officer Jack Dunne walked in just then, and Ben turned abruptly away from Morgan.

"Take her down to the station along with the others. Book them for trespassing—no, make that breaking and entering."

Morgan gazed at him in shock, forgetting completely about the photo. "Breaking and entering? You can't be serious."

"I'm dead serious," he said icily. "If you want to play your Hollywood games, Morgan, then you're going to learn that here in Rocky Bluff, you pay the consequences." He wore a grim, sad expression. "I thought we were past playing games."

Jack Dunne hung back awkwardly. Morgan took a step closer to Ben. "I thought so too," she said angrily. "But you're too stubborn and pigheaded to even listen to explanations. Everything has to be your way, doesn't it? Well, you can't control everything, Ben."

"Maybe not. But I can keep you and your high-and-mighty friends out of my hair for a while."

"I did not break into this place."

"Yeah, that's what Bergson claims too. He conveniently found the back door ajar."

"The lock was broken. It was on the floor," Morgan insisted.

"Right now it's in a little plastic bag. The lab is going to check it for fingerprints." He glanced over his shoulder at the uniformed officer. "Well, what are you waiting for? Take her in."

Jack Dunne, looking decidedly uncomfortable, moved toward Morgan. When he took hold of her arm, she jerked away.

"We could always add resisting arrest—" He stopped mid-sentence, staring at the officer and then at Morgan. They had all picked up the acrid smell at the same time. Smoke.

Ben was the first one out the door, Jack and Morgan close on his heels. They raced down the stairs.

The smoke was coming from Charlotte's bedroom. Morgan gasped as Ben cautiously opened the door.

Charlotte's bed was on fire. Small curls of flame leapt from the mattress. In another few moments they would shoot up into torches of fire. Ben grabbed a blanket and began hitting at the flames, while Jack ran next door to the bathroom with the china pitcher. Ben managed to squelch the flames and Jack doused the embers with a good deal of cold water.

Ben looked over at Morgan. She stood framed in the doorway in her flowing white dress, her face almost as pale as the cloth. For a moment all Ben could think about was that she looked incredibly beautiful. And terribly upset. He walked slowly over to her, while Jack Dunne once again hung back, focusing his eyes on the burned mattress.

There were tears in her eyes, salty droplets

staining her cheeks. Ben felt an overwhelming need to comfort her, despite his anger and disappointment. He could feel her hurt as if it were his own. He didn't really comprehend it, nor did he imagine Morgan could. But whatever mysterious forces were operating here in this strange, foreboding house, there was no denying that they both experienced them. He reached out for her, taking her into his arms.

She fell against him like a rag doll. All of her energy, anger, and fight were drained. She just clung to him, burying her head against his chest, secure only in the steady, if quickened, beat of Ben's heart.

Jack Dunne cleared his throat, breaking the silence and the moment. "I'll send someone up to remove the mattress."

Ben dropped his arms to his sides, his expression once more grim. "Let's all get out of here before we have any more thrills in this . . . horror house. Take her in." He allowed no feeling to enter his voice.

Morgan felt sorely bruised as Ben relinquished his hold. This time she did nothing to resist Officer Dunne's light clasp on her arm. Ben strode out the door first. By the time Morgan stepped outside, Ben's car was tearing out of the driveway.

There were two police cars out front. A second officer, an older man with white hair, thick, rimless glasses, and a drawn, tired expression, sat at the wheel of one of the cars. In the backseat, all looking very petulant and bearing the faintest trace of fear, were Lloyd Bergson, Françoise Perrin, and Joe Shaeffer.

Jack whisked Morgan into his cruiser before she had any opportunity to talk with her companions in crime. But there'd be plenty of time for a reunion down at the tiny back-room police station. She found herself wondering just where the Rocky Bluff police were going to put all of them.

She found out when Jack Dunne pulled up behind the other cruiser at the Rocky Bluff Memorial Library. He ushered Morgan, Lloyd Bergson, and Joe Shaeffer inside the building while Françoise Perrin was driven to have her ankle checked before getting booked.

It was nearly eleven P.M., and it so happened that forty-three-year-old Valerie Lester, who lived with her mother in a small house directly across from the library, was just coming home from the nine o'clock movie at the Prince Cinema. She loved movies and saw almost every film that hit the Prince. She had secret crushes on a number of movie stars, but her most passionate dreams these past two years had revolved around the darkly handsome Joe Shaeffer.

When she saw him step out of the cruiser, her first thought was that she must be dreaming. She actually pinched herself, not only to make certain she wasn't in a fantasy, but to start her heart beating again. Joe Shaeffer, here in Rocky Bluff already. She, along with just about every other citizen of the town, had heard about the possibility of *Windswept* being filmed in Rocky Bluff. But Valerie hadn't been prepared for it to all start happening so soon.

Why, she pondered from her vantage point across the street, had her dream hero been in Harvey Schumacher's police cruiser? And what was he doing being escorted into the Rocky Bluff Memorial Library at eleven o'clock at night by Jack Dunne? She was so caught up in her thoughts about the hypnotic Joe Shaeffer that she ignored the other man walking beside him. However, she did pay attention to the fact that Morgan Gerard was also being led into the library. Something big was up. Valerie Lester was certain of it.

Before midnight a good half of the town knew that Joe Shaeffer was being held prisoner at the library. Although most of the townsfolk were not late-night people, a fair-sized crowd gathered at Elk Ridge Road hoping to get a glimpse of the famous movie star. When the lovely Françoise Perrin arrived in Harvey Schumacher's cruiser at twelve fifteen and limped to the stairs of the library on the policeman's arm, a small throng converged on the pair.

Jack Dunne scurried outside to settle things down.

"Go on, folks. Go home," he called out. He spotted his younger sister in the group and groaned. He wouldn't be surprised if his mother showed up soon. Ever since she'd heard about this dumb movie, she'd been talking about it nonstop. Why, she was even thinking about renting out the two guest rooms on the second floor to some of those Hollywood characters. Officer Dunne was clearly on Mayor Ben Corbett's side in all this. He'd been looking forward to a nice peaceful summer. If this was any example, peace was the last thing he would be getting.

"What's going on, Jack? Why are you holding Shaeffer and Françoise Perrin?"

Several people threw that question at him as he and Harvey Schumacher hurried the actress inside the library. Without an answer Jack waved the crowd to disperse them and bolted the door. Of course, none of them budged. And Jack had his hands too full to cope with that minor problem. They'd grow tired soon enough and amble back to their homes.

Morgan sat with a glum-looking Françoise Perrin in the larger of two offices in the basement of the library. Jack Dunne had just set up cots for them.

"Can I get you anything else?" he asked timidly. He hated to admit it, but he did feel slightly awed by the ravishing foreign movie star who stared at him with cool disdain. She mumbled something under her breath. Jack couldn't make it out, but he never had studied French in school. Even if he had, he probably wouldn't have been taught that particular phrase.

When he walked out, locking the door behind him, Morgan glanced down at Françoise's wrapped ankle.

"How is it?"

"The doctor says a sprain. All I know is, it hurts. When I asked him for a painkiller, he gave me a

155

suspicious glare and dropped a vial of aspirin in my palm."

Morgan's lips curved into a small smile. "The price of fame."

Françoise gingerly lifted a long, graceful leg up on an empty wooden chair and looked at Morgan blankly. "Does he actually think I'm going to sleep on that?" She gave the army cot a grimace of disgust.

Morgan stood up, stretched, and moved to one of the cots. "I don't know about you, but I've slept on worse." She stretched out on the cot, closing her eyes, picturing that first night she and Ben had huddled together in the jail cell. Oddly, it seemed so long ago. She took in a long, steadying breath and turned her head to Françoise.

"What happened tonight?"

"What happened?" Françoise exclaimed. "I'll tell you what happened. Your mad American director led me into a nightmare, that's what happened. I don't know what ever possessed me."

"What did possess you?" Morgan asked pointedly.

"To go into that house?"

"No. To scream when you did."

"I—I saw something." Françoise paused, her dark-blue eyes widening a little. "Someone. I saw someone running toward the stairs."

"A woman?" Morgan felt herself stiffen.

Françoise shook her head. "No. It was a man. I'm certain of that."

"What did he look like?" Morgan's mind flashed

on that photo of Eliot. "Was he tall, slender, dark-haired?"

Françoise shrugged. "My flashlight wasn't strong enough. But he wasn't tall. And he was"—she gestured with her hands forming two arcs—"full. Stocky, you would say."

Morgan gaped at her. "Stocky?"

"I am wrong?"

Morgan shook her head slowly, as if clearing away the fog from her mind. It hadn't been Eliot or Charlotte. Not some ethereal spirit at all. Morgan thought again about the locket lying on the floor and the fire in Charlotte's room. She focused back on the suspicious sounds she'd heard in the basement of the Caspel estate. The place *had* been broken into. But for what reason? Could that fire have been intentionally set? Maybe, Morgan reasoned, someone purposely locked her into the room where Charlotte and Eliot had had their rendezvous. She had no explanation, and yet Morgan knew a pattern was emerging.

She had to talk it over with Ben. She had to make him see that something very suspicious was going on at the Caspel estate, and it had nothing to do with ghosts and goblins. She sighed, closing her eyes again. It would have to wait until he calmed down a little. He'd been so angry at her. Hurt too. But she'd straighten it all out with him. What troubled her more was that eerie photograph of Eliot —a photograph that, had it not been clearly very old, could have easily been a shot of Ben in his mid-twenties.

She remembered Ben telling her he'd come

back to Rocky Bluff fourteen years ago. He was twenty-four years old then. How old had Eliot been in the photo? Close to the same age, she was sure. The vision of that photo crowded in on her. Morgan tried to marshal her thoughts, but nothing coherent materialized. She fell asleep finally. Long after Françoise Perrin had given up sulking and fallen into a deep sleep on her matching cot.

By the next morning word had spread not only through Rocky Bluff and to all the neighboring towns on the Island, but news of the Hollywood foursome's arrest had reached the press coast to coast—thanks to Lloyd Bergson's call to Harris Palmer, telling him to spread the word. It was fantastic publicity. Bergson couldn't have asked for anything better. He seemed oblivious to the fact that all four of them were facing several serious charges. He was absolutely convinced that *Windswept* was destined to be the biggest, most successful film of his career. Everything else, he assumed—correctly, as it turned out—would fall into place.

Donald Glick, of Forsythe and Glick, a powerful New York law firm, was out bright and early the next morning arranging bail. By ten o'clock Lloyd Bergson, Joe Shaeffer, a limping Françoise Perrin, and Morgan Gerard were out of jail—or more accurately, out of the library. Which was just as well, since this was Thursday and the librarian needed time to prepare for her ten-thirty preschool story hour.

Hannah Taggart, the fifty-seven-year-old librarian, had been quite disconcerted to see the huge crowd at the library steps when she walked to work that morning. Not only neighbors and friends had gathered, but reporters, TV cameras, and photographers had also converged on the scene.

Police Chief Moe Hawkins had to cut his fishing trip short, which didn't make him very happy. Neither did all this hubbub over some Hollywood idiots who had no business in his town in the first place. And certainly no business in the old Caspel estate. He didn't go along with this film business any more than Jack Dunne or Ben Corbett. But from the looks of it, it sure seemed like the rest of the town did.

Moe wiped his brow with the back of his hand and set about dispersing the crowd along with Schumacher and Dunne. The townsfolk were a trifle more cooperative then the TV and newspaper people. The media group were far more aggressive and determined to get their interviews. Clusters formed around Bergson, Shaeffer, and Françoise Perrin. Only Morgan Gerard was being spared the questioning. In fact, much to Moe Hawkins's surprise, she joined in to help him clear away people.

Moe noticed that quite a large number of Rocky Bluff residents knew Morgan Gerard and seemed to like her. She spoke to small groups at a time, and when she finished, people smiled and began moving along. He and the two officers concentrated on getting the three notables into a cruiser and whisking them down to the Bluffside Inn, where they were going to stay until the hearing early next week.

When Perrin, Bergson, and Shaeffer were safely inside Dunne's car, Moe Hawkins walked over to Morgan.

"You want a lift over to the inn?"

Morgan hesitated. "No. I have a few things to do in town first. But thank you."

He nodded. He was about to thank her for her help, but then decided not to. From what he could piece out, his shortened fishing trip was a good portion her doing.

Once Bergson and his two stars were gone, the media dispersed, hurrying to their cars to get their stories in before the morning deadline. Hannah Taggart looked out the library window, breathing a sigh of relief. The children would be arriving any minute. She picked up the amusing storybook, *Bobbi's Bad Luck Day*. Then, tapping her fingers meditatively on the cover, she tucked it back into its shelf, selecting one entitled *The Sunshine Gang* instead.

Morgan walked up the street. It was a warm, cloudless day. She hesitated two houses down from Ben's. Had he calmed down yet? she wondered. Chances were slim, considering all of the hectic activity this morning. She silently cursed Bergson for fouling everything up. She was sure Ben would never approve the location shots now. Bergson and his friends had gone and proved Ben absolutely right about turning this little town topsy-turvy.

She gathered her courage and knocked on his

160

door. There were other, more pressing issues to resolve beyond whether or not *Windswept* was filmed here. There was the matter of getting Ben to understand why she'd gone out to the Caspel estate despite his order; the matter of the short, stocky man Françoise had seen stalking up the stairs of the mansion; and not the least, the matter of where this whole mess left their budding relationship.

She slipped her hand into her pocket, feeling the locket she had taken from Charlotte's bedroom. There was also the matter of why Ben Corbett was the spitting image of a long-dead grounds-keeper by the name of Eliot. Morgan hadn't finished her list of strange and curious matters that needed to be resolved, when Ben's front door opened.

Laura Sawyer, Ben's robust, elderly housekeeper, smiled at Morgan.

"I hear there was quite a fuss this morning down at the library."

Morgan smiled. She liked the buxom housekeeper. "Biggest excitement to hit Rocky Bluff this year."

"This year? This century is more than likely. Well"—she paused—"of course there was the big scandal way back about Charlotte Caspel's suicide. But that was before my time."

"Yes," Morgan said softly. "That was the start of it."

Laura looked puzzled by Morgan's remark, but she merely shrugged. "I suppose you want to see Mayor Corbett. He's been down at his office since eight this morning. And the phone's been ringing here ever since. I don't know how I'm going to get any work done here today, that's for sure."

Morgan commiserated with Laura and then hurried over to the town building, which was actually a small cluster of offices over the Rocky Bluff Volunteer Fire Station. She spotted a couple of TV vans in the parking lot. When she got upstairs, pandemonium was reigning supreme. She could hear Ben's voice booming over a host of others and he was sounding anything but happy. Morgan was outside his door when it was opened abruptly.

She was nearly thrown to the floor by two reporters being unceremoniously shoved out of the room by Ben. When he saw her he grabbed her wrist, and before she could regain her balance, he'd tugged her into his office. She fell heavily against him. Ben righted her immediately. He was clearly in a worse frame of mind than last night when he'd found her in the Caspel mansion.

"Sit down," he ordered.

Morgan remained standing, arms crossed over her chest. "Will you please give me a chance to explain?"

Surprisingly he nodded his assent.

For a moment or two Morgan was too stunned to find her voice.

"Well?" he said dryly. "Let's hear it."

"For one thing, I didn't break into—"

"I know."

Morgan looked up sharply. "You do?"

He nodded, offering no other statement.

"Neither did Lloyd Bergson. He swore to me that he found the door—"

"I know that too," Ben said impatiently.

Morgan gazed at him, an expression of frustration and puzzlement on her face. "You know that none of us broke into the estate?"

"That's right."

"But someone did. A short, stocky man. Françoise saw him."

"Moe Hawkins has her statement. I'm pretty sure it's the same prowler who broke in the other times."

"Oh." She stared into Ben's cool eyes. For a moment she thought his stillness would erupt into a tirade of anger. But instead he gave her a weary shrug.

"I guess you'll be getting what you're after," he said sullenly.

She looked baffled.

"I can forget about running for mayor again next fall if I turn Bergson down now. I wouldn't even be able to run for dogcatcher. It seems Joe Shaeffer and Françoise Perrin's arrival on the scene has stirred the town into action." He turned around and grabbed up a sheaf of papers, practically shoving them in her face. "A petition," he announced harshly. "I'd say, except for yours truly and my exhausted, frustrated police force and possibly one or two others, every member of this town has scribbled his or her John Hancock on that paper. I guess Hollywood wins. You can tell Bergson he can go ahead. And the sooner he gets started and gets the hell out of here, the happier I'll be."

"What about me? Will you be happier if I clear out as fast as I can?"

Ben refused to meet her eyes. "I assumed that was your plan."

Morgan swallowed as she stared at Ben's profile. She thought about the shock last night of seeing him walk into the room just after she'd discovered Eliot's photograph. She palmed the locket in her trembling hand. "I don't have any definite plans," she murmured. She wanted to say more, but she found that she couldn't.

Ben turned his gaze on her then. For a long moment he said nothing. "I was so furious at you last night," he said finally. "It wasn't just that you'd gone to the Caspel place after I'd told you to stay away. It wasn't even that you'd called Bergson here."

"I didn't call him, Ben. He called me. That's what I was trying to explain. He left word for me to meet him at the Caspel estate at ten last night. I tried to get hold of him before he left L.A., but I couldn't."

Morgan was taken aback when Ben suddenly pulled her roughly to him. "That isn't the only reason you went back, is it?"

She looked up at him, her turquoise eyes misty. "No," she whispered. "It isn't the only reason." A few tears trickled down her cheeks. "Oh, Ben, I don't understand it. I don't understand any of it. Except—except that I love you. I do, Ben. I love you."

"Morgan," he said hoarsely, imprisoning her in a

fierce embrace, his mouth taking hers in a burning kiss.

When she threw her arms around him, the tiny golden locket fell out of her hand and onto the floor. The clasp opened on impact, the two miniature photos that Morgan had placed side by side earlier, coming into view.

It looked for all the world as if Charlotte and Eliot were staring up at Ben and Morgan, faint smiles on their lips as though they were pleased by what they saw.

CHAPTER TEN

Ben released Morgan. He didn't see the locket lying on the floor at first. Yet he couldn't deny the strange sensation he'd felt of being watched. It was Morgan who looked down first, and Ben's gaze followed hers.

He stared transfixed, and his breathing seemed to stop. Then, very slowly, he knelt down and picked up the open locket. His action was cautious, as if the gold might somehow sear him. He pressed his lips together, drawing them into a tight line.

Morgan put her hand lightly on his shoulder, but he didn't seem to feel her touch.

"Ben," she said, then more forcefully, "Ben."

He looked up at her, startled. "It's amazing," he murmured. "Truly amazing."

She nodded, a soft smile curving her lips. "I found the photo last night. Then you walked in moments later. The likeness is uncanny."

Ben touched his jaw, intent once again on the photo. Then his eyes drifted to the photo of Charlotte. It wasn't that Morgan bore a direct physical resemblance to Charlotte. It was more in their expressions, the depth of emotion conveyed in the eyes. And now Ben, too, was certain that Charlotte's eyes were that rare shade of turquoise that had drawn him so to Morgan.

"It frightened me at first," Morgan continued in a low voice. The din outside the office had settled down somewhat, thanks to Ben's staff. Morgan could hear Ben's strained breathing. "But it doesn't now. I never thought I was the type to believe in destiny." She gripped Ben's arm. "But that must be it. Ben, don't you believe—"

"Let's go back to my house," he cut her off abruptly, snapping the locket closed and tucking it into his breast pocket.

"Your house?"

He took her hand. "Come on."

They made their way hurriedly through the cluster of media people still hanging about the outer office, hoping for another story. Ben gave them all a stoic "No comment."

Morgan had no idea why Ben was so adamant about going home. Maybe he was just too upset to remain at the office. But it seemed that something was driving him, that he had some particular purpose in mind. He didn't say a word as they practically raced the three blocks to his house. And Morgan didn't bother trying to question him, knowing it was unlikely that he would give any explanations.

When Laura greeted the two of them as they walked into the house, she saw immediately that Ben was in a strange state. She'd known him since he was a boy. He rarely bore that look of intensity, but there were times . . .

He hurried up the stairs, Morgan breathlessly rushing after him. Laura, full of curiosity, followed.

Ben stopped in the hallway on the second floor. There was a wooden board cut out in the ceiling with a short string attached to it. As a boy Ben couldn't reach that string, but then, as a boy he'd always been afraid to. It wasn't that he hadn't thought often about sneaking up to the attic when he'd stayed here with his father and grandfather, but he'd never gotten up enough courage to do it. His grandfather, Isaac Corbett, a somber, morose old man, had always told him the attic was off limits. He insisted the floorboards were weak and it was too dangerous.

But Ben had always sensed there was more to it. It was almost as if there was something forbidden up there, something his grandfather kept very private. Ben was convinced of that when, one afternoon, he returned home early from the beach with a bad headache and saw his grandfather climbing up the attic stairs. He stayed there a long time, unaware that Ben was home. Ben never told him, but he knew after that incident that Isaac simply didn't want Ben snooping around.

When Ben had returned as an adult, claiming the house as his own, he was anxious to search that attic and finally resolve the mystery. Laura had been there that day. She'd known his earlier fear of the attic because one night, when Ben was nine, she'd baby-sat for him when he was awakened by a terrible thunderstorm. He was trembling, his young face ashen. He told Laura he'd had an awful nightmare about seeing ghosts in the attic and that they were trying to take him away.

The day he'd finally gone up to the attic, Laura, concerned as ever, remained on the second floor close by the attic stairs. Ben knew that she was there to give him added confidence and though her effort wasn't necessary, he loved her for it.

There'd been nothing very ominous in the attic. It was old and musty and the floorboards did creak. A few cartons, marked by age and yellowed water stains, were scattered about the dark, close space. Beyond them there was nothing except a small desk wedged into the corner under a tiny window. There was one drawer in it. It was locked. Not a very complex lock, certainly one Ben could easily have snapped with a penknife. But he couldn't bring himself to do it. He felt an inexplicable reluctance to open that drawer and see what was inside, as if he'd be violating some unspoken trust. He was convinced the locked drawer guarded a terrible secret. Hurrying down the attic stairs that day he told himself he was being ridiculous, crazy to let himself be caught up in his grandfather's game. Yet in all the years he'd been in the house, he had never once returned to that attic, never once considered opening that desk drawer. In fact, consciously, he'd truly forgotten all about it.

As soon as Ben saw the photo of Eliot in that locket, the image of the old desk flashed in his mind and he knew that the time had finally come to clear away the mystery and put aside concerns he'd carried with him since childhood.

Morgan had no idea of the cause of Ben's anxiety, but she felt it immediately as he drew down the folding attic stairs, his hands straining as they gripped the railing. He stood with his foot poised on the first step, staring up into the dimly lit space.

Laura patted Morgan lightly on the back and smiled softly. Then she quietly walked away, knowing that Morgan was the only one Ben needed now. Morgan waited, saying nothing.

Ben took a deep breath and started the climb. Once begun, his steps were more sure, his nervousness fading. *Yes*, he thought, *it's time.*

Morgan came up after him. He turned to her, taking her hand, guiding her carefully in the shadowy light to the desk. He lifted an old tablecloth from a nearby box and wiped off the attic window. Through the canopy of trees a few rays of sun cast their light on the old mahogany desk. Ben was still gripping Morgan's hand in his.

She squeezed it reassuringly, not altogether sure whom she was reassuring—him or herself. As soon as she'd stepped into the attic, Morgan felt that same odd presence she experienced at the Caspel estate. She was shivering despite the cloying heat up there. It made no sense. But then, so little had made sense since this all began.

Ben pulled his Swiss army knife from his pocket. With remarkably steady hands he attacked the lock. When it gave, he exhaled, having unconsciously held his breath while he'd worked at it.

His hands were less steady as he slowly opened the drawer.

Morgan moved closer, her own breathing strained. She gasped as the drawer was opened fully.

There was a photo on top. Morgan and Ben could now see that the two miniatures in Charlotte's locket were actually snipped from one photo that was a duplicate of this one. Ben glanced at Morgan, then gently lifted the old photograph out. They stared at the young couple, Charlotte in a flowing, sheer cotton dress, Eliot in an open shirt and narrow trousers.

"They look so happy," Morgan said, an odd note of sadness in her voice.

Ben turned the photograph over. In a broad, bold script were the words: *Charlotte and Eliot, May 7, 1907.*

There was a small pile of letters held by a thick rubber-band in the drawer. Ben took them out, slipping the band onto his wrist. The first letter was postmarked May 8, 1907. The writing on the envelope had faded badly, but the letter inside was intact.

Dear Isaac,

I have never known such excruciating pain. She is dead. My love, my beautiful, gentle Charlotte, will never again gaze at me with those remarkable turquoise eyes. How shall I ever bear it?

Ben dropped the paper, looking more closely at the envelope. He could just make out that the letter was addressed to Isaac Corbett in Portland, Maine. It had been sent by Eliot Corbett, Rocky Bluff, New York.

Ben ran his tongue over his dry lips. He lifted the next envelope. There was no writing on this one. Inside was a death certificate made out for Eliot Corbett, who died on the eighteenth day of September, cause being a gunshot wound to the heart.

Morgan saw a small photo fall from the envelope. She bent down and picked it up, her blue eyes widening as she stared at it.

"They were identical twins," she whispered, turning the photo over to read: *Eliot and Isaac, October 1901, Portland, Maine.*

Ben took the photo. "It's as though I'm looking at a double image of myself. So that was the secret my grandfather kept. Eliot was my great-uncle. But why was Isaac so intent on hiding the truth?"

Morgan was looking at another letter as Ben spoke. In a strained voice she said, "I know why."

Ben cocked his head, his brow furrowed. "What do you mean?"

She handed him the letter. There were tears in her eyes.

My Dearest Love,
I mourn for you, my lovely Charlotte—even after twenty long, lonely years. I know that you will never read this letter, but I truly believe my pain, my shame, and yes, my great undying love

172

for you are feelings that you grasp even now. I feel your spirit with me constantly, and I know you take pity on my torment. But still, after all these years, I realize that I must confess to you openly so that I can somehow still the anguish.

When you died my brother Isaac came from Portland to comfort me in my grief. I had stopped writing to him after . . . I still cannot bear the memory. One moment you were there at your window, waving at me. The next . . .

I hated Wescott Caspel almost as passionately as I love you, my darling. When Isaac arrived, I told him the true circumstances of your death. I said that I saw your husband at the window just after you fell, that he had the audacity to smile across the lawn at me afterward.

I had a gun. I had finally gained the courage to do what I knew I must do—destroy Wescott Caspel as he had destroyed the most perfect jewel on this earth. Isaac saw me take hold of the gun. He insisted that I come to my senses. Come to my senses? At that moment I had lost all sense, all feeling except hatred.

We struggled with the gun. It went off, and Isaac clutched at my shirt, then fell into my arms. My brother, the other half of my soul, my dearest friend. Isaac died in my arms.

I was beside myself. But then, gripped by some strange force, I knew what I must do. I carried Isaac in the dark of night to your house. Strengthened by some supernatural force I bore his weight as I made my way up the sturdy vines to your window one last time. . . . Oh, my dar-

ling Charlotte, do you remember those sweet, passionate moments we shared together in our little haven?

I laid my brother down on our bed, carefully wiping the gun and placing it on the floor. You see, I thought, at least, my brother would not have died in vain. I foolishly believed that Wescott would be tried for the murder of Eliot Corbett and get his just punishment. I put in an anonymous telephone call to the police.

But good fortune has never been mine . . . except for those few precious months we were together. Then I knew such perfect bliss.

Wescott must have found Isaac before the police came. By the time they arrived, he had carefully pressed Isaac's limp hand to the gun, fixing the scene to appear to be a suicide. Wescott won after all. And I lost everyone I held so dear.

I disappeared for many years after that. I lived for a while in California. One night I got drunk. I admit that happened frequently. I was so desperately unhappy. All I wanted to do was forget. There was a woman. I met her in a bar. I don't even remember. But several months later she tracked me down and informed me she was pregnant. I did the decent thing and married her to give the baby a name. But when my son was born, Eva ran off, leaving the boy with me.

I thought of you constantly, wanting desperately to return to Rocky Bluff. But I was afraid. When Wescott died several years later, I finally returned. I had to be with you. Pain and torment had taken their toll on my features. No one in

the area even made the connection between my-
self and the long-gone Eliot. So I bought this
small house in town for myself and my son,
called myself Isaac Corbett, and have continued
to live the lie. But you know the truth, my dar-
ling. And I pray my brother forgives me as I beg
you to forgive me.

In the end I was a coward, waiting from afar
for Wescott to die. After my brother's death I lost
all courage. But I have never, in all these twenty
years, lost the passion that will be ours to share
for eternity. I am with you always, my darling
Charlotte.

> *Your most faithful, enduring love,*
> *Eliot*

Ben leaned against the wall. Beads of sweat had
broken out across his brow. He looked at the letter
that had lain in the small desk drawer for all these
years. At last the past and the secrets held in its
grasp were unlocked.

He could feel the fear and confusion leaving
him. A rain cloud concealed the sun, covering the
attic in shadowy light. Ben looked at Morgan.
They shared a tender smile, both feeling remarkably content and at peace. Then he gathered her
in his arms, his warm, moist lips meeting hers.

That night they returned together to the Caspel
estate. Ben let them in with his key to the silent
house. They climbed the stairs, pausing to look
across at Charlotte's room where the fire had
been, then moving on to the third-floor love nest.

At the door Ben reached out to grasp the doorknob and paused. He gave Morgan a curious smile. "Are you sure?"

Morgan's eyes glistened. "Only this once." She placed her hand over his and they turned the knob together.

They undressed each other with unhurried ease, taking exquisite pleasure in the task. Ben lifted Morgan in his arms and carried her to the bed where many years before, Charlotte and his grandfather, Eliot, had known such supreme joy. Eliot had passed that profound passion down to his grandson.

His mouth devoured Morgan's with an intensity that made her tremble, his strong, knowing hands moving familiarly on her slender body. Cupping her chin he gazed for what felt like endless moments into those rare blue eyes. He stroked her cheek, then tenderly traced the beautifully etched features of her face with his fingertips.

"You're more beautiful than Charlotte," he whispered.

Morgan smiled sweetly. "And you're finer than Eliot. He let passion and hate rule him, finally destroy him, really. He lacked the kind of integrity you have. I love you so, Ben." She pressed her lips to his for a tender kiss.

"It *is* destiny," Ben murmured, caressing her breasts, placing his head to her heart. "Sweet destiny."

"We must never destroy what we have," Morgan said breathlessly.

"Never, my darling." He drew her close, their

kisses deepening, their hands caressing, stroking, demanding.

Their past lovemaking had only hinted at the passion and supreme intimacy that exploded inside of them now. Tonight their erotic quest brought them each to new heights.

Morgan's body began to tremble violently as Ben's kisses and caresses consumed her completely. She kept whispering his name, urging him on as she writhed against his hard body, her voice and movements exciting him more, his passionate assault growing fiercer. She accepted his attack greedily, thankfully, her body desperate for release.

He entered her with a smooth, deep thrust; Morgan gasped as she clung to him. The wind carried eerie murmurings in the dark night, but neither Morgan nor Ben heard what almost sounded like the rustle of a long dress across a wooden floor, soft, happy sighs, and gentle laughter. Ben and Morgan were locked in their own world now, Charlotte and Eliot no longer existing for either one of them. They had come here to confront the ghosts of the past, and in so doing had discovered the absolute core of each other.

He held her for a long while afterward on the bed in that simple third-floor room. When they left, the rain had stopped, and dawn was breaking on a new day.

The filming of *Windswept* was in its third week. The cast, crew, and extras had gathered under a tent on the lawn of the Caspel estate. It was nine

P.M. on a stormy night. The crew had had to wait three days for the proper weather for the last interior shots. The cameras were moving into place for the scene where Lauren walked into Charlotte's bedroom and imagined she saw Charlotte at the window staring out at the storm.

Morgan was chatting with some of the extras, all locals from Rocky Bluff. Their work here was completed, but they were all staying around to watch the scene and attend a gala celebration afterward. There was a special air of excitement tonight. Everyone felt it. Perhaps it was because it was the last time Bergson would be shooting at the Caspel place.

Ben pulled up a few minutes after nine, waving at Morgan as he stepped out of the car. After the filming tonight Bergson was throwing a grand bash in the main salon of the mansion. Ben was to be the honored guest, a kind of thank-you from everyone for letting them use the Caspel estate after all.

Ben had to admit, as he made his way through the crowd under the tent, that Morgan had been right about Bergson's running a tight ship. Oh, there had been a fair share of commotion since the arrival of the film people and an occasional speedster on the back roads, but all in all the cast and crew had been quite subdued. No doubt because Bergson worked them all to the bone. By the time they finished on the set, they were probably happy simply to crawl into bed and get some sleep before their five A.M. wake-up calls. Bergson was a man obsessed, and he was determined that this picture be his greatest achievement, his claim to fame for posterity.

Morgan rushed into Ben's arms and gave him a warm, welcoming kiss.

"They've only got this last scene and then it's champagne for everyone."

Ben closed his hand over hers and smiled. He could see the shimmer of excitement in her eyes. Their gazes drifted over to the mansion. Since that night three weeks ago Ben had not been back, Morgan venturing in once or twice, but only for a few brief moments. Her work at the estate was over. Her days were filled with getting everything ready for shoots on an assortment of locations around town.

They had laid some ghosts to rest the night she and Ben had made love in the little room where Charlotte and Eliot used to meet. Yet the eerie, sad sensations still clung to the mansion. Morgan no longer felt drawn to the place. Much to the contrary, she experienced a melancholy emptiness about it. It seemed that the more real and compelling her relationship with Ben, the less powerful the spirits of Charlotte and Eliot. Morgan was back to not believing in ghosts, but she could not quite dismiss the aura the legend of the two dead lovers had created.

She pressed her cheek against Ben's shoulder.

"Oh, there you are," Bergson exclaimed, his features fraught with tension as he spied Morgan. "I was afraid I couldn't track you down in time." He grabbed Morgan's wrist. "I need you desperately."

Ben chuckled. "Isn't that supposed to be my line to Morgan?"

Lloyd gave a begrudging little laugh. "Right. But my needs are different." He looked at Morgan. "Lisa Owens just smashed her finger in a door and someone's had to rush her into town to have it checked. Damn, it's the first bit of bad luck we've had here. But you could easily stand in for her and play Charlotte for this scene. There are no lines and it's a wide-angle shot. We'll do the close-ups later."

Morgan tensed. "Why not just wait for her to come back?"

"The rain is slowing down. Another twenty minutes and we'll lose it. Come on, Morgan. I always said you'd make the perfect Charlotte. Anyway, you've got some special qualities. Who knows? You might make it big in front of the camera."

"Oh, no, thanks." Morgan glanced up at Ben. "As a matter of fact I've been considering giving up my wandering days behind the scenes. There comes a time when the excitement starts to fade, when the thought of yet another mad scramble for an airport, another hotel, another new town, simply loses its appeal. It would be kind of nice to settle down in a quaint little spot."

"Come on," Bergson quipped. "What would you do with yourself? Sit around some cottage with a white picket fence, bringing hubby his slippers and pipe, knitting little booties for the baby?"

Morgan glanced from Bergson to Ben, a warm smile on her face. "Well, the script's slightly off center. . . . I don't need a picket fence. . . ."

180

She laughed softly. "But it might work. It just might work at that."

Ben's eyes sparkled. He put his arm around her. "You know how much I like happy endings."

"Morgan, you can't desert me now. There's no one else who will do. Be a good girl." Bergson really didn't wait for an answer. He practically dragged her away from Ben.

Morgan gave Ben a helpless little shrug. "All right. All right. But only this once. I don't particularly like the idea—"

"Terrific," he cut her off, leading her to Lisa Owens's trailer. "The dress is inside. I'll get Marge to make you up and Tom will fix your hair."

As Morgan was dressing and being attended to inside the trailer, Ben waited nearby under the shelter of an old elm tree. The door opened, the dresser stepping out first, opening a huge black umbrella. Then Morgan stepped out.

She was wearing a dress remarkably similar to the one she'd bought in town, only this had a lace frill along the bodice and the waist cinched more tightly, accentuating the gentle yet voluptuous curve of her hips. Her hair was loose, brushed to a soft sheen, parted in the middle rather than the subtle parting to the side she usually chose. Her face was highlighted by a soft rose blush and pale coral lipstick.

As Ben's eyes traveled over her, he was startled by the resemblance she bore to Charlotte Caspel's photograph. He found it more than a little disconcerting, and when she smiled at him, he found his own smile manufactured. A feeling of dread came over him. He didn't want her to go into that house. Reasoning with himself to no avail he caught hold of Morgan's arm.

She saw the alarm in his face. Kissing him tenderly, she whispered, "We don't believe in ghosts and spirits. It's going to be fine."

Only it wasn't.

He stood resolute, watching her enter the front door. Then, with the rain suddenly coming down hard again, he raced around the house. Although it was cordoned off, Jack Dunne didn't say a word as Ben ran under the ropes. The Kleig lights were illuminated on Charlotte's bedroom. A few moments later he saw Morgan at the window. She smiled down at him.

And then Ben's eyes were drawn to a room down the hall. As a beam of light crossed by its window, Ben thought he saw a small, heavyset man race across the room.

He could be one of the crew, Ben told himself, but he didn't feel convinced. And then he remembered Françoise Perrin's statement about seeing a short, stocky man in the Caspel house. Ben felt a premonition so compelling he shouted to Jack for assistance and headed for the back door, completely disrupting the shoot.

Morgan gazed down at Ben, saw his gesture to the policeman, saw the two of them racing for the house. She was baffled by his strange behavior. Lloyd Bergson was livid.

Before Ben reached the door there was a loud explosion. Several people screamed. Morgan, too shocked to utter a word, stood frozen as she watched smoke creep up the stairs into the open room. Everyone else began running out.

Ben was racing into the house, Jack Dunne and several others behind him. The back staircase was already engulfed in flames. They rushed around to the front one. It, too, was impassable. Ben saw Bergson, Françoise Perrin, and the cameraman rushing to the door.

He grabbed Bergson. "Morgan. Where is she?"

Bergson, overcome by smoke, could only wave vaguely toward the stairs.

"Come on," Ben shouted frantically to Jack and the others who had joined them. "We'll never get her out this way."

Morgan had managed to crawl out the window onto the ledge. She never dreamed she'd actually be here again, she thought, desperately trying to keep herself from panicking. He would come to her. Ben would save her as he had done before.

Smoke was billowing from the window where the explosion had been and was filtering slowly but surely out of Charlotte's window now. Morgan could feel herself starting to fall apart. Terror gripped her and she was struggling to conquer recurrent waves of dizziness. But when she closed her eyes to squelch the sensation, she kept seeing herself crashing down onto the bluff, white dress flowing. . . .

"No!" she cried.

"Morgan!" It's all right, darling. I'm coming. Don't be afraid."

She saw Ben painstakingly making his way up the drainpipe, he'd climbed down that first day.

The difference now was that thankfully it had been repaired by the movie crew. Smoke intermittently clouded her view of him and she grew more frightened for Ben than she was for herself.

Then he was on the ledge, edging toward her, moving faster than he should, but he knew there was precious little time left.

Morgan shook off the terror freezing her into a statue and carefully began edging her way toward him. At last, hands stretched out, their fingers touched. Then he was gripping her arm.

Flames were shooting out of windows now. The rain and smoke made it painfully hard to see. Morgan's eyes filled with tears and she kept blinking them away. It felt like an eternity before they reached the drainpipe.

She was cut and bruised when they landed together on the wet ground, and then people were rushing to their aid. Ben shouted for everyone to clear out. The building was going to fold. The roof had already started to cave in.

He gathered Morgan in his arms, but when they were a safe distance away, she made him stop and set her down. She stared at the blazing mansion, her eyes still filled with tears. Ben knew that it wasn't only because of the smoke.

He put his arm around her. "They're free now, love," he whispered softly. "The ending for them is just the beginning for us."

Morgan smiled through her tears. For a brief moment she imagined she saw a filmy white shadow emerge from the flames. Then she turned away from the crumbling building and put her arms around Ben, drawing his lips to hers for a kiss filled with hope and promise.

They were still in each other's arms when Jack Dunne appeared. He was dragging a very bedraggled-looking short, heavyset man along with him.

"Here's our culprit," Dunne announced. "His name is Vic Altman. He used to work as a janitor down at the bank. Until, so he tells me, he joined forces with three other men to rob the Rocky Bluff Bank. They hid the money in the house. I guess he'd planned on leaving it there for quite a while, before all this started." He looked at Morgan and then at the crowd still gathered a safe distance from the flames. "He was determined to scare people off before anyone found his treasure. It . . . got out of hand, to say the least."

Morgan stared at Vic Altman. "Then it was you that locked us into Charlotte's room that time. And then afterward, you locked me in the little room on the third floor."

Vic rubbed his smoke-smudged face. "I overheard you talking. I knew you were spooked. I figured if I got you scared enough you'd give up the idea of using this place."

Morgan sighed. So now all of the mysterious events had an explanation. It was over. Even the Caspel estate was gone now. The tales of Charlotte's calls on windy nights would die off and the memories would fade.

Ben motioned to Jack to take Vic off. Then he turned to Morgan. She was gazing off into the distance, her incredible turquoise eyes reflecting sparks of the fiery blaze. He covered her hand with his, feeling her warmth, her vibrancy.

"Will you take that part Bergson described? You know, the one about settling down in the house with the white picket fence?" he asked softly.

She looked up at him. "You mean the one where the loving wife brings the pipe and slippers to her hubby?" She cocked her head, giving him a teasing smile. "It's the pipe-and-slippers bit that bothers me."

"I don't smoke a pipe. And I'll toss my slippers in the trash. We'll run around barefoot," he said with a grin.

"And I don't know how to knit."

He pressed her hand to his lips. "We'll make sure you have a little time to learn." He turned her to him. "I love you, Morgan." He paused. "It's bound to be a quiet life after the career you've had."

"I like the idea of starting a new career. Helping the mayor of a thriving seaside town could be a big job . . . what with learning how to be a wife . . . and how to knit booties as well. Actually, it sounds like a dream come true." She kissed him tenderly. "I love you, Ben. For eternity," she whispered.

He gathered her in his arms. "For eternity." Then they turned their backs on the past and walked away hand in hand.

*Rekindle your secret
yearnings for
romance and passion
with the splendid
historical novels
of*

Vanessa Royall

M